W9-CYT-858

The United States
and the USSR
in a Changing World

The United States
and the USSR
in a Changing World

Soviet and
American Perspectives

EDITED BY
Andrei G. Bochkarev
Moscow Institute of Agricultural Engineers

Don L. Mansfield
Northern Arizona University

Westview Press
BOULDER • SAN FRANCISCO • OXFORD

Woods Hole Oceanographic Institution
Purchase Order No. 04026
8 Jan 1992

All rights reserved. No part of this publication may be reproduced or transmitted in any form or by any means, electronic or mechanical, including photocopy, recording, or any information storage and retrieval system, without permission in writing from the publisher.

Copyright © 1992 by Westview Press, Inc.

Published in 1992 in the United States of America by Westview Press, Inc., 5500 Central Avenue, Boulder, Colorado 80301-2847, and in the United Kingdom by Westview Press, 36 Lonsdale Road, Summertown, Oxford OX2 7EW

Library of Congress Cataloging-in-Publication Data
The United States and the USSR in a changing world : Soviet and American perspectives / [edited by] Andrei G. Bochkarev and Don L. Mansfield
    p. cm.
  Includes index.
  ISBN 0-8133-8381-1.—ISBN 0-8133-8382-X (pbk.)
    1. United States—Foreign relations—Soviet Union. 2. Soviet Union—Foreign relations—United States. 3. United States—Foreign relations—1989–   . 4. Soviet Union—Foreign relations—1985–
I. Bochkarev, Andreĭ Gennad'evich. II. Mansfield, Don L., 1937–
E183.8.S65U56   1990
327.73047—dc20   91-29251
                                                                      CIP

Printed in the United States of America

The paper used in this publication meets the requirements
of the American National Standard for Permanence of Paper
for Printed Library Materials Z39.48-1984.

10   9   8   7   6   5   4   3   2   1

Contents

Foreword

The improvement of relations between the Soviet Union and the United States constitutes one of the central goals of President Mikhail Gorbachev's "new political thinking" in Soviet foreign and domestic policies. As President Gorbachev mentioned in his book *Perestroika and Soviet-American Relations*, "today we are witnessing an upswing in Soviet-American relations, the improvement of which is so necessary to our two nations and to the whole world." With the demise of the Cold War, the possibilities for a substantial improvement in relations are recognized by both nations and both place a high priority on the attainment of this goal.

This book describes the new era in superpower relations and discusses the possibilities for Soviet-U.S. cooperation in resolving international issues during the 1990s and into the next century. Edited by a Soviet professor and an American professor, the text is valuable because it helps to dispel the stereotypical thinking that has plagued Soviet-American relations and resulted in misconceptions on both sides. The unique combination of Soviet and American interpretations provides a perspective on issues that is lacking in other assessments of the topic. The articles selected for analysis were written by outstanding scholars in both countries, including John Gaddis, Zbigniew Brzezinski, Michael Mandelbaum, Henry Trofimenko, Alexei Arbatov, and Georgy Arbatov.

This study includes a discussion of the positive and negative aspects of the Cold War era in superpower relations and describes the events and policies that led to the demise of the global conflict. It also focuses on changes in national security strategy and doctrine, the possibilities for economic cooperation, and the increasing preference of both countries for multilateral negotiation in the United Nations and other international organizations. The dramatic changes in the European and Third World policies of both powers are also considered, with speculation on the possibilities of superpower collaboration on policy development in these crucial areas of the world. The book concludes with a look at future U.S.-USSR relations, with a surprising similarity in the opinions expressed in the Soviet and American commentaries.

The book's comparative approach illustrates the similarities and differences in the policies of the two countries and explores persistent conflict issues as well as opportunities for collaboration. It makes a major contribution to the study of Soviet-American relations and provides a balanced and integrated analysis for scholars, policymakers, and students of international studies.

Despite the recent turbulent events in the Soviet Union, in which conservative forces in the Communist party attempted a coup against President Gorbachev, the positive changes in Soviet-American relations highlighted in this text are expected to prevail in the future.

Inna Rybalkina
Researcher, Institute of
African Studies of the USSR
Academy of Sciences, Moscow

Preface

This text examines Soviet-American relations for the 1990s from both the Soviet and American perspectives. The topics selected for analysis are considered to be central to the Soviet-American relationship and those that are most likely to undergo significant change during the present decade. We have chosen authors, both Soviet and American, whose arguments enhance our understanding of various aspects of an issue and who effectively place the issue within the context of other foreign policy concerns of the two countries. The essays reflect a diversity of viewpoints: Some are written by government officials, others by academics, and a few by concerned citizens. Their perspectives cover the political spectrum, from liberal to conservative, in their respective countries. The selections were drawn from a variety of sources, including scholarly journals, books, newspapers, and government documents. With only a few exceptions, the essays have been excerpted to emphasize only those issues that are central to Soviet-American relations.

Because the Soviet-American relationship is constantly changing, the selections are all recent. Indeed, only a few of the essays were written before 1990. One difficulty in treating such a dynamic topic is that some of the articles speculate on issues that have been resolved or nullified even before the book went to press. For example, several references discuss the prospects for German reunification. Others consider the long-term prospects for the Warsaw Treaty Organization (WTO). Even though Germany is now unified and the WTO is no longer a functioning organization, we have included references to these issues because it is instructive to understand the policy preferences of each superpower and how the "resolution" of the problem affected their changing relationship.

Although the text generally juxtaposes the Soviet and U.S. positions on a particular issue in order to highlight policy similarities and differences, we have not held rigidly to this format. Moreover, in many cases the commentaries illustrate areas of cooperation and agreement, rather than just points of conflict. In fact, in this era of "new thinking" in foreign policy for both countries, there is a conscious effort by some authors to stress policy similarities and de-emphasize differences.

The United States and the USSR in a Changing World: Soviet and American Perspectives is intended to be a supplementary rather than a basic textbook. However, because of the dynamic nature of the topic, it is difficult to find an up-to-date text; therefore, this reader could serve as the primary textbook for a course (supplemented with the most recent materials available on each topic).

One final point: as a Soviet professor and an American professor jointly preparing a text on the relations of our two countries, we believe that we have shown in a small way the opportunities for cooperation between our two countries. We have enjoyed our association and the opportunity to work together on what we considered to be a worthwhile project. We were periodically reminded that such a collaborative effort would have been exceedingly difficult only a few years ago. It was both interesting and perplexing to note that many of the issues that have served to divide our countries have become, in a surprisingly short interval, irrelevant to the bilateral relationship. The reader will detect this somewhat euphoric attitude in the way that we have structured the text and selected essays.

Both editors would like to express their appreciation to Earl Backman, dean of the College of Social and Behavioral Sciences, Northern Arizona University, and Karl Webb, dean of the College of Arts and Sciences, for providing the monetary support for Professor Bochkarev to instruct and conduct research at Northern Arizona University during 1990-1991. We would also like to express our appreciation to Louella Holter of the Bilby Research Center for the professional preparation of the text and her editorial assistance. Arlene Bauer and Michelle Diaz also provided invaluable typing assistance. We are especially grateful to Inna Rybalkina, researcher at the Institute of African Studies of the USSR Academy of Sciences, who spent many hours reviewing articles in Moscow and forwarding them for our consideration.

We also wish to express our gratitude to Susan McEachern and Alison Auch of Westview Press for their support and counsel throughout the publication process.

Andrei G. Bochkarev
Moscow Institute for
Agricultural Engineers

Don L. Mansfield
Northern Arizona University

About the Editors and Contributors

Editors

Andrei G. Bochkarev, doctor of history, is chair of the Department of Political History at the Moscow Institute of Agricultural Engineers. The author of numerous articles on international affairs, he was a visiting professor at Northern Arizona University during 1990-1991.

Don L. Mansfield is a professor of political science at Northern Arizona University. Associate dean of the College of Social and Behavioral Sciences, he has also served as chair of the Department of Political Science. He is the coeditor of *Conflict in American Foreign Policy: The Issues Debated.*

American Contributors

Zbigniew Brzezinski served from 1977 to 1981 as national security advisor to the president of the United States and is the author of *The Grand Failure: The Birth and Death of Communism in the Twentieth Century.*

Alton Frye, vice president of the Council on Foreign Relations, was staff director for Senator Edward W. Brooke (R-Mass.).

John Lewis Gaddis is professor of history at Ohio University. His books include *The United States and the Origins of the Cold War, 1941-47; Russia, the Soviet Union, and the United States: An Interpretative History*; and *The Long Peace: Inquiries into the History of the Cold War.*

David R. Jones is director of Dalhousie University's Russian Micro-Project and former research associate of the Harvard Russian Research Center. A prolific author, he is also editor of the *Military-Naval Encyclopedia of Russia and the Soviet Union* and the *Soviet Armed Forces Review Annual* volumes.

Meryl A. Kessler, a Soviet specialist, is a fellow at the Kennedy School's Center for Science and International Affairs, Harvard University.

Steven Kull is a senior research asssociate at Global Outlook in Palo Alto, California.

F. Stephen Larrabee is a senior staff member at the RAND Corporation in Santa Monica, California.

S. Neil MacFarlane is associate professor of government and foreign affairs and director of the Center for Russian and East European Studies at the University of Virginia. He is the author of *The Idea of National Liberation, Intervention and Regional Security*, and *Gorbachev: Third World Dilemma*.

Michael Mandelbaum is the Christian Herter Professor of American Foreign Policy at the Paul H. Nitze School of Advanced International Studies of Johns Hopkins University and the director of the project on East-West relations at the Council on Foreign Relations.

Charles William Maynes is the editor of *Foreign Policy* magazine.

John J. Mearsheimer is professor and chair, Department of Political Science, the University of Chicago.

Lt. General William E. Odom, USA (Retired), is director of national security studies at the Hudson Institute and adjunct professor of political science at Yale University. He was director of the National Security Agency at the time of his retirement from the U.S. Army in 1988.

Edward L. Rowny was the first U.S. START negotiator. He retired from the post of special advisor to the president and secretary of state for arms control matters in June 1990 after nearly half a century of public service.

Stanley R. Sloan is the senior specialist in International Security Policy at the Congressional Research Service, Washington, D.C. His books on European security and arms control include *NATO in the 1990s* and *NATO's Future: Toward a New Trans-Atlantic Bargain*.

Adlai E. Stevenson, former U.S. Senator (D-Ill.), is a counsel at the Chicago law firm of Mayer, Brown, and Platt.

Thomas G. Weiss, former executive director of the International Peace Academy and a United Nations staff member, is the associate director of the Institute of International Studies, Brown University.

Soviet Contributors

Alexei G. Arbatov, doctor of history, is head of the Department of Disarmament and Security, Institute of World Economy and International Relations (IMEMO). An expert on military affairs, his books include *Security in the Nuclear Age and Washington's Policy, Space Weapons: Dilemma for Security, Disarmament and Security*, and *Lethal Frontiers: A Soviet View of Nuclear Strategy, Weapons and Negotiations*.

Georgy A. Arbatov is director of the Institute of U.S. and Canadian Studies of the USSR Academy of Sciences. He is an expert in U.S. foreign and domestic policies. He is the author of *Soviet-American Relations During the Great Patriotic War, 1941-1945* and *U.S. Foreign Policy at the Turn of the 1980s*; and coauthor of *The Soviet Viewpoint*.

Pavel Bayev, candidate of sciences (history Ph.D.), is a senior researcher in the Institute of Europe of the USSR Academy of Sciences. He is the author of *The Gulf: From the Impasse of Confrontation to the Political Alternative* and *Tactical Nuclear Weapons in Europe*.

Mikhail Bezrukov is a research fellow at the Institute for U.S. and Canadian Studies. His specialty is international security affairs. He is a contributor to *Typological Studies of Social and Political Processes in the U.S.*

Yuriy Davydov is head of department at the Institute for U.S. and Canadian Studies and holds the academic rank of professor. His specialty is European affairs. His books include *The U.S.A. and the European Process* and *The U.S.A. and the European Problems of Detente*.

Sergei Karaganov, doctor of history, is deputy director of the Institute of Europe of the USSR Academy of Sciences. A specialist in U.S. politics, he is coauthor of *Reasonable Sufficiency and New Political Thinking* and *U.S.A.: The Transnational Corporation in Foreign Policy*.

Valeri Karavayev, doctor of economics, is a leading researcher at the Institute of Economy of the World Socialist System of the USSR Academy of Sciences. An expert on the world economy, he is the author of *Integration and Investments: The Problems of COMECON Countries' Cooperation* and *Economic Relations of the Socialist Countries with the Capitalist World*.

Andrei Kolosov is a political analyst and the author of numerous articles on international affairs.

Andrei Kozyrev, candidate of sciences (history Ph.D.), is chief of the International Organizations Department of the USSR Ministry of Foreign Affairs. His publications include *No! To Arms Trade; Arms Trade in the Policy of Imperialism;* and *The Arms Trade: A New Level of Danger.*

Lev Lvovich Lyubimov, doctor of history, is head of the Department of North American Research of the Institute of World Economy and International Relations (IMEMO). A specialist in economic problems, he is the author of *The Burning (Actual) Problems of U.S. Economic Development, State-Monopoly Capitalism in the U.S.A.,* and *The World Ocean: Arena of Confrontation and Cooperation.*

Alexei Pushkov, candidate of sciences (history Ph.D.), is a consultant to the International Department of the Central Committee of the CPSU. He graduated from the Moscow Institute of International Relations, defending the thesis "Crisis of the Main Political Concepts in English-American Sovietology."

Victor Shein, candidate of sciences (history Ph.D.), is head of a department in the Institute of Europe of the USSR Academy of Sciences. He is the author of *U.S. Dictatorship in NATO* and *U.S.A. and NATO: Evolution of the Imperialist Partnership.*

Henry Trofimenko is chief analyst at the Institute of U.S. and Canadian Studies of the USSR Academy of Sciences. For fifteen years he directed that institute's department for the study of U.S. foreign policy. His books include *The U.S. Military Doctrine, Peaceful Coexistence in the Nuclear Age,* and *USSR-U.S.: Half a Century of Peaceful Coexistence.*

Vitali Zhurkin is a corresponding member of the USSR Academy of Sciences, director of the Academy's Institute of Europe, and acting academic secretary of the Academy's Section of World Economy and International Relations. He is the author of a number of works, including *The U.S.A. and International Political Crisis, The USSR-U.S.A.: The 1970s-the 1980s,* and *The U.S. Global Strategy under the Scientific and Technological Revolution.*

Copyright Information

1. From John Lewis Gaddis, "Looking Back: The Long Peace," *Wilson Quarterly* (1989), pp. 42-65. Reprinted by permission of the *Wilson Quarterly*, published by The Woodrow Wilson International Center for Scholars, and The Oxford University Press, publishers of *The Long Peace*, from which the article was drawn. Copyright © 1987. Article composed in 1987.

2. From Lev L. Lyubimov, "The New Thinking and Soviet-American Relations," in Steve Hirsch, ed., *MEMO: New Soviet Voices on Foreign and Economic Policy* (Washington, D.C.: BNA Books, 1989), pp. 403-419. Excerpted and reprinted by permission of BNA Books. Copyright © 1988 by the Institute of World Economy and International Relations (IMEMO). English language rights copyright © 1989 by The Bureau of National Affairs, Inc., Washington, D.C.

3. From Zbigniew Brzezinski, "Ending the Cold War," *The Washington Quarterly*, Vol. 12, No. 4 (Autumn 1989), pp. 29-34. Excerpted and reprinted by permission of The MIT Press, Cambridge, MA, copyright © 1989. (Some footnotes have been deleted; those remaining have been renumbered.)

4. From Henry Trofimenko, "The End of the Cold War, Not History," *The Washington Quarterly*, Vol. 13, No. 4 (Spring 1990), pp. 21-35. Excerpted and reprinted by permission of The MIT Press. (Some footnotes have been deleted; those remaining have been renumbered.)

5. Original chapter for this volume, copyright © 1992 Westview Press, Inc.

6. From David R. Jones, "Domestic and Economic Aspects of Gorbachev's Foreign Policy," in Carl G. Jacobsen, ed., *Soviet Foreign Policy: New Dynamics, New Themes* (New York: St. Martin's Press, 1989). Reprinted by permission of St. Martin's Press (North American rights) and the Macmillan Press (world rights). Copyright © 1989.

7. From Michael Mandelbaum, "The Bush Foreign Policy," *Foreign Affairs*, Vol. 70, No. 1 (America and the World, 1990/1991). Excerpted and reprinted by permission of *Foreign Affairs* (1991). Copyright © 1991 by the Council on Foreign Relations, Inc.

8. From Steven Kull, "Dateline Moscow: Burying Lenin," *Foreign Policy*, No. 78 (Spring 1990), pp. 172-191. Excerpted and reprinted with

permission from *Foreign Policy* 78 (Spring 1990). Copyright © 1990 by the Carnegie Endowment for International Peace.

9. From Alexei Pushkov, "Is an Ideological Concert Possible?" *International Affairs* (Moscow), No. 6 (June 1990), pp. 42-49.

10. From Alexei Arbatov, "How Much Defense Is Sufficient?" *International Affairs* (Moscow), No. 4. (April 1989), pp. 31-44.

11. From William E. Odom, "Gorbachev's Strategy and Western Security: Illusions vs. Reality," *The Washington Quarterly*, Vol. 13, No. 1 (Winter 1990), pp. 145-155. Excerpted and reprinted by permission of The National Strategy Information Center. Copyright © 1990.

12. From Alexei Arbatov, "Deep Reductions in Strategic Arms," in Steve Hirsch, ed., *MEMO: New Soviet Voices on Foreign and Economic Policy* (Washington, D.C.: BNA Books, 1989), pp. 453-470. Excerpted and reprinted by permission of BNA Books. Copyright © 1988 by the Institute of World Economy and International Relations (IMEMO). English language rights copyright © 1989, by The Bureau of National Affairs, Inc., Washington, D.C.

13. From Edward L. Rowny, "Arms Control and the Future of U.S.-Soviet Relations," *Strategic Review*, Vol. 19, No. 1 (Winter 1991), pp. 17-25. Reprinted with permission of *Strategic Review*. Copyright © 1991 by the United States Strategic Institute.

14. From Thomas G. Weiss and Meryl A. Kessler, "Moscow's U.N. Policy," *Foreign Policy*, No. 79 (Summer 1990), pp. 94-112. Reprinted with permission from *Foreign Policy* 79 (Summer 1990). Copyright © 1990 by the Carnegie Endowment for International Peace.

15. From Andrei Kozyrev, "The USSR's New Approach to the U.N.," *International Affairs* (Moscow), No. 7 (July 1990), pp. 12-19.

16. From Adlai E. Stevenson and Alton Frye, "Trading with the Communists," *Foreign Affairs*, Vol. 68, No. 2 (Spring 1989), pp. 53-71. Excerpted and reprinted by permission of *Foreign Affairs* (Spring 1989). Copyright © 1989 by the Council on Foreign Relations, Inc.

17. From Valeri Karavayev, "Eastern Europe Is Opening Itself to the World," *International Affairs* (Moscow), No. 4 (April 1990), pp. 35-44.

18. Excerpted from F. Stephen Larrabee, "The New Soviet Approach to Europe," *Proceedings of the Academy of Political Science*, Vol. 38, No. 1 (Winter 1991), pp. 1-25. Reprinted by permission of the Academy of Political Science. Copyright © 1991. Excerpted by permission of the author. (Some footnotes have been deleted; those remaining have been renumbered.)

19. From Sergei Karaganov, "The Problems of the USSR's European Policy," *International Affairs* (Moscow), No. 7 (July 1990), pp. 72-80.

20. From Stanley R. Sloan, "NATO's Future in a New Europe: An American Perspective," *International Affairs* (U.K.), Vol. 66, No. 3

(July 1990), pp. 495-511. Reprinted by permission of *International Affairs*. Copyright © 1990 by The Royal Institute of International Affairs. Excerpted by permission of the author. Article composed in mid-1990.

21. From Mikhail Bezrukov and Yuriy Davydov, "The Common European Home and Mutual Security," in Richard Smoke and Andrei Kortunov, eds., *Mutual Security: A New Approach to Soviet-American Relations* (New York: St. Martin's Press, 1991). Reprinted by permission of St. Martin's Press (North American rights) and the Macmillan Press (world rights). Copyright © 1991.

22. From John. J. Mearsheimer, "Why We Will Soon Miss the Cold War," *The Atlantic Monthly*, Vol. 266, No. 2 (August 1990), pp. 35-50. Excerpted and reprinted by permission of the author.

23. From F. Stephen Larrabee, "The New Soviet Approach to Europe" (see Reference 18). Pages 14-20 of this same article were excerpted by permission of the author for this chapter.

24. From Pavel Bayev, Sergei Karaganov, Victor Shein, and Vitali Zhurkin, "Is a Third Zero Attainable?" *International Affairs* (Moscow), No. 4 (April 1990), pp. 4-12, 23.

25. From S. Neil MacFarlane, "Superpower Rivalry in the 1990s," *Third World Quarterly*, Vol. 12, No. 1 (January 1990), pp. 1-25. Excerpted and reprinted by permission of the *Third World Quarterly*. Copyright © 1990.

26. From Andrei Kolosov, "Reappraisal of USSR Third World Policy," *International Affairs* (Moscow), No. 5 (May 1990), pp. 34-42.

27. From Georgy A. Arbatov, "Where Should We Go from Here?" in Graham Allison and William Vry, eds., *Windows of Opportunity: From Cold War to Peaceful Competition in U.S.-Soviet Relations* (New York: Ballinger Publishing Company, 1989). Excerpted and reprinted by permission of Ballinger Publishing Company. Copyright © 1989.

28. From Charles William Maynes, "America Without the Cold War," *Foreign Policy*, No. 78 (Spring 1990), pp. 3-25. Excerpted and reprinted with permission from *Foreign Policy* 78 (Spring 1990). Copyright © 1990 by the Carnegie Endowment for International Peace.

INTRODUCTION

In the aftermath of the recent abortive coup in the Soviet Union, one of the first individuals contacted by President Mikhail Gorbachev was the president of the United States. President Gorbachev wanted to express his appreciation for President George Bush's support during the crisis and also assure him that the progress made in improving superpower relations would not be sidetracked by the coup attempt. Such an exchange would have been inconceivable just a few years earlier and illustrates the importance that both countries attach to the new "post-confrontational" phase of their relationship.

It is evident that Soviet-American relations have been transformed to a degree that was completely unforeseen just a few years ago. With the apparent end to the Cold War, both countries have modified their foreign policy objectives to take advantage of the demise of bipolar politics and the evolution into a "new world order." "New thinking" in Soviet foreign policy and the positive American response to these changes has enabled the countries to normalize their relations and to explore opportunities for mutually beneficial cooperation. What are the prospects for further superpower accommodation in the post-Cold War era? Is there a strong interest on the part of both powers to work more cooperatively to resolve issues? What aspects of their relationship are likely to continue to be a source of tension between the two powers? Will they be able to maintain peaceful relations? This book attempts to answer these questions by analyzing significant issues in U.S.-Soviet relations from both the Soviet and American perspectives.

The volume is divided into eight parts. Part One, "The Evolution of Soviet-American Relations in the Post-War Era," describes the nature of the superpower conflict during the Cold War and draws some conclusions regarding both the negative and positive aspects of the confrontation. Consideration is also given to policy revisions and the resulting chain of events that led to the termination of the Cold War. The question as to who "won" this struggle of the post-war superpowers is also addressed, with some disagreement on this point among the contributing authors.

Part Two, "Soviet and American Foreign Policies After the Cold War," is oriented toward the radical changes in Soviet foreign policy since General Secretary (and later president) Mikhail Gorbachev introduced the concept of "new thinking" in Soviet foreign policy. Both the Soviet and American interpretations of the causes and effects of the new Soviet policies are presented, followed by an explanation of the Bush administration's reactions to these unprecedented events and policy adaptations. Also included in Part Two is a consideration of the extent to which Soviet "new thinking" has "de-ideologized" U.S.-Soviet relations. If the optimistic assessments presented in both the Soviet and American essays are correct, then the prospects for improved relations between these former ideological adversaries are great indeed.

In Part Three, "National Security Issues," the selections assess the extent to which these foreign policy revisions have influenced the military strategy and doctrine of the two superpowers. The American essays stress that, despite severe economic and political constraints, the Soviet Union is still a military superpower and it would be unwise to ignore this fact. The Soviet articles place greater emphasis on doctrinal adaptations and the negative domestic impact of excessive defense spending in both countries. In the essays on arms control there is general agreement by both the Soviet and U.S. arms control specialists that, now that the Cold War is over, arms control in the 1990s must adapt to the changes in U.S. and Soviet relations. In fact, they see unprecedented opportunities for arms control breakthroughs and recommend that both countries place an extremely high priority on reducing the risk of devastating conflict.

Part Four, "The Role of the United Nations," outlines how changes in Soviet-American relations have given a new life to the United Nations. Both selections focus on the Soviets' new approach to the U.N., but treatment of recent changes in the U.S. perspective of the international organization is also included.

Trade relations between the East and West in general, and the Soviet Union and United States in particular, are addressed in Part Five, "Economic Rivalry and Cooperation." The articles illustrate the economic vulnerability of both the United States and the USSR and suggest that improved economic relations would be mutually beneficial. One issue addressed is whether a nation should provide economic assistance, and/or improved trade relations, with an opposing military superpower. The obvious commercial benefits of the relationship are highlighted, but some consideration is also given to the "functional" attributes of greater economic interaction and the diminished possibility for warfare between such integrated states.

Part Six, entitled "Europe After the Cold War," is devoted to various aspects of Soviet-American relations in the new Europe. Several selections consider the radical transformation of Europe and the extent to which changes in superpower policies—and particularly Soviet "new thinking"—served as a catalyst for the collapse of communism in Eastern Europe and the reunification of Germany. Others consider how this collapse of bipolarity in Europe will affect the long-term stability of the region—with some rather pessimistic conclusions. Other selections address the appropriate role of NATO now that the Warsaw Pact has disintegrated, as well as alternative security systems that might include all European states as well as the superpowers. Significant breakthroughs in European arms control agreements during recent years, with the INF and CFE treaties being the most conspicuous examples, are also discussed in this section. The implications of a "nuclear-free" Europe for European stability and U.S.-Soviet relations is addressed in the final two articles in this section.

Although the changes are not as dramatic as those found in Europe, superpower rivalry in the Third World has shifted markedly during the past few years. As discussed in Part Seven, "Third World Issues," both superpowers are displaying an increased reluctance to continue the nonproductive "zero-sum" game that has dominated U.S.-Soviet relations in the Third World. Furthermore, there is increased recognition that the costs of past conflict in these areas have exceeded the gains and that superpower cooperation in North-South disputes can be beneficial to all nations involved.

The final section, Part Eight, "The Future of Soviet-American Relations," provides a long-term perspective of U.S.-Soviet relations in a transformed world. The proposals may appear overly optimistic to those who are leery of the prospects for Soviet-American cooperation in world affairs, but the recommendations deserve serious consideration.

PART ONE

The Evolution of Soviet-American Relations in the Post-War Era

Section 1
THE U.S.-SOVIET RIVALRY
IN PERSPECTIVE

Who could mourn the passing of the Cold War? While the world was divided into two conflicting camps, there was the ever-present danger of nuclear war between the superpowers. Defense spending was at such high levels that the economies of both the Soviet Union and the U.S. were adversely effected. The conflict was on a global scale, with the "zero-sum game" approach to Soviet-American relations evident even in the Third World. The result was that both superpowers had the propensity to impose their conflict upon local conflict throughout the world. It was an ideological struggle that isolated the two nations from one another and produced xenophobia among their citizens. It was a hostile, risky, and wasteful period in the history of both nations. We welcome its demise and are already questioning the causes of such an odious relationship.

Despite this euphoria as the superpowers enter a new era of relations, political commentators and strategists have been quick to point out that the Cold War did have its positive features. In fact, some have gone so far as to suggest that the Cold War was actually a blessing, or at least a very useful thing. There is some logic to this view: During the Cold War there was a tested method of maintaining the semblance of world order by means of the bipolar rivalry, of dividing the world into two blocs headed by two military superpowers. It was a crude but effective device, which, John Gaddis argues, could be credited with maintaining the "long peace." These "benefits" of the Cold War are now being compared to the possible consequences of its demise—the disintegration of stable alliances, political fragmentation throughout the world, the instability associated with a multipolar international system, and nuclear proliferation.

In "Looking Back: The Long Peace," John Gaddis writes that it would be well for us to question why the great-power peace during the postwar era survived despite so much provocation. It is important for us to understand, in other words, why there has been no Third World War. Gaddis contends that the primary reason that war was avoided is that the bipolar structure of the world encouraged stability. So also did certain inherent characteristics of the bilateral Soviet-U.S. relationship. To a surprising degree the two countries were mutually independent. Despite the appearance of two opposing political systems, locked in a struggle to the death, the author points out that the domestic structures of the two states were not likely, in themselves, to produce war.

Nuclear deterrence was the most distinguishing characteristic of the military struggle and it provided a mechanism to control conflict escalation. It was one of the primary reasons that statesmen of the two superpowers were extremely cautious—particularly when compared to their predecessors—about risking war between the two countries. Somewhat paradoxically, he argues "that the development of nuclear weapons has had, on balance, a stabilizing effect on the postwar international system." Technology has also played a role in postwar stability, because the "reconnaissance revolution" reduced the likelihood of a surprise attack. Furthermore, despite the antagonistic rhetoric, the two powers have actually moderated their ideological objectives to the common goal of international stability. Finally, Gaddis argues that great power stability was possible because implicit "rules of the game" developed in the Soviet-U.S. relationship. For example, neither side directly challenged the other's sphere of influence.

His conclusion is that the Cold War, although perhaps not fully appreciated at the time, was a self-regulating system that accommodated a variety of shared superpower interests. As a result the postwar period is more aptly described as the "long peace" rather than a time of instability and warfare.

While Gaddis emphasizes the stability of superpower relations during the Cold War era, Lev L. Lyubimov, in his essay "The New Thinking and Soviet-American Relations," vividly recounts the intense rivalry between the two powers while the world was divided into antagonistic blocs. He also reminds us that the mutual stereotypes that colored the relationship were a barrier to any efforts to normalize Soviet-U.S. relations. Even though there was some movement away from confrontation toward "peaceful coexistence" in the early 1970s, détente was short lived. In the mid-1970s, Soviet-American relations deteriorated primarily because of a policy reversal by the Reagan administration and right-wing Republicans. He admits that General Secretary Brezhnev was partially responsible for the decline in détente, but the Soviets had little choice because the United States "was not contemplating relations based on equality...." The United States sought to restrict Soviet strategic arms, weaken the USSR's influence in the developing world, and "ideologically 'soften up' the countries of the socialist commonwealth." Lyubimov is not hesitant to assess blame in this so-called "Second Cold War": "the return to confrontation was carried out exclusively by the U.S., which bears political and historical responsibility for doing so."

It is the author's opinion that the Reagan administration also contributed to the economic stagnation experienced by the Soviet Union in the mid-1980s. The "ruling circles" in the United States recognized the economic advantage they had over the Soviet Union and took steps to undermine the Soviet economy. This was accomplished primarily by reviving the arms race, but there were also efforts to restrain Soviet exports, prevent technology transfer to the USSR, and undermine any prospects for economic cooperation between the USSR and developed capitalist or developing countries. The U.S. also exacerbated regional conflicts to force the Soviets to shoulder additional expenditures. "The U.S. policy toward the USSR became an element of its policy of global revenge and a part of its efforts to restore its world standing."

But now Soviet-American relations are entering a new phase, and this is due to the foreign-policy component of *perestroika. In the author's opinion, the new Soviet foreign policy has "forced the West to recognize that the initiative had shifted to Moscow," because the Soviets had denounced the "reactive" model of international behavior that characterized the Cold War period.*

Now, as the superpowers enter into a new phase of their relationship, he sees some opportunities for cooperation but suggests that a great deal needs to be clarified. Therefore, a certain degree of caution is justified while the two countries work together to develop "stable models of interaction."

1

Looking Back:
The Long Peace

John Lewis Gaddis

I should like to begin this essay with a fable.

Once upon a time, there was a great war that involved the slaughter of millions upon millions of people. When, after years of fighting, one side finally prevailed over the other and the war ended, everyone said that it must go down in history as the last great war ever fought. To that end, the victorious nations sent all of their wisest men to a great peace conference, where they were given the task of drawing up a settlement that would be so carefully designed, so unquestionably fair to all concerned, that it would eliminate war as a phenomenon of human existence. Unfortunately, that settlement lasted only 20 years.

There followed yet another great war involving the slaughter of millions upon millions of people. When, after years of fighting, one side finally prevailed over the other and the war ended, everyone said that it must go down in history as the last great war ever fought. To everyone's horror, though, the victors in that conflict immediately fell to quarreling among themselves, with the result that no peace conference ever took place. Within a few years, the major victors had come to regard each other, and not their former enemies, as the principal threat to their survival. Each sought to ensure that survival by developing weapons capable, at least in theory, of ending the survival of everyone on earth.

Paradoxically, that arrangement lasted twice as long as the first one, and as the fable ended, showed no sign of collapsing anytime soon.

It is, of course, just a fable, and as a rule one ought not to take fables too seriously. There are times, though, when they can illuminate reality more sharply than conventional forms of explanation. This may be one of them.

For it is the case that the post-World War II system of international relations, which nobody designed or even thought could last very long—which was based not upon the dictates of morality and justice but rather upon an arbitrary division of the world into spheres of influence, and incorporated some of the most bitter antagonisms short of war in modern history—has now survived twice as long as the far more carefully designed World War I settlement. Indeed, it has approximately equaled in longevity the great nineteenth-century international systems of Metternich and Bismarck....

To be sure, the term "peace" is not the first that comes to mind when one recalls the history of the Cold War. The period, after all, has seen the greatest accumulation of armaments the world has ever known, a whole series of protracted and devastating limited wars, an abundance of revolutionary, ethnic, religious, and civil violence, as well as some of the most intractable ideological rivalries in human experience. Nor have those more ancient scourges—famine, disease, poverty, injustice—disappeared from the face of the Earth.

Is it not stretching things a bit, one might ask, to take the moral and spiritual desert in which the world's nations conduct their affairs and call it "peace"?

It is, of course, but that is just the point. Given all the conceivable reasons for having had a major war during the past four decades—reasons that in any other age would have provided ample justification for such a war—it seems worthy of comment that there has not in fact been one; that despite the unjust and wholly artificial character of the post-World War II settlement, it has now persisted for the better part of half a century. This may not be grounds for celebration, but it is at least grounds for investigation: for trying to comprehend how this great-power peace has managed to survive for so long in the face of so much provocation, and for thinking about what might be done to perpetuate that situation. After all, we could do worse.

Stability, Not Justice

Anyone attempting to understand why there has been no third world war confronts a problem not unlike that of Sherlock Holmes and the dog that did not bark in the night: How does one account for something that did not happen?

The question involves certain methodological difficulties, to be sure: It is always easier to account for what did happen than for what did not. But there is also a curious bias among students of international relations that reinforces this tendency: "For every thousand pages published on the causes of wars," Geoffrey Blainey has noted, "there is less than one page directly on the causes of peace." Even the discipline of "peace studies" has given more attention to what we must do to avoid the apocalypse than it has to the equally interesting question of why it has not happened so far.

One difficulty is that our actual experience is limited to the operations of a single system—the balance of power system—operating within either the "multipolar" configuration that characterized international politics until World War II, or the "bipolar" configuration that has characterized them since. Alternative systems remain abstract conceptualizations in the minds of theorists, and are of little use in advancing our knowledge of how wars in the real world do or do not occur. But in "systems theory," one can find a useful point of departure for thinking about the nature of international relations since 1945.

A valuable feature of systems theory is that it provides criteria for differentiating between stable and unstable political configurations: This can help to account for the fact that some international systems outlast others. It is characteristic of a stable system that it has the capacity for self-regulation: the ability to counteract stimuli that would otherwise threaten its survival, much as the automatic pilot on an airplane or the governor on a steam engine would do.

A system of self-regulating mechanisms is most likely to function when there exists some fundamental agreement among major states on the objectives they are seeking to uphold by participating in the system, when its structure reflects the way in which power is distributed among its members, and when agreed-upon procedures exist for resolving differences.

Does the post-World War II international system fit these criteria for "stability"?

Certainly its most basic characteristic—bipolarity—remains intact, in that the gap between the two greatest military powers and their nearest rivals is not substantially different from what it was four decades ago. At the same time, neither the Soviet Union nor the United

States nor anyone else has been able wholly to dominate that system; the nations most active within it in 1945 are for the most part still active today. And of course the most convincing argument for stability is that, so far, World War III has not occurred.

We can all conceive of international systems that would combine stability with greater justice and less risk than the present one does, and we ought to continue to think about these things. But short of war, which no one wants, change in international relations tends to be gradual and evolutionary. It does not happen overnight. This means that alternative systems, if they ever develop, probably will not be total rejections of the existing system, but rather variations proceeding from it. All the more reason, then, to try to understand the system we have, to try to distinguish its stabilizing characteristics from its destabilizing ones, and to try to reinforce the former as a basis from which we might, in time and with luck, do better.

Bipolarity's Bounty

Any such investigation should begin by distinguishing the structure of the international system in question from the behavior of the nations that make it up. The reason for this is simple: Behavior alone will not ensure stability if the structural prerequisites for it are absent, but structure can, under certain circumstances, impose stability even when its behavioral prerequisites are unpromising. One need only compare the settlement of 1945 with its predecessor of 1919 to see the point.

If the intentions of statesmen alone had governed, the Paris Peace Conference of 1919 would have ushered in an era of stability in world politics comparable to that brought about in Europe by the Congress of Vienna almost a century earlier. And, at least as far as self-determination was concerned, the Versailles settlement did come as close as any in modern history to incorporating the principles of justice.

Unfortunately, in so doing, it neglected the realities of power. It broke up the old Austro-Hungarian Empire, a move that accurately reflected the aspirations of the nationalities involved, but that failed to provide the successor states of Poland, Czechoslovakia, Austria, and Hungary with the military or economic means necessary to sustain their new-found sovereignty.

Even more shortsightedly, there was no effort to accommodate the interests of two nations whose populations and industrial strength were certain to guarantee them a major influence over postwar European developments—Germany and Soviet Russia. It should have been no surprise, therefore, that when the Versailles system finally broke down in

1939, it did so largely as the result of a deal cut at the expense of the East Europeans by these two countries whose power had been ignored, twenty years earlier, in the interests of justice.

Nobody, in contrast, would picture the post-World War II settlement as a triumph of justice. That settlement arbitrarily divided sovereign nations such as Germany, Austria, and Korea, not because anyone thought it was right to do so, but because neither the United States nor the Soviet Union could agree on whose occupation forces would withdraw first. It did nothing to prevent the incorporation of several of the countries whose independence the 1919 settlement had recognized—for example, Poland, whose independence Britain had gone to war in 1939 to protect—into a Soviet sphere of influence. It witnessed, in response to this, the creation of an American sphere in Western Europe, the Mediterranean, and the Pacific.

What resulted was the first true polarization of power in modern history. The world had had limited experience with bipolar systems in ancient times, it is true: Certainly Thucydides's account of the rivalry between Athens and Sparta carries an eerie resonance for us today; and statesmen of the Cold War era could not forget what they had once learned, as schoolboys, of the antagonism between Rome and Carthage. But these had been regional conflicts: Not until 1945 could one plausibly speak of a *world* divided into two spheres of influence, or of the *superpowers* that controlled them.

Now, bipolarity may seem to many today—as it did four decades ago—an awkward and dangerous way to organize world politics. Simple geometric logic would suggest that a system resting upon three or more points of support would be more stable than one resting upon two. But politics is not geometry. The passage of time and the accumulation of experience have made clear certain structural elements of stability in the bipolar system of international relations that were not present in the multipolar systems that preceded it:

1. The bipolar system reflected the facts of where military power resided at the end of World War II—and where it still does today. In this sense, it differed from the settlement of 1919, which made so little effort to accommodate the interests of Germany and Soviet Russia.

It is true that in other categories of power—notably the economic one—states have since arisen that are capable of challenging or even surpassing the Soviet Union and the United States in the production of certain commodities. But as the *political* position of nations such as West Germany, Brazil, Japan, South Korea, Taiwan, and Hong Kong suggests, the ability to make video recorders, motorcycles, even automobiles and steel efficiently has yet to translate into anything approaching the capacity of Washington or Moscow to shape events in the world as a whole.

2. The post-1945 bipolar structure was a simple one that did not require sophisticated leadership to maintain. The great multipolar systems of the nineteenth century collapsed in large part because of their intricacy: They required a Metternich or a Bismarck to hold them together.

Neither the Soviet nor the American political system has been geared toward identifying statesmen of comparable prowess; demonstrated skill in the conduct of foreign policy has hardly been a major prerequisite for leadership in either country. And yet, a bipolar system, because of the high stakes involved for its major actors, tends to induce in the personalities involved a sense of caution and restraint, and to discourage irresponsibility. "It is not," Kenneth Waltz notes, "that one entertains the utopian hope that all future American and Russian rulers will [embody] nearly perfect virtues, but rather that the pressures of a bipolar world strongly encourage them to act internationally in ways better than their characters may lead one to expect."

3. Because of its relatively simple structure, alliances in this bipolar system have tended to be more stable than they were during the nineteenth century and during the 1919-1939 period.

It is striking to consider that the North Atlantic Treaty Organization has now equaled in longevity the most durable of the pre-World War I alliances, that between Germany and Austria-Hungary; it has lasted twice as long as the Franco-Russian alliance, and much longer than any of the tenuous alignments of the interwar period. Its rival, the Warsaw Treaty Organization, has been in existence for almost as long.

The reason for this is simple: Alliances, in the end, are the products of insecurity. So long as the Soviet Union and the United States each remain for the other (and the other's clients) the major source of danger, neither superpower encounters much difficulty in maintaining the coalitions it controls. In a multipolar system, sources of insecurity can vary in much more complicated ways—and alliances tend to shift to accommodate these variations.

4. At the same time, and probably because of the stability of the basic alliance systems, defections from both the U.S. and Soviet coalitions—China, Cuba, Vietnam, Iran, and Nicaragua, in the case of the Americans; Yugoslavia, Albania, Egypt, Somalia, and China again in the case of the Russians—have been tolerated without the disruptions that might have attended such changes in a more delicately balanced

multipolar system. The fact that a state the size of China was able to reverse its alignment twice during the Cold War without dramatic effect says something about the stability bipolarity brings. Compare this record with the impact, prior to 1914, of such apparently minor episodes as Austria's annexation of Bosnia and Herzegovina, or the question of who was to control Morocco. It is an odd consequence of bipolarity that although alliances are more durable than in a multipolar system, defections are at the same time more tolerable.

In short, without anyone's having designed it, the nations of the postwar era lucked into a system of international relations that, because it has been based upon realities of power, has served the cause of order—if not justice—better than might have been expected.

"Good Fences"

But if the structure of bipolarity encouraged stability, so too did certain inherent characteristics of the bilateral Soviet-American relationships.

It used to be fashionable to point out, before the Cold War began, that, despite periodic outbreaks of tension between them, Russians and Americans had never actually gone to war with each other. The same claim could not be made for either country's relations with Britain, Germany, Italy, Austria-Hungary, Japan, or (if the Americans' undeclared naval war of 1798-1800 is counted) France. This record was thought to be all the more remarkable in view of the fact that, in ideological terms, the Russian and American systems of government could hardly have been more different.

The onset of the Cold War made this argument seem less than convincing. To assert that relations between Russia and the United States had once been good, students of the subject now suggested, was to confuse harmony with inactivity. Given the infrequency of contacts between Russia and the United States during the nineteenth century, their tradition of "friendship" had been decidedly unremarkable. Once contacts became more frequent, as they had by the beginning of the twentieth century, conflicts quickly followed, even before Western statesmen had begun to worry about bolshevism or the imminence of the international proletarian revolution.

But even after this breakdown in cordiality—and regardless of whether it had been real or imagined—the point remained valid: There still had been no Russian-American war, despite the fact that Russians and Americans had at one time or another fought virtually every other major power. This raises the question of whether there are not structural elements in the Russian-American relationship itself that contribute to stability, quite apart from the policies actually followed by Russian and American governments.

It has long been an assumption of classical liberalism that the more extensive the contacts that take place between nations, the greater are the chances for peace. Economic interdependence, it has been argued, makes war unlikely because nations who have come to rely upon one another for vital commodities cannot afford it. Cultural exchange, it has been suggested, encourages people to become more sensitive to one another's concerns, and hence reduces the likelihood of misunderstandings. "People-to-people" contacts, it has been assumed, make it possible for nations to "know" one another better; the danger of war between them is, as a result, correspondingly reduced.

These are pleasant things to believe, but there is remarkably little historical evidence to validate them.

As Kenneth Waltz has pointed out, "the fiercest civil wars and the bloodiest international ones are fought within arenas populated by highly similar people whose affairs are closely knit." Consider the costliest military conflicts of the past century and a half, using the statistics conveniently available now through the University of Michigan "Correlates of War" project: Of the ten bloodiest interstate wars, every one of them grew out of conflicts between countries that either directly adjoined one another, or were involved actively in trade with one another. Certainly economic interdependence did little to prevent Germany, France, Britain, Russia, and Austria-Hungary from going to war in 1914; nor did the fact that the United States was Japan's largest trading partner deter that country from attacking Pearl Harbor in 1941.

Since 1945, there have been more civil wars than interstate wars; that fact alone should be sufficient to call into question the proposition that interdependence necessarily breeds peace.

The Russian-American relationship, to a remarkable degree for two nations so involved with the rest of the world, has been one of mutual independence.

The simple fact that they occupy opposite sides of the earth has had something to do with this: Geographical remoteness has provided little opportunity for the emergence of irredentist grievances comparable in importance to historic disputes over, say, Alsace-Lorraine, or the Polish Corridor, or the West Bank, the Gaza Strip, and Jerusalem. In the few areas where Soviet and U.S. forces—or their proxies—have come into direct contact, they have erected artificial barriers like the Korean demilitarized zone or the Berlin Wall, perhaps in unconscious recognition of an American poet's rather chilly precept that "good fences make good neighbors."

Nor have the two nations been economically dependent upon one another in any critical way. The United States requires nothing in the form of imports from the Soviet Union that it cannot obtain elsewhere. The situation is different for the Russians, to be sure, but even though the Soviet Union imports large quantities of food from the United States—and would like to import advanced technology as well—it is far from being wholly dependent upon these items, as the failure of attempts to change Soviet behavior by denying them has shown. The relative invulnerability of Russians and Americans to one another in the economic sphere may be frustrating to their policymakers, but it is probably fortunate, from the standpoint of international stability, that the world's two most powerful nations are also its most self-sufficient.

But what about the argument that expanded international communication promotes peace? Is not the failure of Russians and Americans to better understand one another a potential source of instability in their relationship?

Obviously it can be, if misunderstandings occur at the level of national leadership. The most serious Soviet-American confrontation of the postwar era, the Cuban Missile Crisis (1962), is generally regarded as having arisen from what appear to have been quite remarkable misperceptions of each side's intentions by the other. But "people-to-people" contacts are another matter. The history of international relations is replete with examples of familiarity breeding contempt as well as friendship: There are too many nations whose people have known each other all too well and have, as a result, taken an intense dislike to one another—French and Germans, Russians and Poles, Japanese and Chinese, Greeks and Turks, Arabs and Israelis—to lend very much credence to the proposition that getting to know other nations invariably means getting along with them.

It may well be, then, that the extent to which the Soviet Union and the United States have been independent of one another rather than interdependent—the fact that there have been so few points of economic leverage available to each, the fact that two such dissimilar people have had so few opportunities for interaction—has in itself constituted a structural support for stability in the countries' relations, whatever their governments have actually done.

Seeking the Roots

Structure can affect diplomacy from another angle, though: one that has to do with the domestic roots of foreign policy.

It was Karl Marx who first noted the effect of social and economic forces upon political behavior. John A. Hobson and Vladimir Lenin subsequently derived from this the proposition that capitalism causes both imperialism and war. Meanwhile, Joseph Schumpeter was working out an alternative theory that placed the origins of conflict in the "atavistic" insecurities of aristocracies, bureaucracies, and certain leaders. Historians, both Marxists and non-Marxists, have stressed the importance of domestic structural influences in bringing about World War I, and there has been increasing scholarly interest in the role of such factors in interwar diplomacy. But to what extent can one argue that domestic structures have shaped the behavior of the Soviet Union and the United States toward each other since 1945?

There has been a persistent effort to link the structure of the American economy to foreign policy, most conspicuously through the assertion that capitalism requires an aggressive search for raw materials, markets, and investment opportunities overseas in order to survive. The theory pre-dates the Cold War, having been suggested by Charles A. Beard during the 1920s and 1930s. But it was left to William Appleman Williams to work out the most influential characterization of what he called "open door" expansionism in his classic work, *The Tragedy of American Diplomacy* (1959). Recently—in a more sophisticated way—the linkage between economic structure and foreign policy has stressed the role of "corporatism": the *cooperation* of business, labor, and government to shape a mutually congenial environment.

Both the "open door" and "corporatist" models have been criticized, with some justification, for their tendency toward reductionism—the explanation of complex phenomena in terms of single causes. But what is important here is that these most frequently advanced arguments linking the structure of American capitalism with American foreign policy do not assume, from that linkage, the inevitability of war.

One of the advantages of the "open door," Williams has noted, was precisely the fact that it *avoided* confrontations. It was a way to "extend the American system throughout the world without the embarrassment and inefficiency of traditional colonialism"; "it was conceived and designed to win the victories without the wars." Similarly, "corporatist" historiography stresses the stabilizing rather than the destabilizing effects of U.S. intervention in Europe after World Wars I and II: American attempts to replicate domestic structure abroad are credited with reinforcing rather than undermining international systems.

Neither the "open door" nor the "corporatist" paradigm, therefore, offers evidence sufficient to confirm the old Leninist assertion that a society committed to capitalism is necessarily precluded from participation in a stable world order.

There have been, if course, Schumpeterian as well as Leninist explanations of how domestic influences affect American foreign policy. C. Wright Mills some three decades ago stressed the interlocking relationship of businessmen, politicians, and military officers; this "power elite" had imposed a form of "naked and arbitrary power" upon the world. Subsequent analysts, no doubt encouraged by Dwight D. Eisenhower's perhaps inadvertent endorsement of the term, transformed Mills's argument into a full-blown theory of a "military-industrial complex" whose interests effectively prevented any significant relaxation of world tensions.

There were, to be sure, certain difficulties with this model: It did not plausibly explain the Truman administration's low military budgets of 1945-1950; nor did it deal easily with the shift from defense to welfare expenditures presided over by Richard Nixon during the early 1970s. It neglected evidence that a "military-industrial complex" existed inside the USSR as well. But even if one overlooked these problems, it was not clear how the existence of such a "complex" necessarily made war any more likely, given the opportunities deterrence offered to develop a profusion of military hardware without the risks war would pose to one's ability to continue doing precisely this.

But what about the Soviet Union? In attempting to understand the effect of international influences on Soviet foreign policy, American analysts have found Schumpeter a better guide than Lenin; they have stressed the extent to which the requirements of legitimizing internal political authority have affected behavior toward the outside world. It was George F. Kennan who most convincingly suggested this approach with his portrayals, in 1946 and 1947, of a Soviet leadership at once so insecure and so unimaginative that it felt obliged to cultivate external enemies in order to maintain itself in power.

Whatever the validity of this theory—Kennan himself considered its application limited to the Stalin era—the characterization of a Kremlin leadership fated by its own nervous ineptitude to perpetual distrust remains the most influential explanation in the West of how domestic structure influences Soviet foreign policy.

But this theory, too, did not assume the inevitability of war. Institutionalized suspicion in the USSR resulted from weakness, not strength, Kennan argued. As a consequence, the Kremlin was unlikely to initiate military action. With rare exceptions, U.S. officials ever since have accepted this distinction between the likelihood of hostility and the probability of war; the theory of deterrence has been based upon the assumption that paranoia and prudence can coexist. By this logic, then, the domestic structures of the Soviet state, however geared they may have been to picturing the rest of the world in the worst possible light, have not been seen as likely, in and of themselves, to produce war.

One should not make too much of these attempts to attribute to domestic constraints the foreign policy of either the United States or the USSR. International relations, like life itself, are a good deal more complicated than the models tend to suggest. But it is significant that these efforts by scholars to link internal structure to external behavior reveal no obvious proclivity on either side to risk war; that despite their differences, Soviet and American domestic structures appear to have posed no greater impediment to the maintenance of a stable international system than has bipolarity itself or the bilateral characteristics of the Soviet-American relationship.

Confronting Mortality

Even if the World War II settlement had corresponded to the distribution of power in the world, even if the Russian-American relationship had been one of minimal interdependence, even if domestic constraints had not created difficulties, stability in the postwar era still might not have resulted had there been, in either of the dominant powers, the same willingness to risk war that existed in the past.

Students of the causes of war have pointed out that war is rarely something that develops from the workings of impersonal social or economic forces, or from the direct effects of arms races, or even by accident. It requires deliberate decisions on the part of national leaders. More than that, it requires calculations that the gains to be derived from war will outweigh the possible costs.

"Recurring optimism," Geoffrey Blainey has written, "is a vital prelude to war. Anything which increases that optimism is a cause of war. Anything which dampens that optimism is a cause of peace."

Admittedly, those calculations are often in error: as Kennan, in his capacity as historian, has pointed out, whatever conceivable gains the statesmen of 1914 might have had in mind in risking war, they could not have come anywhere close to approximating the costs the ensuing four-year struggle would actually entail. But it seems hard to deny that it is from such calculations—whether accurately carried out, as Bismarck seemed able to do in his wars against Denmark, Austria, and France during the mid-nineteenth century, or inaccurately carried out, as was the case in 1914—that wars tend to develop. They are not something that just happens, like earthquakes, locust plagues, or (some might argue) the selection of presidential candidates in the United States.

For whatever reason, statesmen of the post-1945 superpowers have been exceedingly cautious, compared to their predecessors, in risking war between their countries. Consider the crises in Soviet-American relations: Iran, 1946; Greece, 1947; Berlin and Czechoslovakia, 1948; Korea, 1950; the East Berlin riots, 1953; the Hungarian uprising, 1956; Berlin again, 1958-1959; the U-2 incident, 1960; Berlin again, 1961; the Cuban Missile Crisis, 1962; Czechoslovakia again, 1968; the Yom Kippur war, 1973; Afghanistan, 1979; Poland, 1981; the Korean airliner incident, 1983. One need only run down the list to see how many occasions there were that in almost any other age, and among almost any other antagonists, would eventually have produced war.

That war was avoided cannot be chalked up to the invariably pacific temperaments of the nations involved: The United States participated in eight international wars involving 1000 or more battlefield deaths between 1815 and 1980; Russia participated in nineteen. Nor can this restraint be attributed to any unusual qualities of leadership on either side: The vision and competency of postwar Soviet and American statesmen does not appear to have differed greatly from that of their predecessors. Nor does weariness stemming from participation in two world wars fully explain this unwillingness to resort to arms: During the postwar era both nations have employed force against third parties—the United States in Korea and Vietnam; the Soviet Union in Afghanistan—for protracted periods of time, and at great cost.

It seems inescapable that what has really made the difference in inducing this unaccustomed caution has been the workings of the nuclear deterrent.

Consider, for a moment, what the effect of this mechanism would be on a statesman from either superpower who might be contemplating war.

In the past, the horrors and costs of wars could be forgotten with the passage of time. Generations like the one of 1914 had little sense of what the Napoleonic Wars—or even the American Civil War—had revealed about the brutality, expense, and duration of military conflict. But the existence of nuclear weapons—and the fact that we have direct evidence of what they can do when used against human beings—has given this generation a painfully vivid awareness of the realities of war that no previous generation has had. It is difficult, given this awareness, to generate the optimism that historical experience tells us prepares the way for war; pessimism, it seems, is a permanent accompaniment to our thinking about war. And that, as Blainey reminds us, is a cause of peace.

That same pessimism has provided the superpowers with powerful inducements to control crises resulting from the risk-taking of third parties. It is worth recalling that World War I grew out of the unsuccessful management of a situation neither created nor desired by any of the major actors in the international system. There were simply no mechanisms to put a lid on escalation—to force each nation to balance the short-term temptation to exploit opportunities against the long-term danger that things might get out of hand. The nuclear deterrent provides that mechanism today. As a result, the United States and the Soviet Union have managed a whole series of crises—most notably in the Middle East—that grew out of the actions of neither but that could have involved them both.

None of this is to say that war cannot occur: If the study of history reveals anything at all it is that one ought to expect, sooner or later, the unexpected. Nor do I claim that the nuclear deterrent could not function equally well with half, or a fourth, or even an eighth of the nuclear weapons now in the superpowers' arsenals. Nor do I intend to deprecate the importance of refraining from steps that might destabilize the existing stalemate—whether through the search for technological breakthroughs that might provide a decisive edge over the other side; through so mechanical a duplication of what the other side has that one fails to take into account one's own, quite different security requirements; or through strategies that rely upon the first use of nuclear weapons in the interest of achieving economy, abandoning the far more important tradition of never employing these weapons in combat.

I am suggesting, though, that the development of nuclear weapons has had, on balance, a stabilizing effect on the postwar international system. They have served to discourage the process of escalation that has, in other eras, too casually led to war. They have had a sobering effect upon a whole range of statesmen of varying degrees of responsibility and capability. They have forced national leaders, every day, to confront the reality of what war is really like, indeed to confront the prospect of their own mortality.

That, for those who seek ways to avoid war, is no bad thing.

Technology's Gift

But although nuclear deterrence is the most important behavioral mechanism that has sustained the postwar international system, it is not the only one. Indeed, the very technology that has made it possible to deliver nuclear weapons anywhere on the face of the earth has functioned also to lower greatly the danger of surprise attack, thereby supplementing the self-regulating features of deterrence with the assurance that comes from knowing a great deal more than in the past about adversary capabilities. I refer here to what might be called the "reconnaissance revolution," a development that may well rival in importance the "nuclear revolution," but one that rarely gets the attention it deserves.

The point was made earlier that nations tend to start wars on the basis of calculated assessments that they have the power to prevail. But it was suggested as well that they have often been wrong about this: They either have failed to anticipate the nature and the costs of war itself, or they have misjudged the intentions and capabilities of the adversary they have chosen to confront.

Now, it would be foolish to argue that Americans and Russians have become any more skillful at discerning one another's *intentions.* Clearly the U.S. invasion of Grenada surprised Moscow as much as the Soviet invasion of Afghanistan surprised Washington. The capacity of each nation to behave in ways that seem perfectly logical to it but quite unfathomable to the other remains about what it has been throughout the Cold War. But both sides are able—and have been so for at least two decades—to evaluate each other's *capabilities* to a degree unprecedented in the history of relations between great powers.

What has made this possible, of course, has been the development of the reconnaissance satellite—a device that, if rumors are correct, allows the reading of automobile license plates or newspaper headlines from a hundred or more miles out in space—together with the equally important custom that has evolved among the superpowers of allowing these objects to pass unhindered over their territories. The effect has been to give each side a far more accurate view of the other's military capabilities—and, to some degree, economic capabilities—than could ever have been provided by the best spies in the history of espionage.

The resulting intelligence does not rule out the possibility of surprise attack, but it does render it far less likely, at least as far as the superpowers are concerned. And that is no small matter, if one considers the number of conflicts—from the Trojan War down through Pearl Harbor—in whose origins deception played a major role.

The "reconnaissance revolution" also corrects, to a degree, the asymmetry imposed upon Soviet-U.S. relations by the two nations' different forms of political and social organization.

Throughout most of the early Cold War years the Soviet Union enjoyed all the advantages of a closed society in concealing its capabilities from the West; the United States and its allies, in turn, found it difficult to keep anything secret for very long. That problem still exists, but the ability now to peer visually and electronically into almost every part of the Soviet Union helps to compensate for it. And, of course, virtually none of the limited progress the two countries have made in arms control would have been possible had Americans and Russians not tacitly agreed to the use of reconnaissance satellites and other techniques to monitor compliance.

There is no little irony in the fact that these instruments, which have contributed so much toward stabilizing the postwar international system, grew directly out of research on the intercontinental ballistic missile and the U-2 spy plane. Technological innovation is not always a destabilizing force in the Soviet-American relationship; there may be again instances in which the advance of technology, far from increasing the danger of war, could actually lessen it. It all depends upon the uses to which the technology is put, and that, admittedly, is not easy to foresee.

The Power of Ideas

If technology has had the potential to stabilize or unsettle the international system, that cannot as easily be said of ideology.

One cannot help but be impressed—when one looks at the long history of national liberation movements, or revolutions against established social orders, or racial and religious conflict—by the continuing capacity of ideas to move nations, or groups within them to fight. It is only by reference to a violent and ultimately self-destructive ideological impulse that one can account for the remarkable career of Adolf Hitler, with all of its chaotic consequences for the postwar international system. Since 1945, the ideology of self-determination has induced colonies to embroil colonial masters in protracted and costly warfare; it has also led factions within newly independent states to seek forcibly their own separate political existence.

Ideologically motivated social revolution, too, has been a prominent feature of the postwar scene, with major upheavals in nations as diverse as China, Cuba, Vietnam, Cambodia, and Nicaragua. But the most surprising evidence of the continuing influence of ideology has come in the area of religion. Conflicts between Hindus and Muslims, Arabs and Israelis, Iranians and Iraqis, and even Catholics and Protestants in Northern Ireland provide little reason to think that ideas— even those once considered to have relevance only for historians—will not continue to have a major potential for disruption.

The U.S.-Soviet relationship has not been free from ideological rivalry; it could be argued, in fact, that these are among the most ideological nations on earth. Certainly their ideologies could hardly be more antithetical, given the self-proclaimed intention of one to overthrow the other. And yet, since their emergence as superpowers, both nations have shown an impressive capacity to subordinate antagonistic ideological interests to a common goal of preserving international order.

The reasons are worth examining.

If there ever was a moment in which the priorities of order overcame those of ideology, it would appear to have been when Soviet leaders decided that war would no longer advance the cause of revolution.

That had not been Lenin's position: International conflict, for him, was good or evil according to whether it accelerated or retarded the demise of capitalism. Stalin's attitude was more ambivalent: He encouraged talk of an "inevitable conflict" between the "two camps" of communism and capitalism in the years immediately following World War II; but, shortly before his death, he appears also to have anticipated the concept of "peaceful coexistence." It was left to Georgii Malenkov to admit publicly, after Stalin's death in 1953, that a nuclear war would mean "the destruction of world civilization."

Nikita Khrushchev subsequently refined this idea (which he had initially condemned) into the proposition that the interests of world revolution, as well as those of the Soviet state, would be better served by working within the international order than by trying to overthrow it.

The reasons for this shift are not difficult to surmise.

First, bipolarity—the defining characteristic of the postwar international system—implied unquestioned recognition of the Soviet Union as a great power. It was "no small thing," Khrushchev noted in his memoirs, "that we have lived to see the day when the Soviet Union is considered, in terms of its economic and military might, one of the two most powerful countries in the world."

Second, the international situation during the 1950s and early 1960s seemed favorable, especially because of the decline of colonialism and the rise of newly independent nations likely to be suspicious of the West, to the expansion of Soviet influence in the world.

Third, and most important, the growth of nuclear capabilities on both sides had confirmed Malenkov's conclusion that in any future war between the great powers there would be no victors at all, capitalist or communist. "The atomic bomb," Soviet leaders reminded their more militant Chinese comrades in 1963, "does not observe the class principle."

The effect was to transform a state which, had ideology alone governed, should have sought a complete restructuring of the international system, into one for whom that system now seemed to have definite benefits, so much so that the goal of overthrowing capitalism had been postponed to some vague point in the future. Without this moderation of ideological objectives, it is difficult to see how the postwar great-power stability could have been possible.

Ideological considerations have played a less prominent role in shaping American foreign policy, but they have had influence nonetheless. The Wilsonian commitment to self-determination, revived and ardently embraced during World War II, did a great deal to alienate Americans from their Soviet allies at the end of that conflict. Nor had their military exertions moderated Americans' long aversion to collectivism—of which the Soviet variety appeared to be the most extreme example. But there had also developed, during the war, an emphatic hostility toward "totalitarianism" in general: Governments that relied upon force to stay in power at home, it was thought, could hardly be counted on to refrain from the use of force in the world at large.

Demands for the "unconditional surrender" of Germany and Japan reflected this ideological stand: There could be no compromise with regimes for whom a totalitarian rule was a way of life. What is interesting is that although the totalitarian model came to be applied as easily to the Soviet Union as it had been to Germany and Japan, the absolutist call for unconditional surrender was not.

To be sure, the United States and the USSR were not at war. But levels of tension during the late 1940s were about as high as they can get short of war, and we now know that planning for the *contingency* of war was well under way in Washington—as it presumably was in Moscow.

It is not easy to explain why Americans failed to commit themselves to the eradication of Soviet totalitarianism with the same determination they had applied to German and Japanese totalitarianism. One reason, of course, would have been the daunting prospect of attempting to occupy a country the size of the Soviet Union. Another was the fact that, despite the hostility that had developed since 1945, U.S. officials did not regard their Russian counterparts as irredeemable. The very purpose of "containment" had been to change the *psychology* of the Soviet leadership, but not, as had been the case with Germany and Japan, the leadership itself.

But Washington's aversion to an unconditional surrender doctrine for the Soviet Union stemmed from yet another, less obvious consideration. It had quickly become clear to American policymakers, after World War II, that insistence on the total defeat of Germany and Japan had profoundly destabilized the postwar balance of power. Only by assuming responsibility for the rehabilitation of these former enemies, as well as the countries they had ravaged, was the United States able to restore equilibrium. Even then it was clear that the U.S. role would have to be a continuing one.

It was no accident that the doctrine of unconditional surrender came under fire after 1945 from a new school of "realist" geopoliticians, who were given to viewing international stability in terms of the wary toleration of adversaries rather than, as a point of principle, their annihilation. Largely as a result of such reasoning, U.S. officials at no point during the Cold War seriously contemplated, as a political objective, the elimination of the Soviet Union as a major force in world affairs.

All of this would appear to confirm the proposition that systemic interests tend to take precedence over ideological interests.

Both the Soviet ideological aversion to capitalism and the American ideological aversion to totalitarianism could have produced policies—as they had done in the past—aimed at the overthrow of their adversaries. That such ideological impulses could be muted to the extent they have been during the past four decades testifies to the stake both Washington and Moscow have had in preserving the existing international system. The moderation of ideologies must be considered, then, along with nuclear deterrence and reconnaissance, as a major self-regulating mechanism of post-war politics.

Playing Games

The question still arises, though: How can order emerge from a system that functions without any superior authority? Even self-regulating mechanisms like automatic pilots or engine governors need someone to set them in motion; the prevention of anarchy, it has generally been assumed, requires hierarchy, in both interpersonal and international relations.

Certainly the statesmen of World War II expected that some supranational structure would be necessary to sustain a future peace—whether in the form of a new collective security organization to replace the ineffectual League of Nations, or through perpetuation of the great-power consensus that Churchill, Roosevelt, and Stalin sought to forge. All would have been surprised by the extent to which order has been maintained since 1945 in the absence of effective supranational authority of any kind.*

This phenomenon has forced students of international politics to recognize that their subject bears less resemblance to local or national politics, where order does in fact depend upon legally constituted authority, than it does to the conduct of games.

In a game, order evolves from mutual agreement on a set of "rules" defining the range of behavior each side anticipates from the other. The assumption is that the particular "game" being played promises

---

* The United Nations, regrettably, cannot be considered such an authority.

sufficient advantages to each of its "players" to outweigh whatever might be obtained by trying to upset it. In this way, rivalries can be pursued within an orderly framework, even without a referee. Game theory thus helps to account for the paradox of order in the absence of hierarchy that characterizes the postwar superpower relationship; it provides a sense of how rules establish limits of acceptable behavior on the part of nations who acknowledge only themselves as the arbiters of behavior.

These rules are, of course, implicit rather than explicit. They grow out of a mixture of custom, precedent, and mutual interest that takes shape quite apart from the realm of public rhetoric, diplomacy, or international law. They require the passage of time to become effective; they depend for that effectiveness upon the extent to which successive generations of national leadership on each side find them useful.

They certainly do not reflect any agreed-upon standard of international morality; in fact, they often violate principles of justice adhered to by one side or the other.

No two observers of superpower behavior would express these "rules" in precisely the same way; indeed, it may well be that the rules' very vagueness has made them more acceptable than they otherwise might have been.

What follows is my own list, derived from an attempt to identify regularities in the postwar Soviet-American relationship whose pattern neither side could now easily disrupt.

1. *Respect spheres of influence.* Neither Russians nor Americans officially admit to having such "spheres," but in fact much of the history of the Cold War can be written in terms of the efforts both have made to consolidate and extend them. One should not, in acknowledging this, fall into so mechanical a comparison of the two spheres as to ignore their obvious differences. The American sphere has been wider in geographical scope than its Soviet counterpart, but it has also been a much looser alignment, participation in which has more often than not been a matter of choice rather than coercion. What is important from the standpoint of superpower "rules" is the fact that, although neither side has ever publicly endorsed the other's right to a sphere of influence, neither has ever directly challenged it.

Thus, despite publicly condemning it, the United States never seriously attempted to undo Soviet control in Eastern Europe; Moscow tolerated, though never openly approved of, Washington's influence in Western Europe, the Mediterranean, the Near East, and Latin America. A similar pattern held up in East Asia, where the Soviet Union took no more action to oppose U.S. control over occupied Japan than the Truman administration did to repudiate the Yalta agreement, which left the Soviet Union dominant, at least for the moment, on the northeast Asian mainland.

Where the relation of particular areas to spheres of influence had been left unclear—e.g., the Western-occupied zones of Berlin prior to 1948, and South Korea prior to 1950—or where the resolve of one side to maintain its sphere appeared to have weakened, as in the case of Cuba following the failure of the Bay of Pigs invasion in 1961, attempts by the other to exploit the situation could not be ruled out: The Soviets' Berlin blockade, the Communist invasion of South Korea, and Khrushchev's decision to place Soviet missiles in Cuba can all be understood in this way. But it also appears to have been understood, in each case, that the resulting probes would be conducted cautiously. They would not be pursued to the point of risking war if resistance was encountered.

Defections from one sphere would be exploited by the other only when it was clear that the first either could not or would not reassert control. Hence, the United States took advantage of departures from the Soviet bloc of Yugoslavia and—ultimately—the People's Republic of China; it did not seek to do so in the case of Hungary in 1956, Czechoslovakia in 1968, or (in what was admittedly a more ambiguous situation) Poland in 1981. Similarly, the Soviet Union exploited the defection of Cuba after 1959, but made no attempt to contest the reassertion of American influence in Iran in 1953, Guatemala in 1954, the Dominican Republic in 1965, or Grenada in 1983.

2. *Avoid direct military confrontation.* It is remarkable, in retrospect, that at no point during the Cold War have Soviet and American military forces engaged each other in sustained hostilities. The superpowers have fought three major limited wars since 1945, but in no case with each other: The possibility of direct Soviet-American military involvement was greatest—although it never happened—during the Korean War; it was much more remote in Vietnam and has remained so in Afghanistan as well. In those few situations where Soviet and U.S. units have confronted one another directly—the 1948 Berlin blockade, the construction of the Berlin Wall in 1961, and the Cuban Missile Crisis the following year—great care was taken on both sides to avoid incidents that might have triggered hostilities.

Where the superpowers have sought to retain or to expand areas of control, they have tended to resort to the use of proxies or other indirect means. Examples include the Soviet Union's decision to sanction a North Korean invasion of South Korea, and its reliance on Cuban troops to promote its interests in sub-Saharan Africa. On the U.S. side, covert intervention has been a convenient (if not always successful) means of defending spheres of influence. Clients and proxies have come to serve as buffers, allowing Russians and Americans to compete behind a facade of "deniability" that minimizes the risks of open—and presumably less manageable—confrontation.

The superpowers—unlike their predecessors in history—have also been careful not to let the disputes of third parties embroil them directly. This has been most evident in the Middle East, where there had been no fewer than five wars between Israel and its Arab neighbors since 1948; but it holds as well for the India-Pakistan conflicts of 1965 and 1971, and for the recent struggle between Iran and Iraq.

3. *Use nuclear weapons only as an ultimate resort.* One of the most significant of the superpower "rules" has been the tradition that has evolved, since 1945, of maintaining a sharp distinction between conventional and nuclear weapons, and of reserving the latter only for the extremity of total war. In retrospect, there was nothing inevitable about this.

The Eisenhower administration announced its willingness to use nuclear weapons in limited war situations; Henry Kissinger, though he later repudiated the position, strongly endorsed such use in his 1957 book, *Nuclear Weapons and Foreign Policy,* as a way to keep alliance commitments credible. Soviet strategists as well have traditionally insisted that in war both nuclear and conventional means would be employed.

Thus it is remarkable that the world has not seen a single nuclear weapon used in anger since the destruction of Nagasaki more than four decades ago. Rarely has the *practice* of nations so conspicuously departed from proclaimed *doctrine.* Rarely, too, has so great a disparity attracted so little public notice.

This pattern of caution did not develop, as one might have expected, solely from the prospect of nuclear retaliation. As early as 1950, at a time when the Soviet Union had only just tested an atomic bomb and had only the most problematic means of delivering it, the United States had nonetheless ruled out the use of its own atomic weapons in Korea because of the opposition of its allies, the fear of an adverse reaction in the world at large, and uncertainty as to whether they would produce the desired military effect. And despite his public position favoring the use of atomic weapons, Eisenhower would repeatedly reject recommendations to resort to them in limited war situations.

It was precisely this sense that nuclear weapons were qualitatively different from conventional ones that most effectively deterred the United States from employing them during the first decade of the Cold

War—when the tradition of "non-use" had not yet taken hold, ample opportunities for their use existed, and the possibility of Soviet retaliation was not great. The idea of a discrete "threshold" between nuclear and conventional weapons, therefore, may owe more to the moral—and public relations—sensibilities of U.S. officials than to any actual fear of escalation.

By the time a credible Soviet retaliatory capability was in place, at the end of the 1950s, the "threshold" concept was also firmly fixed: One simply did not cross it, short of all-out war. Subsequent limited war situations—notably Vietnam for the Americans, and Afghanistan for the Russians—have confirmed the continued effectiveness of this unstated "rule" of superpower behavior. So have the quiet but persistent efforts of both sides to keep nuclear weapons from the hands of others who might not abide by the rule.

4. *Prefer predictable anomaly over impredictable rationality.* One of the most curious features of the Cold War has been the extent to which the superpowers—and their clients, who have had little choice in the matter—have tolerated a series of awkward, artificial, and apparently unstable regional arrangements. The division of Germany is the most obvious example. Others would include the Berlin Wall, the position of West Berlin itself within East Germany, the partition of the Korean peninsula, the existence of an avowed Soviet satellite some 90 miles from Florida, and not least, the continued functioning of an important U.S. naval base within it.

There is in all of these arrangements an appearance of wildly illogical improvisation. None could conceivably have resulted, it seems, from any rational and premeditated design. And yet, they have had a kind of logic: The fact that these jerrybuilt but rigidly maintained arrangements have lasted so long suggests an unwillingness on the part of the superpowers to trade familiarity for unpredictability.

5. *Do not seek to undermine the other side's leadership.* There have been repeated leadership crises in both the United States and the Soviet Union since Stalin's death. One thinks especially of the decline and ultimate deposition of Khrushchev following the Cuban Missile Crisis, of the Johnson administration's all-consuming fixation with Vietnam, of the collapse of Nixon's authority after Watergate, and of the recent paralysis in the Kremlin brought about by the death of three Soviet leaders within less than three years. And yet in none of these instances can one discern an effort by one side to exploit the other's vulnerability. Indeed there appears to have existed in several of these situations a sense of frustration, even regret over the rivals' difficulties.

From the standpoint of game theory, a rule that acknowledges legitimacy of leadership on both sides is hardly surprising: There have to be players for the game to proceed. But when compared with other situations in which that reciprocal tolerance has not existed—e.g., the long history of dynastic struggles in Europe up through the wars of the French Revolution—its importance as a stabilizing mechanism becomes clear.

Stability is not the same thing as politeness. It is worth noting that, despite levels of hostile rhetoric unmatched on both sides since the earliest days of the Cold War, the Soviet Union and the United States have managed to get through the 1980s without a single significant military confrontation. Contrast this with the record of Soviet-American relations in the 1970s. That was an era of far greater politeness in terms of what the two nations said about one another, but it was marred by potentially dangerous crises over Soviet submarine bases and combat brigades in Cuba, U.S. bombing and mining in Vietnam, and Soviet interventionism in Angola, Somalia, Ethiopia, South Yemen, and Afghanistan. There was even a major American nuclear alert during the Yom Kippur war in 1973—the only one since the Cuban Missile Crisis—at the height of what is now wistfully remembered as the era of détente.

What stability does require is a sense of caution, maturity, and responsibility on both sides. It requires the ability to distinguish posturing—in which all political leaders indulge—from provocation. It requires recognition of the fact that competition is a normal state of affairs in relations between nations, much as it is in relations between major corporations, but that this need not preclude the identification of certain common—or corporate, or universal—interests as well.

It requires, above all, a sense of the relative rather than the absolute nature of security—i.e., that one's own security depends not only upon the defensive measures one takes, but also upon the extent to which these create a sense of insecurity in the mind of one's adversary.

It would be foolish to suggest that the Soviet-American relationship today meets all of these prerequisites. But to an extent, the relationship has taken on a new maturity. To see that it has, one need only compare the current mood of wary optimism with the lack of communication that existed at the time of the Korean War, or the swings between alarm and amiability that characterized the late 1950s and early 1960s, or the inflated expectations and resulting disillusionments of the 1970s. This new maturity would appear to reflect an increasing commitment, on the part of both nations involved, to a "game" played "by the rules."

How to End the Dance?

What all of this suggests is that for a long time there has been a good deal more to the Soviet-American relationship than immediately met the eye. At the level of public awareness, the mood has shifted from détente to confrontation, and back again. But at a less conspicuous level, policymakers in both Moscow and Washington have quietly accommodated themselves to the system within which their very different nations have functioned since 1945.

The result has been progress toward self-regulation—i.e., perpetuation of the system—at a steadier rate than appearances might have led one to expect. That progress, in turn, has produced a surprising array of shared Soviet and American interests. It is almost enough to convince one that the Marxists are right in seeing both surface and subsurface processes at work in history—except that few if any Marxists would have predicted this outcome.

But can it last? International systems, after all, are not wholly under the control of the states that make them up. Changes in their structure can alter great-power relationships despite the wishes of great powers, who may not even be aware of what is happening. It is worth thinking about whether the current system—whose indefinite perpetuation neither side can guarantee—can continue to provide as benign a framework as it has for the emergence of common Soviet-American interests.

Consider the system's most prominent characteristic: its bipolarity. Whatever the structural prerequisites for this phenomenon were, they have long since disappeared. The power vacuums of 1945 have long since been filled; ideological bipolarity exists now only in symbolic terms; the post-war world economy was never bipolar at all, but instead evolved from unquestioned U.S. hegemony to an uneasy European-American-Japanese triumvirate, with the Russians remaining almost entirely irrelevant to that process. It is only a behavioral feature of the system—the decision of the Soviets and the Americans to remain nuclear superpowers—that sustains bipolarity, and that raises an interesting problem. Behavior is normally thought to be more volatile than structure; if behavior shifts, what happens to the international system in the absence of structural support?

The possibility that the superpowers might shift their behavior with respect to nuclear weapons would have seemed remote prior to 1986, but that was a surprising year. It saw the Soviet government, headed by Mikhail Gorbachev, abruptly endorse the abolition of all such weapons by the year 2000. It also witnessed, at Reykjavik, an American administration unable to state with any clarity why that might not be a good idea. Neither side seemed to be giving much thought to what a nuclear-free world—or even a nuclear-minimal one— might imply for the future of bipolarity, which many students of international systems now regard as the mainstay of post-war stability. How might we sustain bipolarity over the long haul if our avowed goal is to do away with the most important force—nuclear deterrence—that keeps it functioning?

We should also be thinking about the future of interdependence. If the relative independence of Russians and Americans from one another accounts in part for the historic absence of direct military conflict between them, can that situation continue as contacts grow?

An ironic consequence of perestroika may well be an increased capacity on each side's part to influence the other. Moscow's current enthusiasm for "joint ventures" with Western capitalists could give the West— if not the United States acting alone—some capacity to shape future Soviet economic development. The Russians' newly acquired skills in public relations—another consequence of perestroika—have already influenced Western opinion. Polls now show Americans holding almost as favorable a view of the President of the Soviet Union as they do of the President of the United States.

It is also worth considering what a more democratic political system inside the Soviet Union might imply for that nation's relations with the West. If the historical record is any guide, the result could be to lessen still further the danger of military confrontation: Wars between democratic states have been rare indeed.

It is significant that analysis of Soviet-American relations used to see the Kremlin as requiring a hostile outside world to meet certain domestic political priorities; indeed, a case could be made that something like this happened in the United States during the late 1970s and early 1980s. One can conceive of circumstances in which this pattern might reassert itself, with consequences for stability that would be hard to predict.

All these are ways in which Soviet and American behavior might alter the international system. But the system itself could also change, quite apart from what the major actors within it choose to do. For one thing, there is no guarantee that the nature of power itself remains the same over time. Even today there are strong indications that military power—at least in the hands of "great powers"—counts for less than it did in 1945; whether this results from the existence of nuclear weapons and inhibitions about using them, or whether it would have happened in any event, remains unclear. But what does seem apparent is that the "metric" of power in international relations is shifting away from the military dimension. Toward just what it is moving—whether economic, cultural, or even religious power—is difficult to say.

This trend, in turn, raises the question of competitors. If the international system does shift, what rivals to the United States and the Soviet Union are likely to emerge on the world scene, and what would the implications be for Soviet-American relations? The possibilities are familiar yet remote: They obviously include China, Japan, and Western Europe. But it is equally obvious that none of these potential rivals will attain "superpower" status—according to the traditional definition of that term—anytime soon. Yet neither is it inevitable that this will never happen.

If and when it does, the Russian and American response could be either to "bandwagon," i.e. to align unilaterally with new centers of strength, or to "balance," to act cooperatively against them. Historical evidence suggests the latter to be at least as likely a possibility as the former, but no one can say for sure.

What does seem clear is that relative Soviet and American influence in world politics is more likely to decline than to increase over the next several decades. It would be helpful if great powers could approach senility at roughly the same rate—that way imbalances of power would not develop. But history is rarely so accommodating. The more frequent situation is for one great power to decline relative to another. That becomes dangerous, because desperation may override prudence before the capacity to harm one's rivals or oneself has ceased to exist. As Paul Kennedy reminds us in his best seller, *"The Rise and Fall of the Great Powers* (1987), during the past 500 years no such country has ceased to be "great" without having been either defeated or weakened in war.

The remarkable reception Kennedy's book has received suggests that he has touched a sensitive nerve. But in their preoccupation with what he has said about American decline, many of Kennedy's critics have missed an important point, which is that he sees Soviet decline as likely to precede—and to exceed in its extent—that of the United States.

This possibility has received confirmation—at least by implication—from a most authoritative source: Mikhail Gorbachev in his own best seller, *Perestroika: New Thinking for Our Country and the World* (1987).

> Historical experience has shown that socialist society is not insured against the emergence and accumulation of stagnant tendencies and even against major socio-political crises. And it is precisely measures of a revolutionary character that are necessary for overcoming a crisis or pre-crisis situation.

All of which raises an interesting problem for the future of Soviet-American relations. The preservation of stability in the face of decline—and particularly asymmetrical decline—may require something new in international relations: the realization that great nations can have a stake, not just in the survival, but also in the success and the prosperity of their rivals. International systems, like tangos, require at least two reasonably active and healthy participants. And it is always wise, before allowing the dance to end, to consider with what one will replace it.

The task of maintaining a stable international system, it has been suggested, is a bit like riding a bicycle: If one thinks too hard about how one does it, one is apt to fall off. That may be, but where the future of Soviet-American relations is concerned, such an approach leaves a lot to chance—and to the instinctive capacity to maintain equilibrium. Might it not be better to begin to think, in a cautiously exploratory way, about how we have thus far managed more than four decades of superpower peace; about how we might maintain a comparable Soviet-American relationship in a shifting international system; about how we might pinpoint those areas where stabilizing maneuvers lie within our freedom of action; and about how we might be aware—lest we blame ineffectiveness on each other—of those areas which do not?

2

The New Thinking and Soviet-American Relations

Lev Lvovich Lyubimov

... Following the end of World War II, in which the USSR and the United States were allies, the Cold War, marking an extended period of Soviet-American confrontation, began almost immediately. Once the defeat of fascist Germany and militaristic Japan had been completed, the narrowness of the mutual basis for political cooperation became apparent. The Soviet Union's development into a real power and serious rival in the international arena resulted in a decisive parting of the ways, something that had been delayed solely by the inertia of the countries' having had a common strategic goal in World War II. Other objective causes of the sharp deterioration in Soviet-American relations include the time it took to recognize the consequences and realities of the nuclear age and the mutual inertia of established military and political concepts and doctrines (the thesis of the inevitability of a military confrontation between capitalism and socialism; the idea that it was possible to wage a nuclear war and obtain unilateral military advantages; the notion that a new world war, by analogy to the results of Worlds Wars I and II, would inevitably have revolutionary consequences). Undoubtedly, subjective circumstances, such as the views of specific leaders, a distorted interpretation of the other side's actions, also played a negative role.

...In contrast to the United States, the Soviet Union was prepared, of course, to continue cooperation in the postwar period. But the concept of such cooperation that we put forward had been rejected previously, in the 1930s, and it did not move Washington to abandon its policy of hard-line confrontation.

... The Cold War was probably unavoidable. At the same time, it could have taken on somewhat more moderate forms if the sides had not been guided exclusively by the tug-of-war concept that constantly led to an impasse.

The struggle of the Cold War era became the engine of races in both nuclear and conventional arms, which resulted in squandering of vast resources on both sides. In the United States the strategy and policies of confrontation were institutionalized in the establishment and rapid growth of the military-industrial complex, which became an extremely important component of the domestic political and economic structure. Mutual stereotypes also took root in public and political thinking and became a barrier that was to stand for many years in the way of any constructive efforts in the sphere of Soviet-American relations. The adherence to these stereotypes resulted in numerous crises, starting with the Korean events and ending with the West Berlin and Caribbean crises in 1961 and 1962.

In the late 1950s and the 1960s Soviet-American relations slowly began to emerge from a state of political anabiosis. The basic impetus to this process was provided by the USSR's new political approaches developed at the 20th CPSU Congress. Many entrenched stereotypes underwent radical reexamination, and certain premises that had interfered in the USSR's development of a constructive policy in the international area were discarded.

The rethinking of the premise concerning the inevitability of wars between socialism and capitalism gave dynamism to Soviet policy. The realities of the nuclear age came to be increasingly well recognized in both Moscow and Washington. The Eisenhower-Dulles hard line toward the USSR and the other socialist countries not only failed to produce results but caused growing criticism of the United States in Western Europe. The Suez crisis and the revolution in Cuba, the defeat of the counterrevolution in Hungary, events in Lebanon, the launchings of the first Soviet space satellites, the crisis in relations between the United States and Latin America following U.S. intervention in Guatemala—all this led, in the final analysis, to certain changes in U.S. policies on a number of international problems.

The resumption in 1959 of the Geneva conferences of the foreign ministers of the USSR, the United States, Great Britain, and France on the German question, and the conclusion of the Antarctic Treaty that same year marked a certain stabilization in Soviet-American relations, which was subsequently developed in the diplomacy of the Kennedy administration. Starting with a worsening of relations and experiencing the lessons of the Bay of Pigs and Caribbean crisis, the U.S. leadership at that time was forced to recognize the impossibility of nuclear war, the fact that the USSR and the United States had a number of coincident interests, and the necessity of ending the Cold War. One result of those changes was the 1963 Moscow Treaty banning nuclear tests in three environments.

The Soviet Union's attainment of parity with the United States in strategic arms (which created a qualitatively new basis for Soviet-American relations), and the military defeat of U.S. imperialism in Vietnam, along with the weakening of the United States' world economic positions, forced the American leadership to begin to reexamine its policies both toward the Soviet Union and on other problems. It should be noted that the new situation for the United States was, for the most part, correctly assessed by the U.S. leadership, which stopped the aggression in Vietnam, acknowledging defeat, and agreed with the need to limit the arms race and take a number of other positive steps in foreign policy.

The détente period began; it ended the first cycle of postwar Soviet-American relations, a cycle that had passed through the Cold War stage and a transitional stage toward a more stable and positive model. The negotiation method came to replace the policy of military pressure, which proved to have been substantially undermined. The United States, albeit not without vacillation, recognized its own role as a party to such negotiations, rather than their presiding officer.

The détente years were marked by major accomplishments in Soviet-American strategic-arms-limitation negotiations and in preparations for solving a considerable number of global problems, and by a sharp increase in the role of multilateral diplomacy. Relations between the United States and the USSR embarked on a course of ensuring greater security for each one and its partners, saving or using the national resources spent for military purposes more efficiently, and developing bilateral contacts on a broad range of issues. But the main result of détente was a certain movement away from confrontation and toward peaceful coexistence. The United States' readiness to undertake fundamental steps aimed at reducing tension and creating stable relations with the USSR was an important feature of that period. In showing such readiness, the United States was by no means contemplating the development of those relations on the basis of equality and partnership. Its concept of "participation in détente" included such components as restricting the quantitative growth of the USSR's strategic arms (with a view to subsequently shifting its own efforts to a race in the qualitative aspects of arms), weakening or at least stabilizing the USSR's influence in the developing world, and ideologically "softening up" the countries of the socialist commonwealth.

Of course, the Soviet Union had no intention of following the rules of the game proposed by Washington. After achieving strategic parity with the United States, it showed a persistent desire to maintain it. The Soviet Union, of course, was no passive observer of events taking place in the developing countries, although events in Angola had already proven to be a severe trial for the U.S. maintenance of a positive attitude toward détente. Finally, the Soviet thesis concerning the exacerbation of the ideological struggle was taken by Washington as evidence that its intention in that area had no serious chance of being realized. On the other hand, the USSR regarded the United States' inability to realize its plans as a natural result of changes in the correlation of forces in favor of the forces of peace and progress, and it saw this both as proof that the policy of détente was correct and as a pledge that it was irreversible.

At the same time, the fact that experience continued to confirm the inability to attain all the goals that the United States had set for itself when it became involved in the détente process reduced to nil that country's interest in continuing the process. Our policy failed to duly take this circumstance into account....

I would like to emphasize that in the 1970s the question of the relationship between the actual content of détente and the limits within which the Soviet Union was prepared to make its compromise-based contribution to that content became especially pressing. Today that question has become even more important. After all, it is now that we are beginning to give adequate answers to it. For example, in the concrete conditions of the 1970s, notions of the relationship between détente and the ideological struggle that were based on the thesis concerning the exacerbation of that struggle and the "intensification of ideological confrontation between the two systems" resulted in our being unprepared to take a new approach to the so-called humanitarian problems. Moreover, in interpreting the thesis concerning the exacerbation of the ideological struggle, a certain bias had developed toward depicting that process as one that took place on the level of propaganda and "psychological warfare." Yet in the atmosphere of détente it more clearly and openly reflected the historical dispute over which system was more effective in economic, social, and political terms.

Or consider the following example. An academic approach was taken toward the Third World as a zone that was supposedly characterized throughout by the "growth of socialism," and as our natural ally in all cases in the struggle against imperialism without taking differentiation into account. This approach caused us to be drawn into regional conflicts. After Angola came events on the Horn of Africa and then—Afghanistan. This sharply intensified Soviet-American rivalry and polarized the two powers' positions on an issue to which they should have sought and evidently found mutually acceptable solutions.

Finally, a whole series of our established legal doctrines pertaining to the international sphere failed to accord with the emerging tendency in the mid-1970s to deal with certain issues on the basis of international law. Thus, the objective requirement that the functions of binding regulation of some types of states' activities be turned over to certain international organizations came into conflict with our doctrine, developed back in the prewar years, that denied any such right to international organizations on the grounds that it was a violation of state sovereignty, in all cases without exception. This put us in a situation where, while putting forward urgent and objectively necessary disarmament proposals, we simultaneously denied the right of effective mutual verification of disarmament measures. The concepts of verifying implementation, liability for violations (e.g., damages), and the mutual presentation of reliable information fared particularly badly. Yet the problems of international law that arose in huge numbers in the 1970s were an important part of the overall political context in which the détente process developed. Providing for the stable support and expansion of that context meant ensuring one of the basic conditions for détente, peaceful coexistence, and cooperation among states. And we cannot rule out the possibility that in the 1970s, and later, the United States took direct advantage in its policies of its knowledge of our stereotypes and its confidence that we would rely on them in any given instance. The United States' present maneuvers on verification issues, now that we have proposed radical steps in that area, show this theory's validity.

The period of détente proved short-lived. In the mid-1970s Soviet-American relations began to worsen, and by the first half of the 1980s there was already talk of a second Cold War. A new cycle set in that was characterized by higher costs of confrontation, with unprecedented amounts of money being spent on the military, political, and diplomatic "servicing" of confrontation. For the first time, a constant—not just crisis-related—threat of global nuclear disaster arose. A whole set of regional crises arose in which the symmetrical interests of the two great powers became involved.

The transition to this cycle resulted from a number of factors. The strengthening of conservative forces in the United States that began in the second half of the 1970s and brought the Reagan administration to power in the 1980 elections did not just accompany but supported this process. The uniting of the positions of the new rightists, traditional right-wing Republicans, and right-wing Democrats, and their attainment of power at the beginning of the 1980s in both Congress and the White House brought about major changes in U.S. foreign policy as a whole and its policy toward the USSR in particular. If the factors contributing to the "departure" of détente from international relations were created by all sides, albeit to different degrees, the return to confrontation was carried out exclusively by the United States, which bears political and historical responsibility for doing so.

At the end of the 1970s U.S. ruling circles for the first time recognized their advantage when the dynamics of the economic growth of their country and the Soviet Union were compared. Stagnation-related phenomena in the Soviet economy and social development, which led in the mid-1980s to the emergence of economic contradictions that were pre-crisis in form, interrupted an almost 50-year trend under which the Soviet national economy had shown faster growth rates than that of the United States.

In the United States these events were taken as a signal to add the burden of a new spiral of arms expenditures that, in its view, would be "critical" to undermining the Soviet economy. In the late 1970s and early 1980s, U.S. policy toward the USSR consisted of efforts to restrain Soviet exports, prevent the import of medium- and high-technology products into the USSR, and undermine any form of economic cooperation between the USSR and developed capitalist countries or developing countries. To all intents and purposes, the United States was trying to bring about the USSR's economic isolation. By sharply exacerbating regional conflicts and throwing hundreds of millions, even billions, of dollars into them, the United States attempted to force the Soviet

Union, too, to shoulder the burdens of additional expenditures in those regions.

The Reagan administration's intention to change the existing correlation of forces in its favor was also demonstrated by such actions as its rejection of disarmament negotiations and of ratification of agreements that had already been achieved, as well as its attempt to revise those agreements; its revival of doctrines aimed at the attainment of military superiority; its adoption of the concepts of "acceptable losses," "limited" nuclear war, and the possibility of victory in a nuclear clash; its sharp increase in the military budget; its unbridled "psychological warfare" against the USSR and the other socialist countries; and its outright interventionist actions in Grenada, Libya, and Lebanon.

The United States' policy toward the USSR became an element of its policy of global revenge and a part of its efforts to restore its world standing, including its standing with the developing countries, Western Europe, and Japan. Whereas American diplomacy had showed a readiness in the mid-1970s to accept certain compromises in the North-South dialogue, as apprehensions regarding a raw materials shortage disappeared, that readiness diminished and ultimately gave way to the policy of a hard-line reexamination of American stands on all the problems involved in that dialogue.

At the same time, with growth rates of the American economy proving somewhat higher than those of the West European economies and nearly on a par with those of the Japanese economy, the illusion arose in the United States that it could stabilize and possibly recover its lost positions in the world economy. This was indeed an illusion, since American reckoning was based on the obsolete philosophy of a world community that was divided and steadily being further divided, and in which the struggle to advance selfish, separate interests was the rule.

Another reason this was an illusion is that, in reality, a drop in growth rates in a competitor country or group of countries no longer inevitably results in changing the relative positions of centers of power in the world capitalist economy. The real correlation of forces among the centers is neither exclusively nor even principally determined by these growth rates. In the age of the scientific and technological revolution, the constant improvement of the quality and efficiency of products used is taking the place of the quantitative increase in personal and production consumption. Therefore, in order to evaluate the United States' real place in the world economy, it is far more important to look at such factors as the rapid drop in its share of world trade in high-technology products; its negative foreign-trade balance in such products, which manifested itself for the first time in 1986; its growing imports of means of production; and the growing share of foreign products purchased with capital investments in U.S. industry, transportation, and communications. The unprecedented combination of a rise in imports and a drop in the exchange rate of the dollar sharply exacerbated the problem of the competitiveness of American goods on both the internal and external markets. The transformation of the United States into a debtor nation was also a new phenomenon.

The deterioration of the developing countries' economic situation also negatively affected the United States' world standing. Backwardness inevitably leads to social and political instability, creating dangerous hotbeds of conflict that take on an international dimension and draw states located beyond the region of conflict into their orbit. Backwardness—instability—conflicts—militarization—international tension—the slowing of development: such is the logical pattern of processes rooted in the poverty of peoples. The accumulation of tremendous debts reduces guarantees that they will be repaid, undermines the stability of the world currency and credit system, and may lead to unpredictable political decisions and economic consequences. The current deterioration in the developing countries' economic situation is automatically resulting in a reduction of their imports from the developed states, including the United States. In 1985 and 1986, U.S. exports to the African countries dropped by 5.8 percent and 22 percent respectively; in the same two years, its exports to West Asia dropped by 12.8 percent and 13.3 percent; and in 1985 its exports to Southeast Asia dropped by 16.1 percent.

Finally, the U.S. policy established in the 1980s of exacerbating the USSR's economic problems and achieving its own military superiority also stemmed from the philosophy of the past. In practical terms, it caused a rise in international tension and in the real danger of nuclear war and the destruction of civilization. Today when you lay a trap for the other party you risk laying one for everyone, including yourself....

Of all aspects of the early 1980s' policy of global revenge, the most dangerous for humanity was the proclamation of a crusade against the USSR and socialism. Here the U.S. administration's policy increasingly took on the features of an apocalyptic movement based on the illusion of its own side's ability to survive a nuclear war. But in the 1984 elections it became obvious that the movement was evoking a growing sense of fear both among Americans themselves and among West Europeans. The prospects of global catastrophe had moved from the future to the present. The buildup of nuclear arsenals had reached not only a dangerous but a senseless point.

Tension in Soviet-American relations reached its highest point at the end of 1983, when the deployment of American medium-range missiles began in Europe. A crisis arose not just in bilateral relations but concerning the fate of human civilization. It was vitally necessary to seek a way out of that crisis and a real response to the cry "civilization in danger!" The campaign for revolutionary transformations in the USSR that began with the CPSU Central Committee's April 1985 Plenum created the possibility of making that search.

The beginning of a new phase in Soviet-American relations was due primarily to the foreign-policy component of perestroika... The USSR's foreign policy in the past few years forced the West to recognize that the initiative had shifted to Moscow. People in the United States came to realize more and more clearly that the new Soviet approach and the Soviet leadership's specific steps reflected the USSR's intention to abandon the "reactive" model of behavior in the international arena that was being imposed on it, a model according to which reaction to one's adversary's actions dominates foreign-policy practice, raising the level of confrontation. The fact that the creative element was coming to prevail in Soviet strategy, when seen against the backdrop of the Reagan administration's rigid subordination of its policy to the obsolete concepts with which it had come to power, was causing increasing concern in the U.S. establishment.

The first major result of the new foreign-policy thinking was the effective policy of taking steps to remove the "obstructions" that had arisen in previous years both in Soviet-American relations and in key issues related to averting the world nuclear threat. The December 1987 summit provided the first real results on the path toward creating a comprehensive system of international security—the Treaty on the Elimination of Medium- and Shorter-Range Missiles. An agreement that just a short time before had been regarded in the United States, Western Europe, and many other countries as unattainable became a reality thanks to the new thinking.... Now real preconditions were created for making progress in strategic arms reduction as well.

Today, Soviet-American relations are entering a new phase. The USSR and the United States are only at the very beginning of the latest stage in their relations, a point at which a great deal has not yet been clarified. The stage that is beginning will evidently be a transitional one. Its main content should consist of developing stable models of interaction between the two powers. A tremendous, probably even decisive, influence on the process of forming those models will be exerted by perestroika, which is already evoking a mixed reaction in the United States. This reaction contains on the one hand, elements of concern that the USSR may become a more serious rival and competitor and on the other, disbelief that it will succeed in carrying out its plans. Both variant appraisals are already being seriously taken into account in creating a future model for the American stance toward the USSR.... The successes of Soviet perestroika will have a tremendous influence on public attitudes in the United States and, consequently, on development of a concept for doing business with the USSR, a concept which might differ significantly from those to which the United States had previously adhered.

In addition to perestroika, a considerable influence on that process would be exerted by the Soviet Union's maintaining the foreign-policy initiative and taking steps that might bring about a radical change in Western ideas about alleged Soviet aggressiveness—ideas which form the political and philosophical foundation of NATO—and draw the United States and Western Europe more deeply into the détente process. In addition, the interrelated goals, means, and structure of Soviet-American cooperation require careful study. In particular, it would be of fundamental importance to define mutual interests in two spheres where the aspirations of the whole human race and prospects for the future especially require the support and responsible action of the two great powers. We are referring, in the first place, to universal human problems, and in the second place, to the problems of providing support in international law for global cooperation, of which humanitarian problems should be a part. One of the most important accomplishments of current Soviet foreign policy has been to single out, from the whole complex of Soviet-American relations, the issues that together form the common human agenda. Finally, a genuinely broad and long-term basis should also be found for economic cooperation between the two powers....

Section 2
THE END OF THE COLD WAR

Is the Cold War over? In recent years there has been a debate among academicians, government officials, and journalists as to whether the changes brought about by Mikhail Gorbachev have ended the Cold War. Early during 1989 the New York Times editorialized that "The Cold War Is Over." At about the same time, Margaret Thatcher also declared the Cold War to be over. However, National Security Affairs Advisor Brent Scowcroft's reaction was much more cautious. The academic community has been divided. George Kennan has said that it is over. Other specialists on Soviet affairs have been more hesitant.

Writing before the Communist governments of Eastern Europe fell during the second half of 1989 and before the fate of Germany was decided in the first half of 1990, Zbigniew Brzezinski was of the opinion "that the Cold War was not yet over but it would be if certain changes occurred." His recommendations are interesting because they present criteria that might be used to determine whether the Cold War is actually "history."

In his commentary, "Ending the Cold War," Brzezinski indicates that there are different interpretations of the Cold War's demise because the question is not nearly as easy to answer as it may appear. The orientation toward the Soviet Union of the individual making the determination is the first consideration. Those who have been quick to proclaim the end of the Cold War are generally those who place a high value on accommodation with Soviet policy. These individuals are more apt to view the Cold War as a "conundrum of reciprocal misunderstandings" rather than an inevitable ideological struggle. On the other hand, those who fail to accept the suggestion of the

Cold War's end are those who view the conflict as a "philosophical crusade."

Brzezinski contends that whatever his long-term goals, Mikhail Gorbachev was forced to ask for an "armistice" in the Cold War. The economic and political crisis in his country impelled the Soviet leader to reduce tensions with the West and move from "conflictual to accommodative relationships." As encouraging as this may be, Brzezinski stresses that the Soviet Union is still a military superpower, a fact difficult to ignore in determining whether Soviet-American relations have entered a new era. Somewhat ironically, the Soviet Union has had to assign very high priority to the maintenance of military power because the losses in the economic and ideological realms have been so devastating.

Because the Cold War will not be over until the security issue is resolved, the author states that the West needs to develop an overarching framework for ending the Cold War. Basically this means that Western policy must address the security dimensions of the changing East-West relationship in Europe. In his view, the alliance structure in Europe should be maintained because it provides a stable structure that will accommodate substantial political and economic change. "Neither Europe's security nor East-West accommodations would be served by attempts to dismantle the Warsaw Pact alone or to disband both of the alliances." Furthermore, some assurance that the Brezhnev Doctrine of "limited sovereignty" has been repudiated by the Soviet Union would be necessary to conclude that the Cold War was over.

Having addressed the security aspects of the relationship, the West should then enact a comprehensive program of economic and technological assistance to promote irreversible change in the Soviet Union. This should include large-scale credits, and the easement of existing debts.

Henry Trofimenko, in "The End of the Cold War, Not History," begins his essay by stating that he does not intend to assess who "won" and "lost" the Cold War. He sees little merit to such a debate because it is irrelevant to future Soviet-American relations. In the same vein, he disagrees with those in the West who claim that the end of the postwar bipolar conflict signifies a triumph of "Western liberalism" over the "great socialist idea." It is true, he states, that socialism as portrayed by Karl Marx remains unfulfilled in the Soviet Union. But, on the other hand, he sees little in the practical application of *"liberalism"* in Western capitalist states to suggest that the goals of that ideology have been fully realized.

The central issue is not who won or loss the Cold War, nor is it the triumph of one ideology over another. The important issue is whether the two superpowers are able to take advantage of the change in international relationships and develop cooperative methods for the mutual resolution of persisting world problems. Actually, if the two powers can agree on the central issues to be resolved, he contends, they will have established criteria for finally terminating the Cold War. He proposes a number of significant issues that should be addressed and submits that *"those who would agree with this list, could conclude that East and West essentially have moved beyond the Cold War."*

Trofimenko sees progress in the new superpower relationship. For example, in his opinion there has been a marked decrease in Soviet-U.S. confrontation in the Third World. For another, superpower adjustments to the dramatic changes in Europe seem to have established the foundation for a *"new and truly postwar international order."*

In conclusion, the author suggests the two great powers should agree on common goals as they work to develop a more cooperative relationship. They should seek to avoid nuclear war at all costs. They should also appreciate the role that each can play in protecting the global environment, in providing for the basic needs of the people in their own societies and throughout the world, and in promoting democratic principles of government.

3.

Ending the Cold War

Zbigniew Brzezinski

A central question resonates today both in Europe and in the United States: is the Cold War over? This question is being asked repeatedly by journalists, by students, by statesmen. It is posed with earnestness and with hope. Its being asked is in itself an important indicator of historical change.

This question is actually not easy to answer. What is more, the debate over the Cold War has itself paradoxically become a part of the Cold War. The louder some observers in the West affirm the continued existence of the Cold War, the easier it is for General Secretary Mikhail Gorbachev wistfully to affirm his desire to end the conflict and to stigmatize as mindless proponents of the Cold War those who dispute his view—thereby actually scoring points in the political contest that has come to be known as the Cold War. Thus, even the debate over the Cold War's alleged demise becomes part of the waging of that war.

Complicating matters even further is the reality that any answer not only risks oversimplifying a complex historical process but also may serve as a screen for hidden ideological preferences. On one hand, those who hastily proclaim the Cold War's end tend to be (though with some striking exceptions) those who have traditionally placed the highest value on accommodation with, rather than on firm opposition to, Soviet aggressiveness; who have in the past advocated concessions in the face of such unilateral acts of Soviet assertiveness as the deployment of the SS-20s or the invasion of Afghanistan; and who have viewed the Cold War not as a profound philosophical collision but as a conundrum of reciprocal misunderstandings. Last but not least, some among them are eagerly seeking to make a quick buck in the East.

On the other hand, those who firmly reject—maybe even with a touch of anxious nostalgia—the notion of the Cold War's end tend to be those who have viewed the Cold War largely as an ideological crusade; who have more often than not exaggerated Soviet power and who have been overly preoccupied with the prospects of Soviet invasion; who almost automatically have labeled any agreement with the

Soviet Union as appeasement; and who particularly fear that popular acceptance of the notion of the end of the Cold War will mean the unilateral disarmament of the fallible West.

Although the contrasts are stark, they are not overstated to propound the all-too-easy conclusion that the right answer lies somewhere in the middle. Rather, decision makers must derive policy from analysis of what has been happening lately in East-West relations, looking at the situation from all angles.

The Bush administration's comprehensive review of East-West policy was long overdue. During the last two years of the Reagan administration, the U.S.-Soviet accommodation acquired a momentum of its own. However, in its latter phases it was propelled more by Gorbachev's calculated amiability and President Ronald Reagan's fascinated responsiveness than by a deliberate Western strategic design. Some of the current confusion regarding the status of the Cold War results partly from the festivals of feigned friendship in Washington and Moscow that became substitutes for policy. The new president and his top foreign-policy advisers—probably the best U.S. team since the early 1950s—realize the danger that policy based on the lowest common denominator of interagency consensus lacks the requisite historical vision and the desired strategic thrust.

In fact, circumstances call for a Western policy that is historically ambitious and conceptually innovative. Today, the Soviet world is in the midst of the most serious crisis of its entire history. Both its ideology and its system have failed. What is more, everyone knows it, including the ruling Communist elites. This failure could lead at some point to convulsive outbreaks and even spasms of violence. Although it is far from clear what the continuous agony of communism will yield, some points are clear.

First, the internal Soviet systemic crisis will preoccupy the Soviet leadership for a long time to come. This author has elsewhere defined the essence of the Soviet multilateral empire's internal dilemma as involving a basic contradiction between the requirements of economic progress and the imperatives of political stability. Desired economic progress can only be purchased at high cost to political stability, and political stability can only be sustained at the price of economic progress.

The insoluble tension between these irreconcilable objectives has already constrained the external Soviet freedom of action. The failure to win in Afghanistan speaks for itself. Indeed, to remedy its internal malaise, the Soviet Union needs a major accommodation and even economic help from the West. It needs a breathing spell (*peredyshka*) in order to pursue its *perestroika*. As a result, in a move reminiscent of

Lenin in Brest Litovsk in 1918, Gorbachev has asked for an armistice in the Cold War. That was the real message of his address in December 1988 to the United Nations General Assembly.

Second, as the internal crisis percolates, Soviet control over Eastern Europe inevitably will decline further. The term Eastern Europe is a political concept, connected with the Cold War, and Eastern Europe, simply put, wants again to be central Europe. In other words, it wants to be itself. Some Soviet spokesmen are already beginning to signal that the Kremlin might not even be adverse to a neutral status for some of the East European states. Hungary has been explicitly mentioned recently. Such thinking could augur a substantial redefinition of the Soviet concept of its geopolitical interest in Eastern Europe—an issue certainly worth pursuing. Even Gorbachev's slogan of "a common European house" could be exploited to further such change.

Third, the patterns of change in Eastern Europe will likely be highly differentiated and, indeed, in some cases potentially quite violent. Although Hungary and Poland are leading the way toward some form of political pluralism—thus toward a major break not only with the Stalinist but also with the Leninist tradition—no Communist-ruled state has yet crossed the elusive dividing line between a state-controlled and a genuinely free market economy and between one-party monopoly of power and a genuinely open multiparty political system....

Fourth, although the Soviet Union remains a major military power, it is a giant with powerful hands and rotten innards. Today the Soviet Union is only a one-dimensional global power, that is, noncompetitive economically, socially, or ideologically but very strong militarily. The West must take into account that enormous Soviet military might in any comprehensive policy response to the dramatic crisis of the Soviet world. The Kremlin continues to assign very high priority to the maintenance of that power, especially as the political importance to the Kremlin of its military might has risen in recent years precisely because the Soviet Union has come to be viewed worldwide as an economic and ideological loser.

In that complex setting, the West must fashion a policy that simultaneously advances the positive aspects of economic and political change in the East and enhances wider European regional security. In brief, this requires a policy designed to translate the *peredyshka* that the Soviet leadership needs into a genuine *perestroika* of East-West relations that everyone wants.

To be politically appealing and historically relevant, such a wider response should meet the following requirements. First, it must entail the definition and articulation of the Western concept of the Cold War's termination—a definition that is truly symbolically compelling and politically substantive. A simple and attractive definition of what the end of the Cold War actually should mean to everyone in the West and in the East is a political necessity. This is especially true because of Gorbachev's success in focusing public attention on the atmospherics of the East-West relationship, thereby diverting attention from the precipitating causes and from the more enduring issues of the Cold War. Unfortunately, he has had help in this respect from some Western statesmen who have joined in a chorus of less than thoughtful pronouncements on the general subject of the Cold War, thereby further obfuscating the issue.

The key point here is very simple: if Westerners want more than a mere armistice in the Cold War, they have to define the actual meaning of its end. They have to express this message in terms that are capable of mobilizing public support.

Second, Western policy must respond to the political-economic crisis of the Soviet world in a manner that constructively encourages and consolidates genuinely irreversible change. That sets a higher standard for policy than either passivity based on wishful thinking or a headlong rush to pour capital into the East, which makes it easier for those Communist elites who merely want to repair the status quo to have their cake and eat it, too.

A critical and discerning approach to historic changes in the East should not be an excuse for Western indifference. Without substantial Western aid, the process of change, notably in Hungary and Poland and soon also in Czechoslovakia, could simply provoke breakdowns, even revolutionary outbreaks, then repressive reactions and even a belated Soviet intervention. That would have terminal consequences for any genuine democratization. Therefore, the West must unambiguously convey that it holds the view that violent change in Eastern Europe would be counterproductive from everyone's point of view and that arbitrary impediments to peaceful change are likely to provide the most powerful impulses for such revolutionary violence. The need for discriminating involvement in the internal processes of change will face an even greater challenge in the case of the Soviet Union itself. There, both on economic issues and especially in the case of mounting national problems, the evolving situation is at a very delicate stage, with future trends considerably more uncertain than in the case of Eastern Europe.

Third, Western policy must address the security dimensions of the changing East-West relationship in Europe. This is especially the case because the progressive fragmentation of the Soviet empire must be breeding fears in the Kremlin that the North Atlantic Treaty Organization (NATO) may soon be aiming to extend its sphere of influence to the Bug River and perhaps even attempt to foster instability within the Soviet Union itself. That fear would become particularly strong if the West, in seeking to promote peaceful change, appeared also to be seeking to reopen the German geopolitical question.

Westerners must therefore find a policy formula that enhances East-West stability even as it facilitates the desirable and perhaps even inevitable political and economic change within the Soviet sphere. In that context, it is particularly important that the United States eschew anything that conveys the impression that it seeks a new Yalta with the Soviet Union, a new geopolitical arrangement contrived over the heads of the East Europeans and maybe even of all Europeans. Any ambiguity on that score would simply breed resentments and suspicions.

The quest for a security formula that is congenial to political change yet reinforces the state of stability also has to take into account the strategic level. The enhancement of security in Europe must go hand in hand with the reinforcement of both U.S. and Soviet strategic security. Obviously, it can hardly be either the U.S. or the Soviet objective to make Europe more secure for the Europeans while the American and Soviet peoples remain, or even become more, strategically vulnerable.

In brief, the issues—some symbolic, some political, some economic, some military and even strategic—are a complex web. The response needs to be equally comprehensive. It should be presented as a broad framework for terminating the Cold War, not just dribbled out in bits and pieces. A historically ambitious design would stand a better chance of winning public support and even of mobilizing popular support in the East for a substantive, not just symbolic, East-West accord.

In explicitly defining the meaning of an end of the Cold War, the West should not be shy in focusing on the symbolic and philosophical. The fundamental issue has been, and still is, freedom of choice versus coercive ideological orthodoxy. Let us not forget that human rights have been the central stake in the Cold War, and the West's identification with human rights has been its greatest moral strength. The Berlin Wall and free elections are not just slogans; they are the substance of the political contest....

People on both sides of the East-West divide would understand such a definition of the Cold War's end. It is a historically and politically more relevant definition than the exchange of flirtatious smiles between Gorbachev and Western leaders. Such a definition would also facilitate the eventual progressive departure from central Europe of major portions of U.S. and Soviet forces, whose prolonged presence there has been a major manifestation of the Cold War. The West should therefore not be shy in proclaiming the important connection between the philosophical and the military symptoms of the Cold War. It should also reaffirm clearly that, indeed, the West's central goal is to end the Cold War.

In fostering political and economic conditions actually congenial to ending the Cold War, the West—in which at this point one should also include Japan as an interested party—should undertake a comprehensive program of staged economic and technological assistance to foster peaceful change within the Communist world. If peaceful changes continue, some Communist states will soon need help in technical expertise, in resources, and in financing. Even on such a specific matter as parliamentary procedures and operations, the prospectively more influential legislators in some Communist-governed countries lack the essential experience and techniques. Special training and exchange programs in this area, and in many others, will be needed, should be developed, and should be offered both to the East European states and to some of the Soviet republics.

Western nongovernmental actors can play a particularly constructive role in this regard. Trade unions, press associations, environmental groups, and others have now a greater opportunity than ever before to forge links with their incipient counterparts in the East. Some have already been doing so, thereby fostering the social and political pluralism that is fundamentally incompatible with totalitarianism.

More important still is the need in the East for large-scale and long-term credits, as well as for an easement of existing debts along the lines of the Brady Plan for Latin America. A major trilateral effort in this area is urgently needed, and special trilateral planning machinery to that end should be created.

At the same time, the recipients must match Western initiative with solid commitments to institutionalize economic and political pluralism. Without a firm schedule for the adoption of such comprehensive reforms and a reciprocal step-by-step schedule for comprehensive and constructive Western assistance, there is the risk of repeating the wasted credit flows of the 1970s, a fact that even the Communist elites acknowledge.

Finally, the West's proclaimed goal for European security ought to be the transformation of the Warsaw Pact from an ideological to a purely geopolitical alliance designed to maintain the territorial status quo in Europe. Neither Europe's security nor East-West accommodation would be served by attempts to dismantle the Warsaw Pact alone or to disband both of the alliances. The first would be strenuously, and probably effectively, resisted by Moscow. The second could only yield a neutral and vulnerable Europe.

What is needed is an overarching framework of security based on the two alliances within which peaceful political and economic change can be accommodated. In such a context, the progressive dismantling of the largely artificial communist systems in Eastern Europe and their transformation into forms more palatable to their people's traditions and aspirations would not automatically represent a danger to Moscow. A social democratic Hungary or a christian democratic Poland, which would remain members of the Warsaw Pact, would not tip the balance of power in Europe to the West's advantage.

It therefore follows that the West, beyond seeking equitable conventional force reductions in the Vienna negotiations, should also seek formal assurances from Moscow that the Brezhnev Doctrine has been invalidated—at the same time reassuring Moscow that the West's political goal is not the defection of member-states from the Warsaw Pact. Perhaps at some point, the Brezhnev Doctrine could yield to a joint East-West statement, formally affirming both the role of the two alliances in the maintenance of European stability and explicitly excluding the use of either alliance for the imposition of any particular ideological orthodoxy on its members.

In conclusion, the issue exceeds the superficial and short-term query—should the West be helping Gorbachev?—and involves the larger issue of the Western response to the general crisis of communism. Even if the West should fashion such a comprehensive strategy for ending the Cold War, the conflict's actual end will be a protracted process, not a single event. This will be so even if the West designates some symbolic events (for example, the removal of the wall) as history's milestones. Ultimately, the Cold War's end will be perceived with greater clarity only with the benefit of hindsight. However, if Westerners act with the requisite strategic resolve, they are more likely to ensure that such a perception will coincide with the recognition that the peaceful ending of the Cold War was tantamount to the West's historic victory in it.

4

The End of the Cold War, Not History

Henry Trofimenko

... The new attitude of the U.S. leadership toward *perestroika* somehow makes irrelevant the debate about who won and who lost in the East-West, or Soviet-U.S. confrontation of the past forty-five years. President Bush evidently believes it more productive and important to build constructive relations with the Soviet Union than to clash regarding the theoretical problem of victory and defeat. This attitude is shared by the Soviet leadership, Mikhail Gorbachev, and the new Soviet parliament. They are working toward common understanding and cooperation between the Soviet Union and the United States, and are seeking higher forms and methods of close mutual engagement in order to solve outstanding international problems, such as environmental degradation and the threat of war.

Nevertheless, the media debate continues about who won and who lost the Cold War and why, and is especially loud in the United States. It appears that U.S. experts and journalists, particularly of the conservative Republican type, desperately wish to underscore that present international developments actually are the result of the United States having won the Cold War and the Soviet Union sort of having capitulated. Practically speaking, such assertions seem to have two aims. One aim is to push the Soviet Union into a corner, showing that it has no way out other than to succumb to whatever demands the United States and the West might make. In line with this approach, Graham Allison has been advising in *Foreign Affairs* that U.S. policymakers ought to use "what may be a historic chance to push actively for specific and major steps by Moscow that advance Western interests."[1] The second aim is to attempt to justify the continuation of the old policy of arms buildup because the power base it created ostensibly helped the United States and the West "win" the Cold War.

The intention is not to recommence herein the discussion of who is to blame for the Cold War. Joseph Stalin probably is more responsible for its beginning than Harry Truman, although both sides later were engaged actively in it. Nevertheless, it should be remembered that it was the United States that officially declared the Cold War as its main foreign policy strategy.[2] For the past several years, the Soviet Union vehemently and categorically has denounced the Cold War, saying that it no longer plays that game. The pronouncements of some U.S. politicians and journalists, however, seem to rejoice at the so-called achievements of the Cold War, advising more of the same in dealing with the Soviet Union. It seems clear, therefore, that whatever the Soviet Union does, it remains difficult to move out of the established rut if the other side is not supportive. That is why even as great a Cold War game practitioner as Dr. Zbigniew Brzezinski aptly has remarked that "the debate over the Cold War has itself paradoxically become a part of the Cold War."[3]

Some people in the Soviet Union also feel nostalgic about "the good old days" when there was a "remarkably stable and predictable set of relations among the great powers."[4] It was during the Cold War that the Soviet Union became a superpower militarily on a par with the United States. There are quite a few people in the Soviet Union who believe that the superpower status was the main factor that made the United States switch to more equitable rules of the game for all the players in the international arena. As a result of the Cold War competition, the Soviet Union became efficient in producing ballistic and cruise missiles. Experts well remember the famous Khrushchev remark that the country was producing missiles like sausages! Those waxing nostalgic hold that if the Soviet Union were obliged to recommence the competition, it still would be proficient in making missiles and even aircraft carriers, notwithstanding the decline in expertise in the production of soap and edible sausages.

At the same time, it is gratifying to observe that the debate on winning or losing the Cold War is running out of steam rather quickly. The majority of people, whether in the United States or in the Soviet Union, are tired of the nervousness and tensions of the Cold War atmosphere, preferring the breeze of fresh air in the new positive developments in Soviet-U.S. relations that are taking place after the Malta summit.

The Great Liberal Idea and
Learning Marx Firsthand

Some sophisticated members of the U.S. academic elite seem desperate, however, to prove the triumph of the "American idea," but not in such a primitive way as putting forth the contention about winning the

Cold War. Hence, the well-publicized, brilliant article written with tongue-in-cheek by Francis Fukuyama about the end of history, whose gist is the eulogy of "the triumph of the West, of the Western *idea*."[5]

"What we may be witnessing," writes Fukuyama, "is not just the end of the Cold War, or the passing of a particular period of postwar history, but the end of history as such: that is, the end point of mankind's ideological evolution and the universalization of Western liberal democracy as the final form of human government."[6] He then goes on to say that it was Karl Marx, "who believed that the direction of historical development ... would come to an end only with the achievement of a communist utopia that would finally resolve all prior contradictions."[7] A communist utopia has failed to materialize, stresses Fukuyama, but its Western alternative, liberalism, has triumphed. This triumph could be considered a resolution of all prior contradictions, although in a way diametrically opposed to the Marxist one. Thus, one has the end of history, according to Marx and Hegel, from whom Marx borrowed "the concept of history as a dialectical process with a beginning, a middle and an end."[8]

The author's difficulty with Fukuyama is the same as the one his old history teacher had with him, admonishing him to "study the originals, not interpretations or summaries!" Karl Marx actually had said nothing about the *end of history*. He wrote that "the bourgeois relations of production are the last antagonistic form of the social process of production ...; at the same time the productive forces, developing in the womb of bourgeois society, create the material conditions for the solution of that antagonism. This social formation brings, therefore, the *prehistory* of human society to a close" (author's emphasis).[9] Marx thought that the creation of a new harmonious social order based on his teachings would mean the *beginning* of the history of humankind, not the end of it. Real history is when a human being finally has shed his or her beastly, servile past, having done away with economic and other forms of exploitation, having been freed from the necessity to sweat for the meager daily ration, having put an end to the institution of armed strife, and having gained by scientific and technical prowess the time for self-perfection, engagement in literature, the arts, philosophy, sports, etc. Succinctly put, real history is when a human being finally has attained Manifest Destiny, to use the popular American expression.

Regretfully, the social experiment that was started in Russia in 1917 did not work out that way. Usurping dictatorial powers, Stalin unrecognizably distorted the Marxist idea of a non-antagonistic, classless social association in which "the free development of each is the condition for the free development of all."[10] The concept of the individual was crushed by the tremendously oppressive superstructure of the proletarian state. State terrorism, a greatly misused word in the Soviet press, really did reign supreme. That is why many Soviet intellectuals now are convinced that there is more socialism in Sweden or Switzerland, than in the socialist Soviet Union. Perestroika, started in the country under the leadership of Mikhail Gorbachev, is aimed to rectify that situation, through the restoration of the original humanitarian values of the socialist idea by radically overhauling the present society. Today, the greatest debate in the Soviet Union is how radical that overhaul should be, with the majority of people leaning toward the point of view that so far it has not been radical enough.

However, the failure in the Soviet Union to implement the basic humanitarian features of a socialist idea does not confer automatically on Western liberalism the title of the winning side, as Fukuyama, in trying to trick the reader into accepting, would say by default. What is so-called *Western* liberalism? To consult the great authority on the *Western idea*, Oswald Spengler:

> ... in eighteenth-century England, first the Parliamentary elections and then the decisions of the elected commons were systematically managed by money; England, too, discovered the ideal of a Free Press, and discovered along with it that the press serves him who owns it. It does not spread 'free opinion'—it generates it. Both together constitute liberalism (in the broad sense).[11]

Thus wrote the author of *The Decline of the West*, speaking about "the successful utilization of the bourgeois catchwords in politics."[12]

However, one doubts that Dr. Fukuyama had this meaning in mind. He treats liberalism as an embodiment of universal human values, and the notion of humanity's right to freedom and a system of government based on the consent of the governed as prime among them.

Is not the legacy of Marx, untainted by Stalinist interpretations, an integral part of that liberalism as much as the legacies of Peter Chaadayev, Alexander Herzen, Leo Tolstoy, Feodor Dostoyevski, Nikolay Feodorov, Nicolas Berdyayev, and dozens of other great Russian thinkers who contributed to the development of a universalist liberal idea? No Western economic or sociologist worthy of naming did not flirt, at one time or another, with Marxist ideas. Several achievements of the liberal welfare society, among them the eight-hour workday, equal rights for men and women, social security, and workers' compensation, were copied from the legislation and practices of postrevolutionary Russia.

As soon as the debate reemerged about which idea finally had triumphed, not a few Soviet authors scrambled to discover the worldwide victory of the basic elements of the socialist idea, despite the fact that it had fared badly in the first socialist country. As one Soviet commentator observed:

> Wherever the [Western] ruling elites proved flexible enough, they were able to put many elements of socialist programmes into practice in due time and to create shock absorbers for social conflicts. Wherever they were reluctant or unable to do this, the period of political instability, the succession of weak democratic governments, populist leaders and military dictatorships dragged on for centuries, dooming the countries to backwardness.[13]

Even if one foregoes discussing the value of the contributions to the development of the great liberal idea that came from different parts of the globe, and, for the sake of argument, grants that the idea totally and purely is Western, one still can inquire how this idea has fared so far in "victorious" societies, especially when the purportedly Marxist socialist scheme, which actually was Stalinist, failed elsewhere. With only an hour's walk in the downtown areas of Western capitals of the liberal societies, one can be approached 10-15 times with the request for spare change, realizing that the proclaimed triumph is still far away. Fukuyama himself admits that "the victory of liberalism has occurred primarily in the realm of ideas or consciousness and is as yet incomplete in the real material world."[14]

As the great socialist idea remains unfulfilled in the Soviet Union, and as the great liberal idea has not materialized completely in the West, it would be prudent to leave the ideas as they are, competing a while longer, and to allow scholars and politicians to concentrate better on the end of history as envisaged in the Bible, but not in the writings of old socialist or liberal thinkers. That is, the focus ought to be on the real possibility of the end of the world and human existence through an atomic apocalypse, if big atomic powers were to use their weapons as a *final argument* in support of this or that great idea. Such an eventuality seems improbable now, in great measure because of the Soviet new thinking on foreign policy and the continuing rapprochement between the United States and the Soviet Union. Nevertheless, as recently as the beginning of the 1980s, East and West, upping the ante in a trial of wills, talked themselves into a frenzied atmosphere that seemed reminiscent of the eve of World War I.

Competition among the various ideas regarding the social order and regarding the advantages and deficiencies of different societal models will endure. Humanity will continue to strive for societal and other forms of perfection, always approaching but never attaining them because the criteria of perfection will change in the process. In order to step out of humanity's somewhat barbaric prehistory or childhood and into real history, with all due appreciation to the vital contributions of previous civilizations, humanity should abolish the milleniums-old institution of warfare. As one writer has noted, "if a nation indulges itself in the illusion that, even with nuclear arms, war is possible, and that 'victory' can be won with them, it risks bringing about its own and the world's extinction by mistake."[15] When U.S. and Soviet leaders unanimously declared in November 1985 that "a nuclear war cannot be won and must never be fought," [16] they made a tremendous stride down the road of history. As the Malta summit demonstrated, both countries purposely are moving forward, albeit gradually, in the implementation of their agreement to make drastic reductions in armaments, to strengthen stability, and to reduce the risk of war.

The Finalized End of the Cold War

As [former] Soviet Foreign Minister Shevardnadze has remarked, the Soviet Union and the United States are moving from mutual understanding to mutual action in various fields of international and bilateral relations. In this way, both countries are leaving the Cold War with its vagaries behind them. In an earlier volume of this journal, [*The Washington Quarterly*], Dr. Brzezinski has suggested that there ought to be

> the definition and articulation of the Western concept of the Cold War's termination—a definition that is truly symbolically compelling and politically substantive. A simple and attractive definition of what the end of the Cold War actually should mean to everyone in the West and in the East is a political necessity.[17]

A sound suggestion, but to be authoritative to the people in the West and in the East, a definition ought to be not just Western, but East-West, or Soviet-U.S., for a start. Taking into account the ideas advanced by Dr. Brzezinski, such a definition might contain the following determinants:

- Termination of the arms race and the strengthening of national military security by agreements reached through multilateral efforts;
- Demilitarization of the Soviet-U.S. competition in the Third World;
- Strict implementation of the principle of freedom of choice for all people and the abandonment of both the Brezhnev and the Reagan doctrines;
- Demolition of the Berlin Wall;

- Progress toward the unity of Europe;
- Cessation of ideological confrontation, recognition of the suprema-cy of universal human values, and a shared approach to the prob-lem of human rights;
- Constructive cooperation of all member-states of the United Nations (U.N.) and its institutions for the solution of outstanding problems;
- Defusing of the Soviet-U.S. naval juxtaposition in the Pacific Ocean;
- The acceptance by the overwhelming majority of the states of the world of the principle of peaceful coexistence, understood not as a class struggle, but as friendly cohabitation and cooperation.

To some, this list may seem too long, or too short, but if something is to be produced, it should revolve around the above-mentioned criteria. Those who would agree with this list, could conclude that East and West essentially have moved beyond the Cold War.

In the area of disarmament, the Soviet-U.S. Intermediate-range Nuclear Force Treaty (INF) was a breakthrough on two points. First, it resulted in not just limitations, but the total destruction of an entire class of weapons. Second, it signified even greater breakthroughs in the attitude of both sides with regard to verification. Following the implementation of INF and its practice, all inspections, including the more intrusive ones, seem acceptable, to the benefit of forthcoming agreements, such as the bilateral START talks, the CFE between the countries of the North Atlantic Treaty Organization (NATO) and the Warsaw Pact, and the multilateral chemical weapons (CW) conven-tion.

Following recent encounters between Gorbachev and Bush and She-vardnadze and Baker, there seems little doubt that the START treaty will be ready to be signed this year....

The Cold War, which one hopes is passing, has been played out by the countries and systems in confrontation with each other, on different planes, or on different "battlefields," so to speak. The nuclear countries understood from early on that it is inconceivably dangerous for them to clash militarily head-on, even in non-nuclear battle, because of the inherent possibility of escalation. Therefore, the context acquired non-military or military-psychological forms, without the actual use of weapons. The Cold War has been waged through propaganda duels or psychological warfare—including a competition for the hearts and minds of the so-called spectators in the nonaligned world—and through the arms race with concomitant political and diplomatic struggles. The only real fields of the war were in the Third World, where the United

States and the Soviet Union had been waging battles by proxy. They supported indigenous conflicting forces and occasionally intervened directly, but only in situations where the other side had not been involved directly.

It is this plane of confrontation that is most difficult for both countries to disengage from, not only because of unwillingness to "betray" old friends and clients, but also because of the predominant mentalities and traditions. In the case of the United States, the mentality of Manifest Destiny, which included assuming the role of the world policeman, found conceptual expression in the various so-called imperial doctrines, from Monroe to Reagan. In the case of the Soviet Union, the difficulty has not centered around the remnants of the Grand Russian mentality as much as the blind dedication to the idea of world proletarian revolution, even in situations where it became absolutely clear that such a revolution is nothing but a *fata morgana*. The last flickering of this mentality is evident in the idea of peaceful coexistence as class struggle and in the concept of so-called international duty, which is known in the West as the Brezhnev doctrine, that postulated some fatalistic obligation on the part of "the first socialist state" to interfere to save so-called progressive regimes, sometimes even from their own populations. Recent auspicious developments in this sphere of Soviet-U.S. relations breed optimism as well.

It seems clear that there has been a marked decrease in Soviet-U.S. confrontation in the Third World. In the past few years, much effort has been expended by both countries to defuse local conflicts. Soviet troops have withdrawn from Afghanistan. The United States has stopped military aid to the contras and the Soviet Union has ceased arms shipments to the Nicaraguan government, both actions opening the way to free elections in that country. With active Soviet and U.S. participation, significant steps have been made toward peaceful resolution of the conflicts in Angola, Sahara, Lebanon, and Cambodia. Free elections under U.N. supervision have been held successfully in Namibia, ending years of strife. There has been some movement toward free elections in the Palestinian territories that remain under Israeli occupation.

Thus, in many cases, both superpowers now perceive their international duty not in helping a particular side win, but in cooperating to resolve local conflict.... Although the so-called Brezhnev doctrine is definitely dead, the Reagan doctrine, which is absolutely analogous to it, is not. The U.S. intervention in Panama is the most vivid demonstration of the latter's longevity.

The greatest challenge to the emerging world order that is based on understanding and cooperation of all the participants of international intercourse are the events on the border between the two blocs in Europe. Because of the explosive events in the German Democratic Republic, the stability on that border is gone, together with the Berlin Wall. Although the demise of the Wall is a welcome phenomenon, the turmoil in a Europe that is trying to shift, in an orderly manner, from the bloc stability of the Cold War to the comfort of a common European home is not....

...[T]he issue of the day is stability and security on the continent. The intensification of the all-European process, the gradual rapprochement between Eastern and Western Europe, the overcoming of the confrontational character of relations between NATO and the Warsaw Pact, and the widespread development of extensive economics, cultural, humanitarian, and other ties among the Europeans should enhance stability and security. Despite all the lip service paid to the benefits of the balance of interests, it suddenly dawned on many in Europe that the balance of power also is not a bad thing. The idea of Dr. Brzezinski that both blocs, while they exist, should shed their ideological mantles, becoming security systems based on geopolitical realities, and, in a way, guarantors of stability during this transition period is taking hold in the corridors of power of the nations concerned.

Other points on the list of criteria for the termination of the Cold War appear self-evident. Nevertheless, it is pertinent to observe that Europe is now the experimental ground where the pillars of the new and truly postwar, international world order are being laid. Monumental developments in Asia, such as liquidation of the Soviet-Chinese military confrontation, and increased participation of Japan, Australia, India, and the countries of the Association of South East Asian Nations (ASEAN) in promoting cooperation in the basins of the Pacific and Indian Oceans enhance tendencies toward global conciliation. It is not necessary to strive for an all-embracing emerging consensus, but for a general agreement on four points:

- The Cold War is over and should not be resumed.
- In order for nations and individuals to survive, it is necessary to do all within human power to prevent nuclear war and the destruction of the environment.
- Survival should mean not just meager subsistence, but the provision for all of abundant food and the good things of life.
- Survival only will be meaningful if people are really masters of their own fate, having the freedom of choice and living with liberty entrenched in their society.

As long as the Soviet Union and the United States remain with some extra influence in the world arena, owing to their superpower status, they should use it in consonance in order to promote these goals, around which not only the proletarians, but all of humanity could unite.

Notes

1. Graham Allison, "Testing Gorbachev," *Foreign Affairs* 68:4 (Fall 1989), p. 19.

2. The famous National Security Council Memorandum No. 68 stated: "Every consideration of devotion to our fundamental values and to our national security demands that we achieve our objectives by the strategy of the cold war, building up our military strength in order that it may not be used." *Foreign Relations of the United States*, vol. 1 (Washington, D.C.: GPO, 1977), p. 291.

3. Zbigniew Brzezinski, "Ending the Cold War," *Washington Quarterly* 12:4 (Autumn 1989), p. 29.

4. Eagleburger, "U.S. Foreign Policy," p. 11.

5. Francis Fukuyama, "The End of History?" *National Interest* 16 (Summer 1989), p. 3.

6. Fukuyama, "End of History," p. 4.

7. Fukuyama, "End of History," p. 4.

8. Fukuyama, "End of History," p. 4.

9. Karl Marx, "Preface to the Critique of Political Economy," Karl Marx and Frederick Engels Selected Works in Three Volumes (Moscow: Progress Publishers, 1976), p. 504.

10. Marx, "Political Economy," p. 127.

11. Oswald Spengler, *The Decline of the West* (New York: Random House, 1962), p. 368.

12. Spengler, *Decline of West*, p. 368.

13. Yegor Gaidar, *Moscow News*, October 8, 1989, p. 11. For an in-depth treatment of the same problem, see Georgi Shahnazorov, "East-West: Concerning the de-ideologization of interstate relations," *Kommunist* (Moscow) No. 3, February 1989, pp. 67-78.

14. Fukuyama, "End of History," p. 4.

15. Jonathan Schell, *The Fate of the Earth* (New York: Alfred A. Knopf, 1982), pp. 159-160).

16. United States-Soviet Summit in Geneva. Joint Statement of November 21, 1985, *Weekly Compilation of Presidential Documents*, 25 November 1985, p. 1422.

17. Brzezinski, "Ending the Cold War," p. 31.

PART TWO

Soviet and American Foreign Policies After the Cold War

Section 1
"NEW THINKING" IN SUPERPOWER FOREIGN POLICIES

Mikhail Gorbachev has made "new thinking" the center-piece of his foreign policy program. The phrase "new thinking" occupies the same exalted place in his discussion of international politics that perestroika and glasnost have assumed in his domestic policy. He has emphasized the necessity of discarding old approaches in favor of new policies more appropriate to a changing world.

Clearly Gorbachev's new foreign policy was designed to create the "breathing space" needed to nurture his revolution at home. It is, therefore, deeply rooted in Soviet domestic needs. This is not new to the Soviet Union; there has always been a close relationship between internal and external affairs in Soviet history. What is distinctive about the current situation is the leadership's sense of urgency about the need to change the nation's international environment so that domestic policy priorities can be realized. Furthermore, it hopes to achieve this without sacrificing the Soviet Union's position as a military and diplomatic superpower. Moreover, this search for reform both home and abroad is taking place in a highly diverse and contentious domestic political context. As the recent coup attempt confirmed, advocates of the old foreign and domestic policy agendas remain entrenched in positions of power and influence. There is the concern that the Soviet Union could return to its previous foreign policy stance if Gorbachev fails in his reform efforts.

In his essay entitled "The Policy of New Thinking in a Changing World," Andrei G. Bochkarev discusses the unprecedented change in Soviet foreign policy since Mikhail

Gorbachev became General Secretary of the Communist Party in 1985. The most important revision in the Soviet perspective on world affairs was the adoption of the philosophy of "new political thinking." The central elements of new political thinking are the unity and interdependence of the world, the supremacy of universal interests, freedom of choice, de-ideologization of state-to-state relations, demilitarization, democratization and humanization of international relations, the comprehensive concept of international security, and the doctrine of reasonable sufficiency.

According to Bochkarev, new thinking has resulted in a visible lessening of international tension. One of the first major achievements of the new policy was the INF (Intermediate-Range Nuclear Forces) Treaty, which was signed on 8 December 1987 and came into force during June of the following year. Another example of the role that disarmament has played in new thinking was Gorbachev's announcement at the United Nations during December 1988 that the Soviet Union would unilaterally reduce its armed forces by half a million.

Another dramatic example of Gorbachev's commitment to the new foreign policy was the Soviet withdrawal of troops from Afghanistan in 1989. Equally important was his policy of nonintervention in Eastern Europe in 1989 when that region erupted into a series of anti-Communist revolutions. A particularly significant development in Soviet-American relations took place during the Moscow Summit meeting in 1991 when the superpowers agreed to reduce their strategic forces by 30 percent.

David Jones, in his article "Domestic and Economic Aspects of Gorbachev's Foreign Policy," emphasizes the extent to which "new political thinking" is rooted in Soviet domestic needs. In the early 1980s Soviet officials, both political and military, were warning of the dangers of economic backwardness. When Gorbachev became General Secretary of the CPSU in 1985 he admitted that there was "stagnation" in the Soviet system. Despite the introduction of perestroika and glasnost, the economic and political system continued to deteriorate. Gorbachev became increasingly concerned that the USSR was in danger of becoming a third-rate power. Gorbachev's solution was to develop a modern and efficient economic system in the USSR so that the nation might maintain its great-power status into the twenty-first century.

While directing resources to domestic needs, he sought to guarantee the country's security by attempting to reduce the threats against it. Arms control was a key element in a revised security doctrine because it would free funds for the civilian sector. Subsidies to client states and to Third World nations would have to be curtailed. An aggressive campaign to improve international trade relations would be launched to parallel the new approach to political diplomacy. Expanded trade contracts with the European Economic Community were to be pursued as well as closer relations with GATT (General Agreement on Tariffs and Trade). Overtures were made to the IMF (International Monetary Fund) and the World Bank.

Whether Gorbachev, as a progressive leader, would have taken these steps to normalize international relations if the Soviet Union had not been in severe decline is an interesting question. It is clear, however, that the "new thinking" in foreign policy that was initiated in mid-1987 has the Soviet Union's survival as a nation-state as its primary goal.

America's reaction to Gorbachev's "new thinking" was initially diffident. At first the Bush administration dismissed as premature what appeared to most observers to be unprecedented opportunities to collaborate in areas where American and Soviet interests intersected, and it responded negatively to many of Mikhail Gorbachev's dramatic concessions. The administration seemed to fear that the Soviet Union under Gorbachev was not necessarily less threatening than it had been during the Cold War. The administration's review of Soviet policy during the first four months in office reflected little response to changes in the Soviet Union. Bush later sought to dispel the image of unresponsiveness in the Soviet-American relationship when he announced that America's goal was to "integrate the Soviet Union into the community of nations." At the annual meeting of NATO in May 1989 he pledged to "move beyond the era of containment." It was later that same year, when the Communist regimes in Eastern Europe collapsed, and claims were made that the Cold War had come to an end, that the American administration recognized that Soviet-American relations were entering a new era.

Michael Mandelbaum describes these changes in American foreign policy in his essay entitled "The Bush Foreign Policy." Mandelbaum states that while the revolutions in Eastern Europe essentially ended the Cold War, the American president and his advisors were more "spectators than participants." The United States stayed in the background and no bold new programs were forthcoming. Furthermore, the Bush administration avoided actions that might provoke the Soviet Union. Mandelbaum suggests that the administration acted wisely in not suggesting that the future of Eastern Europe would have to be negotiated by the superpowers. In the author's opinion, "the president deserves high marks for the six eventful months that may be seen in retrospect as the final crisis of the Cold War."

Now that superpower relations have entered a new era, Mandelbaum sees the administration moving from a policy of containment to a policy of "reassurance." Although no grand scheme has been proposed, the author sees a postwar international agenda taking shape. By necessity U.S. foreign policy will be transformed because there has been nothing less than a revolution in international politics, and this has had "a revolutionary impact on America's relations with the rest of the world." As a consequence, "there will be a greater discontinuity in foreign policy between the first and second halves of the Bush presidency than between any two administrations in the postwar period."

5

The Policy of New Thinking in a Changing World

Andrei G. Bochkarev

Since 1985 when Mikhail Gorbachev became the General Secretary of the Communist Party of the Soviet Union, the Soviet Union has undergone unprecedented change.

As the end of the twentieth century approaches, it becomes clear that we will face a future considerably more international than ever believed possible in the past. Nuclear proliferation, regional conflicts, the energy crisis, world food shortages, and environmental problems threaten to involve us all. Many of the previous distinctions between foreign and domestic policies have become artificial. National interests can no longer be defined in strictly ideological terms. Nations with different ideological commitments must begin to cooperate to resolve common strategic, economic, humanitarian, and environmental concerns. Our world is becoming increasingly smaller and global interdependence has become a reality. As Rene Dubos, the 1969 Pulitzer Prize recipient once stated, "It becomes obvious that each of us has two countries, our own and the planet earth."

In our ever-changing world, change is the one certainty. By the end of the century the Soviet Union will not exist in its present form, and politically the world will be very different in the future from what it is today. Today we face a different world and we must seek a different road to the future. This road must draw on the accumulated experience of yesterday, yet be fully aware of the fundamental differences between the circumstances of yesterday and those of today and tomorrow.

This article contains a brief analytical exposition of the changes that have come about in Soviet foreign policy, its philosophy, and progress, which are a result of the evolving concept of new political thinking and the early steps toward putting this policy into practice.

The Philosophy of New Thinking

Many new problems face humanity. The social changes of the century are significantly altering the conditions for the further development of society. New political, economic, scientific, and environmental factors are beginning to operate. The interconnection between nations and peoples is increasing. This new interdependence demands the entire world community join efforts in addressing these global issues and implementing a policy of new thinking.

The dawn of the philosophical concept, new political thinking, began with major political documents submitted by Mikhail Gorbachev to the 27th CPSU Congress, the 19th All-Union CPSU Conference, and other important political and governmental documents.

Without feigning claim on the innovation of new political thought the Soviet government looked toward many various international political and social movements, i.e., humanitarian, environmental, military disarmament, etc., which have struggled against the common dangers faced by humanity in our time. On this threshold of a new era, the USSR is renewing a socialist idea, which has by no means exhausted its possibilities or potentialities. The concept of new thinking, inspired by concern for peace, universal solidarity, individual rights and freedoms, and the natural and intellectual environment of humanity, is equal to offering civilization its own alternatives and choices in social development.

The main points underlying the foundation of new political thinking are the unity and interdependence of the world, supremacy of universal interests, freedom of choice, deideologizing state-to-state relations, demilitarization, democratization and humanization of international relations, comprehensive concept of international security, and the doctrine of reasonable sufficiency.[1]

Unity and interdependence of the world, fundamentally, has a new quality. It proceeds from the premise that now, more than ever, social progress demands that there should be constructive and creative interaction between governments and peoples throughout the entire world. It is essential that international problems, and particularly security issues, be resolved jointly in the interests of all concerned and on the basis of cooperation. Thus, the interests of individual countries and governments should be subordinated to the interests of the world community.

This leads to the second point of supremacy of universal interests. Today the destinies of all nations are more closely intertwined than ever witnessed in history. This reality places more demands on world politics and on the efforts of the world community to solve global problems. It is here that the role of the United Nations becomes irreplaceable. Progress toward these problems in this new epoch demands an essentially new level of international cooperation where each social group can realize its aspirations more fully if it correlates them to the good of humanity as a whole.

Another key aspect in the concept of new political thinking is the principle of freedom of choice. Freedom of choice affirms that there is no unidimensional standard to which the world can evaluate the many various forms of social consciousness and social being. It respects and addresses the multidimensional standard of social development in every nation. Respect can only manifest itself through the security that every nation, large or small, has the inviolable right to choose its own course of development, and that the axiom for any country must be noninterference in another nation's internal affairs. However, even this is not enough. International law must ensure the progress from formal to actual equality through either bilateral, regional, or global mechanisms. Therefore, it is through conditions of diversity, and not through forced artificial leveling, that the world can achieve genuine unity.

Regardless of the distinctions in ideology, all nations must learn to cooperate, to respect one another, and to seek common ground. Individual interests of all nations must be respected. Foreign policy ideological principles must not be built around a particular section of humanity. This aspect of new political thinking presupposes renunciation of the concept of confrontation as a principle in foreign policy and is aimed at deideologizing state-to-state relations.   New principles and new approaches to the task of eliminating ideologized, confrontational stereotypes have made it possible to build civilized relations between nations.

The fragility of today's world, as a result of the possible destruction brought into being by man, makes it imperative to demilitarize, to gradually reduce armaments and promote the abolition of these weapons. Our modern world has become much too small and fragile for wars and policies of strength. The continuation of life cannot be saved and preserved if the acceptance of wars and armed conflicts is not shed. Weapons of mass destruction are endangering the very existence of life on Earth. Consequently, the Soviet Union rejects war as a means of resolving political, economic, and ideological disputes between countries. The circumstances could easily become such that nuclear war will no longer depend upon the intelligence or will of political leaders, but may become captive to technology. The arms race can bring no political gain to anyone. Today the interdependence and involvement of nations in global politics urgently calls for the democratization and humanization of international relations.

Lastly, the principle of reasonable sufficiency is related to that of parity and is mostly defined by the correlation between the military potentials of governments and international and regional political situations. The advancement of this principle aroused a great deal of interest, especially among democratic publics, around the world. It calls for stopping the arms race and beginning arms reductions. The principle of reasonable sufficiency was specifically outlined on 15 January 1985, after a Soviet reappraisal of military political principles called for an extensive program for the elimination of nuclear arms and other weapons of mass destruction by the year 2000.[2] The principle is influenced by various factors, e.g., times of international crises and conflicts versus peacetime, economic capabilities, etc. Nevertheless, impressive results have been achieved between the United States and the Soviet Union in this area, and the USSR-U.S. summit meetings in Geneva, Reykjavik, Washington, and Moscow have played a tremendous role.

New Thinking in Practice

Changing political thinking, shifting from power politics to peace-oriented policies is probably one of the greatest challenges that faces humanity.

New political thinking in Soviet foreign policy has been met with tremendous public response. It has touched all spheres of the world community, and has had a far-ranging consensus of support in addressing new approaches to the problems of human survival. As a result of people's diplomacy and international dialogue the barriers of incomprehension, alienation, and distrust are vanishing. This is improving international political relationships and creating an environment conducive to the practical solution of international issues.

New thinking has resulted in a visible lessening of international tensions. Yet while the menace of war has receded and favorable conditions for perestroika in Soviet foreign policy have been created, these positive changes have yet to become irreversible. The situation in the world today is complicated and there remains considerable resistance to the initiatives of new thinking. It is too early to rule out the possibilities of recurrences of policies developed from positions of strength, flare-ups of tensions and retreats, etc., and unfortunately, the concept of comprehensive security has been slow in gaining ground at the U.N. and in international practice.

One of the first achievements in new thinking was the INF Treaty, which was signed on 8 December 1987, and came into force on 1 June 1988. On the road to nuclear disarmament this genuine breakthrough no longer left doubt as to whether or not the task of phasing out nuclear arms was utopian. A further step in the disarmament process was made on 7 December 1988 in a historic speech before the United Nations. Gorbachev announced a unilateral reduction and demobilization of Soviet armed forces by half a million.

Additionally, the 1989 pullout of troops from Afghanistan was one of the USSR's biggest international achievements of new thinking. It relieved the Soviet Union from an oppressive moral and material burden. The removal of these troops was possible only through radical revisions of Soviet foreign policy and through agreements reached by the Afghan and Pakistani governments in Geneva in 1988, along with guarantees from the United States and the Soviet Union which provided for an end to foreign interference in the affairs of Afghanistan. A corollary of the principles of new thinking and interdependence is the essential role the Soviet Union wants to give the United Nations in solving regional conflicts—conflicts which are found in such places as Angola, Namibia, Cambodia, Afghanistan, and most recently Iraq.

Equally important were Gorbachev's actions last year in Eastern Europe when the Soviet Union maintained an approach of noninterference to the changes and transitions occurring in those regions. The Soviet Union has become a strong advocate of nonintervention in the internal affairs of other countries. The foreign policy principles of new thinking must operate without fail in relations between socialist countries. There is no longer, nor can there be, two systems of values: one for the USSR and the other for Eastern Europe. The relations between the Soviet Union and these countries is now marked by a more creative use of the opportunities offered by universally recognized standards of state-to-state relations. Throughout all the problems and difficulties which are now facing Eastern Europe, as they adjust to new realities, the USSR's relations with them are acquiring a new context.

It was during the 28th Party Congress that Eduard Shevardnadze, Minister of Foreign Affairs of the USSR, underlined the claim that the USSR would not place any obstacles on the process of the destruction of administrative-command systems and totalitarian regimes. To do otherwise would be in direct opposition to the principles of new thinking and the logic of perestroika. Even if the changes in Eastern Europe contradict Soviet interests, the USSR would continue to exclude the possibility of interfering in their internal affairs. Today such interference is not acceptable because the USSR recognizes not solely by words, but by deeds, the equality of all nations, noninterference in other's internal affairs, the sovereignty of people, and the right for freedom of choice.[2]

Another major achievement of Soviet foreign policy in the era of perestroika is the normalization of Soviet-Chinese relations. These new relations have ended a prolonged and painful period of alienation, distrust, and occasional hostility between the two socialist powers. The May 1989 meeting in Peking between the top leaders of these countries, the first in thirty years, ushered in a qualitatively new stage in mutual relations.

An indication of the success of Gorbachev's policy of new political thinking was illustrated in October 1990 when President Gorbachev was awarded the 1990 Nobel Peace Prize for his decisive role in the dramatic rapprochement between East and West.

According to Marshall Goldman, a well-respected Sovietologist, Gorbachev's efforts in changing Soviet foreign policy on the basis of new thinking not only could not have been predicted, but have stunned the entire world. As a result of these dramatic efforts, Goldman credits President Gorbachev with "making our lives more secure." The Norwegian Nobel Committee stated that "Confrontation has been replaced by negotiations. Old European nation states have regained freedom. The arms race is slowing down and we see a definite and active process in the direction of arms control and disarmament."[4]

Doing so more perseveringly and imaginatively, and borrowing all that is constructive and sound, it is the objective of Soviet foreign policy to implement a philosophy based on new thinking. The First Congress of People's Deputies of the USSR emphasized that this is "not a tactical ploy, not a zigzag, not a concession to anyone, but a well-founded strategy expressing the interests of the Soviet people and meeting the interests of humanity as a whole."[5]

The recent resignation of Soviet Foreign Minister Eduard Shevardnadze has caused concern among the international community. Speculation about the many possible consequences in Soviet foreign policy has been rampant. However, Shevardnadze's departure does not inherently bring with it obstacles which would block further positive changes in foreign policy. These changes, and future changes in foreign policy, are irreversible. In our nuclear age, new thinking doesn't have any reasonable alternative.

Notes

1. Mikhail Gorbachev, *Political Report of the CPSU Central Committee to the 27th Party Congress*, Novosti Press, Moscow, USSR. 1986, pp. 80-96.

2. Daniil Proektor, *Politics and Power*, Novosti Press, Moscow, USSR. 1989, pp. 47-49.

3. Eduard Shevardnadze, "Report on the 28th Congress of the CPSU," *Pravda*. 5 July 1990, p. 2.

4. Doug Mellgren, Associated Press, "Gorbachev Wins Nobel Prize," *The Arizona Republic*. 16 October 1990, pg. A-10.

5. Congress of People's Deputies of the USSR, *Documents and Materials*, Novosti Press, Moscow, USSR. 1989, p. 112.

6

Domestic and Economic Aspects of Gorbachev's Foreign Policy

David R. Jones

The special Party Conference convoked by Mikhail Gorbachev in early July 1988 had little to say directly about foreign policy as such. Having given approval to the INF missile treaty and the plans for withdrawing Soviet troops from Afghanistan, its resolutions then concluded with a paragraph that closely linked such issues to internal concerns. "Foreign policy activity" they read, "should contribute ever more to releasing the country's resources for peaceful construction, for *perestroika*, and should be closely tied in with the democratization of society, including making decisions and verification of compliance with the decisions made."[1]

It is, of course, a truism to state that a nation's foreign policy is in large part determined by its domestic politics and economic potential. Similarly, few would disagree that military power has always been a necessary element in international relations. But since 1945—the dawn of the nuclear era—military power seems to have become *the* major element. Indeed, over the past four decades the dominance of 'strategists' and 'strategic thinkers' in discussions (at least in the West) of inter-state and 'inter-system' relationships has been so great that some speak of the 'militarization of diplomacy'.[2]

Along with politics, diplomacy was long considered to be 'the art of the possible', carried out by skilled and subtle practitioners who spend most of their careers seeking to adjust competing national interests in the passionless atmosphere of *realpolitik*. For these men, war was just one—and usually the last—'means of continuing politics'. In fact, by 1914 many diplomats regarded the resort to force as a sign of their failure, and many feared a general conflict might 'put out the lights' of the civilized world as they knew it. Since then, many have regarded the outbreak of war in that year as a tragedy resulting from a process in which military considerations finally overrode political ones, and military strategists overcame the scruples of saner politicians and diplomats.

Yet in the highly charged ideological world of today's superpower politics, diplomacy has been demoted to second place. Since 1945, it has generally been seen as a handmaiden to generals and strategic theorists. Despite occasional summits and the hopes aroused by the SALT process of the 1970s, by the early 1980s East-West diplomacy seemed useful only as a means to justify limited incidents of violent intervention (e.g. Afghanistan and Grenada), and as a mechanism for helping to avoid a systemic cataclysm. For despite widespread recognition that such a nuclear war would be a global catastrophe, the focus of the superpowers still seemed to be on maintaining sufficient military strength to deter each other, and to 'win' just such a conflict, should it somehow occur.

These tendencies reached their apogee during the late 1960s, 1970s and early 1980s. Faced with a worsening international climate and humiliated over Cuba in 1962, the Soviet Union set out to obtain military-strategic, and so, it hoped, political, parity with the USA. But after a brief period of détente and successful efforts at arms control, the USA became disenchanted with the Soviets' behavior and fearful over their apparent 'unprecedented military build-up'. The result was the reinvigorated American program of defense spending begun by President Carter and continued at still higher levels by his successor, Ronald Reagan. Ironically, just as the Soviet military-political establishment seemed at long last to be readjusting its doctrine to the realities of nuclear weapons, and to be revising its military doctrine so as to accept unambiguously the concept of 'mutually assured destruction' (MAD) as a de facto constraint on their utility, officials in Washington began talking of developing a war-fighting capability for a 'protracted' nuclear conflict. As diplomacy languished in an atmosphere of highly charged rhetoric, President Reagan's Strategic Defense Initiative (SDI) suddenly threatened to upset the existing strategic diplomacy, to doom immediate hopes for arms control and reductions, to send superpower arms racing into a new and expensive spiral, and to extend the theaters of any future conflict to the Cosmos.

By 1985 the future seemed bleak indeed. Nonetheless, beneath the surface other developments were occurring that would improve the picture. In the first place, within both superpowers, let alone elsewhere, there were large constituencies—often spurred on in the West by active and articulate peace-activists—calling for a reversal of the trends just outlined. Second, and perhaps of more importance, in both superpowers there was a growing and sharpening awareness of the disastrous economic and domestic impacts of this competition in armaments. And third, the year 1985 saw a new generation of political leadership finally come to power in Moscow. After the two years of uncertainty that had followed the death of Leonid Brezhnev, Mikhail Gorbachev finally emerged as General Secretary of the Communist Party and gave Soviet reformers firm leadership for a program of internal economic and social *perestroika* (restructuring), *glasnost* (openness) and *demokrati-satsiia* (democratization).

Perestroika and 'New Thinking'

The new Soviet leader has accompanied his program of domestic reforms with calls for 'new thinking' in the realm of foreign relations. In practice, this has been demonstrated by Moscow's increased flexibility and willingness to compromise in the arms reduction and other East-West negotiations, in Soviet efforts to settle regional issues in the Third World and reduce tensions with China, and in the aggressive promotion of economic, cultural and other ties with the outside world in general.

More theoretically, these initiatives have been accompanied by claims that Soviet military doctrine has been further revised to give it a purely 'defensive' character, that the accompanying arms programs seek only to assure 'adequate security', and that this latter should be sufficient in a world that guarantees both the 'mutual security' of the long-time rivals, as well as the increased intercourse between them.[3] In fact, this new thinking seems to presage nothing less than a switch of attention from the purely military aspects of international relations, and an effort to bring interstate relations back into the less ideological atmosphere of realpolitik. Indeed, in June 1988 one leading official openly admitted that in the past, "we lacked a realistic view of the world." He therefore urged that future policies "acknowledge the world in all its complexity" and recognize the de facto "interdependence" that exists between modern states.[4]

As a consequence, the Soviet leaders appear to have embraced the 'demilitarization' of diplomacy and appear to be increasingly interested in the practice of this time-honored means of pursuing national interests in general, of reducing the perceived level of external threat faced by the Soviet state, and of promoting that state's internal health as well as its external security. In fact, Foreign Minister E.A. Shevard-nadze had already gone so far as to announce that it is time to "'economize' our foreign policy." He went on to point out that to sacrifice realism to ideological formula means one loses much, "including the ability to improve the economic position of one's own country and, in this way, to expand the range of its political influence in the world."[5]

This new thinking, as well as President Reagan's alleged desire to be remembered as a 'peacemaker', go far to explain the abrupt improvement in superpower relations since 1985. But despite this, Gorbachev's own personal charm and the apparent rationality of his policies, one would be naive to believe that the Soviet Union has adopted its new stance for motives of pure idealism. It is equally misguided to assume cynically that this new thinking represents merely a fleeting change in Soviet tactics, or an elaborate exercise in *maskirovka* (deception) designed to mask a continuing drive for military and political hegemony. Undoubtedly, the Soviet leaders would prefer to attain such a position, and some of them may believe that someday history will bring their cause just such supremacy. But for the moment, as competent 'realpoliticians' they have recognized that real military superiority is an unattainable dream, and that the domestic economic realities of their state demand urgent attention. Or as Gorbachev himself put it to a cheering throng of automobile workers, "a strong, healthy economy provides the guarantee for a policy of peace. This is the link between domestic and foreign policy."[6]

Domestic Determinants

In the past numerous scholars have discussed the various domestic determinants underlying Russian and Soviet foreign policy. These have included ideological conviction, the ebb and flow of bureaucratic interests within the government, the need for external distractions from internal difficulties, and so on. But in the speech just quoted, Gorbachev himself made clear the domestic goal that requires his new thinking in international relations, as well as a new political thinking with regard to domestic policies. This is his determination to provide his state with a powerful, modern and efficient economic system, which in turn will be the basis for the USSR's continued prestige, power and influence abroad.

When Secretary Gorbachev maintains the Soviet economy is in crisis, few Western specialists disagree. True, since 1962 the USSR, thanks to strenuous efforts, has gained military parity with the USA and the right to the title 'superpower'. Nonetheless, the costs have been great indeed and even Soviet specialists admit that defense expenditures—in spite of their official stability throughout the 1970s—have been both a "very important part" of, and "no small burden" on, the state budget.[7]

Gorbachev himself admitted in February 1987 that defense "is a load on the economy, apart from all else because it diverts enormous resources that could be redirected, and it is well known where, we have plenty of problems."[8] But as he also noted: "You can rest assured when it comes to defense, that is point number one, and point number two as well." While some analysts interpret this and similar statements to mean that "Gorbachev's view of the future places the military as uppermost in the long run,"[9] the implications of his policies are not necessarily as straightforward as they suggest. For while the general secretary had promised the military the traditional "everything necessary," this was now limited only to "the requirements of a sensible, sufficient defense."[10]

While the future demands of such sufficiency remain the subject of debate, the price of the existing military establishment is depressingly evident. Its economic base continues to be the highly centralized and bureaucratized economic structure created by Joseph Stalin. For the first three decades after the Second World War, this gave the USSR the sustained annual growth rate (3-4 percent in estimated Gross National Product or GNP during the early 1970s) that permitted it to occupy center stage in the world arena. As a result, an optimistic leadership happily permitted an annual growth in defense spending of 4-5 percent, and simultaneously pledged—in Brezhnev's words of 1974—"to attain a full abundance of high-quality foods and consumer goods, and to provide each family with a well-appointed apartment."[11] But by 1976 the economy already showed signs of stagnation, and by 1978 the annual estimated growth in GNP had dropped to a miserable 1.6 percent. Further, although the growth rate of defense expenditures also slowed to about 2 percent annually, the U.S. Central Intelligence Agency estimated that its share of GNP had actually risen from 13-14 to 15-17 percent.[12]

As a result of these factors, as well as the by-now endemic inefficiency of the Stalinist economic model, Brezhnev's pledge remains not only unfulfilled, but the quality of Soviet life is such that caustic Western critics dismiss the USSR as a mere "Upper Volta with missiles." If some feel this description is unnecessarily harsh, it nonetheless accords with many aspects of Russian reality. For example, the CIA has reported that the per capita Soviet income is roughly $7000 (U.S.) annually (the same as Britain and Italy), but many disagree. Thus one Western observer in Moscow told reporter Daniel Ford that in reality the "Soviet economy should be compared with Mexico's or Malaysia's or Portugal's", and insisted that real "GNP per capita is about a third of what the CIA says ... I prefer to use simple standards—health standards, average life expectancy, infant mortality ... and when I do [the] Soviets end up with those comparable to countries at about $2500 per capita."[13]

Other Western authorities support this view. A report published by the U.S. Congress's Joint Economic Committee in late 1987, for instance, remarks on the primitive nature of new housing being built in the countryside. It cited a survey that showed that as late as 1985, only 30 percent had water, sewer services and central heating, and that 42 percent of this housing "was built with no amenities whatsoever."[14] As for the Soviet-Mexican comparison, an estimate in May 1988 maintained that the number of car owners in the USSR was 42 per 1000 of the population. This compares with 552 per 1000 in the USA, 329 per 1000 in Great Britain, and 65 per 1000 in Mexico. Indeed, in terms of car owners in the fourteen countries surveyed (the eight East Bloc nations included), the USSR surpassed only Egypt (15 per 1000), Romania (11 per 1000), and India (2 per 1000). In fact, the Soviets were runners-up to the Poles, who in relative terms owned over twice as many autos as did their Russian 'allies'.[15]

Soviet officials and journals have recognized many of these specific problems. Here two examples will suffice: Egor Ligachev's admission in January 1988 that almost half of Soviet schools lacked indoor plumbing, and the newspaper *Trud*'s recognition in May that year, that the USSR had an infant mortality rate more than double that of the USA and most developed nations—a situation it blamed on poor sanitation and incest.[16] More important still, they have also had to face the fact that these problems are only especially visible symptoms of a deteriorating economic and social system that has been reflected in stagnating growth rates, increasing resource constraints, commodity shortages, a rise in the rates of alcoholism, crime and corruption, low sanitary standards, and a general atmosphere of cynicism.[17]

By the early 1980s political and even military commentators, of whom the most prominent was the then Chief of the General Staff, N.V. Ogarkov, were warning of the dangers of economic backwardness.[18] Or as Gorbachev himself admitted to the Central Committee's Plenum in January 1987, "at some point our country began to lose its momentum, difficulties and resolved problems started piling up, and elements of stagnation and other phenomena appeared that are alien to socialism." Naturally these conditions "seriously affected the economy and the social and spiritual spheres" of Soviet life. As a result, he charged that under Brezhnev, "[c]onservative attitudes, inertia, the tendency to brush aside anything that did not fit conventional patterns, and an unwillingness to face up to pressing socio-economic matters prevailed in policy-making and practical activities."[19]

According to one American diplomat, Gorbachev had been so deeply troubled by this situation that he had "concluded that the USSR is in danger of becoming a third-rate—not a second-rate—power in the twenty-first century."[20] This assessment also may be too extreme, but the new party secretary obviously entered office determined to launch his nation on another of its periodic efforts at reform designed both to modify its social structure and to maintain its position among the foremost world powers. In fact, Gorbachev had made this clear even before assuming office in March 1985. On the previous 10 December he had pointed to radical problems "of vast dimensions" and the "titanic task" of innovation involved in "increasing the working people's prosperity, ensuring the consolidation of the USSR's positions on the international scene, and enabling it to enter the new millennium in a manner worthy of a great and prosperous power." This aim, he insisted, could only be realized by "the transition to an intensive economy that is developed on the basis of the most up-to-date scientific and technological changes." This in turn would require "extensive changes in the economy and throughout the system of social relations." And as a good Marxist, he warned that bringing the USSR to "a new stage in the socio-economic process" meant that changes in production relations "must also extend to the system of political relations," and hence usher in "a new level in the development of socialist democracy."[21]

Economic Perestroika

Here in a nutshell is the justification of the new political thinking, as well as the nexus of perestroika, glasnost and demokratisatsiia. The details of the resulting programs have been examined elsewhere and need not concern us. For our purposes it will be sufficient to note the main planks of the general secretary's economic program as enunciated by the reformist economists, of whom Abel Aganbegian has been most prominent. These include modernization of an aging industrial plant, especially the important machine-building sector, by accelerated investment in new technology and the introduction of modern techniques from the defense industrial sector; an increase of the resources devoted to consumer production so as to provide a higher standard of living and greater incentives to the labor force; and to transform the extensive Stalinist command economy into a more efficient, intensive one by decentralizing its planning and administrative structures, introducing market mechanisms, encouraging more cooperative and private enterprises, and forcing large state-owned enterprises to work on a profit basis. In the context of this radical 'restructuring', glasnost is conceived as a necessary prerequisite for technological transfers and innovation. Meanwhile, the criticism inherent in even a limited process of demokratisatsiia can serve as a means of rooting out corruption and inefficiency, as well as a spur to the increased participation by labor that Gorbachev has insisted is necessary for the success of his initiatives.[22]

Above all else, this ambitious and far-ranging program demands a greater resource investment in industry so as to increase the factor productivity of capital. For while many of the most visible and dramatic campaigns associated with economic restructuring have concerned the drive against alcoholism and for greater discipline in the workplace, the factor productivity of labor has in fact been rising steadily since the mid-1960s. Nonetheless, Soviet industry still requires roughly three times the inputs of all kinds to provide a similar quantity (quite apart from quality) of goods to that produced in the West.

It is, rather, the productivity of capital that has been declining continuously, and so retarding the growth rate of GNP, during the same period. As for the implications of this program for spending on security and defense, to date these remain unclear. The Soviet leaders may have hoped, as some argue, that they could develop the non-defense sphere of industry by introducing more efficient management and productive techniques from military industry, and then use the resulting gains to reinvest in, and so reinvigorate, the civilian sector. Yet it seems very unlikely that these measures can provide either the 80 percent increase (above the 1981-1985 level) in capital investment in civilian machine-building demanded by Gorbachev for 1986-1990, or the resources necessary to develop the "fundamentally new instruments, computer-controlled machine tools, robot equipment, and the latest-generation computers," that even military men recognize are desperately needed.[23]

Implications of the New Thinking
for Security Policy

As a result, most Western analysts now agree that sooner or later, the Soviet leadership will face hard choices about cutting defense spending or curtailing the investment for the industrial transformation that the general secretary and his supporters believe is vital for their nation's future. And indeed, some believe they have already faced these choices, and that as a consequence, military spending has been curtailed.[24]

In terms of realpolitik, a state may seek to guarantee its security by relying on its own military potential, by combining the latter with the potential of allies, or by seeking to reduce the threats facing it. During past Russian efforts at domestic reform and economic renewal (e.g. the 1860s, 1880s-1890s and 1920s) its leaders have chosen to place heavy emphasis on the third alternative: that is, on the diplomacy of threat reduction. And give the inspiration he claims to have found in the example of Lenin's New Economic Policy (NEP) of the early 1920s, it is not surprising that Gorbachev has done likewise.

Many Western commentators, especially those wedded to the idea of continuing Party-military tension within the USSR, assume that Gorbachev must have faced considerable opposition when he began introducing his new thinking into security affairs in 1985.[25] Yet this assumption overlooks the fact that the foundations were already laid on which he has built. For example, movement toward ending the stalemate of arms control in general, and on Euromissiles in particular, had been evident under Yuri Andropov. Similarly, by the late 1970s Soviet analysts were becoming increasingly disillusioned about the chances of radical revolution in the nations of the underdeveloped, and frequently pre-industrial, Third World, and so doubted that the USSR had much to gain by involving itself closely in their affairs.[26] But most important of all, the changes in declared Soviet military doctrine since 1976 meant that by 1985 most military thinkers accepted both the necessity for economic renewal, and the uselessness of nuclear weapons as a means of waging war. Indeed, in May 1985 no less a personage than Marshal N.V. Ogarkov suggested—perhaps as a result of higher political pressure—that the destructiveness of nuclear weaponry not only negated the possibility of nuclear war, but of systemic world war in general.[27]

For these reasons, Gorbachev's proclamation of new thinking to the 27th Congress was hardly novel. "The nature of today's weapons" he told the delegates, "leaves no state with the hope of defending itself by technical military means alone—let us say, with the creation of a defense, even the most powerful one. Ensuring security is more and more taking the form of a political task and it can be solved only by political means." And he insisted that "first and foremost," the powers must find "the will ... needed to go along with disarmament."[28]

But despite this emphasis, arms control was only one aspect of a much larger effort at threat reduction. This rapidly became apparent in the increased flexibility and offers of compromise, of which acceptance of the 'zero option' for Euromissiles was the most dramatic example, that Soviet negotiators have demonstrated throughout the range of East-West discourses. This has gone far to reduce the sense of international tension that existed when Gorbachev became general secretary in March 1985, which in turn has doubtless worked to his advantage as he pushed military doctrine toward its new, self-proclaimed 'defensive' formulation.

The advantages of this revised security doctrine for domestic economic reform are obvious. To begin with, arms control agreements in themselves—as Aganbegian recently suggested—may "free investment funds for the civilian sector."[29] Nonetheless, the direct savings from such agreements as that on Euromissiles, or even one on strategic nuclear systems, will be small. For contrary to popular belief, nuclear missiles consume only a small part of either superpower's defense budget. Only much deeper cuts either in other aspects of procurement, or in the manpower drafted, or in both, will allow a major diversion of resources to the civilian sector.[30] Hence the real value of these measures is that they promote an atmosphere in which Gorbachev can argue for such radical steps at home, and in which his newly demilitarized diplomacy can seek to improve relations elsewhere in the world arena.

Another aspect of the new thinking both promotes this same goal of reduced tensions and offers financial savings. As pointed out above, by the early 1980s Soviet analysts of Third World affairs were becoming increasingly dubious of the advantages to be gained in most developing states. They argued that Moscow should reserve real support only for those nations in which Soviet prestige was intimately involved (Cuba, Vietnam, and perhaps Afghanistan), which offered strategic bases (South Yemen) or opportunities to irritate the USA (Nicaragua), which provided hard currency for Soviet arms (Libya and Angola), or which were already well along the road to industrialization (India). Apart from any hopes that might be raised by ideologically satisfying currents within the last group, aid to them might also open to the USSR new avenues of access to modern technology.[31]

In any case, while Gorbachev has sought to maintain a close relationship with New Delhi, his policies elsewhere in the Third World have gone well beyond even the earlier recommendations of the pessimistic analysts. Throughout the developing world Soviet initiatives have recently been marked by a new stinginess. Even such long-time clients as Cuba and Vietnam, not to mention newcomers such as Nicaragua, seem to be finding their subsidies reduced significantly. Meanwhile, it can hardly be doubted that Moscow is encouraging Havana to proceed with negotiations for a withdrawal from Angola. Most stunning of all was Gorbachev's embrace of diplomacy as a means of ending the large-scale Soviet presence in Afghanistan—a step that few believed likely even a year earlier. While Moscow's final plans for influence in the mountain nation remain obscure, acceptance of the Geneva agreement was obviously another move to improve relations with the USA, as well as with a suspicious China and the Muslim world.[32]

In the climate of glasnost and demokratisatsiia, these initiatives in East-West arms control and in reducing Soviet commitments abroad may bring Gorbachev useful domestic dividends of a non-economic nature as well. While public opinion plays a very different role in the Soviet Union from what it does in the West, it remains a significant consideration. Indeed, Western analysts admit its importance when they discuss the future of his economic reforms. Given the expectations aroused by the General Secretary, and the poor economic performances of 1987 and early 1988, as well as the disruption that is bound to occur when price subsidies are ended, they note that perestroika may be threatened by popular impatience before the reforms have time to bear fruit.[33] In such a situation, successes in foreign affairs may help to placate such discontent. Thus the withdrawal from Afghanistan is undoubtedly popular, and successful arms reductions can only be welcomed by a populace well aware of the impact of war and, through civil defense, the effects of nuclear weaponry. In addition, reduced subsidies abroad will be equally agreeable to a populace resentful of supporting others while their own shops remain almost empty. In this manner, international successes may well bring Gorbachev much-needed respite until his reforms take root, while Pizza Huts, Big Macs and Pepsi Cola become earnests of the more abundant future to come.

External Economic Initiatives

Nonetheless, the General Secretary and his advisers may regard the economic and domestic benefits outlined above as being peripheral to the main goals of domestic perestroika. Instead, all the above measures, as well as concessions on Jewish emigration and other aspects of human rights, are motivated by the argument that "the improving political climate ... would help economic relations."[34] And given the overriding priority accorded domestic economic restructuring, it is not surprising to find that parallel to its new program of political diplomacy, Moscow has launched an aggressive campaign of economic diplomacy. Aimed at obtaining Western technology and investment credits to support what Gorbachev has called his plans for "in-depth, truly revolutionary transformations," this has resulted in what American intelligence analysts call the "reaching out for Western capital in a manner unparalleled since the 1920s."[35]

This diplomacy is naturally much less dramatic than that associated with arms reductions, force reductions and troop withdrawals. But in the long run, its implications may be crucial for the Soviet Union and perestroika. It involves nothing less than an attempt to integrate the USSR and the Council for Mutual Economic Assistance (CMEA) much more closely with the world economic system. Further, as a consequence of an expected increase in quantity and quality of Soviet manufactures for export, the Soviet leadership hopes to become less reliant on energy and raw material exports, and "so create a trade structure more suited to a large industrial nation."[36]

To this end, Moscow has expanded its trade contacts with the Euro-

pean Economic Community, and is seeking closer relations with the
General Agreement on Trade and Tariffs (GATT). The Soviets have
also expressed interest in the International Monetary Fund and World
Bank which, despite Western reservations about the seriousness of
intent, still continues. The CIA has suggested the motives behind these
latter approaches may be mainly political since "the USSR may feel
that its world power status requires that it be a major player with
major world bodies." Even so, even its analysts admit that Soviet
spokesmen have explained this interest by an expectation that association with these major institutions may open new opportunities
regarding trade, especially through reduced tariffs.[37]

In this regard, the reorganization of the Ministry of Foreign Trade in
1986 was obviously another major aspect of this program. There has
also been an ambitious publicity program highlighted by Gorbachev's
personal meeting with representatives of U.S. businesses to urge expansion of both trade and investment. Meanwhile, other Soviet delegations have toured nations like Canada with similar aims. But if Soviet
exports of manufactured goods, arms excluded, are still relatively
small, they have recently scored some modest successes. Thus a new,
subcompact Lada, named the Samara, has been selling reasonably well
in Canada, the United Kingdom, West Germany, and elsewhere, while
India has imported two enriched uranium nuclear power plants.[38]

Other examples could be cited but, to date, these are still only straws
in the wind. For the moment, Moscow's trading efforts continue to be
hampered by inefficient central planning, low reserves of hard currency, and the poor quality of many products thanks to distorted pricing
and the poor incentives still offered Soviet workers. Even so, if Gorbachev's plans are implemented, even these long-term obstacles may be
overcome. Indeed, advisers like Aganbegian have ambitious goals and
hope eventually that the present level of U.S.-Soviet trade ($2 billion
plus annually) can be raised from 1 percent to 5-10 percent of his nation's
overall foreign trade.[39]

One method adopted by Moscow to overcome these difficulties and
generally advance his program has been the promotion of joint ventures
between Soviet enterprises and Western companies. According to guidelines set down in early 1987, the latter firms could hold up to 49 percent
of equity—this restriction was later rescinded—repatriate profits, and
participate in management (although Soviet citizens must serve as
board chairmen and directors-general). With regard to the actual
ventures, the Soviet authorities have called for proposals for a wide
range of projects in the light, food and machine-building industries,
electronics and communications, petrochemicals, the development of
energy and other resources in Siberia and the Kola peninsula, the auto-

mobile industry, grain transport and storage facilities, and so on. Although the program has had a slow beginning, by April 1988, American firms had filed over 50 proposals, and deals had been consummated between Aeroflot and Pan American Airways, Combustian Engineering (Stamford, Conn.) and the Soviet Ministry for Oil Refining and the Petrochemical Industry, for publication of a computer magazine, for a joint software enterprise known as Dialogue, and so on.[40]

It would seem that Soviet planners see two major advantages in such joint ventures. First, they obviously regard them as a means of acquiring capital investment and Western technology, such as that provided by Porsche for the Samara, without having to provide hard currency in advance. Second, the recent allocation of 30 percent of the Soviet stock in one joint venture to a metal plant may set a precedent by which Soviet enterprises eventually may obtain capital for modernization directly from foreign currency profits made in other sectors of the economy.[41]

The most successful aspect of Gorbachev's economic diplomacy concerns Soviet financial operations abroad. Apart from modernizing the domestic banking system, by 1987 Soviet banks in the West had increased the use of acceptance facilities and began employing modern financial instruments. More impressive yet was the Soviets' first participation in an international bond issue and, in an echo of past battles, their settling with Britain over the last Imperial Russian bonds. Speculation that Moscow was planning its own bond issue quickly proved correct in January 1988 when an official Soviet bond issue was floated in Switzerland. By that time May negotiations in West Germany were concluded for a bank loan for 3.5 billion marks ($2.1 billion) for modernizing Soviet industry, as well as for a second bond issue, this time for 300 million marks ($180 million). Although U.S. Secretary of Defense Frank Carlucci warned such financing might permit a sustained rate of defense expenditure, other officials rejoiced that Western nations had expanded opportunities for profit. As for the Soviets, such activities undoubtedly helped diversify their sources of funding, and reduced the borrowing costs, whatever the end purposes of the credits obtained.[42]

Conclusion

Gorbachev's new political thinking, then, remains deeply rooted in Soviet domestic needs. If the political program of glasnost and demokratisatsiia reminds historians of the Russia of Aleksandr II in the 1860s, the economics of perestroika are more reminiscent of the policies of Tsarists finance ministers in the 1880s-1890s. And like their predecessors a century earlier, the economic reformers of today's USSR are using the diplomacy of realpolitik to reduce external threats, and thus justify restraining, if not cutting, military spending to free resources for investment elsewhere. Precedents for these aspects of the new thinking, active arms control included (e.g. the First Hague Conference), are all to be found in the Russia of Sergei Witte.[43] But so too is the lesson of dependence on foreign fiscal resources. Aganbegian had made it clear that the Soviets today are mindful of this. Although he used modern Hungary as his cautionary example, he has stressed to American audiences that since the aim of perestroika is economic independence and prosperity, the USSR is "not going to become a great debtor nation."[44]

Notes

The writer wishes to thank the Canadian Institute for International Peace and Security for funding the research project of which this chapter is one result.

1. *New York Times*, 5 July 1988, p. 9.

2. Stephen F. Cohen, *Sovieticus, American Perceptions and Soviet Realities*, New York, Norton, 1986, pp. 139-142, makes this point about American diplomacy, but it is applicable to superpower relations in general.

3. A typical Soviet exposition of the new 'defensive' doctrine is Marshal S. Akhromeev, "Doktrina predotvrashcheniia voiny, zashchity mira i sotsializma," *Problemy mira i sotsializma* 1987, no. 12, pp. 23-28. For recent Western assessments of its purport see my "Gorbachev, the Military and Perestroika," *International Perspectives*, May-June 1988, pp. 10-12; and Gerhard Wettig, "New Development of Military Doctrine," *Aussen Politik*, 1988, no. 2, pp. 169-181.

4. Vadim Zagladin, *Pravda*, 13 June 1988, p. 1.

5. *Vestnik Ministerstva innostrannykh del SSSR*, 10 September 1987, pp. 3-6. For another recent Soviet study connecting foreign policy with economic factors, and calling for realism in military matters, see A.I. Iziumov and A. Kortunov, "The Soviet Union in the Changing World," *International Affairs*, Moscow, 1988, no. 8, pp. 46-56.

6. M.S. Gorbachev, *Bystree perestraivat 'sia, deistvovat' po novomu*, Moscow: Politizdat, 1986, pp. 43-45.

7. See, for example, M.I. Piskotin, *Sovetskoe biudzhetnoe pravo*, Moscow, Finansy, 1971, p. 11; and F.S. Massarygin, *Finansovala sisterna SSSR*, Moscow, Finansy, 1968, pp. 119-120. In this regard, R.A. Faramazian's comments about the USA in *Razoruzhenie i ekonomika*, Moscow, Mysl'; 1978, seem equally applicable to the Soviet Union.

8. TASS International Service, "Speech to the All-Union Congress of Trade Unions," Moscow, 25 February 1987.

9. U.S. Defense Intelligence Agency, *Statement to the Subcommittee on National Defense Economics Joint Economic Committee*, Washington, 14 September 1987, p. 8.

10. "Speech to All-Union Congress of Trade Unions."

11. *Pravda*, 15 June 1974, p. 1.

12. CIA/DIA, Joint Submission to the Subcommittee on Economic Resources, Competitiveness and Security Economics, Joint Economic Committee, U.S. Congress, *The Soviet Economy Under a New Leader*, Washington, 16 March 1986, p. 35.

13. Daniel Ford, "A Reporter at Large (*Perestroika*)," *New Yorker*, 28 March 1988, p. 68. For a recent Soviet response to the "Upper Volta" type of comment see A.I. Iziumov, "Ekonomika SSSR: Vzgliad s Zapada," *Politicheskoe sarnoobrazovanie*, 1988, no. 13, p. 68ff.

14. Cited by Ford, "A Reporter at Large," p. 68.

15. *New York Times*, 8 May 1988, pp. F1, F26.

16. , 19 February 1988, p. 1; 20 February 1988, pp. 1-2; *New York Times*, 7 May 1988, p. 4.

17. See, for example, the informed assessments of Allan H. Meltzer, "The 'System' is Still the Problem," *Los Angeles Times*, 29 May 1988, p. IV.2; and Philip Taubman, "The Russians Hear Dazzling Ideas, While They Wait for Delivery," pp. E1-E2.

18. N.V. Ogarkov, *Vsegda v gotovnosti k zashchite Otechestva*, Moscow: Voenizdat, 1982, p. 30ff.

19. "O perestroika i kadrovoi politike partii," *Sovetskala Rossiie*, 28 January 1987, p. 1.

20. Ford, "A Reporter at Large," p. 68.

21. JPRS, *USSR National Affairs, Political and Social Developments*, 28 May 1985, pp. R1-R3.

22. For typical descriptions of Gorbachev's economic reforms see the articles by John E. Tedstrom and others in *Problems of Communism*, July-August 1987, passim; C.P. Armstrong and T. Rakowska-Harmstone, *Gorbachev, "Reform," and the USSR*, Toronto, Mackenzie Institute, 1987; Gertrude E. Schroeder, "Anatomy of Gorbachev's Economic Reform," *Soviet Economy*, July-September 1987, no. 3, pp. 219-241; and the numerous items listed in J.M. Battle and T.D. Sherlock (eds.), *Gorbachev's Reforms: An Annotated Bibliography of Soviet Writings, Part I: 1985-June 1987*, Gulf Breeze, FL, Academic International Press, 1988. For a Soviet analysis of Western treatments of the economic reforms see Iziumov, "Ekonomika SSSR," p. 69ff.

23. For discussions of the productivity issue see *The Soviet Economy Under a New Leader*, passim; the CIA's/DIA's more recent *Gorbachev's Economic Reform: Problems Emerge*, Washington, 13 April 1988, p. 9ff; and Richard R. Kaufman's paper "Industrial Modernization and Defense in the Soviet Union" presented to the NATO Economics Colloquium in Brussels, 1-3 April 1987, p. 15.

24. The predictions of Jones, "Gorbachev," p. 12, and James T. Westwood, "The USSR's 12th Five-Year Plan and Its Zero-Growth Defense Budget," D.R. Jones (ed.) *Soviet Armed Forces Review Annual 11: 1987-1988*, Gulf Breeze, FL, Academic International Press, 1989, have seemingly been confirmed by Army

General Vitali Shabanov, the Deputy Minister of Defense for Armaments. Speaking at a news conference in late July 1988, he connected a decrease in defense spending and military procurement with the new "defensive" doctrine, *Washington Post*, 27 July 1988, pp. A1, A18.

25. See, for example, Jeremy R. Azreal, *The Soviet Civilian Leadership and the Military High Command, 1976-1986*, Santa Monica, CA, Rand R-3521-AF, June 1987, and Abraham S. Becker, *Ogarkov's Complaint and Gorbachev's Dilemma: The Soviet Defense Budget and Party-Military Conflict*, Santa Monica, CA, Rand R-3541-AF, December 1987.

26. Jerry Hough, "Russia and the Third World: The Revolutionary Road Runs Out," *The Nation*, 1 June 1985, pp. 666-668. Also see the later similar if more cautious assessments of Francis Fukuyama, *Moscow's Post-Brezhnev Reassessment of the Third World*, Santa Monica, CA, Rand R-3337-USDP, February 1986; and Harry Gelman, *The Soviet Union in the Third World: A Retrospective Overview and Prognosis*, Santa Monica, CA, Rand OPS-006, March 1986.

27. N.V. Ogarkov, *Istorooa uchit bditel 'nosti*, Moscow, Voenizdat, 1985, pp. 50-51.

28. M.S. Gorbachev, "Politicheskii doklad Tsentral 'nogo komiteta KPSS XXVII s'ezdu Kommunisticheskoi partii Sovetskogo Soiuza," *XXVII s'ezd Kommunisticheskol partii Sovetskogo Soluza. Stenograficheskii oichet*, Moscow, Politizdat, 1986, pp. 86-87.

29. Hedrick Smith, "On the Road with Gorbachev's Guru," *New York Times Magazine*, 10 April 1988, p. 42.

30. In their report *Gorbachev's Economic Program: Problems Emerge*, p. 36, the CIA and DIA argue that the short-term savings from agreements such as the INF Treaty are questionable, but that the long-term impact could be more substantial if the plant and workers involved in these and other systems are switched to civilian production. For a recent Soviet study of such possible 'conversions' see A.I. Iziumov, "The Other Side of Disarmament," *International Affairs*, Moscow, 1988, no. 5, pp. 82-88, 114. A more pessimistic appraisal of the possible benefits is that of J.O. Dendy, "The Soviet Military Challenge," in Brian MacDonald (ed.), *The Soviet Military Challenge*, Toronto, Canadian Institute for Strategic Studies, 1988, pp. 157-169.

It must also be remembered that relative to the total military budget, nuclear and strategic systems absorb a comparatively small percentage. Thus the CIA regularly estimated that during 1967-77, the time of the "sustained military build-up," the service most involved with such weapons (the Strategic Rocket Forces) consumed only 8-10 percent of the total operating and investment budgets. The Ground, Air and Air Defense Forces, on the other hand, took up jointly 52-68 percent of the total. In addition, total operating expenditures have always outstripped the combined funds allocated to investment and research and development. For these reasons, serious savings from the defense budget may well demand a radical 'restructuring' of the Soviet Armed Forces that will significantly reduce their overall numbers. For typical CIA assessments see the National Foreign Assessment Center's *Soviet and U.S. Defense Activities, 1971-80: A Dollar Cost Comparison*, Washington: SR 81-10005, January 1981, pp. 2-4, and *Estimated Soviet Defense Spending: Trends and Prospects*, Washington, SR 78-10121, June 1978, p. 3.

31. Hough, "Russia and the Third World," pp. 667-668.

32. These developments will be assessed in other chapters in this volume, but one should note that Moscow has already moved farther in reducing its Third World commitments than either Fukuyama or Gelman anticipated (note 26).

33. See, for example, Bill Keller, "The Consolidator: Why a Stronger Gorbachev Might Not be Strong Enough," *New York Times*, 9 October 1988, P. E1.

34. Smith, "On the Road with Gorbachev's Guru," p. 42.

35. *New York Times*, 25 April 1988, p. 25. Also see the CIA/DIA submission to the U.S. Congress Joint Economic Committee's Subcommittee on National Security Economics, *Gorbachev's Modernization Program: A Status Report*, Washington, 19 March 1987, pp. 33-34, and *Gorbachev's Economic Program*, pp. 39-42.

36. CIA/DIA, *Gorbachev's Modernization Program*, p. 33.

37. CIA/DIA, *Gorbachev's Modernization Program*, p. 34; Paul L. Montgomery, "Soviets' European Trade Bid," *New York Times*, 11 June 1988, p. 42. Also see following chapters.

38. *New York Times*, 7 May 1988, p. 4; 8 May 1988, p. F1; and Ivan D. Ivanov, "Restructuring the Mechanism of Foreign Economic Relations in the USSR," *Soviet Economy*, July-September 1987, p. 192.

39. Smith, "On the Road with Gorbachev's Guru," p. 42.

40. On the joint ventures see CIA/DIA, *Gorbachev's Modernization Program*, p. 33; *Gorbachev's Economic Program*, p. 41; and Smith, p. 42.

41. *New York Times*, 8 May 1988, pp. F1, F26. The present writer was informed of the stock transfer by Dr. Joseph Mastro of North Carolina State University in May 1988.

42. Smith, "On the Road with Gorbachev's Guru," p. 42; *New York Times*, 11 May 1988, p. 31.

43. On Tsarist efforts at arms control and economic development, see Theodore H. Von Laue, *Sergei Witte and the Industrialization of Russia* (New York: Columbia University Press, 1963), pp. 155-156.

44. Smith, "On the Road with Gorbachev's Guru," p. 42.

7

The Bush Foreign Policy

Michael Mandelbaum

In 1989 the greatest geopolitical windfall in the history of American foreign policy fell into George Bush's lap. In a mere six months the communist regimes of Eastern Europe collapsed, giving the West a sudden, sweeping and entirely unexpected victory in its great global conflict against the Soviet Union. Between July and December of 1989 Poland, Hungary, East Germany, Czechoslovakia, Bulgaria and Romania ousted communist leaders. Their new governments each proclaimed a commitment to democratic politics and market economics, and the withdrawal of Soviet troops from Europe began. All this happened without the West firing a single shot.

The revolutions in eastern Europe ended the Cold War by sweeping away the basic cause of the conflict between the two great global rivals: the Soviet European empire. They did so on George Bush's watch, a term that seems quite appropriate. As the revolutions occurred, he and his associates were more spectators than participants—a bit confused, generally approving, but above all passive. The president kept the United States in the background. In response to the most important international events of the second half of the twentieth century, the White House offered no soaring rhetoric, no grand gestures, no bold new programs. This approach served America's interests well. Events were moving in a favorable direction; staying in the background, taking care not to insert the United States into the middle of things, was the proper course of action. The qualities most characteristic of the Bush presidency—caution, modest public pronouncements and a fondness for private communications—were admirably suited to the moment.

The end of communism in Europe need not have proceeded so smoothly. There were pitfalls and blind alleys, alternative policies that had serious advocates. The Bush administration steered clear of them all. In so doing, it steered the United States into a new world.

But with the end of the Cold War the familiar guideposts of American foreign policy have disappeared. The revolutions in eastern Europe, taken cumulatively, were a revolution in international politics, and they have had a revolutionary impact on America's relations with the rest of the world. There will be greater discontinuity in foreign policy between the first and second halves of the Bush presidency than between any two administrations in the postwar period.

The post-Cold War international agenda is beginning to take shape. It is not likely to be dominated by military confrontations between great nuclear powers, or even by crises like the one in the Persian Gulf. Instead, economic issues will predominate, particularly as formerly communist Europe and countries in other regions move toward market institutions and practices. For these challenges President Bush's style of leadership seems less appropriate. The attributes he lacks—the capacity to define clearly American interests abroad and the policies necessary to pursue them, a mastery of the intricacies of economic affairs, and a determination to redress the chronic imbalances of the American economy—may well be the qualities required for effective leadership in the post-Cold War era.

The end of the Cold War took place in two stages. In the last half of 1989, the communist governments of Eastern Europe fell; in the first half of 1990, the fate of Germany was decided. In both stages, plausible alternatives existed to the approaches adopted by the Bush administration; at each stage, the administration chose the proper policy.

The president could have done what many wanted him to do: exult in the West's triumph. He could have celebrated victory more publicly, more frequently and more emphatically. Doing so, however, would have jeopardized the necessary condition for the revolutions of 1989: Moscow's willingness to tolerate them.

There was no doubt more than one reason that the Soviet leaders decided not to stop the process of political change in eastern Europe in 1989, as their predecessors had done in Hungary in 1956, in Czechoslovakia in 1968 and, indirectly, in Poland in 1981. Mikhail Gorbachev and his colleagues were aware of the weakness of their country's international position. They were preoccupied with internal affairs, especially deteriorating economic conditions and the rising rebelliousness of the non-Russians. Whether or not they recognized that they could end their conflict with the West only be relinquishing eastern Europe, they were plainly convinced that they could give up the empire that Stalin had acquired without putting Soviet security in mortal jeopardy.

That conviction might have wavered had the West ostentatiously celebrated the retreat of Soviet power. By what it refrained from doing publicly, as much as by whatever private messages it may have conveyed to Moscow, the Bush administration avoided embarrassing, threatening or otherwise provoking the Soviets. This was the most important contribution to the events of 1989 that the United States was in a position to make.

The administration might also have followed the opposite policy. It could have made common cause with the Soviet Union to try to control the process of change in eastern Europe. Secretary of State James A. Baker was reported in March 1989 to be favorably disposed to discussing that subject with Moscow.[1] The idea was far from absurd. When communist governments in eastern Europe were challenged in the past, the Soviet Union intervened to keep them in power, bringing bloodshed and repression and poisoning relations with the West. There was every reason in 1989 to try to avoid a similar sequence of events.

The Bush administration acted wisely in not making the political future of eastern Europe the subject of Soviet-American negotiations. Such negotiations would have severely damaged relations with the Europeans themselves, both east and west, who objected to what they termed a "second Yalta"—the two great powers decided Europe's fate without European participation. Negotiations, as it turned out, were unnecessary. The Soviet Union did not intervene. The Bush administration correctly calculated that the interest of the United States lay in allowing the authentic, peaceful, democratic revolutions to run their course. Washington encouraged this process by reassuring Moscow that the course of events did not jeopardize legitimate Soviet interests. This middle course with the Soviet Union, between collaboration and confrontation, was an important and underappreciated achievement of American foreign policy. If one of the tests of each presidency after 1945 has been the capacity to manage crises, the president deserves high marks for his policies during the six eventful months that may be seen in retrospect as the final crisis of the Cold War.

No sooner had the last East European revolution been completed—in Romania—than Europe and the two great nuclear powers had to confront the issue of German unity. The march toward the merger of the two Germanys—or, rather toward the collapse of East Germany and its takeover by the West—was not initially intended by any government, including Bonn. It was the product of the spontaneous initiative of hundreds of thousands of East Germans. By moving to the West in large numbers, even after the opening of the inner-German border, they voted with their feet against the continued existence of a separate state. They also voted for the end of East Germany in March 1990 in a more familiar way; the first free elections ever held in the G.D.R. yielded a resounding majority in favor of rapid unification.

In light of the four decades of peace that a divided Europe had enjoyed and the havoc that Germany had wrought when it had been powerful and independent, it was hardly surprising that German unity was not universally welcomed. British Prime Minister Margaret Thatcher and French President François Mitterrand each indicated that they were not happy at the prospect. Commentators in the United States were not wholeheartedly enthusiastic either, and for the same reasons: the Germans could not be trusted; or, even if they could be, discarding the security arrangements that had served so well for so long was unacceptably risky. Had Washington also shared and acted on these reservations, it could have slowed and perhaps even blocked German unification. The United States—as well as Britain and France—would have in effect declared that, while every other nation in Europe, and all peoples elsewhere, were entitled to choose their own political arrangements, the Germans were not. Such a declaration would have stirred the same kind of resentment at unequal treatment that Hitler exploited in the 1930s in order to win power and launch his ruinous policies. Although it would not have pushed Europe into war, it would have discredited in the eyes of Germans the important roles the Federal Republic played in the postwar period—in NATO, in the European Community and in other international organizations.

The Bush administration declined to place obstacles in the path of German unity. Without American support no other country, or combination of countries, could have hoped to block German unification. But Washington was no more prescient than any other capital about the pace of events in Germany. It was motivated in part by a short-term concern that a fight over unification between West Germany and its allies would bring to power Germany's Social Democrats, who might adopt a dangerously neutralist foreign policy. Support for Chancellor Helmut Kohl was nonetheless consistent with the proper long-term American approach to the German Question: that is, support for the right of Germans to decide their own fate, combined with efforts to create conditions in which the German decision, especially if in favor of unity, would not make others, or Germans themselves, feel insecure.

The key to maintaining a secure Europe was to keep the newly united Germany firmly anchored in an American-led security community. The Bush administration waged a successful diplomatic campaign on this issue within the framework of the "two plus four" negotiations. These talks involved the two Germanys plus Britain, France, the Soviet Union and the United States—the four powers whose victory in World War II gave them special prerogatives in Germany. In the first half of 1990 the administration used this forum to obtain Soviet acquiescence on Germany's continuing membership in NATO.

The final details of the terms of German unity were worked out without the United States, Britain or France, in the summer of 1990 in a meeting between Chancellor Kohl and President Gorbachev at the

Soviet leader's home in Stavropol. The meeting raised the specter of Soviet-German collusion against the interests of the rest of Europe. Without reconciliation between Germany and Russia, however, there could be no end to the Cold War. Peace in Europe was impossible without an accommodation between its two largest powers. For most of the hundred years between the fall from power in 1890 of Bismarck, the original architect of German unity, and the 1990 unification of the two German states, Germany and Russia had defined their interests in Europe in ways unacceptable to each other. This ongoing Russo-German antagonism caused much of the tension, rivalry and war on the continent in that period. It may now be hoped that the events of 1990 have brought that era to an end.

The Soviet-German rapprochement is not dangerous to others, provided it takes place within a European security framework that includes a continuing American presence. It is just such a framework that the Bush administration was instrumental in designing, and is apparently committed to maintaining.

Just as America, the Soviet Union and the European nations were beginning the task of constructing a new post-Cold War Europe, Saddam Hussein interrupted them. His invasion, occupation and declared annexation of Kuwait—and the American response—dominated U.S. foreign policy in the latter half of George Bush's second year as president.

President Bush dispatched to the Middle East the largest expeditionary force since the Vietnam War and organized an impressively wide coalition against Iraq. The American intervention in the gulf, whatever its outcome, will exert a major influence on future American policy in the region. It may also prove to be the decisive event of George Bush's presidency. Success could assure his reelection and strengthen his hand at home and abroad; failure could have the opposite effects. Even a limited victory for Saddam Hussein would increase the power of forces opposed to the United States and its friends, and have adverse and perhaps disastrous consequences for the entire Middle East.

The gulf crisis is not, however, a preview of international politics beyond the Cold War. It is an important development, to be sure, that cannot help but influence American foreign policy in years to come. But it is not the seminal event from which America's new international role will emerge.

The Iraqi invasion demonstrated that some features of the Cold War persist, even in the absence of the Soviet-American rivalry. There are still dangerous people abroad who have the power to jeopardize Western interests. It also demonstrated that when those interests must be defended by force the principal responsibility continues to rest with the West's leading military power, the United States. The gulf crisis also illustrates the changes that the end of the Cold War has produced in international politics. The United States and the Soviet Union find themselves on the same side of the conflict. In part because of this harmony, it proved possible to assemble an international coalition of unprecedented breadth to oppose Saddam Hussein.

Soviet-American cooperation also made possible a prominent role in the gulf crisis for the United Nations, whose machinery, especially the Security Council, had for most of its history been paralyzed by the great schism between its two strongest members.

Most important of all, the end of the Cold War and the newfound solidarity between Washington and Moscow allowed the United States to undertake military operations on a large scale in the Middle East, without the fear of triggering a larger conflict with the Soviet Union and uncontrolled escalation to World War III. This was an enormous military advantage for the United States.

The gulf crisis, however, does not offer a reliable guide to the post-Cold War world. The United States sent forces to the Middle East for two reasons: to support the principle that stronger powers must not swallow up weaker neighbors; and to prevent a large fraction of the world's oil reserves from coming under the control of a brutal, aggressive and unpredictable tyrant. The principle of sovereign independence is important. Where it is challenged in the years ahead the United States will surely support beleaguered small states—but not by sending 400,000 troops to liberate them. Oil is a uniquely valuable resource, one that makes the Persian Gulf the only part of the Third World where Western interests are sizable enough to justify a large war.

In the minds of American policymakers, the various conflicts of the Cold War were all connected. The Greek civil war, the Korean War, the Vietnam War and others were seen as part of a global struggle against communism. Each was consequential not only for what was directly at stake, but for its effect on the Western position in other parts of the world. The confrontation with Iraq, by contrast, is not connected to anything beyond the Middle East. Important as the Middle East is to the United States and the rest of the West, it does not provide the basis for a global foreign policy, as did the conflict with the Soviet Union.

During the Cold War, wars and conflicts outside Europe derived their importance for the United States from their connection to the Soviet Union. With the end of the Cold War, they will be far less consequential for American foreign policy. The Persian Gulf excepted, the United States is considerably less likely to dispatch forces abroad in the post-Cold War era. In this sense the gulf crisis belongs to the past, not the future, of American foreign policy.

There is still a military role for the United States to play, but the regions where American forces will remain useful are those where they were concentrated during the conflict with the Soviet Union: Europe and East Asia. Their mission, however, will be different from those they have become accustomed to carrying out.

Deterrence of the Soviet Union has ceased to be the all-consuming international concern of the United States. Moscow is withdrawing its troops from Europe, and drawing down its forces in East Asia as well. Equally important, the sources of an expansive Soviet foreign policy— the commitment to the principles of Marxism-Leninism and the determination to spread them abroad—have all but disappeared.

The end of the Cold War, however, does not bring an end to the system of relations among sovereign states in which threats can arise. The difference is that, henceforth, the dangers to the security of America's friends in Europe and Asia are likely to be more distant and nebulous than the sharply defined threat the Soviet Union was seen to pose over the last four decades. Dangers could still arise, and there is still a role for the United States to play in dealing with them. West Europeans will continue to share a continent with a Soviet Union that, whatever form it ultimately takes, will be both large and heavily armed. Europe will need to counterbalance that military power; perpetuating the American commitment is the best way to do so.

The newly united Germany in particular will need some form of protection. German-Soviet relations are now cordial. But Soviet military force, particularly Soviet nuclear weapons, give Moscow considerable potential for leverage over Germany should some new disputes arise between them. Without some form of protection, Germans will be vulnerable to Soviet pressure. A Germany without a security tie to the United States might well feel the need to strengthen its own armaments, perhaps even with nuclear weapons. A German nuclear arsenal would not arise from aggressive impulses. Rather, it would be a prudent, defensive response to a new set of geopolitical conditions. But however benign its motives, a Germany armed with nuclear weapons would create uncertainty, alarm and instability in Europe. Perpetuating the American commitment to western Europe is a hedge against this undesirable and potentially dangerous sequence of events. This is why the Bush administration's determination to maintain the basic structure of NATO is well advised.

Such a commitment would be designed not so much to deter an immediate threat from the Soviet Union as to reassure all of Europe—

including Germany and the Soviet Union—that it need not fear a power vacuum. Such a vacuum might compel European nations to recalculate their military requirements, perhaps in ways others would consider as threatening.[2]

In East Asia, as in Europe, the Soviet threat to America's principal ally, Japan, has diminished considerably. Yet the American military presence there remains useful for the same reason. If the United States were to withdraw completely from the region, Japan, like Germany, might feel the need to adopt a more independent military role, including the acquisition of a nuclear arsenal. A nuclear-armed Japan would likewise alarm neighboring countries. In the post-Cold War era, American military forces in East Asia, as in Europe, can serve as a buffer among countries that, while no longer avowed adversaries, continue to be suspicious of one another and might conduct more aggressive foreign policies without a reassuring American presence.

Providing reassurance will require America's continued military cooperation with other countries, which may prove difficult. The United States may not retain all the overseas military facilities and basing rights of the Cold War. The American presence in the Philippines, for example, is already contracting; the United States has agreed to withdraw its fighter aircraft from Clark Air Force Base. Similarly, although the German government will welcome the continuation of an American security guarantee, the German people may be increasingly reluctant to play host to American forces, especially American nuclear weapons. If the political difficulties of deploying armed forces abroad will multiply in the wake of the Cold War, however, the forces that the United States will need to deploy will be more modest. The military requirements of reassurance in Europe and Asia will surely be less demanding than those of deterrence.

The greatest difficulty in sustaining a policy of reassurance, ironically, may lie in winning support for it in the United States . The forty-year rationale for stationing American troops abroad is gone. The Cold War provided a succession of American presidents with a powerful justification for stationing troops overseas and occasionally sending them into battle. The simple, compelling purpose of the nation's global military deployments was to check the Soviet Union. To the American public, the new purpose—reassurance—is liable to seem vague, implausible, the product of tortured logic, or simply not worth the risk.

In the absence of a Soviet threat the Bush administration floundered in finding a public justification for its military buildup in the Persian Gulf. This president and his successors may well encounter comparable difficulties in persuading the public to continue to support an American military presence overseas. The same question that was raised about troops in the gulf is likely to be directed at the continuing American deployments in Europe and Asia: Why are they there?

To answer that question, and to rally public support for a continuing American military presence abroad, what is needed is what this administration notably lacks: vision—the capacity to paint a vivid, convincing picture of the new world and America's interests in it. Vision requires the ability to communicate not only privately to other leaders, but publicly to the American people. If this president and his successors are able to present the appropriate vision, if they are able to make a persuasive case for keeping enough forces in Europe and Asia to reassure the countries of both regions, then political and military disputes of the kind that dominated the Cold War era are likely to recede. For with the end of the Soviet-American rivalry and the retreat of Soviet power, the basis for many, though by no means all, of these conflicts has vanished....

Notes

1. Thomas Friedman, *The New York Times,* 28 March 1989.

2. On the distinction between deterrence and reassurance see Michael Howard, "Reassurance and Deterrence: Western Defense in the 1980s," *Foreign Affairs,* Winter 1982/83.

Section 2
THE ROLE OF IDEOLOGY

One key element of Gorbachev's "new thinking" is the new tone and orientation that he has brought to the discussion of foreign policy in the Soviet Union. An attempt is being made to "de-ideologize" foreign-policy decision making. As a result, little is said about the eternal, unchanging truths of Marxism-Leninism. The new emphasis on interdependence and the need for cooperation between East and West is a far cry from the traditional Soviet view that saw the outside world as implacably hostile. This de-emphasis on ideology, and the internal changes in the Soviet Union, have clearly had an impact on American thinking about the Soviet Union. As glasnost continued, and as the Soviet Union instituted both political and economic reform, the American image of the Soviet Union as a repressive ideological state bent on general domination changed—and with it the American perception of threat.

Steven Kull's article "Dateline Moscow: Burying Lenin" explores this aspect of the new Soviet foreign policy. He maintains that "new thinking" represents a departure from traditional Marxism-Leninism. Whereas Leninism speaks of the inevitability of state conflict, Gorbachev maintains that world unity is a fundamental aspect of the modern era. In an even more radical departure, Gorbachev claims that the world is moving toward pluralism rather than socialism.

However, despite these pronouncements that some elements of Leninism "belonged to their own time," the break with the ideology is far from complete. Soviet policy makers equivocate on many key ideological issues and Lenin is still revered. Furthermore, Gorbachev still claims that "new thinking" is based on Leninist principles. Given this equivocation among the policy makers, Kull points out that "distinct inconsistencies within the foreign policy elite regarding questions of ideology are hardly surprising."

In his essay "Is an Ideological Concert Possible?" Alexei Pushkov considers the impact of ideology in East-West relations and specifically in Soviet-American relations. He emphasizes that the "Cold War was the most visible manifestation of the clash of ideological movements," but now that the world is changing he expects a radical decline in the level of ideological hostility. He admits that during the détente period ideological differences were de-emphasized, but suggests that only minimal changes actually occurred.

This new era in Soviet-American relations is fundamentally different, the author suggests, and the confrontational aspects of ideologies are weakening. The range of differences in outlooks is narrowing because nations are experiencing similar problems, and this has broadened the opportunities for cooperation between them. This is leading to the emergence of "trans-systemic" elements in ideologies with the philosophy of "interdependence" as the common denominator.

How are these ideological changes affecting the foreign policy thinking of the USSR and United States? The author suggests that Soviet policy now sees a world of states with common interests rather than a world with "mutually exclusive civilizations" in conflict. Yet the picture is quite different in the United States, he argues. The United States still expects all the world to conform to "democratic values of the West." This stance suggests that the Soviet Union must conform to this idealized model as a prerequisite for complete termination of the Cold War. He contends that American foreign policy, despite some adaptations to a changing environment, is still based on continuing rivalry with the Soviet Union. But the author is encouraged by the fact that even those who speak of limits to Soviet and U.S. cooperation seem nevertheless to accept the fact that the relationship will be a form of "state rivalry" rather than an ideological conflict.

8

Dateline Moscow: Burying Lenin

Steven Kull

As declarations of the Cold War's end become commonplace and the United States moves toward greater economic cooperation with the Soviet Union, some Americans still feel uneasy. Although the Soviets seem to be moving in the right direction, some observers wonder whether the Soviets are pulling in their horns only temporarily because of their economic problems. Underlying this question is a more fundamental concern about whether the Soviets, deep in their hearts, are still committed Marxist-Leninists ultimately intent on fomenting socialist revolution around the world.

This is a legitimate concern. Shortly after the 1917 revolution Vladimir Il'ich Lenin said, "Our victory would be a victory only when our cause succeeded in the entire world, because we launched our action exclusively in the expectation of a world revolution." He called on his comrades to persist until they had "conquered the whole world." Even as recently as 1986, the Communist party program embraced the centrality of the "historical competition between the two world sociopolitical systems" and asserted that "the present epoch ... is an epoch of transition from capitalism to socialism and communism.

However, in more recent government statements, in Soviet literature, and in interviews with more than 70 Soviet officials from the Central Committee, the Foreign Ministry, the Ministry of Defense, the military, and various think tanks, important signs indicate that Soviet "new thinking" involves a genuine break with the aspirations of traditional Leninism. To an extent that has not been fully recognized in the West, Gorbachev has repudiated some of the pivotal tenets of Lenin's thinking.

This break is not yet complete, however. Soviet policymakers equivocate on a number of key ideological issues, and there are indications of some persistence of traditional Leninist thought. The tension between new and old thinking was illustrated by a recent controversy over the disposition of Lenin's body. In April 1989 a guest on a Soviet talk show suggested that Lenin's body be removed from its mausoleum on Red Square and buried in the ground. This idea elicited a storm of protest calling it immoral in view of Lenin's "sacred" character, and the official responsible for the show was fired. The idea of burying Lenin was not an offhand comment: The person proposing it was presumably trying to make explicit the discontinuity between Lenin's thought and Gorbachev-era new thinking.

According to Lenin, reality is fundamentally dialectical and therefore conflictual. In the social realm class struggle is inevitable and the ultimate goal is the victory of the working class. Gorbachev, by contrast, maintains that the most fundamental reality is the unity of the world. The interdependence of the peoples of the world, especially given the mutual vulnerability engendered by nuclear weapons, dictates that ultimate values transcend class interests and are universal in nature.

In an even more heretical assertion, Gorbachev claims that the world is not ultimately moving toward socialism but that, "the world is moving to a pluralism which is natural for the new times." He implicitly rejects Lenin's notion of the fundamental illegitimacy of capitalism in conflict with socialism. Instead, Gorbachev's embrace of pluralism "presupposes equality" of all countries and seeks relations "on the basis of balanced interests." Capitalist and socialist states must "learn to live side by side while remaining different.... Thus, the question is of unity in diversity."

According to Soviet specialists this kind of thinking is actually not so new: The notion of living "side by side" originated with Lenin's concept of peaceful coexistence. For Lenin, however, such a posture was temporary: "It is inconceivable for the Soviet Republic to exist alongside of the imperialist states for any length of time. One or the other must triumph in the end." Peaceful coexistence was considered necessary to attain a "breathing spell" allowing socialism to build up its economic and military reserves and the domestic forces of discontent in the capitalist countries to grow. Such thinking flourished through Leonid Brezhnev's years in power. Brezhnev insisted that peaceful coexistence under détente "creates favorable conditions for the struggle between the two systems and for altering the correlation of forces in favor of Socialism."

Gorbachev, however, has unequivocally rejected such notions, saying that it is "no longer possible to retain ... the definition of peaceful coexistence of states with different social systems as a 'specific form of class struggle'." He admits that "there have been changes in Lenin's concept of peaceful coexistence," explaining that while Lenin considered peaceful coexistence a tactical device, in the nuclear age it should become a permanent condition. In Gorbachev's view international relations should be de-ideologized—they should no longer constitute an arena for ideological competition. Only in this way can the human value of peace be preserved.

Gorbachev has been quite direct in acknowledging that this emphasis on human values conflicts with traditional Marxism. Gorbachev recognizes that: "It may seem strange to some people that the communists should place such a strong emphasis on human interests and values. Indeed, a class-motivated approach to all phenomena of social life is the ABC of Marxism." But on another occasion he says:

> The vitality and creative potential of Marxism-Leninism by no means lies in the idea that every single line that its founders wrote is of absolute and everlasting significance.... Many ideas, including major ideas that they put forward under specific historical circumstances, belong to their own time. They have "exhausted" their usefulness and receded into history.

Even Gorbachev is not an unalloyed proponent of his own heresy. Having ideologically disrobed Lenin, Gorbachev often tries to insist that the emperor is as well-clothed as ever. The Soviet leader even claims that his new thinking is not really new, but rather follows in the footsteps of Lenin. A veritable cottage industry has emerged with Soviet scholars scouring Lenin's works for quotations that can be bent to support the thesis that Lenin was the original new thinker.

Equivocation at the Top

This form of doublethink reflects widespread feelings in the Soviet Union. On one hand Soviets are losing faith in the state "religion" established by Lenin. For decades, rapid domestic economic growth and the regular appearance of new socialist governments around the world made Soviets confident of riding the wave of the future. Now this wave seems to have dissipated as communist countries slip ever further behind their capitalist counterparts. It is hard to maintain Leninist convictions about the tide of history when one's own allies keep drifting further away from socialism and one's economy can barely keep afloat.

Nevertheless, Lenin is still revered. He remains the ultimate father figure, the Moses who led Russia out of backwardness into superpower glory. Gorbachev has yet to prove himself the Soviet people's new prophet. He may be their best hope, but he must first bring the Soviet economy out of its doldrums. Moreover, many Soviets are not convinced that Gorbachev's vision for the USSR is spiritually satisfying. Russians, even before the revolution, have held a mystical belief in their unique role in the world. In the highly secular world of socialism, Lenin's vision of the Soviet Union as a vanguard for a utopian global order has fed this belief, assuming a function similar to the one religion plays in other societies. While Gorbachev does hold out the visionary idea that the Soviet Union will lead the world away from the threat of nuclear war, his means for doing so require relinquishing absolutist dreams and accepting greater chaos and diversity in the world. Hence, until Gorbachev believes that the Soviet people are fully resigned to the bitterness of his medicine, he may well hedge his bets by continuing to deny contradictions between his thinking and Lenin's dogma.

Given the equivocation at the top, distinct inconsistencies within the foreign policy elite regarding questions of ideology are hardly surprising. On one hand some Soviets go beyond Gorbachev in breaking with Lenin. One political analyst interviewed stated, "We reject the dogma that the proletariat should achieve socialism in the world.... I think that the Marxist theory that capitalism will be replaced by socialism is wrong."

Others go further, arguing that the evolution toward socialism, far from advancing, may actually be losing ground. Military academician Major General Kim Tsagolov contends: "The eighties showed that the highest wave was over for both the world revolutionary process in general and the socialist orientation in particular." Similarly, Georgi Mirsky, a political analyst at Moscow's influential Institute of World Economics and International Relations, states that "at present there is not a single revolutionary process carrying the national liberation struggle further and deeper." Instead, he argues, among Third World governments "the overwhelming majority ... are by no means interested in the defeat of imperialism. They are fighting to win a place in the sun within the world capitalist family."

A high-level official in the Central Committee asserted that a movement toward socialism in the world continues, but he redefined socialism to mean humanistic values in general and backed the heretical notion that socialist countries and the Communist party no longer lead this process. He even supported the idea that the values of socialism have been fulfilled more successfully in West Germany and Sweden than in the USSR. Similarly, Soviet government statements have described socialism as an abstract "world process" and Gorbachev has de-emphasized the central role of the Communist party in social progress, saying that both Social Democrats and Communists represent the aspirations of the working classes. Also gaining in popularity is the once heretical view that socialism and capitalism will ultimately converge. Military officers as well as officials in the Central Committee and the Foreign Ministry talked during the interviews conducted of an ultimate "synthesis" of capitalism and socialism.

Finally, some Soviets have even broached a heretofore forbidden province: direct criticism of Lenin. Central Committee academic Alexander Tsipko has suggested that some of the distortions of Stalinism may have originated with Lenin. Vasily Grossman's recently unbanned 1963 novel, *Forever Flowing,* even portrays Lenin as a ruthless tyrant.

On the other hand, there is ample evidence of resistance to new thinking and of the perseverance of traditional Leninism. Ideological statements regarding "the historical inevitability of all nations arriving at socialism" continue to appear in the Soviet press. Directly contradicting Gorbachev's statement that class conflict should no longer be the cornerstone of Soviet foreign policy, [former] Politburo member Yegor Ligachev has said, "We proceed from the class nature of international relations. Any other formulation ... only introduces confusion into the thinking of Soviet people and our friends abroad."

At the same time, however, such individuals often feel a need to explain how their ideas fit into new thinking or even form the most correct interpretation of new thinking. Ligachev, for example, in reference to the notion of universal human values, has said that "Active involvement in the solution of general human problems by no means signifies any artificial 'braking' of the social and national liberation struggle." Yuri Krasin, rector of the Central Committee Institute of Social Sciences, has argued that the correctness of new thinking will promote the ultimate victory of socialism, even though new thinking negates that very concept. He says, "An assured peace and disarmament will ... enable [socialism] to reveal more fully its advantages in the peaceful competition with the capitalist system. The struggle for peace does not certainly solve the 'who will win' question." He goes on to say, "Marxists are firm in their belief that socialism will gain the upper hand." Krasin asserts that "New political thinking does not imply giving up the socio-class goals of the struggle for social and national liberation."

These attempts to sustain traditional Leninist perspectives within the framework of new thinking show that old thinking is still very much alive. More important, however, they show to what extent it is on the defensive and probably in an irreversible decline.

The processes and tensions found in Soviet ideological discourse today are reflected in the conduct of Soviet foreign policy. They particularly affect the Soviet Union's active efforts to defend and promote socialism in the world.

The Sinatra Doctrine

The region where the Soviets have expanded the most military and political capital in the service of such aims is, of course, Eastern Europe. After World War II the Soviets ensured the installation of the region's socialist governments. In 1956 and 1968 they even used military force on a large scale to suppress counter-revolutionary trends. In 1968, in what Westerners call the "Brezhnev Doctrine," the Soviets declared that socialist countries have a limited form of sovereignty that affords other socialist countries a right, even an obligation, to intervene militarily to prevent any deviation from socialism.

Given recent Soviet acquiescence in political changes that have brought noncommunist governments to power in Eastern Europe, however, there is no question that the Brezhnev Doctrine is now dead. Soviet Foreign Ministry spokesman Gennadi Gerasimov seemed to relish the announcement of its demise in October 1989 when he said: "In the Soviet Union of today we have replaced the Brezhnev doctrine ... with the Frank Sinatra doctrine, from the title of one of his famous songs, 'I Did It My Way.'... I think, in fact, that each Eastern country is doing it its own way."

There is thus substance as well as style in new Soviet policy. The Soviet Union has gone beyond acquiescing to the changes in Eastern Europe: It has promoted them actively. In August 1989, when the new Polish government was being formed, Gorbachev reportedly telephoned leaders of the Polish Communist party and successfully pressed them to be more accommodating to the interdependent trade union movement Solidarity. Shortly after Gorbachev's visit to East Germany in October [1988], President Erich Honecker resigned and the government launched into a series of dramatic reforms, including freedom of travel to the West. In November Gorbachev reportedly called then Czechoslovak Communist party chief Milos Jakes to urge him to loosen his grip over Czechoslovak society. And in December the Soviets not only openly supported the forces overthrowing the Communist party regime of Nicolae Ceausescu, but even sent them medical and relief aid. The West may find this type of intervention actually attractive rather than deplorable.

Despite such important moves the Soviets apparently still aim to maintain the Warsaw Pact and to preserve some form of socialist identity. As a result, ambiguities remain about the freedom of East European countries to determine their own fates. One unresolved question is whether Warsaw Pact members may give up socialism. There are strong indications that they may indeed do so. In a speech to the Council of Europe in July 1989, Gorbachev appeared to accept that a socialist country might abandon socialism, saying "social and political orders of one country or another changed in the past and may change in the future as well." In September, when a group of deputies from the communist Polish United Workers party proposed removing the constitutional guarantee of the party's "leading role," an article in the newspaper *Izvestia* said that this move "attests to a sense of realism and a rejection of one of the widespread myths." When Nikolay Shishlin, a member of the Soviet Communist Central Committee, was asked whether Poland was still a socialist state, he shrugged: "You know, we even ask ourselves if we are a socialist state."

Yet some Soviets exhibit signs of unease with the idea of East European countries departing from socialism. In February 1989, the prominent academic Oleg Bogomolov declared that there would be no danger even if Hungary became a Western-style bourgeois democracy. But only a few days later then Politburo member Nikolay Talyzin publicly disagreed with Bogomolov's statement.

Even Gorbachev has equivocated on the issue of East European countries shelving socialism. In July 1989, for example, he admonished that "some would like to see the problem of Europe solved by the displacement of socialism, but I think this is unreal and even dangerous." He later tied himself into knots trying to reconcile this position with other statements implying complete freedom of choice:

> If you and I agreed that the construction of a common European home does not mean, and will not mean, the ousting of ... this or that system ... but on the contrary ... each remaining the same as he is, but at the same time changing too ... it would mean that each people would retain its freedom of choice.

Another ambiguous issue is whether East European countries are free to withdraw from the Warsaw Pact. When Vadim Zagladin, an adviser to Gorbachev, was confronted with this question in April 1989, he said that Warsaw Pact members are as free to leave their alliance as NATO members are to leave theirs—apparently implying that it would be acceptable. But when Gerasimov was asked in October whether Poland or Hungary could become neutral, he said that they still have obligations to the alliance—the apparent implication being that these obligations may not be terminated....

Even though the Soviets have tried to impose some constraints on the behavior of their East European allies, the Brezhnev Doctrine is not necessarily in effect anymore. For the USSR to use military force against its allies is all but inconceivable. Ironically, the Soviets are more apt to look to the West for help in keeping their allies in line. And it appears that Western leaders are discouraging Warsaw Pact members from trying to upset the existing alliance structure. Manfred Woerner, secretary general of NATO, has called the existing military-political groupings inviolable, and U.S. Secretary of State James Baker has said that instability in Eastern Europe "would not be in the U.S. interest."

Soviet involvement in the Third World is another key area in which tension between old and new thinking is evident. The Soviet Union traditionally has considered the Third World as a principal arena for advancing the socialist revolution. The Soviets have supported insurgent movements such as the African National Congress, the South-West Africa People's Organization, and the Vietcong in their wars of "national liberation" against colonial or repressive governments. They have also backed socialist governments, such as those of Angola, Ethiopia, Mozambique, and Nicaragua, fighting insurgencies of their own. In Afghanistan, they intervened militarily on a large scale. The USSR has also developed a global military presence with a powerful navy expressly designed to support socialist forces abroad. In addition to operating major naval facilities at Vietnam's Cam Ranh Bay and Syria's Tartus, its ships dock in such far-flung countries as Cuba, Guinea-Bissau, and South Yemen.

Now, as part of their effort to de-ideologize foreign policy, the Soviets are insisting that they want to retreat from this large-scale operation. From pursuing socialist victories in civil conflicts they have moved to supporting the process of national reconciliation, which generally leads to internationally supervised elections with fair representation for all feuding factions. They have explicitly proposed this approach for Afghanistan, Cambodia, Nicaragua, South Africa, and apparently, in a quieter way for Angola.

Moscow has also consistently expressed an interest in reducing the superpowers' global military presence. It has proposed that both superpowers abandon all foreign bases and withdraw all troops outside their national borders. It has supported the various proposals for Zones of Peace, Friendship and Neutrality, which call for the superpowers mutually to withdraw their forces from the Indian Ocean, the Mediterranean, the South Atlantic, and Southeast Asia.

In addition, the Soviets have unilaterally reduced their naval activities in distant waters and hinted at the possibility of further reductions. Foreign Minister Eduard Shevardnadze, on a visit to the Philippines in December 1988, implied that the Soviets might withdraw unilaterally from Cam Ranh Bay.

However, the Soviets in some ways still maintain an active and ideologically oriented involvement in the Third World. They supply vast quantities of arms to socialist governments fighting insurgencies.

Soviet officials still occasionally speak of supporting national liberation movements, and at the Central Committee's Institute of Social
Sciences one still sees young cadres from Third World countries trekking
off to receive ideological instruction. Soviet economic and military aid
is still apportioned along ideological lines, and the Soviet Union maintains a larger navy than warranted by its territorial security needs.

At the same time there is a strong feeling that this kind of activity
will continue to ebb. Even those Soviet officials interviewed who
explicitly supported an activist and ideological policy in the Third
World considered this development inevitable. They were resigned to
the rapid erosion of the Soviet public's support for such activities.
They felt this arose in part from disappointing and painful experiences
in the Third World, especially in Afghanistan, but more significantly
from the influence of Soviet economic problems on the public's willingness to make the necessary sacrifices. *The Christian Science Monitor*
reported in April 1989, for example, that some Soviet citizens had
revised a song of praise for Cuba that begins "Cuba my love, island of
purple dawn" to read "Cuba, give back our bread; Cuba, take your sugar;
Cuba, Kruschev is long gone; Cuba, get lost." It is particularly striking
that the Soviet officials interviewed expressed no hope that the Soviet people's interest in promoting Third World socialism would ever be
reignited. Even those most unhappy about this state of affairs simply
hoped that the United States would not try to impose hegemony but
rather would cooperate in a regime of mutual constraint allowing Third
World countries to follow their own path of development....

9

Is an Ideological
Concert Possible?

Alexei Pushkov

Having subordinated political practice to themselves, the ideologies and the doctrines obtaining from them have made a deep imprint
on twentieth-century history. The Cold War was the most visible
manifestation of the clash of ideological movements. None of the
factors traditional for international relations, such as competition

between states, geopolitics and the struggle for the spheres of influence, could have led to such a total rivalry between the sides, either by themselves or in combination with others. This rivalry was made possible only by the confrontation between the polar world views and the profoundly different principles governing the organization of society and the economy.

However, the world is changing right before our eyes. The thesis on the interdependent, contradictory, and yet united world does not need any confirmation and is rather a reality today. Besides, the time has come to move from the interdependence (that may be both negative and positive) to definitely positive unity and interaction in the solution of global problems of civilization. And there a question arises: What to do with the ideology? Today we have every reason to try to look beyond the bounds of the ideological dichotomy. Is it fair to deny the possibility of the evolution of ideologies themselves and view them as something frozen once and for all? Is it not wiser today to speak of their interaction, of the fact that they are turning from a factor of confrontation into one of a drawing closer of states?

There have been periods in the history of the relations between the USSR and the Western powers when ideological hostility receded to the background, giving way to common interests. However, all of these periods were relatively brief and were accompanied by only minimal changes in how the sides perceived each other.

Today is fundamentally different in that there has arisen a host of prerequisites for a shift to qualitatively new relations with the West. The role of the ideological factor is changing substantially in them even now. *Under the impact of natural global challenges and imperatives of socio-economic development, the range of difference in outlooks is narrowing, and common ground and converging elements are appearing in ideologies that used to stand diametrically opposed to each other.* Let us explain this thought.

The 1970s and 1980s were a time of the formation of what could be termed a critical mass of interdependence. Now added to the "traditional" task of removing the nuclear threat is the extremely urgent need to jointly prevent an ecological collapse, elaborate the optimal model of world economic development, and resolve the demographical and other global problems. Of course, dangers connected with them existed in the past, too. And the sides took certain steps to neutralize them. However, they were insufficient and inconsistent. The scope of the tasks at hand and the true degree of the unity of the world were not realized either in the East or the West.

The deeply ideologized vision of the world is also gradually retreating as the role of socio-universal, class-neutral processes enhances international cooperation. The points at issue are the scientific and technological revolutions, the development of the productive forces, internationalization of production and societal life, and rationalization of social structures and management functions. The diverse coincidences of interests of all states in these spheres, including the bearers of different ideologies, are quite obvious. What is more, the objective nature of such processes is leading to the appearance of similar features and common patterns in development in states with different social systems, which again broadens the foundation for cooperation between them.

All this is leading to the emergence of extra-, or rather, transsystemic elements in ideologies. Unambivalently opposed to each other in the past, they are today coming together on the level of antinuclear and ecological thought. One can speak of the appearance of a new phenomenon—the philosophy of interdependence and its taking root in the public consciousness, which is winning over ruling quarters and the social and intellectual elite. Universal value orientations are forming which are increasingly determining notions of the paths of social progress.

In the past, ideological factors used to restrict the possibilities for pursuing a constructive line in the world arena, while the sober steps that were nevertheless taken were carried out contrary to ideological postulates. Today, however, other elements are taking shape in ideologies, elements which function no longer as an inert, dogmatic and fundamentalist force but as a catalyst to international cooperation. What is more, shifts in many components of public consciousness are clearly outstripping the possibilities of real policy and a practical solution of the disarmament problem and are coming up against the inertia of the arms race, military-political alliances inherited from the past, and structures for insuring the strategic interests of states.

As a result, confrontational aspects of ideologies are weakening, and elements of growing interdependence, responsibility and the commonality of both sides are increasingly manifest. Over the long term this can lead to a situation where the opposing ideologies will become an atavism and reveal their historical limitedness.

The reality of this prospect is borne out by the entire logic of social development, above all by the orientation of the sweeping changes taking place in Eastern Europe and the USSR. Societal life is being reexamined here on the basis of the principles of pluralism, a multiparty system, political democracy, a rule-of-law state, and a market economy. Principles and forms of organization and functioning of society, principles that used to be unconditionally rejected as "alien" but which have proved their universality, are being introduced into socio-economic practice.

The transition taking place (albeit differently in different countries) by institutions and mechanisms tested by human experience is being accompanied by a true ideological revolution. It is developing along two major paths. Sweeping changes in the content of the dominating ideology with preservation of the basic orientation to socialist values together with an intensification of ideologies opposed to it are typical of one. An elbowing out of the formerly dominant ideologies by alternative ones unambiguously geared to the liberal market model is typical of the other.

In Western societies such radical changes do not take place; they demonstrate both ideological and political stability. On this basis "the complete victory of the liberal democratic model" is being proclaimed in the West. In his sensational article "The End of History?" the American political scientist Francis Fukuyama draws the conclusion of the "universalization of Western liberal democracy as the final form of human government."[1]

Without delving into a debate over this concept, all we will note is that in a number of respects this very model was developed with an eye to the socialist idea and absorbed many elements of social existence obtaining from it.

In our day it is incalculably far removed from its classical capitalist version. Today, democratic tendencies, including on the level of suffrage and self-government, are enhancing in the industrialized societies of the West. State regulation of the economy is being carried out. An ever-increasing role is being played by such types of ownership as joint-stock and cooperative, i.e., those which have striking social aspects. Ramified systems of social security have been established. Basic political and social rights of citizens are being ensured.

However, the evolution of these societies was lengthy, taking up as it did an entire period in history and, therefore, it has been smooth. The upheavals they experienced, for example, in the early 1930s and the late 1960s were catalysts to further changes.

However, until just recently, the East remained mesmerized by variants of authoritarian, totalitarian socialism that had been established between 40 and 70 years ago. The very serious alarms which sounded in 1953 in the GDR, in 1956 in Hungary, in 1956 and 1970 in Poland, and in 1968 in Czechoslovakia and which attested to extreme trouble, were muffled, or in any event, not perceived in full measure. Even if some changes were planned, they proceeded extremely slowly and inconsistently, with relapses, and were in any event extremely far removed from social needs. That is why the current renewal in these countries bears the nature of a revolutionary, tectonic shift, when the political, social and psychological springs that were compressed in the societies for a long time are being released.

Thus, from the standpoint of adaptability, the capacity to perceive all that is new and dictated by the interests of progress, and social and political flexibility, the liberal market type of development has truly proved its advantage over the authoritarian socialist one. However, developing within the framework of Western societies, the socialist democratic idea has been constantly winning victories, victories that may be small, but ultimately very weighty, over the "traditional" Western liberalism. The point at issue is precisely the idea, not the practice, of the socialist countries or its "influence," since the task of social justice and democratic rule in these countries has not been implemented. Aside from everything else, the establishment of Social Democracy as one of the main political and ruling forces in these societies has become an important manifestation of this.

Thus, universal elements of political, economic and societal life which are functioning as prerequisites for social development and are indivisible from it are crystallizing in the course of historical evolution and mutual influence of ideologies. Typically, for all their differences, political parties in Western countries (aside from extremist groupings) are coming together on the basis of a certain consensus with regard to the principles of democracy, the legal and social protection of citizens, and assurance of their political rights and freedoms. The same general democratic consensus is taking shape at present in the East European societies among the main political forces in existence there.

In today's world there is still no unity regarding such universal values as freedom, democracy, political pluralism and the supremacy of law. Different societies interpret them differently, and varied notions of their economic and political foundations are possible. However, it is also indubitable that these values cannot be of a different order. There exists a universal understanding of them, a certain agreement regarding the forms of the activity of society and the norms and institutions existing in it beyond which agreement notions of human rights and democracy lose all meaning. The final document of the Vienna meeting can serve as a real, mutually acceptable platform ensuring a basic concurrence of the sides' approaches in this sphere.

I think that the reason for the positive attitude to the Soviet *perestroika* on the part of both the Western public and the ruling quarters is largely the fact that we are beginning to arrive at a similar understanding of human rights, political freedoms, access to information, the activity of democratic institutions, and much else. The USSR's readiness to bring its domestic legislation in line with its international commitments is unquestionably imparting additional stability to the current shift in East-West relations. Thus, this shift is going much farther than the détente of the 1970s, for it affects not merely the forms but the very foundations of the interaction of the states belonging to the two systems....

Of course, since different socio-economic systems exist there are still differences in the ideologies dominant in them; for example, those that deal with the goals of progress, social ideals and ways of achieving them. There are also extraneous elements which feed on mutual distrust, the pressure of stereotyped thinking inherited from the past, and the force of political and ideological inertia. The existence of military, industrial and propaganda structures which have become solidly ingrained in the social organism, are based on the logic of conflict, are incapable of existing without the presence of an enemy, and constantly generate its image constrains by itself changes in the way the sides perceive each other. However, it is in the ideological sphere that tendencies toward convergence are developing the most rapidly, outstripping the possibilities for the transformation of the political, economic and military institutions inherited from the past.

How are these dynamics affecting the foreign policy thinking of the sides, say, the USSR and the U.S.A.—the states with the traditionally most ideologized foreign policy?

The foreign policy course of the Soviet Union is based on the model of the evolution of the world which obtains from the possibility of the crisscrossing but independent development of states of the two systems, a model which assumes broad international cooperation. According to this model, the present-day world is not two mutually exclusive civilizations, but one common civilization, in which universal values and the freedom to choose paths of social development dominate. This principle is viewed as one of universal importance. Parallel movement of East and West from the political, military-strategic and ideological heritage of the Cold War to disarmament, co-development, and to a new world based on the principles of humaneness and justice, is assumed.

In the U.S.A., the picture is different. Here a vision of the outlook for world developing which links it with global establishment of the "democratic values of the West" still dominates. The principle of freedom of choice is interpreted as the triumph of the liberal market structure of society everywhere. In relations with the East European countries the emphasis is placed on their evolution in a Western direction. This is what determines the attitude of the exponents of the traditional ideologized thinking to the Soviet Union. The U.S.A.

views the transition of the world to social uniformity in essence as a prerequisite for a full end to the Cold War.

However, in the American foreign policy establishment there is no longer the former consensus regarding the USSR that used to be based on the logic of confrontation. A new approach is beginning to take shape, one grounded on the altered vision of Soviet society and the prospects for its development. Views are being expressed about the possibilities for forms of ensuring freedom of development that are different from the Western model. This is behind the appeal to render support to the Soviet leadership's effort to carry through perestroika. The supporters of this approach reject the arguments of the rightist-conservative quarters who discern in perestroika nothing but a "respite" for amassing forces to renew the toughened rivalry with the West.

All these ambivalent and frequently contradictory elements are intertwining in American foreign policy today. Even though the ideological motivation in it is preserved, it is undergoing considerable changes. It is no longer prevalent in the shaping of the foreign policy course but is merely one of the sources of its formation—alongside or even after strategic and political interests which, for their part, are no longer identified definitively with ideological ones. A vested interest in the success of the Soviet restructuring drive, in a controlled evolutionary development of events in Eastern Europe that would exclude the danger of freewheeling social explosions and in the maintenance of international stability is advancing to the forefront.

Hence the readiness stressed by the Bush administration to promote the involvement of the Soviet Union in the world community and to proceed to new partnership with it. Hence also the administration's intention to base its East European policy on realism and circumspection and to avoid actions that could help turn a country or region as a whole into a source of international tension. No less typical is the obvious restraint displayed by the administration regarding separatist movements in the USSR, which is evidenced by the U.S. reaction to the developments in Azerbaijan and the Baltic republics.

Perhaps these shifts are not as dramatic as the ones in the Soviet Union, since they do not touch upon the foundations of society but merely affect the perception of the outside world. However, they have rather deep, and far from only psychological, roots. For a long time U.S. policy vis-à-vis the USSR was based on the notion of the virtually unlimited resources of the U.S.A. in "rolling back Communism," which was taken to mean chiefly all-out rivalry with the USSR in all areas of world policy. At present, however, the U.S.A. is increasingly coming to realize both the political counterproductivity and the heavy economic price of this policy, especially in the face of the stiffening com-

petition from Japan and the EEC. Rather broad agreement regarding
the need to reduce the American defense budget is present in Washington's ruling quarters. In this context the administration's declared
intention of extending "beyond the bounds of containment" in relations
with the USSR is not a propaganda ploy but an important element in
the efforts to explore reserves for improving the financial and economic
and international position of the U.S.A.

It would be incorrect, of course, to overstate the significance of the
shifts taking place in American foreign policy thinking. On the whole
it obtains today, too, from the inevitability of the continuing rivalry
with the USSR in the world arena, above all in Europe, in one form or
another.[2] Although the need for stable partnership between the two
countries in arms control, ecology, the joint fight against terrorism, and
cooperation in settling regional conflicts is recognized, the notion of the
limitedness of the concurrence of Soviet and American interests is still
prevalent. Thus the point at issue is a striving to normalize relations
within the framework of regulated competition instead of establishing
wide-ranging positive cooperation. However, such rivalry is increasingly being regarded not as ideological but as state rivalry, i.e., a totally different phenomenon.

However, one cannot but take account of the fact that in the USSR
the new model of the vision of the world is still at the formative stage.
As the recent plenary meetings of the CPSU Central Committee, especially the one held in February, have shown, it is actively being called
into question. Its critics are talking about the inadmissibility of a "one-
sided" review of our foreign policy approaches and regard the current
Soviet policy as a sort of temporary meandering or even a concession to
the West. There is also a tendency to look for those "responsible" for
the developments in Eastern Europe and to regard the sovereign states
situated there as the USSR's "buffer zone." In short, the new thinking
is being countered by the former imperial, ideologized views of international relations and the USSR's role in the international arena.

The political untenability and moral unacceptability of such approaches were amply covered in the addresses of a number of the participants in the Plenum. However, it is expedient to dwell on this in
greater detail, for we are dealing here with recurrences of the stand
that has already brought this country to a historical impasse.

A typical feature of this stand is the supplanting of the genuine interests of the USSR with orthodox ideological criteria. By implication, its policies and actions in the international arena correlate not to
the needs of Soviet society but to some "fundamental principles" which
obtain from the old black-and-white vision of the world. No attention
at all is paid to the fact that, for one thing, these principles them-

selves were initially the product of a mythologized perception of the world, and for another, the underpinnings of the international policy have undergone sweeping changes since the time they were elaborated.

The ideologized reading of Soviet national interests is being accompanied by an inability or reluctance to reckon with present-day realities and to see the real reasons for the social processes unfolding in the world. The developments in Eastern Europe are perceived either as a consequence of an "oversight" of the Soviet leadership or as the result of some intrigues of the West. They subscribe to any interpretation other than the true one, namely, that manifest in them was the historically inevitable aspiration of the East European societies to rid themselves of the forcefully imposed ideological and political framework that hampered their development and self-realization. However, the direction which the changes in these countries took was conditioned by the patent failure of the policies of the parties that ruled there until recently and by their considerable discreditation in the population's eyes.

The trump card of the critics of the new thinking is concern for the security of our state. However, is there little proof that counting on purely strong-arming means of ensuring it has in fact led to a progressive undermining of both the military and economic security of this country and the exhaustion of its economic, natural and psychological resources? And is it unclear that any attempts to keep the East European countries within our orbit by force would bury arms reduction talks, throw the world back to the worst times of the Cold War, lead to a total undermining of trust in the USSR, and play into the hands of the most militarist, anti-Soviet circles in the West?

We think that it is high time to scrap the notion that one can proclaim the ideals of freedom and simultaneously deny other countries' right to freedom of a social science, that one can talk of peaceful coexistence yet make foreign policy an instrument of class-based rivalry in the world arena.

Incidentally, manifestations of the old double standard in Soviet political quarters are taken advantage of very energetically by rightist conservative forces in the West which are closely following developments in this country and are vigorously searching for corroboration of their forecasts regarding the temporary nature of the changes apace in Soviet society. In the U.S.A., for example, this part of the political spectrum accepts the current policies of the Bush administration as tentative and is prepared to go over to a political offensive under certain circumstances. The reserved or even skeptical attitude extant in the U.S.A. toward the prospects for long-term, stable Soviet-American cooperation is largely linked with the continuing uncertainty about the results of perestroika, above all about the future nature of Soviet foreign policy.

It is also high time for us to rid ourselves of the "parity syndrome"; i.e., we should not render our every action in the world arena toward de-confrontation and disarmament conditional on an automatic and equitable change in the West's stands. The main reason for this is that changes favorable to us are constantly taking place there, and manifest in this is the cumulative effect of Soviet foreign policy initiatives and approaches. What is most important, however, is that we ourselves need a reexamination of the idea of socialism, a renewal of the foreign policy course, and a scuttling of outmoded dogmas and myths.

A distorted vision of the world played its role in that the USSR in effect bowed out of the world community in a number of respects. Clearly, this did much more harm to us than to the Western states. The price for the self-delusion on which our mythologized world outlook was based proved too great for our country. It was manifest above all in our sort of self-imposed isolation, which is inadmissible in the modern world, even though within the framework of the socialist system. We, not the West, have in effect to integrate into the world economy, become involved in the activities of international financial and crediting institutions and the international division of labor; in short, we have to rejoin the European Community of Nations.

Nor can Soviet society be harmed by ridding itself of a number of outmoded ideas and tenets that were the fruit of purely theoretical arguments which failed to be corroborated in the course of social development. The danger of these tenets has increased in the context of the interdependent world. Although they ran counter to its logic, these notions largely determined until very recently the type (lest we say "stereotype") of Soviet behavior in the world arena and were the substantiation for, say, the Afghan adventure and other actions which undermined the USSR's international posture and did not accord with the needs of our society.

It is impossible even to gauge the harm that was done to it by the simplistic class approach incompatible both with notions of the integrity of the modern world and with the priority of universal principles. In conditions when neutral class factors have become so prominent, it acted in the reverse direction and greatly hampered an adequate perception of reality. Specifically, it did not make for a proper attitude toward criticism on the part of our foreign friends (as a result of which we lost many of them) and all the more so the ideological foes of socialism, and rendered it impossible to single out the constructive, potentially useful elements in it. Today, however, it is being discovered that a number of Sovietologists who used to be unconditionally considered falsifiers in the USSR, drew quite fair conclusions on the functioning of our economy and social development in their works.

Another feature of this approach is one-sidedness, which runs counter to a dialectical perception of reality and of a vision of its different, often conflicting, facets. This is but one example. In the 1970s the USSR gave a hostile reception to the human rights campaign inaugurated by the West, above all the U.S.A., unequivocally assessing it as hostile to us and our allies. This hostility was indeed present in it, since the U.S.A. largely used the extensive campaign as a political weapon. However, was this reason to ignore the growing international importance of the human rights problem itself and the fact that it had become a global problem?

As a result, for many years the official stand in this sphere boiled down to defensive moves with periodic attacks against the West that were usually fair but did not relieve us of our own share of the responsibility. This stand in effect played into the hands of our foes in the West and did enormous damage to Soviet interests.

Today we are talking a great deal about morality in politics. For a long time the simplistic class approach implanted factual political amorality. We now have to deal with its fruits—we have to apologize to Czechoslovakia for "1968," and struggle out of the Afghan conflict which has cost us many thousands of lost or crippled lives and huge material resources.

Nikolai Berdyayev wrote very perceptively about the essence of this phenomenon back at the beginning of the century. According to him, " the so-called class-based viewpoint ... in the hands of the greater part of its adherents is proving to be a weapon against universal logic and universal ethics and therefore excludes the possibility of any logical or morally obligating argumentation."[3] Yes, our world, being interconnected, remains contradictory and torn apart by numerous passions and conflicts, including those of a class-based nature. However, its specific nature is that the criterion of class holds true only when it constantly correlates to universal interests and needs and the demands of morality.

In short, while restructuring and renewing in every way, including in terms of world view, we should not put the blame on the West's sluggishness. Unquestionably, it also has to effect some sweeping changes. But the quicker we ourselves proceed to comprehending realities, to an understanding of our national interests that is cleansed of the old ideological extraneous features, the better we will be prepared to meet the future and its challenges.

Notes

1. Francis Fukuyama, "The End of History?" *The National Interest*, Summer 1989, p. 4.

2. See Alexander Yanov, "The New Thinking and American "Brezhnevism." *International Affairs*, Nos. 2-3, 1989.

3. N. Berdyayev. *Sub Specie Aeternitatis. Philosophical, Social and Literary Essays (1900-1906)*. St. Petersburg, 1907, p. 100 (in Russian).

PART THREE

National Security Issues

Section 1
MILITARY STRATEGY
AND DOCTRINE

As part of his policy of "new thinking" Mikhail Gorbachev has sought to change fundamentally both the image and the underlying nature of Soviet defense policy. While the Soviet Union is still to remain a superpower in military terms, it is to present a less threatening appearance to other nations. Prevention of war and a new defensive doctrine are to be the guiding themes. Security is to have a political dimension much more than a military one. Arms control is to be accorded a high priority in this new strategy. As a result, the military instrument of foreign policy has been greatly reduced. One indication of this is Gorbachev's decision to unilaterally reduce forces and defense spending.

As part of this new military strategy, Gorbachev had embraced the concept of "reasonable sufficiency." He argues that the Soviet Union should not aspire to military superiority over the West nor even to strict parity in all weapons systems. Rather, what is needed is sufficient military strength to deter an attack on the Soviet Union and defend the homeland in the event of war. In conjunction with this concept of sufficiency, Soviet commentators have also begun to explore the idea of a "non-offensive defense." It is suggested that all nations, the Soviet Union included, should restructure their arms forces so that their own territory can be defended without posing a threat to other nations.

Gorbachev can point to considerable successes for his new strategy. The Soviet Union is being seen in the West as much less threatening, and the western military establishments are beginning to respond in the form of spending and force reductions.

Alexei Arbatov's "How Much Defense Is Sufficient?" presents a policy proposal to revise Soviet military strategy and reduce military spending. He explains that Soviet military doctrine and strategy have already experienced some revisions in conjunction with "new thinking," but suggests that the reshaping of military policy has really just begun.

His starting point for a revision of doctrine and strategy is this one key assumption: victory in a world nuclear war is impossible. Furthermore, it is very unlikely that a limited, protracted war would not escalate to world nuclear war. Victory in any large-scale conventional war, particularly in Europe, is also out of the question. Escalation to nuclear warfare is practically inevitable, and how can there be a "victor" when Europe is destroyed?

This suggests that the new Soviet military doctrine of "reasonable-" or "defensive-sufficiency" is not simply a reduction in troops and armaments but requires a thorough revision of strategy, operational plans, and force structure. The central purpose is to greatly strengthen the country's defenses for the long term.

The combat task of strategic offensive forces in the new strategy is to prevent a U.S. nuclear attack by surviving a first strike and retaliating against the "life centers" of the enemy. The reality is that it is impossible to reduce one's damage in a nuclear war by hitting the aggressor's strategic forces. For example, 30-70 percent of U.S. weapons are invulnerable to attack. Furthermore, such an attack would mean a first strike, and the Soviet Union is committed to no first-use of nuclear weapons. In terms of reasonable-sufficiency, targets suited for retaliation are the aggressor's economic centers. "A mere 400 nuclear warheads ... could destroy up to 70 percent of the U.S. industrial potential."

The task of conventional forces is also not to conduct offensive operations, but to defend against attack. Nor should the USSR be prepared to fight protracted war on two fronts simultaneously. The likelihood of a two-front war is extremely remote at the present time.

Soviet naval operations will be restricted to defending the Soviet coastline against strikes from the sea or amphibious landings. It would be foolhardy to extend naval confrontation with the U.S. in distant seas.

Arbatov is convinced that these changes need to be made to put Soviet military doctrine more in line with "new thinking." He also sees economic benefits to his proposal. It is possible, he says, that these doctrinal changes could reduce military spending by 40-50 percent in the next five-year period.

William Odom, in his article entitled "Gorbachev's Strategy and Western Security," gives a rather cautious assessment of the changes in Soviet military strategy. He admits that Gorbachev and his military advisors have recast the basic framework in which military strategy and doctrine must operate. It is also true, he believes, that the role of the military in Soviet foreign policy has changed during the past few years. His concern is that Western analysts may fail to understand the "structural situation" that confronts Soviet military policy and strategy. More specifically, he argues that these analysts may have failed to distinguish between Soviet rhetoric and actual military behavior.

Odom contends that the underlying motives for these changes in military strategy should give some indication as to whether these military revisions are only temporary, and therefore, "tactical" in nature. The primary reason, he asserts, that Gorbachev changed Soviet military doctrine is because the USSR could not keep up with the United States in the arms race. And if the arms race has contributed to reforms and political change in the Soviet Union up to this point, it can continue to do so. Furthermore, because the United States must be convinced that the Soviet Union is transforming its political system rather than just revitalizing the old one, it makes no sense to radically change U.S. military strategy until it is sure.

The author further questions the extent to which Soviet military strategy has switched from an "offensive" to "defensive" doctrine. The Soviets may make this claim, but he sees little change in the operational tactics, organization structure, and training of the Soviet military. The West may have seen some of these changes on the Central Front (i.e., European theater of

*operations), he says, but these changes must affect the military
establishment in its entirety to be convincing.*

Odom concludes that the Soviet Union has actually retained
an offensive capability despite claiming a shift to a defensive
military doctrine.   The United States, therefore, he argues,
*"must be wary of arms control reductions that leave us with
forces that are either too small or wrongly structured to retain
operational wartime significance."*

10

How Much Defense
Is Sufficient?

Alexei G. Arbatov

The plans we announced for a unilateral reduction in Soviet Armed
Forces showed that the adoption of a defensive military doctrine and
perestroika in the Armed Forces are not merely declarations, as the
West has alleged, but a practical policy of the Soviet Union and its
allies. It is clear, however, that we have only just set out on a long and
arduous journey to reshape our doctrine, strategy and operational plans,
the quantitative levels and structure of our Armed Forces, their deployment and training system, programs for modernizing their armaments
and combat equipment....

Our defense potential and our plans for improving it are not a "thing
in itself" existing outside political time and space. On the contrary,
they are the most important factor in disarmament talks and in general
political relations between the Soviet Union and other powers. This
implies that people, agencies and research centers directly responsible
for these talks and relations are duty-bound to contribute their share to
the framing of our military policy. Otherwise they will be doomed to
clear *ex post facto* the "mess" resulting from decisions they had nothing
to do with....

Official documents adopted by the Soviet Union and the WTO in
recent years, as well as statements by political and military leaders,
contain key provisions offering a starting point for a revision of military doctrine and strategy. I refer first of all to the fact that victory in a

world nuclear war is recognized as impossible (because the damage it would cause could not be reduced to an acceptable level), as is the waging of a limited and protracted nuclear war. Victory would also be out of the question in a large-scale conventional war in Europe between the WTO and NATO because of the disastrous consequences which even conventional hostilities would have for the population, economy and environment of the continent and in view of the practically inevitable nuclear escalation of such a conflict....

We can infer from the foregoing some further and more specific amendments to the strategy of defensive sufficiency without forgetting, of course, that generalizations of this nature are relative and inevitably open to question:

- Until such time as all nuclear weapons are eliminated under relevant agreements, the combat task of offensive and defensive strategic forces will be not to limit damage in the event of nuclear war (which is impossible in any circumstances), nor to defeat the aggressor's armed forces, but to deliver a crushing blow against its life centers.
- The task of armed forces and conventional armaments is not to conduct offensive strategic operations in the main European and Asian theaters of war, but to engage in defensive operations in order to frustrate offensive operations by the enemy.
- A protracted conventional war is impossible and the task of the armed forces is to prevent the enemy from winning the upper hand in intensive short-term combat operations and from resorting to nuclear escalation with impunity.
- A war on two fronts simultaneously (that is, against the United States and its allies and against China) is very unlikely in the foreseeable future.
- No future use of limited Soviet forces in international conflicts or in internal conflicts in developing countries shall be envisaged.

Such analogies, though artificial, may be described in simplified terms as a transition from the strategy of two-and-a-half wars to a strategy of one war, or rather the ability to stave it off on the basis of a reliable defense potential....

Thus, what we mean by reasonable or defensive sufficiency is not simply a reduction in troops and armaments, but a thorough revision of strategy, operational plans and armed forces, in part by reducing them, revising modernization programs, and redeploying forces, primarily with the aim of greatly strengthening the country's defenses on a long-term basis.

Strategic nuclear forces and conventional armed forces differ fundamentally in tasks, the pattern of financing and requirements from the point of view of keeping up an acceptable military balance. Hence, there can be no standard approach to assessing their sufficiency or cutting the costs involved. The greater part of spending on strategic armaments is necessitated, with rare exceptions, by their development and testing and by investments in production capacities. This spending depends to a relatively lesser degree on the amount of serial production (that is, the number of produced models) and the maintenance costs of deployed forces. This is why expenditures for strategic offensive forces (SOFs) depend chiefly on the diversity of new systems put into service in place of or in addition to existing ones and not on the quantity of delivery vehicles or warheads.

It should be noted that Soviet and U.S. SOF delivery vehicles and warhead totals plainly tend to become stabilized (with the number of delivery vehicles even going down), and this irrespective of the course of talks on their reduction. The arms race in this sphere generally consists in replacing old with new and more effective weapons systems that are also costlier and are therefore manufactured in smaller quantities.

Consequently, the principle of sufficiency in this area demands a justified and consistent decision not only on how many delivery vehicles and warheads we need altogether, but more important, on how many and what new systems we need to introduce so as to counter the American ones. Our answers to these questions will be decisive for establishing how far we can cut economic costs in this sphere. A mere reduction in the total number of SOFs is unlikely to produce a large savings, if—in spite of lower numerical limits set on delivery vehicles and warheads—the renewal systems, by introducing new generations, go on as intensively as before, if in somewhat smaller series.

The task of our strategic offensive weapons is defined by the new military doctrine as preventing a U.S. nuclear attack, through the possibility of surviving a U.S. first strike and causing the enemy unacceptable losses by retaliation. A convincing capability for a devastating response is what constitutes our defensive potential and a guarantee of our security until nuclear weapons are destroyed completely and everywhere under international agreements.

The strategic and military-technological reality now is the following: it is impossible to reduce one's damage in a nuclear war by hitting the aggressor's strategic forces. Indeed, it implies delivering a first strike—that is, assuming the role of aggressor and taking responsibility for a holocaust. This is unacceptable either politically (in light of our commitment to no-first-use of nuclear weapons) or technically (since from 30 to 70 percent of U.S. weapons, such as those carried by submarines and bombers, are invulnerable to attack).

The idea of striking back at U.S. SOFs is evidently strategic nonsense too. Why should the United States leave part of its forces as targets after it has delivered a first strike? In terms of reasonable sufficiency, targets suitable for retaliation are the aggressor's economic facilities. A mere 400 nuclear warheads of the megaton class could destroy up to 70 percent of the U.S. industrial potential. Defense will be ensured if this many of them survive any attack and reach their targets. All further weapons and operations involving the use of SOFs would be doubtful in any respect and evidently unnecessary in terms of sufficiency.

Our current military programs,therefore, raise certain questions from the point of view of the declared principle of reasonable sufficiency. To judge by the information published in foreign sources, we have responded to each SOF system deployed by the United States at this stage in the arms race with two new systems of our own simultaneously....

Are not quantity-oriented mechanisms typical of other echelons of the command system at work here? Are such "asymmetric" responses inevitable? They suit those Americans who advocate wearing out the Soviet Union economically, encouraging them to carry on talks from "positions of strength." This is all the more so because countermeasures in the ratio 2:1 will be even harder for us to adopt in the event of signing a treaty on a 50 percent reduction in SOFs and on a drastic lowering of strategic force levels and sublevels. We could probably effect a serious reduction in economic expenditures without undermining our security while strengthening and not weakening our negotiating position if we followed a ratio of 1:1, or better still 1:2, with the emphasis on the qualitative aspect of new strategic systems and on the high efficiency of their command-control-communication and early warning system.

The strategic task of the MX ICBM system and the new Trident 2 SLBM is admittedly to hit Soviet silo-based missiles. It follows that to maintain our capability for adequate retaliation, we could envisage as a countermeasure against both systems one new system (instead of the present two systems) of land-based mobile ICBMs with either a single warhead or MIRV missile depending on the system's combat tasks and targets....

To reinforce land-based missile forces, it would apparently be enough for us to have one new long-range submarine missile system capable of hitting targets from near the Soviet coast and hence making it unnecessary to venture on the high seas through enemy antisubmarine barriers....

Furthermore, increasingly, experts in the United States recognize that the B-1B bomber (280 billion [sic] dollars per item) is an ill-advised and unreliable system. And even stronger doubts are relevant to our analogous aircraft, Tu-160, called Blackjack in the West. The U.S. bomber is intended to penetrate deep into our large-scale air defense system. But the U.S. practically lacks such a system, for it dismantled almost completely the one it had in the 1960s. To support our ICBMs and SLBMs (if necessary at all, since they are redundant anyway), it would be quite enough to have one type of bomber carrying ALCMs (based on, say, Tu-95s or new wide-bodied, high-capacity aircraft) and capable of hitting targets over a long distance without entering deep into U.S. airspace. Finally, would it not be enough to have one type (instead of two) of sea-based cruise missile?...

The country's system of air defense against strategic weapons is doubtful for at least three reasons. First, it could hardly intercept all U.S. airborne strategic weapons, especially with the deployment of cruise missiles on heavy bombers, that is, many thousands of "Rusts" carrying 200-kiloton warheads. After all, to intercept 60, 70 or 80 percent of them would not mean more than intercepting none. The 20 or even 10 percent of heavy bombers and cruise missiles that could break through carrying 400-800 nuclear warheads with a yield ranging from 200 kilotons to 9 megatons would be able just the same to inflict disastrous, unsustainable damage. It is like a bridge reaching to the middle or spanning two-thirds of a river: no matter how wide, solid or fine, no matter how expensive, it would be as useless as if it had not been there at all. Nor is that all.

Second, radars, the launch sites of air defense missiles and the airfields of interceptors are in themselves entirely vulnerable to ballistic missiles. Incidentally, the U.S. actually plans, in the event of war, a "precursor" strike with sea-based missiles to open "corridors" for its bombers in air defense zones.

Third, land- and sea-based ballistic missiles (some 8000 warheads in all) could, if necessary, hit practically all targets by themselves, without the aid of heavy bombers. The chief reason now given for preserving and renewing them in the U.S. (B-1B, Stealth) is that the Soviet Union will have to spend many times more on modernizing its air defenses, which means that this is seen as one of the most advantageous lines of economically exhausting the Soviet Union....

... However, we admit at the official level and it is part of our doctrine that a wide-ranging war in Europe, even one fought with conventional arms, would lead to a catastrophe and develop almost inevitably into a nuclear holocaust. It follows that a conventional air war is still less likely. (The U.S. does envisage the possibility of using its strategic bombers carrying conventional weapons in a conventional war in Europe against WTO second echelons, communications and ships as well as for strikes against third countries. But official sources say nothing about using heavy bombers for non-nuclear attacks on the Soviet Union. If there are any secret plans for this, they may be dismissed as a strategic absurdity responding to which would be as much of an absurdity.)

A far more modest air defense system is certainly necessary for an early warning of attack, controlling airspace in peacetime and safeguarding the country against possible terrorists. Certain events have suggested that this is something to work on. We also need an air defense system at the tactical, non-nuclear level to shield troops from air strikes. As for the doctrine of averting nuclear war, military-technological and strategic realities demand admitting explicitly and without qualification that the concepts of "repulsing missile space attack" and "destroying the armed forces and military potential of the enemy" are hopelessly outdated. They are a typical instance of projecting prenuclear military thinking into the solution of the historically unprecedented problem of security in the nuclear and space age, which calls for fundamentally new approaches....

... The United States, for one, spends roughly 15 percent of its military budget on strategic forces and over 60 percent on its conventional forces. True, personnel whose share in conventional armed forces is much greater, costs considerably more in the U.S. than in the Soviet Union. But our conventional armed forces have a larger personnel than those of the U.S., and we produced many more types and modifications of weapons systems than that country—doing it, moreover, in larger series and replacing combat equipment by new models more frequently than the U.S....

We declare officially that a protracted large-scale conventional war with NATO in Europe is impossible and unacceptable. This presumably applies also to the United States and Japan in the Far East and in still greater measure to China, a great Asian socialist power. In line with our new doctrine and strategy, we could apparently disband without detriment to our defenses all divisions whose combat readiness is low, scrap the enormous stockpiles of obsolete arms and equipment and abolish the unwieldy system of mobilizing industry for war with due regard to the realities of the quick pace and supertechnologization [sic] of modern warfare. The new doctrine calls for a more compact, more combat-ready and well-paid army having the latest equipment.

As a protracted conventional war on two fronts is highly improbable, it is hardly right to keep major forces on a permanent basis for independent, large-scale military operations in Europe, Asia and the Far East. We could, for instance, effect through demobilization radical cuts in the number of divisions deployed along the frontier with China and in the Far East.

Generally speaking, the surest way to dissipate our resources and wear ourselves out economically is to build a sort of Chinese Wall (in the form of major forces) along all the greatly extended boundaries of the socialist community. The other way of safeguarding security, that is, the intensive way, is apparently to set up a rear infrastructure, including facilities for storing arms, supplies and equipment, plus proper ground and air communications (needed also for economic development, by the way), that would make it possible to quickly redeploy major forces to any threatened area....

Special mention should be made of naval forces in view of the high cost and complexity of modern surface ships and submarines and of the time it takes to build them. Logically, defense sufficiency in the case of these forces implies restricting their combat tasks to defending the Soviet coast against strikes from the sea by carrier task forces and amphibious landings of the West as well as defending [against] strategic submarine enemy forces.

Such functions as interdicting Atlantic and Pacific communications are hardly consonant with a defensive strategy, especially where ground troops and air forces dependably ensure defense in the main continental theater.

An even more doubtful mission is that of searching for and destroying strategic submarines of the United States, Britain and France on the high seas which are dominated by the hostile navy. As the range of modern SLBMs of the Trident 1 and Trident 2 types enables them to be launched from Uruguay and New Guinea, to chase strategic missile carriers there would be as absurd as sowing selected seeds in the Kara Kum desert. It would divert resources from important tasks to unattainable goals. Defense against sea-based strategic and nuclear cruise missiles (as well as against ICBMs and heavy bombers) should be ensured by means of a capability for preventing nuclear aggression, i.e., for delivering a devastating retaliatory strike, and not through the ineffective and costly hunt of submarines.

The extension of naval confrontation with the U.S. in distant seas, in conflict areas involving developing countries—the Mediterranean, the Indian Ocean, the South China Sea, the South Atlantic—is for objective geostrategic reasons the most disadvantageous sphere of rivalry for us, an extremely costly area having no direct bearing on the security of the Soviet Union or its main allies.... Unlike our country, the U.S. has free access to the oceans of the world. Its fleets are in a position rapidly to reinforce each other and are supported by a vast network of bases on foreign soil, and it does not have to bear a burden comparable to ours in supporting defense in continental theaters....

Hence it would be useful to seriously revise plans for the construction of a large surface fleet, including aircraft carriers, nuclear-powered cruisers and landing ships. The forces we have are plainly sufficient for defending our littoral and protecting our sea-based strategic forces equipped with long-range missiles in coastal seas. Henceforward, we ought apparently to concentrate on building multipurpose submarines in smaller numbers and in smaller variety but with higher qualitative indices and armed with anti-ship missiles and torpedoes—plus, if necessary, long-range, sea-based nuclear cruise missiles. Land-based naval missile-carrying aircraft within the range of escort fighters would give powerful support to submarines and surface ships carrying out strictly defensive operations.

According to foreign sources, Soviet ground troops today deploy three types of tanks and three types of combat vehicles and armored carriers simultaneously (against one of each in the United States); non-strategic air and naval forces, seven models of fighters, strike planes and bombers (against three in the U.S.); naval forces, five different classes of warships and three multipurpose submarines (against four and one, respectively, in the U.S.). The same sources claim (while ours are silent) that from 1977 to 1986, the Soviet Union produced twice as many fighters and submarines as the U.S., three times as many tanks and combat helicopters and nine times as many artillery pieces and anti-aircraft missiles. It was only in the construction of large warships that the U.S. found itself ahead of us (by 10 percent). As far as nuclear weapons are concerned the USSR produced four times as many ballistic missiles and thirteen times as many heavy and medium bombers.

These data cannot be taken at face value. But if they reflect the actual state of affairs, at least to some degree, then perestroika in this field should include a whole set of measures such as broader discussion on key programs from the standpoint of defense sufficiency and stricter selection of them on the principle of comparing cost and effectiveness. There is also the need to end unnecessary duplication and introduce healthy competition between construction bureaus and in industry, limit output series and effect renewal at longer intervals while taking bigger leaps in quality....

With the acute deficit of information on our Armed Forces and military budget, it is very difficult to estimate the likely economic effect of the proposals I have set out. However, tentative calculations indicate that their implementation in the next five-year plan period could reduce our defense spending by 40 to 50 percent, and this, most important, not weakening but strengthening the country's defense, to say nothing of other security aspects, both economic and political.

These proposals certainly lay no claim to offering solutions for all problems or showing the only correct course of action. They merely suggest one of the possible approaches put in very general terms and requiring critical analysis by many experts in strategy, technology and economics, who should use our own authentic facts and figures and not foreign data.

It is occasionally said that the military has "no stake" in cutting armaments or military expenditures or in extending military glasnost. It is hard to accept this view. There is no reason whatever to deny that in this area, as in other spheres of our society and state, there are sincere supporters of perestroika, just as there are staunch opponents and those who hold forth about perestroika yet would like to reduce it to cosmetic adjustments.

11

Gorbachev's Strategy and Western Security: Illusions Versus Reality

William E. Odom

Behind the fog of changing Soviet strategy and foreign policy are four realities. First, the Soviet military is in the process of a major transformation and it may decline rather dramatically, but we can understand the transformation only by a continuing assessment of its numerous dimensions. Second, how NATO in general and the United States in particular respond in their own force developments, particularly in arms control negotiations, is critically important. Third, there is a serious danger that we will mistake Soviet force cuts as evidence of a less aggressive Soviet foreign policy, missing the political implications of a changed military posture in Central Europe. Finally, as the Soviet military threat to the Atlantic alliance declines, other problems will make us nostalgic for the formerly awesome Warsaw Pact.

At the root of all the discussion about what is happening in the Soviet Union is a simple but difficult question: is Mikhail Gorbachev bent on transforming the Soviet system or merely revitalizing it? Evidence for either answer exists in Gorbachev's speeches and policies. Indeed, if he is a systemic reformer, it can be argued that he must not show his hand too early for fear of stimulating the forces of resistance. It can be argued with equal cogency that if he does not show his hand early enough, he will lose the support of the liberal reformers because they will become demoralized and unwilling to take the necessary risks.[1] In other words, while we can argue compellingly for both viewpoints, we really do not know what Gorbachev intends, much less his chances of success.

If this were merely a matter observing of Soviet internal politics, we could take a benign stance, watching it with scholarly detachment. Because it affects directly our security, we must take an involved stance, realizing that misperceptions could cost us dearly. That means that we should be cautious and look at the evidence as it unfolds. Getting Western publics to be equally cautious, of course, is not easy.

The Question of Defensiveness

Our main effort should be to see the facts of Soviet behavior in a meaningful context. We have Gorbachev's official change in military doctrine: it is now to be wholly "defensive" and is based on "reasonable sufficiency." Is this a military policy gambit to support his scheme of revitalizing the old political system in the Soviet Union? Or is it a candid statement of the military policy that must accompany his scheme for transforming that political system? In other words, is it truly a sign that the Soviet Union has become a status quo power? Are we seeing in this military policy a strategic deception on the scale of "peaceful coexistence" and the New Economic Policy of the early 1920s? Or are we seeing military evidence of what Zbigniew Brzezinski calls the grand failure of communism and early stages of its funeral procession?

Following Hegel's stricture that "the owl of Minerva spreads its wings only with the fall of dusk," let us declare that we cannot know in advance the answers to these questions. However, we can determine in advance the kinds of Soviet behavior over the next two to five years that would compel us to take the new Soviet military policy as a serious indication of changed Soviet capabilities. Both Western governments and publics can use them for making their own judgments. To know what we must see happen in order to be reassured, we must understand the structural situation that confronts Soviet military policy and strategy. Let us begin, therefore, with a description of the situation.

The Soviet political and military leadership engaged in a long debate in the 1920s about the proper military doctrine for the Soviet state. The losers insisted that Marxism did not have all that much to offer military science, that both the defensive and offensive forms of war retained full relevance for Soviet military doctrine. The winners argued that Marx had uncovered the objective cause of all wars as private property and class struggle. They also insisted that the offensive form of war was the only scientifically appropriate basis for the military doctrine of the new socialist state.

The resulting doctrinal orientation was not challenged for decades. All force development, all doctrine on tactics, operation, and strategy, including doctrine for the nuclear age, has been based on the primacy of the offensive.

With the coming of the information age and its new technologies, the Soviet military perceived another technical revolution in military affairs. They worked through the doctrinal and force structure implications of this new age, and they set about adapting to it over ten years ago.[2]

Whether the military leadership or the political leadership first became aware is not clear, but they perceived that the Soviet science and technology base and the industrial base were not up to the tasks that the altered military doctrine imposed. The sustained U.S. military buildup, begun in the Carter administration and continued in the Reagan administration at an accelerated pace, faced the Soviet military with a qualitative arms race they knew they could not win.

Many other factors, to be sure, must have affected General Secretary Gorbachev's decision to pursue major reforms, but the qualitative arms race and the inadequacy of the Soviet economy to meet the changing military requirements must have weighed heavily in his decisions. Both Army General Yazov, minister of defense, and Army General Moiseyev, chief of the General Staff, have written recently that the Soviet Union must not let the United States lure them into these kinds of arms races, an open admission of the impact of the qualitative arms competition.[3]

It is critically important that Western governments and publics not lose sight of this factor in understanding the dramatic policy shifts by Gorbachev. They are not the result of a belated recognition that the United States is a peace-loving nation. They are the result of the recognition of realities in the correlation of military, economic, and social forces between East and West.[4]

This is not the first such occasion when the Soviet leadership has perceived adverse trends in the correlation of forces. They reached the same conclusion in the early 1920s, and Stalin quietly did the same in the immediate postwar period. On these occasions, they cut their military forces much more sharply than they propose to do today. They shifted resources to key industrial sectors in order to acquire more modern military power later on. They succeeded.

While the present situation is analogous in some regards, it is different in others. First, such a shift is easier immediately after a war than after a long military buildup accompanied by a long period of economic stagnation. Postwar reconstruction generally brings rapid growth quite easily for a time. The present stagnation has created profound structural inefficiencies that cannot be changed easily or quickly.

Second, on this occasion, the regime has pronounced officially a reversal of its long insistence on the primacy of the offensive form of war. This must be a jolting turn for an officer drilled in the belief that Marxism-Leninism requires offensive doctrine. If the new acceptance of the primacy of the defensive form is to be implemented in the military-technical aspect of doctrine, the required changes are sweeping.

Such changes should include first of all a revision in strategy, operations, and tactics. In other words, the officer education and training system must undergo dramatic revisions. Much of what officers have learned must be unlearned. Since military education is based on historical analysis, much of Soviet military history must be rewritten and reinterpreted. We have seen a few small signs of the trend....

Another major area for change is organization. The structure of divisions, armies, and fronts must be altered. The unilateral force reduction in Eastern Europe, as it is described, involves changes in the tank and motorized rifle division structure. Beyond the announced changes, the number of airborne divisions should decline by half or more. The structure of frontal aviation should alter in favor of interceptors over fighter-bombers. The big expansion of *spetsnaz* forces should be reversed; they are designed primarily to support rapid and deep offensives. Many additional changes must follow, not only involving combat organizations but also logistical and combat support units....

Finally, a third area where change should be evident is training. Military exercises should alter dramatically, shifting from primarily offensive to mainly defensive scenarios. Officer training courses in schools and academies must change to emphasize defensive operations and tactics. Textbooks must be rewritten accordingly. The vast network of training ranges for drills by companies and battalions is wholly oriented toward offensive combat; the utility of such networks should decline sharply as drills take on a defensive character.

These changes, of course, concern primarily the Soviet forces committed to land war on the Central Front. A truly defensive doctrine should also have an impact on the Soviet naval forces, particularly in the Northern and Pacific fleets. One would expect naval infantry forces to decline. The drive for a blue-water naval capability that could attack U.S. surface lines of communications to Europe and Korea should abate.

Soviet airlift has always been limited. It should not grow and perhaps even decline. The same is true for sealift of combat power.

Soviet power projection capabilities that can reach Third World states not contiguous to the Soviet Union should decline if the doctrine of defense is truly a strategic orientation. Arms transfers and military assistance training personnel should cease to expand and drop below their present levels. Some basic changes in the traditional Soviet-Cuban relationship should occur, changes that cut back their power projection activities in Africa and Central America. The Soviet naval use of the Caen Fuegos submarine base in Cuba should decline, perhaps stop. Soviet naval exercises in the Gulf of Mexico would be hard to explain as a feature of defensive doctrine.

Changes in strategic forces must not be overlooked. The patrols of Soviet nuclear-missile submarines off the coast of the United States have no place in a defensive doctrine. Nor do bomber sorties over the Arctic Ocean approaching Canadian and Alaskan air space.

Soviet intercontinental and submarine-launched ballistic missile capabilities are clearly more than required for a retaliatory force. Reloadable silos and an expanding mobile missile force suggest a capability designed for sustained nuclear war operations, not just a retaliatory strike....

As we reflect on this rather extensive set of changes that a truly defensive Soviet military doctrine should bring, we can see that too much attention to the Central Front at the expense of the larger Soviet offensive posture and set of activities could lead to misjudgments. We also can draw faulty inferences if we do not insist on seeing solid evidence in all three areas of Soviet military affairs—doctrinal change, organizational change, and change in exercises and operations.

Confidence that we actually have witnessed changes in all three areas and the whole range of Soviet forces, not just those on the Central Front, always will be a matter of judgment. Western intelligence means can detect many of them. Others may prove beyond those capabilities. Over a period of several years, however, I believe we could make high confidence judgments about what actually has occurred. Deception will be a problem, but by maintenance of a healthy level of perseverance and paranoia, we can overcome it.

This is a very elementary first cut at identifying the kinds of Soviet behavior that we need to see to be confident that a defensive doctrine does, indeed, guide Soviet force development, training, and operations. How much of it we must see and in how many areas are matters that need the careful attention of intelligence analysts. A comprehensive approach could be worked out, however, that would allow us to assess the extent and degree of the shift in actual Soviet war preparations and plans for operations. We could see some of the changes fairly quickly. Others would require time, perhaps several years. Until they have occurred across the board, Soviet force reductions on the Central Front merely change the time required for the regeneration of the previous offensive capabilities. In theory, such reductions give us additional warning time; in practice, however, that warning is likely to be ambiguous, the kind that will not inspire an adequate level of popular political support to react in parallel with a Soviet regeneration effort.

The Western Agenda

If Western publics can be educated to take seriously these indices of Soviet military behavior, then the West's debate about how to respond to arms control pressures and disarmament campaigns is likely to be much more realistic and less subject to the glitter of Mr. Gorbachev's public relations gambits. We cannot merely wait, however, to see what the Soviet military does. In the meanwhile, we are compelled to think about our responses. We already have seen the effects of the Soviet peace offensive on NATO's governments and their effort to deal with the public pressures it creates at the NATO summit of May 1989. Let me, therefore, suggest the kinds of changes in U.S. force structure that should be considered if we see reassuring behavior on the Soviet side. I am not recommending that we act soon on any of them. Rather, I am suggesting them to frame the arms control discussion in ways that are least likely to be harmful to Western security.

As a general rule, we should do things that least restrict our ability to regenerate combat power where we now have it deployed. The most difficult things to reintroduce in Europe are corps, division, and battalion flags, that is, staffs and equipment. Cadre battalions, battalions needing additional platoon and company complements of troops to regain full combat readiness, could be permitted in each division. Weapons and vehicles, however, should stay in Europe. Periodic exercises to test our ability to regenerate prior force levels would need to be frequent, something we could do without major political decisions required. They should be a normal part of training activity. Whether this would reduce costs is a question. The airlift requirements to redeploy might equal or exceed the savings. Tactical air power is easier to redeploy than ground forces. Moving squadrons back to the United States, perhaps putting them in the reserves with a short mobilization requirement, might be prudent. Another option is to reduce naval deployments to the Mediterranean and the Northern flank. These steps could reduce costs without seriously impairing our capability to regenerate forces in Europe....

It would be a mistake to undercut or impede a sustained qualitative modernization of land warfare forces. We are in an age of significant technological change. The material and operational developments achieved under the concept of AirLand Battle should be maintained. There is no reason to drop out of the qualitative arms race. It already has contributed to reforms and political change in the Soviet Union. It does not threaten the Soviet Union with invasion, and the Soviet General Staff has long recognized that. We do not have adequate forces at the present levels to pretend to plan such an offensive. Moreover, our joint and combined system of command and control is not up to the challenge. It needs improvement, and in the years ahead, we should work to master effective combined-arms operations just as the Soviet Union has done over the past couple of decades.

Finally, we must be wary of arms control reductions that leave us with forces that are either too small or wrongly structured to retain operational wartime significance. In the dynamics of public opinion and the negotiating process, it is easy to forget about the military operational significance of the residual forces. One frequently hears comments in the United States that we can afford to reduce our forces by "x" percent or by "y" thousands, but they never follow up and explain what missions we will give these residual forces. Will they remain capable of NATO's forward defense strategy? Is there another strategy they are capable of executing that we could accept? Journalists, political leaders, diplomats, and even generals and admirals sometimes find it easier to ignore this issue. At some point, the size of the U.S. force in Central Europe could reach a level that leaves them unable to conduct significant military operations in the face of the Warsaw Pact forces....

The Political Logic of Soviet Strategy

Beyond these narrow military factors—evidence of changes in Soviet military behavior and capabilities and criteria for how NATO, particularly the United States, should judge appropriate responses in Western military reductions—Western publics need to pay attention to the political logic of Soviet strategy. While it is commonplace to acknowledge that military power is a large factor in the overall political equation, it is not so common to show how that is true in particular cases. There is a serious danger that people focus so centrally on the

details of the East-West military equation that they will fail entirely
to recognize how the political equation is changing. In assessing the
realities of Soviet strategy, therefore, we could find fairly compelling
evidence that the Soviet military has shifted to a defensive doctrine
and yet miss the larger rationale of Soviet strategy. It is imperative,
therefore, that we take a second look, seeking to divine the political
scheme of things and how the military component fits in.

Mr. Gorbachev has made many people in Europe and the United
States believe that the Soviet military threat has gone away. It has
not, of course, but there are some signs that it will decline. Several
Soviet spokesmen, supporters of Gorbachev, have emphasized that
Soviet strategy has not been served well by the large Soviet military
capabilities. Reliance on them for political influence and for security
frequently has been too great and the use of nonmilitary means of competition too often has been neglected. The Gorbachev strategy is not at
all defensive. Rather, it is based on a different mix of military, political, and other instruments of competition. As the weight is shifted to
nonmilitary means, a defensive military doctrine can be a more effective component of an overall offensive strategy than an offensive
military doctrine. It looks more peaceful. It can affect adversely our
attitudes about staying in the competition....

Evidence for this judgment is not wholly circumstantial. Three
specialists from the Moscow-based Institute for the USA and Canada
wrote in December 1987, that unilateral force reductions need not lead
to a lessening of Soviet security. Citing a 37 percent reduction in 1955-
1958, they explained that by accompanying the cuts with a wide-scale
peace offensive in the West, Moscow's status improved, and Western
governments were prevented from increasing their military power.[5]

Gorbachev's strategy clearly has been more successful in changing
public attitudes in the West than it has been at home. One can argue,
however, that Gorbachev may intend an offensive strategy based on a
peace offensive and military reductions, but that forces beyond his
control in the Soviet Union and Eastern Europe are bringing changes
that no Soviet leader can reverse. If that is true, then his strategy may
have the objective consequence of a genuine long-term reduction of the
real Soviet menace to the West, no matter what Gorbachev's intention.
This is a serious argument not to be dismissed lightly. The political
trends in Poland and Hungary, the national minorities' demands for
autonomy in the Soviet Union, and the dismantling of the official
ideology hardly can be an orchestrated deception in support of a Soviet
peace offensive....

Not Chess, but Poker

Gorbachev is playing a weak hand, but he is playing it shrewdly. A glimpse into Soviet calculations is provided by the recent play by Shatrov, called "Breskii mir." It is about the risk Lenin took in signing the ignominious Brest-Litovsk Treaty in March 1918. All but two members of Lenin's Central Committee opposed him. Giving up to Germany a third of European Russia looked to his colleagues like a sure formula for losing popular support and eventually political power. Lenin insisted that the Bolsheviks could do that, gain breathing space, and recoup their losses.

To Moscow audiences the message is clear: Gorbachev is taking a gamble on the scale of Lenin's gamble of 1918. It was a defensive move required as part of a large offensive strategy which succeeded. We are compelled to conclude that Gorbachev has a larger offensive aim, notwithstanding his shift to a defensive military doctrine.

The stakes in this contest are not simply the military balance and Gorbachev's success in his domestic programs. Our challenge is not to help the reforms in the Soviet Union—that is Gorbachev's challenge. Our challenge is to maintain the North Atlantic alliance during a period of political change in Central Europe.... Only when we have done that can we decide what changes we can or must make in our military deployments in Europe. They may or may not involve reductions and redeployments, the removal of more nuclear weapons, or the modernization of extant nuclear systems in Europe.

Distinguishing illusions from realities in Soviet strategy traditionally has not been so difficult for those who fully wanted to know the difference. In some regards that is still true today, but some possible objections to my efforts to decipher it deserve to be taken seriously. The West is not the only part in this contest subject to illusions. Let us suppose that Gorbachev genuinely intends a systemic reform, abandonment of socialism, and, eventually, creation of a liberal democratic government. In his analysis of authoritarian reformers, Samuel Huntington notes that there generally have been two types, those who followed a Blitzkrieg strategy and those who followed a Fabian strategy.[6] The former make their goals clear early and try to overwhelm the opposition. The latter reveal only limited goals, a few at a time, keeping the opposition from coalescing to a degree that blocks reform outright.

If Gorbachev is a Fabian reformer, then he is trying to delude the conservative opposition in the Soviet Union. In that case, we can take his peace offensive at face value, but we still risk Western security on his eventual success. If he is a Blitzkrieg reformer, then the outlook is not good because the record of Blitzkrieg reformers is poor. In either event, the argument that I am misreading Gorbachev's genuine intentions by ascribing to him a strategy of the offensive against the West and of deception against political opposition at home, is really beside the point. In both cases prudence dictates that we assume his strategy is offensive. It is safer, and it probably will not affect his domestic result. Western prudence may even facilitate Soviet reform, because Russia's tradition has been to turn to systemic reform only in the face of enormous foreign opposition—usually successful military opposition— for example, the Great Reforms after the Crimean War, the October Manifesto after the Russo-Japanese War, and the Provisional Government after exhaustion in World War I.

Yet another variant in the argument against my analysis is that the subject of illusion is Gorbachev and the Communist Party of the Soviet Union. Suppose my analysis of their strategy is accurate. Gorbachev's reforms are unleashing forces that eventually he and the party will not be able to control. He continues on his course because he has deluded himself into believing he indeed can determine the outcome. Systemic changes may well occur in spite of Gorbachev's intentions to stop with system revitalization. This line of reasoning cannot be dismissed lightly. Things may well get out of control, but they are unlikely to lead to a peaceful evolution toward liberal democracy. Civil war and disorder followed by a reassertion of authoritarianism seem more probable. One never can be certain—perhaps the Soviet empire could decolonize peacefully, but that would require enormous political skill.

If we could be certain that those being deluded are Gorbachev and his colleagues, should we approach our security problems any differently? We certainly should not be belligerent, unnecessarily challenging politically, but should we not keep rather strong conventional military forces ready in NATO throughout the long period of transformation, no matter what course it takes? If we are to sustain adequate defenses, then it will not be enough to show clearly that we can see through Gorbachev's peace offensive. We must do that and more. We must explain why, no matter what Gorbachev has accomplished and still intends to accomplish, we still have grounds for sustaining prudent levels of military defense.

There is a danger that some of the most distinguished long-time observers of the Soviet Union, those who consistently have seen clearly through Soviet strategies and tactics, can lose their credibility at this precarious time for the reshaping of Western perceptions of Soviet power, when their insights are needed most desperately. Any way one looks at developments in the Soviet Union today, one has to be struck by a sense that some kind of transformation is afoot. Simply to pretend that this is not the case requires an accompanying hypothesis that explains in compelling fashion what we are seeing. In this essay I have tried to set forth some indices of behavior that can help to distinguish between Soviet rhetoric and actual military behavior. If I had to guess, I would predict that we shall see the Soviet military meet several of my criteria. That leads me to think more seriously about the implications of a systemic change in the Soviet Union. What would that really mean for the West? Most of our opinion-making elite clearly believe it means only good things for our security and prosperity. It may, but it also is likely to bring a number of unanticipated and unhappy consequences....

Notes

1. See Samuel P. Huntington, *Political Order in Changing Societies* (New Haven, Ct.: Yale University Press, 1968), pp. 344-369, for a discussion of the strategies of reform.

2. See my "Soviet Military Doctrine," *Foreign Affairs* 67: 1 (Winter 1988/89), pp. 114-134, for details.

3. D. Yazov, *Red Star*, 9 February 1989, and M. Moiseyev, *Red Star*, February 10, 1989.

4. See my "How to Handle Moscow," *Washington Post*, 12 March 1989, Outlook section.

5. V.V. Zhurkin, S.A. Karaganov, and A.V. Kortunov, "On Reasonable Sufficiency," *USA: Economics, Politics, and Ideology* 12 (1987), pp. 14-20.

6. Samuel Huntington, *Political Order in Changing Societies*.

Section 2
ARMS CONTROL

In Alexei Arbatov's "Deep Reductions in Strategic Arms," his second contribution to this volume, he comments on the nature of the arms race between the superpowers as much as making specific proposals to reduce the level of strategic weapons. He points out that in the past forty years the military rivalry between the major powers, especially in the area of nuclear arms, has outgrown the political contradictions that initially caused it. The arms race has acquired a momentum of its own and formed its own mechanism of reproduction. The dynamics of the arms race are fed by the powerful military-industrial complexes in both the Soviet Union and the United States, and secrecy and lack of oversight have put no restrictions on its growth. As a result, the level of military confrontation between the superpowers has a certain momentum of its own that is proving difficult to reverse. It seems apparent, then, that political relations between the two major powers must change significantly before the military component of the relationship can be substantially revised.

But the "balance of terror" is more complicated than this, as he explains. The arms race itself is a source of distrust, so perhaps political relations can not be altered without curbing the arms race. The result is a closed circle. The only way out of the circle is to restrain the arms race by technical arms control agreements, and success in this area will lead to improved political relations. And, of course, an improvement in the political climate could open the door for more technical agreements, and so on.

However, the technical aspects of the arms race should not be taken lightly. Take, for example, the relationship of technical feasibility and the political probability of nuclear war. The real link between the two is determined by the degree of stability maintained. Simply put, stability in the nuclear area is based on the extent to which a first strike is possible in an acute crisis. Because of the speed and range of strategic weapons, as well as the contingency plans for their use, there is the fear that the technical aspects of the balance are presently more critical than the political behavior of the antagonists. For example, a military objective might be to substantially reduce damage in case of a first strike attack. Although this may be a permissible military goal, it "can hardly be accepted as a state's political goal in war." It is a situation where "strategic logic threatens to prevail over common sense."

This suggests that negotiations on Strategic Offensive Arms (SOAs) should focus on mechanisms to strengthen stability as well as on reducing the number of weapon systems. This is where military doctrine plays a role. The Soviet Union, the author points out, does not maintain a first strike capability and therefore the number and type of strategic weapons it maintains is determined solely by its ability to retaliate. The United States, on the other hand, does maintain a "counterforce" capability, so any specific percentage reduction in SOAs should put limits on that particular capability. These are factors that have to be considered in any reduction of strategic arms, explaining why "technocrats" are needed to negotiate and implement "political" decisions.

Edward L. Rowny, in his article "Arms Control and the Future of U.S.-Soviet Relations," points out that arms control, as pursued in the 1970s and 1980s, is irrelevant today. For the past forty years the goals and means of arms control were shaped by the Cold War. Now arms control exists in an entirely different environment, and the old framework is clearly obsolete. Therefore, the United States must adopt a new approach to arms control as part of a foreign policy that goes "beyond containment."

Rowny explains that it is changes in both context and content that have made the traditional approach to arms control obsolete. Whereas arms control was a "narrow setpiece" of superpower dialogue during the 1970s and early 1980s, now the Soviet-U.S. dialogue includes a variety of important issues. Therefore, whereas arms control was formerly regarded as the barometer of U.S.-Soviet relations, it is now the "least common denominator." We should, Rowny maintains, "not mourn this development but welcome it."

With regard to the content of arms control, the author asserts that the Reagan administration produced a breakthrough in arms control negotiations by changing the rules. It did so by (1) accepting asymmetrical reductions to parity, (2) emphasizing reductions that promoted stability, and (3) insisting on high standards of verification. He stresses that these requirements must not be relaxed even though the context of arms control has changed. This is important, he says, because change in the Soviet Union is not irreversible.

Despite some unilateral steps by the Soviet Union on arms control, Rowny believes that the Soviet Union will keep arms control on the U.S.-Soviet agenda for the 1990s. The reason: A strong strategic nuclear force is now the Soviet Union's only claim to superpower status. So, for political as much as military reasons, the Soviets will seek to keep their forces strong.

12

Deep Reductions in
Strategic Arms

Alexei G. Arbatov

On Political Ends and Military Means

... [If] a given level of arms "is the direct consequence" of political relations among states, it is simply impossible to hope for disarmament agreements without changing those relations. But since it is commonly acknowledged that the arms race today is, in and of itself, one of the most serious sources of mutual distrust and contradictions among states, changing their political relations without curbing the arms race is also hardly possible. The result is a closed circle; without breaking out of it, it really is impossible to hope for complete, or even for partial, arms limitation. When the issue is put this way, the basis for practical steps is lost, and all that remains is a subject for endless discussions and mutual accusations.

It seems that there is only one way out of that circle. It must be admitted that, although political conflicts in relations among states really do lie at the original basis of the arms race, in the past forty years the military rivalry between the major powers, especially in the area of nuclear arms, has considerably outgrown the political contradictions that initially gave rise to it and has largely become separate from them.

The arms race has acquired a powerful momentum, formed its own, exceptionally complex mechanism of reproduction, and established its own laws and cycles. That which E.A. Pozdnyakov considers a transient, temporary effect of the "reverse action" of means on policy, an "optical illusion" leading to an exaggeration of the "dimension and significance" of the means,[1] is precisely the key problem today, and a long-range problem at that.

The military sphere is not unique in this regard. It is sufficient to look around to see, in practically every area of society's life, immense problems created because effects have turned into causes, tactics have turned into strategy, and means have become ends in themselves and are generating their own logic of development, leaving the original ends far behind.

These patterns only stand out especially distinctly in the military area. The dynamics of the arms race are fed by the energy of gigantic military-industrial, bureaucratic establishments, the powerful impetus of the scientific and technological revolution, and the tireless refinement of strategic thinking. Multiply this by the solid curtain of secrecy behind which lack of oversight and irresponsibility in the expenditure of vast resources are often concealed, by jingoistic slogans that hide chauvinism and narrow-minded ideas about other peoples, and by a fear, which paralyzes rational thought, in the face of boundless destructive might in the hands of other powers against which there is no defense, and the driving momentum of this flywheel appears in a scale that is closer to reality.

Its ever-faster revolutions have not only long since become divorced from their initial political motivation, they have even outgrown any minimally rational military considerations. (For example, what sort of actions could nearly 200 NATO and Warsaw Treaty divisions conduct in Europe if the two alliances' 7000 to 8000 units of tactical nuclear weapons were put to use, which would make the continent permanently uninhabitable?) From every indication, the levels of military confrontation, military programs, and strategic concepts themselves have turned into an extremely important, although highly specific, area and form of expression of the political relations among states. This area is becoming increasingly isolated from other aspects of international politics, but it represents for those politics the danger of the most destructive and irreparable consequences, consequences with which no disputed issue in contemporary international life is commensurate.

But it is precisely because military-strategic reality is a special form of expression of political relations among states that it is open to political influence; moreover, that influence is also exerted in a specific form of relations: through disarmament negotiations and corresponding agreements. And for major advances to be made along this path, it is not necessary to wait until the political first causes of the arms race are eliminated. Disarmament efforts and steps themselves, which enjoy increasingly wide support from world public opinion, are changing the political relations among states and actively and positively affecting as important an area of those relations as military-strategic relations....

The Problem of Strategic Stability

[There is also] the relationship between the objective military-technological possibility and the political probability of nuclear war. Negotiations on arms reductions influence mainly the former, although agreements in that area unquestionably improve overall political relations among states, and that contributes, in turn, to peaceful settlement of international conflicts whose escalation might lead to a nuclear war. It seems that the link between the physical possibility and political probability of a nuclear war is provided by the degree of stability in the military-strategic situation.

... [T]he most important aspect of stability evidently is the extent to which the constituent elements of the given strategic correlation of forces increase or decrease the possibility of delivering a first strike in a situation of acute crisis, that is, the way in which those elements affect the material aspect of the danger of launching a thermonuclear war.

In this connection, of course, it would be wrong to turn the significance of purely military factors into an absolute. In a conflict, the political prerequisites and goals of states have been and continue to be the determining factors, and their relation to the purely military situation has always been of an extremely complex, dialectical nature as to the danger that a crisis will turn into a war. Under present conditions, however, the influence of military-strategic factors on the development of potential crisis situations substantially increases.

This is due, first of all, to destructive power that has grown beyond all precedent, to the speed and range of the weapons, and to the catastrophic consequences of their use—and, at the same time, to the unprecedented increase in the technical and organizational complexity of military mechanisms. They are geared to previously planned and fine-tuned interaction among a tremendous number of elements and performers that are coordinated to the minute, even the second, and that encompass the land, the sea, and the air—and lately, more and more, outer space as well. This turns the contemporary armed forces of the principal powers, and especially their strategic nuclear "aggregates," into a powerful factor weighing on the choice of steps in a crisis, and increasingly forcing on politicians a special logic of action with a powerful mixture of strategic, operational, and tactical determinants.

Selection of criteria for evaluating the stability of the correlation of forces as the result of different options for reduction of SOAs is dictated to a critical extent by determining what strategic goals an opposing side might pursue in delivering a nuclear strike first.

According to Soviet strategic views, the most probable and primary objective of nuclear aggression might be to reduce retributive might, that is, to prevent a retaliatory strike, or to substantially reduce the damage it would cause.[2]

It should be noted that reducing the damage in a nuclear clash, while a permissible military goal, can hardly be accepted as a state's political goal in a war. After all, the most reliable means of reducing the damage to any state would be to prevent the unleashing of a nuclear conflict in the first place. Nonetheless, a nuclear cataclysm could evidently be the continuation of a certain military strategy that had gotten out of the control of politics and was acting according to its own laws. The political goals of states can clash and result in a military conflict, including one involving their direct use of conventional armed forces and weapons against each other. It is precisely in that situation, when both the stakes and the losses in the course of a conflict have already become substantial, and when the leaders of the hostile states cannot stop the escalation of military actions and settle the conflicts by peaceful means, that strategic logic threatens to prevail over common sense.

As noted by the late, prematurely departed V.I. Gantman, a major Soviet scholar and one of the founders of our theory of international relations,

> after arising as a political relation, an international conflict acquires a certain independence and a logic of its own development, and it becomes capable on its own of influencing, in various ways, other relations

that develop in the context of the given conflict, and even of influencing the nature of the contradictions on which that conflict is based and the means of resolving them.[3]

In a case in which a strategic nuclear strike by the other side seems inevitable or very probable, and in which the estimated difference in damage sustained from a first strike and a second strike is relatively high, an incentive may arise to deliver a preemptive nuclear strike in the calculation that the retaliatory strike will be of less force than it would be under other conditions.

In such a situation, regardless of the states' original political motives and goals, it is precisely the condition of the strategic correlation of forces—the existence of equilibrium or, to the contrary, the superiority of one side—that can be a decisive factor capable of tipping the balance in one direction or another. Negotiations on SOAs should mainly serve the purposes of reducing the probability of a nuclear disaster by strengthening stability at reduced levels of strategic equilibrium.

Both the theoretical and practical importance of the scientific study of the problems of strategic stability is obvious. And it is equally obvious that no progress will be made here without a detailed analysis of the dynamics of the military balance, strategic doctrines and concepts, and the specifics of arms reduction negotiations.

A 50 Percent Reduction in Strategic Offensive Arms

During the Washington summit meeting the sides were able to bring their positions significantly closer in order to prepare joint wording regarding the key elements of the first stage in the reduction of SOAs. In particular, they reaffirmed the previous principles of a 50 percent reduction in SOAs.... They also agreed on a limit of ... heavy ICBMs and ... for nuclear warheads on them.... The joint statement also reflected an agreement that, as the result of reductions, the total throw-weight of Soviet ICBMs and SLBMs [submarine-launched ballistic missiles] would be reduced by 50 percent, and that level would not be exceeded by either side....

At the same time, substantial differences remain between the two powers. The essence of the disagreements between the sides on the reduction of SOAs is rooted in the Soviet Union's and the United States' substantially different approaches to the essence of military-strategic equilibrium and strategic stability.

The concept of strategic stability on which U.S. policy is based postulates that land-based ICBMs are destabilizing, since they are best suited to first strike against the other side's strategic forces (especially their analogous component) for the purpose of weakening them, and at the same time are themselves most vulnerable to such a strike by the enemy. This supposedly creates a dual incentive for their preemptive use. And submarine-launched missiles and bombers carrying cruise missiles are supposedly intended only for a retaliatory strike (the former are insufficiently accurate and have undependable communications with their headquarters, and the latter require many hours of flight time to their targets). Consequently, the more strictly ICBMs are reduced and limited, the less the likelihood of a first strike, and the greater the strategic stability.

Relying on its own understanding of stability, the United States has endeavored to achieve agreement terms that would change the structure, qualitative makeup, and consequently, military capability of the Soviet Union's strategic forces. From the time of the Reykjavik meeting, the American side, in defining ICBMs as the most "destabilizing" type of strategic weapon, has insisted on a treaty's including sublevels that would additionally limit the number of warheads on certain components of the strategic triad (combined ICBMs and SLBMs, and ICBMs separately), and even on certain specific types of land-based ballistic missiles. These terms presuppose a substantial restructuring of the traditional composition of Soviet strategic forces, a composition which stems from the specific features of the Soviet Union's geostrategic situation, its military organizational and technical development, and the history of the development of its military doctrine and strategy.

According to the American proposals, in addition to quantitative sublevels, strict qualitative limits should be placed on heavy ICBMs—traditionally the key element of Soviet SOAs—since it would be forbidden to produce, test, or deploy modernized versions, or to carry out the modification or conversion of their launchers. Another condition would be banning and dismantling mobile land-based ICBMs....

The U.S. condition banning mobile ICBMs is officially based on the difficulties of verification, particularly verification of a ban on the capability to rapidly reload ICBM launchers. It is obvious, however, that given the comprehensive verification methods, including on-site inspection currently being discussed by the two powers, perfectly reliable guarantees could be provided against the possibility of reloading the launchers of mobile land-based ICBMs. It is instructive that this point in the official U.S. position has drawn serious criticism from both the U.S. "strategic community," including its conservative representatives, and from Congress.

The administration has demonstrated a diametrically opposite attitude toward issues of verification where American programs are concerned. The United States is by no means arguing for restrictions on long-range sea-launched cruise missiles, despite the understanding in principle about them reached in Reykjavik. Yet sea-launched cruise missiles are a plainly destabilizing weapon system. They possess heightened accuracy and the capability of destroying highly hardened targets, and their launching and flight are difficult to detect using space and ground early-warning systems, which creates a threat to the other side's strategic forces, as well as to its command and communications system.

The United States is planning to deploy about 4000 sea-launched cruise missiles of the Tomahawk type in 10 various modifications, with nuclear and conventional warheads, on multipurpose nuclear submarines.... It is characteristic that in this case the problem of verification does not worry the U.S. administration, and it refuses to discuss limitations on sea-launched cruise missiles, except for one type that carries a nuclear warhead, although it is practically impossible to distinguish the individual versions of that system on the basis of external features.

One cannot fail to note one circumstance of a general nature. Even without any sublevels and qualitative limitations, a 50 percent reduction in SOAs ... would affect the Soviet Union's strategic forces and programs rather substantially. The point is, first, that the United States has a more balanced distribution of delivery vehicles and warheads among the three components of its strategic triad. Second, in the arms race the USSR, by and large, has responded to U.S. actions with an average lag of five years in the phases of deploying systems. The Soviet strategic forces have more single-warhead delivery vehicles than the U.S. strategic forces....[4] At the same time, the Soviet multiple-warhead ICBMs, SLBMS, and heavy bombers (with cruise missiles) are about five to seven years "younger" than the American ones, and the USSR's most expensive military units (figured in terms of the cost of a prototype), i.e., nuclear-powered submarines carrying missiles with MRVs, are, on the average, 15 years younger than their American counterparts.

This means that the Soviet Union would have to carry out its 50 percent reduction by eliminating systems that are much less obsolete, especially with respect to submarines. The removal of relatively old single-warhead missiles and planes would provide a substantial reduction in delivery vehicles (more than 50 percent), but a very small reduction in warheads (13 percent). By eliminating obsolete single-warhead missiles, multi-warhead delivery vehicles, and old submarines, the United States theoretically could more painlessly reduce its SOAs by 60 percent of its delivery vehicles and 65 percent of its warheads (based on the counting rules.)[5] That would provide its 50 percent reduction and create a certain additional "reserve" allowing the deployment of a new generation of strategic systems....

In any variation, the Soviet Union would have to remove more than 50 ballistic-missile submarines from its SOAs, including some relatively new nuclear-powered ballistic-missile submarines that have been launched since the late 1970s, as well as at least 500 old single warhead ICBMs ... which have come on line since 1975.[6]

As for the U.S. strategic forces, by virtue of the objective circumstances that have been noted, they would be affected somewhat more "mercifully." With the removal of 28 obsolete submarines carrying Poseidon and Trident-1 SLBMs, 260 old B-52 bombers, and 770 Minuteman-2 and Minuteman-3 ICBMs (1965 to 1975), the United States would be able to refit its SOAs with the latest systems with relatively less difficulty....

"Why do we need all these mind-boggling calculations?" ask some supporters of the "political" school. "After all, the political meaning of reducing arms arsenals is much more important." Granted, that is indisputably the case. The treaty will improve Soviet-American relations and the entire world political climate. But just what does that mean, to put the question more specifically? How do you measure the positive changes, how do you weigh the potential negative consequences, and how do you eliminate them? Obviously, the chief political essence of the treaty is that it should help reduce the threat of nuclear war. And that requires more appreciable and stable changes than a good mood among the world public (although that too, of course, plays no small role). These changes should be expressed in a reduction of the material possibility and, therefore—all else being equal—political probability of a first nuclear strike in a hypothetical crisis situation—a first strike that could launch a nuclear war. And here you will not get by with general discussions. You have to calculate, analyze, and formulate well-founded concepts of the sort of strategic goals an adversary might pursue in launching a first strike, the factors in the military balance that contribute to that, the factors that discourage it, and how the relationship between them might change as the result of any given draft treaty.

As noted above, the sublevels and other limitations proposed by Washington are based on a detailed concept of "strategic stability." This concept was developed and widely discussed in the United States over the course of two decades among specialists, politicians, and representatives of the mass media. Although the concept is not monolithic and has a number of variants in the United States, its general propositions provide the basis for both the U.S. negotiating line and its strategic programs as complementary elements of a single policy of "providing security."

In actuality, it has many vulnerable points and has been subjected to serious criticism in Soviet scholarly literature.[7] But since strengthening strategic stability occupies such an important place in negotiations between the USSR and the United States, it is obvious that the Soviet approach to this issue requires more detailed and comprehensive explanation in the context of the disclosure of the USSR's defensive military doctrine. After all, at the present stage, until nuclear arms are eliminated, both the USSR's armed forces and its policy of achieving radical disarmament agreements serve a single goal—preventing nuclear war.

Where it has not yet been possible to reach agreement, the balance must be maintained through military programs that provide deterrence [sderzhivaniye] through the potential for a retaliatory strike. It is advisable to measure that potential according to the principle of reasonable sufficiency, taking into account the other side's forces and programs. But where it is possible to limit U.S. forces through agreements, the need for certain of the Soviet Union's nuclear weapons is eliminated, and they can be given up as part of those agreements. The decisions of the 27th CPSU Congress, which emphasized political means of strengthening security, call for priority to be given to precisely that course. In speaking at the 42nd session of the U.N. General Assembly, V.F. Petrovskiy, USSR deputy minister of foreign affairs, emphasized:

> We proceed from the premise that movement toward a nuclear-free world can be accomplished in stages, in terms of both the participants involved and the weapons covered, and at each stage and over the course of this entire process, there should be a steady strengthening of security and enhancement of strategic stability. At the intermediate stages of that movement, agreements should be reached at least on what constitutes reasonable sufficiency in both nuclear and conventional arms, and on maintaining strategic stability at the lowest possible level of that sufficiency.[8]

A comprehensive explanation of the Soviet concept of stability would persuasively show how our strategy of preventing war and orienting entirely toward a retaliatory strike determines the existing and future structure and the basic quantitative and qualitative characteristics of Soviet SOAs.

Greater glasnost regarding these matters cannot weaken security. After all, the principal aim in Soviet military doctrine (and consequently, in strategy, tactics, and military development) is to prevent nuclear war, and not to "surprise" an adversary, if he should decide to attack. Of course, in a number of respects a certain military uncertainty reduces the likelihood of aggression. The actual details of operational planning and the operation of the command, communications, and warning system, of course, should be kept secret (and incidentally, are kept secret not only by the Soviet Union but by America), so that the other side may not attempt to take advantage of such information to acquire the capability for a "decapitating" or "disarming" strike. Yet uncertainty proves absolutely counterproductive if the other side uses it to launch a campaign about the "Soviet threat" to justify new rounds of the arms race and to try to force inequitable agreement terms on the Soviet Union....

Since the sublevels presently being discussed, as pointed out above, would significantly limit the numbers of Soviet land-based ICBMs, SLBMs, and submarines themselves, we naturally cannot be indifferent to which new systems the United States will start deploying in the 1980s and 1990s within the framework of agreed-upon overall ceilings and sublevels. Cutting SOAs in half should result in strengthening stability and limiting U.S. counterforce potential (especially its ability to strike hardened targets and cover regions where land-based mobile missiles are deployed). That goal would be advanced by establishing certain additional sublevels or structural quotas on the strategic forces that will remain after a reduction.

For example, we are referring to limits on certain weapons systems within each of the components of the strategic triad. Let us recall that at the Washington summit, agreement was reached on a limit of 1540 warheads for heavy ICBMs within a sublevel of 4900 warheads on land-based and sea-launched ballistic missiles. In this connection, it seems, stability would be improved by also establishing special limits within the sea and air components of SOAs, in order to limit the deployment of destabilizing systems. This pertains to new SLBMs of the Trident-2 type (along with their technical analogues in the USSR, of course). Then, instead of deploying Trident-2 missiles on 17 Ohio-type submarines, the United States could deploy them on a smaller number of such boats, and the number of powerful and accurate counterforce weapons, which undermine stability and raise the threat of a first strike, would be reduced accordingly.

As for air-launched cruise missiles, the sublevel of 4900 warheads (out of 6000) on ICBMs and SLBMs presupposes the limitation of air-launched cruise missiles to a maximum of 1100 units. By insisting on a larger number of them, the United States thereby erodes the significance of the 4900 subceiling. After all, the other side could also put forward a proposal to raise that subceiling within the overall limits in order to increase the number of highly survivable retaliatory-strike weapons in other components of the triad. Since the United States insists on limiting ICBM warheads to 3300 units (in October 1987 the USSR proposed a version of that sublevel of 3000 to 3300 units), it would probably be useful to turn that sublevel into a limit on the concentration of warheads (i.e., 50 to 55 percent) in any one component of the triad, whether land, sea, or air.

As noted above, the U.S. terms for a 50 percent reduction assume a serious change in the traditional structure of Soviet SOAs. In this connection a question arises as to whether that structure is something sacred that will tolerate no changes. Obviously, that is not the case. Lately we have witnessed many traditions that once seemed unshakable undergoing revision for the overall good. And incidentally, even the structure of Soviet SOAs has historically changed quite substantially. For example, until 1967 the USSR had absolutely no nuclear-powered ballistic-missile submarines, which both sides' specialists assign to the operational component of SOAs; when SALT II was signed (1972), sea-launched missiles accounted for approximately 20 percent of all Soviet warheads, while in 1986 they accounted for more than 30 percent.[9] The percentage of warheads on heavy bombers, which now amounts to about 5 percent, will increase ... to nearly 20 percent....

So the question lies not in the unalterability of the structure, but in arranging matters in such a way that, within the limits of a 50 percent reduction in SOAs, the USSR's strategic forces are optimally suited to the performance of their main task: preventing an unpunished nuclear strike by relying on their readiness to deliver a retaliatory strike capable of causing unacceptable damage to an aggressor.[10] The principle of reasonable sufficiency, however, does not presuppose a restructuring of SOAs after the American model, toward which agreement terms are pushing us. On the contrary, the reasonable sufficiency principle would actually rule that out. After all, the structure and technical characteristics of the U.S. forces embody certain strategic concepts that are unacceptable to us ("counterforce disarming strike," for example, or "limited and protracted nuclear war"). Neutralizing these plans presupposes not the preparation of analogous plans and weapons, but maintaining the ability to perform the aforementioned task despite any new U.S. strategic arms. In addition, there are objective differences in the two sides' geostrategic situations and technical development....

More radical steps are also possible, especially in light of the USSR's intention not to stop at 50 percent reductions. It makes no sense to put these steps off for long; after all, in the next five to seven years the deployment of new systems, even within lowered quantitative ceilings, could cost immense amounts of money, and that, in and of itself, will make subsequent, deeper reductions more difficult, not to mention the potentially destabilizing effect of a new generation of weapons. In this connection the Soviet scholar A.A. Kokoshin has put forward an important theoretical proposition, which is fully supported by experience: "As opposed to efforts to restore and maintain military-strategic parity," he stresses, "strengthening strategic stability unilaterally is much more difficult, and sometimes almost impossible. Hence an important feature of stability is the requirement that there must be reciprocity in order to achieve it" (that is, to achieve appropriate agreements—*A.A.*).[11]

Notes

1. *MEMO*, No. 10, 1987, p. 31.

2. D.F. Ustinov, "Avert the Threat of Nuclear War" (*Pravda*, 12 July 1982); *For the Sake of Peace on Earth: the Soviet Program for the '80s in Action* [*Radi mira na zemle. Sovetskaya programma dlya 80-x godov v deystvii*], Materials and Documents, Moscow, 1983, p. 184.

3. *International Conflicts of the Present Day* [*Mezhdunarodnyye konflikty sovremennosti*] (principal editor, V.I. Gantman), Moscow, 1983, p. 18.

4. *Pravda*, 8 February 1988.

5. *Pravda*, 17 March 1987.

6. Calculated on the basis of *Pravda*, 12 December 1987; *Pravda*, 8 February 1988; and *Where Does the Treat to Peace Originate?* [*Otkuda iskhodit ugroza miru*], Moscow, 1987, pp. 7-8.

7. See *Strategic Stability Under the Conditions of Radical Reductions in Nuclear Arms*; A.G. Arbatov, A.A. Vasilyev, and A.A. Kokoshin, "Nuclear Weapons and Strategic Stability" (*SShA: ekonomika, politika, ideologiya* [*The United States: Economics, Politics, Ideology*], Nos. 9 and 10, 1987.

8. *Vestnik MID SSSR* [*Bulletin of the USSR Ministry of Foreign Affairs*], No. 9, 10 December 1987, pp. 10-11.

9. Calculated on the basis of *Where Does the Threat to Peace Originate?* [*Otkuda iskhodit ugroza mira*], Moscow, 1987, p. 8; and *Disarmament and the Security Yearbook, 1986*, Vol. 1, p. 39.

10. See D.T. Yazov, *Guarding Socialism and the Peace* [*Na strazhe sotsializma i mira*], Moscow, 1987, p. 34.

11. A.G. Arbatov, A.A. Vasilyev, and A.A. Kokoshin, "Nuclear Weapons and Strategic Stability (First Article)," (*SShA: ekonomika, politika, ideologiya*, No. 9, 1987, p. 10).

13

Arms Control and the Future of U.S.-Soviet Relations

Edward L. Rowny

The traditional approach to arms control that marked the Cold War had a strictly limited goal in keeping with the basic character of the overall U.S.-Soviet relationship. That goal was to cap the strategic arms competition between the United States and the Soviet Union. Arms control negotiations rested on the assumption that a war-threatening "arms race" required attempts to place formal constraints on the nuclear might of the superpowers.

That progress in arms control was an indicator of the state of U.S.-Soviet relations was a dangerously false generalization. For example, the U.S.-Soviet agreement to the ABM Treaty and the SALT I Interim Accord marked the inauguration of the period of "détente." Ironically, it also marked the beginning of the massive quantitative and qualitative buildup in Soviet strategic and conventional forces. Leonid Brezhnev's signature on the SALT II Treaty in June 1979 did not keep the Red Army from invading Afghanistan a scant six months later. Nor did it prevent the Soviet Union from attempting to turn Sandinista Nicaragua into a satellite. Moreover, neither SALT I nor SALT II prevented the quadrupling of Soviet strategic weapons during the 1970s and 1980s.

Today, arms control—in the wake of the political changes sweeping Eastern Europe and the Soviet Union—exists in a wholly new environment. For the United States, arms control must find a role as part of a foreign policy that goes "beyond containment." The old framework for arms control is clearly obsolete. Adherence to an outdated Cold War standard will only result in missed opportunities and mixed up priorities. The United States must adopt a new approach that will make arms control relevant in the 1990s.

Cold War Era Arms Control:
The Record

Arms control as practiced in the Cold War produced decidedly mixed results. Some treaties have offered considerable benefits. For example, the Non-proliferation Treaty (NPT), completed in 1978 and since then signed by 120 countries, places an important brake on the spread of nuclear weapons technology. It has crystallized the commitment to keep nuclear weapons out of the hands of dangerous or unstable governments. While Israel postponed, if it did not terminate, the development of nuclear weapons by Iraq, the NPT played an important role in keeping the fingers of, e.g., Libya and North Korea, off the nuclear trigger. Another example of success was the Intermediate Nuclear Forces Treaty (INF) of 1987 which succeeded in eliminating an entire class of intermediate-range ballistic missiles.

But while some agreements had positive results, others clearly failed in their intent. Examples include the strategic offensive arms agreements of the 1970s: SALT I and SALT II. These agreements were pursued ostensibly as a means to restrict the "arms race" and lessen the danger of nuclear war between the superpowers. However, they did little to constrain the growth of Soviet strategic nuclear capabilities. As former Secretary of Defense Harold Brown put it: When we built, they built. When we stopped building, they continued to build.

But these vintage products of the Cold War have had other effects on arms control well beyond their benevolent political intent. Unfortunately, past agreements limiting strategic arms have often hamstrung efforts to develop more comprehensive, durable and stabilizing security arrangements.

Despite its fatal flaws, SALT II contained some provisions which enhanced security. Accordingly, while never ratified by the U.S. Senate, the United States unilaterally adhered to its limits for seven years—even well after the treaty would have expired. The Reagan administration abandoned the "interim restraint" policy of informal adherence to SALT II limits only after it was clear that negotiations on a strategic arms *reduction* treaty (START) were imminent. By October 1986 the basic outline of the START agreement had been hammered out at Reykjavik.

The future of limitations and reductions of strategic offensive arms is obviously related to the future of limitations on strategic defenses. The AMB Treaty severely limits the strategic ballistic missile defenses that may be deployed by the United States and USSR. As defensive technology progresses, it will be possible to develop defenses against ballistic missiles that are vastly more capable than those of 1972 when the treaty was signed. Yet for many in the arms control community, the ABM Treaty is not so much a treaty designed to serve a purpose of integrating a balance of strategic offensive weapons and defensive systems as it is an icon of an outdated Cold War theory: Mutual Assured Destruction (MAD). Put simply, this theory of deterrence holds that the best way to keep the United States and Soviet Union from war is to make sure they are capable of annihilating one another. As Fred Iklé recently wrote in the *Washington Post* ("Nuclear Gridlock," June 26, 1990), adherents of MAD "mistake a Cold War artifact for a physical constant of the nuclear age." The end of the Cold War should also mark the end of the dogma of MAD.

Today changes in both context and content have made the traditional approach to arms control obsolete. U.S.-Soviet relations, which provide the context of arms control, are in a critical phase of transition now that the Cold War is over. As the context changes, the *content* of arms control must also change to adapt to new realities of international relations.

The Context of Arms Control

The most important contextual change for arms control has been the sweeping change in U.S.-Soviet relations in the last five years. Directly contradicting the idea that arms control agreements would pave the way for better U.S.-Soviet relations, the 1980s proved the reverse to be true: only better relations can pave the way for progress on arms control. U.S.-Soviet relations broadened from a narrow set-piece dialogue on arms control to a broad and increasingly spontaneous exchange on a variety of important issues. This broadening process came about for several reasons.

First, President Reagan doggedly insisted on a broad agenda for top-level U.S.-Soviet talks. Reagan pushed for an agenda incorporating human rights, regional issues, and bilateral affairs, in addition to arms control. He did this out of deep personal conviction that American relations with the Soviet Union could not truly improve unless we addressed the root causes of tension between the two. As he was fond of saying, "Nations don't mistrust one another because they have arms; they have arms because they mistrust one another."

Secondly, the U.S.-Soviet agenda broadened because of Soviet President Gorbachev's willingness—for good reasons of self-interest—to break with the long-standing Soviet practice of focusing exclusively on arms control. Still, Gorbachev did not make the break quickly. At the first summit with President Reagan in Geneva in 1985, Gorbachev opened with arms control despite Reagan's attempts to tackle a broad agenda. But over the course of five Reagan-Gorbachev meetings, Gorbachev moved slowly toward a dialogue on the entire range of issues on which the United States and USSR differ. Internal pressures within the Soviet Union such as the state of the Soviet economy no doubt played a major role in this evolution. To be sure, Gorbachev could hardly promote *glasnost* at home and fail to practice openness in his talks with U.S. officials. He made the transition, as Georgy Arbatov candidly admitted, by "taking away the *image* of the enemy." If the Soviet Union were no longer perceived to be a threat, Gorbachev calculated he could cajole credits from the West and rescue the withering Soviet economy.

The third major reason why U.S.-Soviet ties were broadened was the pressure of developments in Eastern Europe. The rapid collapse of communist governments was the unforeseen result of Gorbachev's policy of glasnost. These events threatened increased isolation for a Soviet Union unwilling to discuss vital issues of the day. It would mean isolation not only from the West but from former satellites now breaking out of its orbit. Engaging on a broad agenda with the United States could help avoid such isolation and promote the perception that the Soviet Union had a hand in fast-breaking political developments.

The net result of this move to a broad framework for the U.S.-Soviet relations has been to prompt a reevaluation of the importance of arms control. Nowhere could the twilight of arms control as the centerpiece of U.S.-Soviet relations be seen more clearly than in the press coverage of the Washington summit in May 1990. Despite the buildup of the summit as a meeting on arms control, media attention centered on questions surrounding German reunification and the Soviet economic blockade of Lithuania. In the seventy minutes of the Bush-Gorbachev joint press conference at the end of the summit, there was not a single question on arms control.

It should be clear in the wake of these observations that while arms control was formerly regarded as the barometer of U.S.-Soviet relations, it is now the least common denominator. We should not mourn this development but welcome it. It means that basic issues separating the United States and the USSR are at long last receiving serious attention as the two presidents square off against one another.

Given this new relationship, the reevaluation of our approach to arms control is timely. William G. Hyland called attention in *Foreign Affairs* some months ago to perhaps the most important characteristic of the post-Cold War period: "The United States does in fact enjoy the luxury of some genuine choices for the first time since 1945."

The Content of Arms Control

Having addressed the changes in the context of arms control, what about changes in its content? The predominant aspect of arms control during the Cold War was military competition. Paradoxically, military competition contained in it the seeds for progress in arms control. By rebuilding U.S. and NATO defenses in the 1980s, the Reagan administration laid the essential groundwork for progress on arms control. It seems clear that without the deployment of U.S. Pershing and cruise missiles in 1983, there would have been no INF Treaty. Without the modernization of U.S. strategic forces and the pressure of the Strategic Defense Initiative, there would have been no progress in START. Similarly, the little-trumpeted Conventional Defense Improvements initiative played an important role in bringing the Soviets to the table on conventional forces.

The pressure applied by building more weapons was, however, only half the story. The other half was the set of radical proposals offered by President Reagan. Here, as in other areas of politics, Reagan simply changed the rules.

Reagan: Changing the Terms of the Debate

At the outset of the Reagan administration, the President's proposals were derisively dismissed by the Washington bureaucracy as "unrealistic" and naive. But President Reagan stuck to his guns. The changes he made were designed to ensure that future agreements would, in fact, make a real contribution to security.

The most significant of Reagan's new proposals was his call for deep reductions of existing weapons. Treaties would no longer simply cap or codify increases in weapons; they would scale them back. He called upon both the United States and the Soviet Union to reduce their arsenals to lower and equal levels. Reagan rejected Soviet proposals for freezes or equal percentage reductions knowing that they would only lock in Soviet advantages.

Secondly, the yardstick for START reductions was changed to a new one that more accurately measured nuclear capability. Rather than counting only the "launchers" of nuclear weapons, START would specifically restrict the number of weapons that could be deployed on ballistic missiles. Using the analogy of hand-held weapons, not only would rifles be limited, but bullets as well.

Thirdly, the types of reductions envisioned by Reagan were designed to have a real impact on security by strengthening stability. They would make it harder for the Soviets to believe they could launch a successful first strike. Rather than accept the Soviet argument that "all nuclear weapons are equal," Reagan's proposals emphasized cuts in those weapons which because of their speed, accuracy and readiness were best suited for a first strike. Accordingly, the spotlight was placed on fast-flying ballistic missiles, especially land-based ICBMs. Because the Soviet Union had invested far more heavily in large, multiple warhead ICBMs, this approach would admittedly require them to accept big cuts in the largest part of their strategic nuclear force. But this fact undercut neither the soundness of the U.S. position nor the President's desire to see it adopted.

Finally, Reagan decided that new treaties would contain higher standards of verification. Comprehensive on-site inspection and clearly defined treaty obligations would supplement "National Technical Means" to create a rigorous system of verification. As a result, in the INF agreement the Soviets for the first time agreed to open their military facilities to on-site inspection and to allow American inspectors to witness the destruction of weapons.

While START will attempt to incorporate these advances, it will have to apply them to a more difficult problem—verifying non-zero limits of different types of weapons systems. This is in contrast to the more easily verifiable limits of one class of weapon zeroed out in INF. Changing technology poses a challenge to verifying arms control agreements in the post-Cold War era. New and perhaps insurmountable problems are being faced as attempts are made to grapple with the problem of effective limits on smaller, dual-capable, and increasingly mobile weapons.

Indeed, traditional methods may not be able to provide strictly verifiable limits on certain types of weapons. For example, dual-capable cruise missiles, that is, cruise missiles capable of carrying both nuclear and conventional warheads, have, so far, defied verification. Mobile ICBMs and short-range nuclear forces also present formidable verification problems. Because they tend to improve military stability since they cannot be targeted for a first strike, mobile ICBMs will continue to be a part of the strategic arsenal of both the United States and the USSR. But without effective limits on their production, inventory and deployment, they also represent a significant military capability that undermines the goals of arms control.

Adapting Arms Control to a New Era

Arms control must adapt to survive the changes in U.S.-Soviet relations or risk declining relevance in a post-Cold War world where long-suppressed political problems assert themselves. There is an old saw that arms control is either impossible or irrelevant: that either the U.S.-Soviet relationship is so antagonistic that real arms control is impossible, or so good that arms control does not matter. This Cold War aphorism can be turned on its head by shedding old thinking on the role of arms control.

But shedding old thinking, to mix metaphors, does not mean tossing out the baby with the bath water. We should keep that which is good and build upon it. Specifically, we should retain three key tenets established by the Reagan administration:

- Asymmetrical reductions to parity
- Reductions that promote stability
- High standards of verification

As noted earlier, perhaps the most notable move of the Reagan years was away from "arms limitations" and toward significant "arms reductions." Previously, the Soviets could only be convinced to accept equality where rough parity already existed. They saw no reason to give up advantages unless we made concessions in other areas. Unfortunately, we had few such advantages to trade away. It is therefore well that asymmetrical reductions to parity have now become a guiding principle in arms control.

Likewise, the principle of seeking reductions that would promote a more stable balance of forces (instead of reductions for their own sake) must be retained to promote reliance on weapons that are clearly second-strike systems.

Finally, verification remains essential to any credible concept of arms control. Moreover arms control cannot make a real contribution to American security if we cannot be confident that an agreement is being observed.

There are those who argue that in the age of glasnost there is increasing trust between the United States and USSR that relaxes the requirement for stringent verification. All we need, they maintain, is to "deter" violations and detect those which are so large as to pose a "militarily significant" threat to the United States.

But there have simply been too many bumps in the road to support this view. A violation has to be detectable to be deterred. The discovery in April 1990 of SS-23 missiles in Eastern Europe—after we believed all SS-23s to be eliminated under the INF Treaty, and five years after the Eastern Europeans say they received them—points up the need for tight verification even today.

This incident points to the continuing need not only for strict verification, but highlights the need for scrupulous insistence on compliance. Even the construction of the **Krasnoyarsk radar**—a cut-and-dried major violation of the ABM Treaty—could not generate support among the public or in the Congress for action. It has proved remarkably difficult for the United States to muster concrete responses even to the most blatant Soviet violations.

Non-strategic Arms Control

So much for retaining that part of the old which is good. But what new thinking should be added? The first adaptation to the 1990s has already been initiated: the application of arms control to non-strategic, and especially, conventional weaponry.

The recently completed Conventional Forces in Europe (CFE) talks provide a case in point. A CFE agreement which enforces compliance will allow the West to use arms control to force the military situation to conform to the political changes continuing to sweep Europe.

CFE addresses what has been the single greatest threat to military stability on the continent of Europe—the huge Soviet conventional advantage. CFE limits the cutting edge, what the Soviets have called "usable" forces. These weapons of first resort are the types the Soviets formerly used in East Germany, Hungary, Czechoslovakia, Poland and Afghanistan. Reducing and limiting Soviet conventional forces by treaty will severely constrain the ability of any future Soviet leader to reimpose his will on Eastern Europe by force. The provisions of the CFE treaty will ensure that reduced Soviet weapons are destroyed, so that they could not reappear in harder times or in other places. Most importantly, CFE makes the most direct contribution to achieving "Europe whole and free" by spurring and codifying the Soviet withdrawal from Eastern Europe.

Enhancing Crisis Stability

A second important adaptation for arms control in the 1990s is to devote greater effort to problems of crisis stability as applied to strategic weapons. START has already reversed the growth of strategic nuclear arsenals. Accordingly, it takes the first short steps toward greater stability. But the world still remains a politically volatile place despite the restraining influence of nuclear weapons. As President Bush so aptly put it, our enemies today are instability and unpredictability. Weapons proliferation and regional conflicts, such as the current Gulf crisis, are factors that could spark superpower conflict. Fortunately, the USSR has been cooperating on the Gulf crisis within the United Nations' framework. Now, a time of better U.S.-Soviet relations, is the best opportunity to gain agreements that can act as an inhibitor of future crises.

Crisis stability can be enhanced through arms control in a number of ways. First, the ratio of hardened strategic targets to hard-target kill ICBM warheads should be reduced. Lowering the ratio of hard-target killers to hard targets complicates a Soviet planner's task and makes the success of a first strike more uncertain.

Second, crisis stability is enhanced by assigning a greater role to confidence-building measures (CBMs). These measures, which limit not the number, but the disposition of military forces, can remove ambiguity from activities that could be regarded as possible threats of hostilities. Here, we can build upon the significant CBMs which have already been agreed. For example, the United States and the Soviet Union have agreements to prevent dangerous military activities at sea, to require the notification of all ballistic missile launches and to give advance warning of a major strategic exercise involving strategic bomber aircraft.

Third, crisis stability is enhanced by improving the command and control of nuclear forces. For credible deterrence we need confidence in our ability to retaliate even after an attacker has done his best to cripple us. This requires better communications between the national command authority and those strategic forces surviving an attack. Great progress has been made in this area in the last decade. The National Emergency Airborne Command Post (NEACP), while no longer continuously airborne, has been upgraded and is on constant alert. The Navy's chief communications links with its ballistic missile submarines, the TACAMO aircraft, have also been upgraded. The ability to re-target U.S. ICBMs has also been improved, increasing the effectiveness and therefore credibility of U.S. second-strike planning.

Finally, strategic defenses can make a major contribution to crisis stability. Defenses can greatly complicate—even confound—an attacker's ability to plan a first strike. Space-based strategic defense would intercept weapons launched against us without regard to their intended targets. Those weapons that made it through the space-based defenses would be scattered randomly among the attacker's intended targets. This "random" effect would be highly disruptive to the careful orchestration necessary to a first strike. And perhaps even more importantly, strategic defenses would allow the President time to assess carefully and deliberately the options he hoped he would never have to face.

Contrary to the conventional wisdom, strategic defenses will be more important to deterrence as strategic offensive reductions take place. As the number of land-based strategic targets goes down, their value will go up. Defenses are needed to deter attack against an American target base that is significantly smaller than that of the Soviet Union.

Strategic arms negotiations following START can profitably put some emphasis on further reductions. But the difference between 5000 and 6000 accountable weapons in START, for example, will not do much to improve security if stability considerations are not factored in. The primary emphasis of START II should be on force restructuring to enhance crisis stability.

The Travails of START

The need to adapt arms control to the current political environment is best exemplified by the travails of the START treaty. Once thought to be too radical, START is now regarded as behind the times. START is a good example not only of how far strategic arms control has come, but how far it has to go.

There is little question that START, if it is effectively verifiable, offers a number of benefits:

- START results in about a 50 percent cut both in Soviet ICBM warheads and in Soviet ballistic missile throw-weight.
- START places an absolute limit of 4900 on fast-flying ballistic missile warheads.
- START promotes reliance on less destabilizing systems by discounting bomber weapons and ALCMs. Bomber-delivered weapons will not be counted one-for-one under START's limit of 6000 "accountable" nuclear weapons.

These are significant improvements over SALT II, and also represent improvements over the situation that would face the United States without START. However, START is far from perfect.

Indeed, START contains several flaws that, while not fatal, represent serious shortcomings. In allowing the Soviets to keep and upgrade their SS-18 force with the Mod 5 missile, START permits the Soviets to escape one of the most important U.S. objectives—reducing, and then eliminating, the unique first-strike threat of Soviet heavy missiles. The original U.S. position banning the testing, production and modernization of heavy missiles would have eventually degraded the reliability of the SS-18 force to the point where the Soviets could not confidently use the missile for its only suitable purpose—a first strike against U.S. ICBMs. Permitting the Soviet Union to continue to produce and test the SS-18 enables them to suffer no loss in the capability—even though START cuts the number of heavy missiles in half. The original U.S. objective—

the gradual atrophy of the SS-18s—was and is a reasonable objective for START.

The Backfire bomber represents another problem area in START. Since the Backfire is capable of striking the United States with nuclear weapons, it should be counted with other Soviet heavy bombers in the treaty. This is true notwithstanding what the Soviets say about their intentions to use the bomber solely for theater missions. If START allows the Backfire to run free, the Soviets will have a loophole to create a massive strategic bomber reserve force.

Finally, it is not clear whether START will provide for adequate verification of mobile ICBMs. This problem is all the more alarming because the Soviet Union continues to produce and deploy mobile ICBMs in great numbers. They have deployed over 250 of their single-warhead SS-25s and about 30 rail mobile, 10-warhead SS-24s. The SS-24s, in particular, pose a destabilizing breakout threat.

Yet, even with its flaws, START provides better crisis stability than would exist in the absence of START. START's limits on ICBM warheads and "discounts" for bomber weapons constrain the Soviet nuclear threat to the United States while allowing needed U.S. modernization. The rub is that nothing guarantees that the United States will adequately modernize its forces.

START: Long-Term Outlook

While START looks relatively good from today's vantage point, its long-term outlook is disturbing. Although it represents a marginal plus for stability when looked at in the presence —as a snapshot—in the longer run—as a moving picture—the trend leads to greater strategic instability. START's failure to zero out heavy missiles will allow the Soviets to maintain a dangerous first-strike capability into the indefinite future. START's failure to reduce adequately the concentration of warheads on MIRVed ICBMs will not force the Soviet General Staff to abandon its first-strike nuclear doctrine. And finally, START will have an inexorable lulling effect on the Congress and the American public that will further undercut necessary U.S. strategic force modernization efforts.

In considering objectives for START follow-on negotiations, American policymakers must, therefore, concentrate on the crisis stability problems left over from the START Treaty. American objectives in the START follow-on negotiations should include the complete elimination of heavy missiles and a phase-out of multiple warhead land-based missiles.

In the Fall 1990 edition of *Foreign Affairs*, Paul Nitze suggested that the draft START Treaty be amended. This amendment would include, among other things, the elimination of multiple land-based missiles. In the preceding paragraph I included this item as a requirement for follow-on negotiations. However, proposing amendments to the draft START Treaty at this time would, in my opinion, scuttle the prospects for a START Treaty. The Soviets have no incentive for accepting far-reaching proposals at this time. Far better, in my opinion, to lock the Soviets into the current START framework and settle for the modest contribution it would make toward improved crisis stability.

Soviet strategic force modernization is continuing apace, unabated either by the improvement in U.S.-Soviet relations or the five-year decline in real defense spending in the United States. The Soviets continue to deploy at a prodigious clip the SS-18 Mod 5, the 10-warhead SS-24, and the road mobile SS-25. Without a doubt, the Soviets will have a thoroughly modern force even after START reductions are implemented. They do not count on START to remove their requirement for first-rate, modern strategic nuclear forces.

American strategic modernization efforts, in contrast, are questionable at best. The B-2 bomber is under sustained attack from those who emphasize its cost without regard either to the B-2's capabilities or its importance to the U.S. deterrent. The B-2, however, is essential to making START work for the United States. The B-2's ability to carry a number of nuclear weapons under the START rules discounting bomber weapons helps offset the relatively much larger Soviet strategic target base.

As for ICBMs, unless the U.S. ICBM force is made mobile, it will only become more vulnerable while Soviet mobile ICBMs become more capable. Failure to modernize amounts to unilateral disarmament. Without it the modest but beneficial effects of START will be negated.

It will be one of the greatest challenges of the Bush administration to convince the American people and the Congress that strategic modernization—of both strategic offenses and defenses—will be needed in the 1990s. Given the perception that there is no longer a threat, despite the Soviets' determination to remain a strategic power, and given our fiscal constraints, the challenge facing President Bush is an awesome one.

The Future of Arms Control

Arms control will face some critical tests in the coming years. Several questions must be raised. Will arms control have outlived its usefulness as a means of enhancing security by seeking lower levels of weapons and greater stability? Is arms control still required as a means of continuing the U.S.-Soviet dialogue when a spate of other issues are on the table?

The security problems addressed by arms control in the U.S.-Soviet relationship will not go away. Maintaining a formidable strategic nuclear force is the Soviet Union's last tenuous claim to superpower status. For this reason alone, the Soviets have a vital stake in keeping their nuclear forces strong. So both from a military and political perspective, the actions of the Soviet Union will keep arms control on the agenda for the 1990s.

Clearly, the Soviets see a continuing political interest in maintaining dialogue on arms control. But desperate rhetoric about "avoiding nuclear war" that made up that dialogue sounds increasingly hollow in an era when the concrete and immediate root causes of conflict can be addressed directly. If we and the Soviets can speak frankly about the future of Europe, do we "need" arms control? One hallmark of the new era is certainly the shift in arms control's place in the U.S.-Soviet relationship from "barometer" to "least common denominator."

As a symbolic exercise, arms control would continue to serve Soviet interests more than ours. As we have seen from the debate on defense spending over the past months, the U.S. defense budget is far more susceptible to cuts made on the basis of "improvement" in the U.S.-Soviet relationship than is the Soviet military budget. While the changing face of the Soviet legislature and Soviet political scene is bringing questions of security policy out from behind the closed doors of the Politburo, it is still a far cry from the freewheeling debate and congressional control of defense spending in the United States.

Whether arms control can retain relevance as a means to greater security depends entirely on whether arms control will be held to new standards of the post-Cold War era. The stringent crisis stability and verification standards of arms control achieved in the 1980s must not be relaxed on the assumption that change in the Soviet Union is irreversible. Indeed, the unprecedented political change underway in the Soviet Union is all the more reason to insist that arms control agreements be rock-solid.

We must recognize that the search for stability may include agreements totally unlike past arms control agreements. The most important test case will be in the area of strategic defenses. Survivable, effective strategic defenses can help create a strategic balance more in consonance with improved political relations. Agreeing to get beyond the once useful, but now obsolescent, mindset of the ABM Treaty is the single biggest test of change in the U.S.-Soviet strategic relationship.

Arms control can have a future in a post-Cold War world. It can prove some vital tests of broader Soviet intentions. Will the Soviets complete their withdrawal from occupied Europe in CFE? Will they abandon their preemptive first-strike strategy through a START agreement that enhances stability? And, perhaps most significant of all, can the U.S.-Soviet strategic relationship grow beyond the Mutual Assured Destruction mindset of the ABM Treaty through an agreement to deploy strategic defenses?

These questions identify a set of important tests for arms control and U.S.-Soviet relations in the 1990s. Posing them can allow arms control to provide a deeper and more enduring test of the new relationship the Soviets say they want with the United States. These questions address issues that are far less dramatic than arms control's traditional and somewhat skeptical mission of avoiding the Apocalypse. But they are, in fact, of far greater practical importance.

PART FOUR

The Role of the United Nations

After forty years of minimal political and financial support for the United Nations, in mid-1987 Moscow signaled a change in policy. In line with Mikhail Gorbachev's "new thinking" on Soviet international relations, Soviet policymakers began to use the United Nations to further political and arms control objectives. Prior to this change the international organization was considered to have limited utility except for isolating the United States or soliciting favor with Third World countries. The "new" Soviet diplomacy at the United Nations represented such a radical change from the previous four decades of confrontation that the United States was not sure how to react. Ironically, during much of the period that Moscow was "discovering" the U.N., the United States seemed to be abandoning it. As a result, Washington was highly skeptical that the international organization could play the role in superpower and global relations that the Soviets were now suggesting. American priorities at the U.N. in the 1980s were limited, and there was considerable skepticism regarding the benefits of multilateral coordination. However, both the substance and tone of American policy began to change with the Bush administration, and the United Nations (as well as other international organizations) was received more favorably than had been the case just a few years prior. Indeed, superpower perspectives on the value of the U.N. evolved to the point that they were surprisingly similar. As a consequence of this change in policy and behavior by both superpowers, the United Nations has been revived. Both the Soviets and Americans are more comfortable dealing with each other at the United Nations than at any time in recent memory. At the 44th General Assembly, an unprecedented joint resolution was submitted by the USSR and

United States calling for a reinvigorated U.N. The new spirit has been shown in unprecedented superpower cooperation during the recent Gulf war. Soviet support of the American-sponsored U.N. resolution to liberate Kuwait after the Iraqi invasion would have been inconceivable just a few short years ago.

Thomas Weiss and Meryl Kessler outline the new Soviet approach to the U.N. in their essay entitled "Moscow's U.N. Policy." They indicate that Gorbachev's new foreign policy has made the Kremlin perhaps the leading advocate for a more dynamic United Nations. In contrast to earlier periods when Moscow viewed the organization as little more than a convenient platform to criticize American and Western policy, the Soviets are now viewing the U.N. as an effective mechanism for resolving international issues. In fact, the authors go so far as to suggest that the Soviet leaders have been converted to "world federalism." The new Soviet approach has resulted in important changes in its stance on a variety of U.N.-related issues. There has also been a change in Soviet rhetoric. The Soviets now speak of "interdependence" and "balance of interests" rather than the inevitable conflict of systems.

As idealistic as the new Soviet policy may appear, the authors see very practical reasons for the change in Soviet policy. The Kremlin appears anxious to reduce foreign commitments without creating a power vacuum, and it sees the U.N. as a less costly and more legitimate way to influence world events. The international organization, for example, may provide a dignified means of disengagement from regional conflicts. This strategy has the benefit of minimizing injury to the Soviet Union's status as a great power.

The new Soviet approach to the U.N. has posed an unexpected challenge to Washington, according to the authors. Initially the United States offered no substantive responses to the various Soviet initiatives. However, recently the Bush administration seems to have begun to recognize some of the opportunities for superpower cooperation in the international organization. It is, however, still too early to tell whether recent developments are harbingers of a new era of superpower collaboration at the U.N. If the United States and Soviet Union move in this direction, the authors conclude, an unexpected peace dividend resulting from the demise of the Cold War will be a more effective U.N.

In "The USSR's New Approach to the U.N.," Andrei Kozyrev describes the "renaissance" in the country's approach to the international organization. He indicates that the USSR's reassessment of the role of the United Nations is a logical consequence of the Soviet Union's "new political thinking." Moscow seems convinced that active participation in the U.N.'s multilateral activities can not only assist the Soviet Union in implementing its foreign policy objectives, but will also enable it to resolve some of its domestic problems.

Kozyrev states that, for some time now, the U.N. has not been an effective mechanism for resolving international problems, but the change in Soviet-American relations has helped to revive the organization. A concrete example of this is the U.N. resolution "to promote international peace, security and cooperation" sponsored by the superpowers. He notes that thaws in Soviet-American relations in the past would tend to enhance bilateral relations to the detriment of multilateral coordination. However, multilateral cooperation through the U.N. is an important part of the new "post-Cold War" dialogue.

Kozyrev points out that Moscow has advanced a series of specific proposals to strengthen the organization because of the "harmony of the ideals of the U.N. and the principles of new political thinking." These proposals have not always been received favorably, he says, because there is a certain degree of inertia in the world body, and it is difficult for some nations to adapt to new conditions. The European Community nations and Canada appear to be the most accommodating. The United States, on the other hand, displays considerable skepticism and is "haughty toward the smaller countries."

What are some of the possibilities for practical utilization of the U.N.? Kozyrev suggests that the organization is now becoming the main universal body for security, for which it was intended. And further enhancement of its peacekeeping potential is an important goal. The resolution of the conflict in Afghanistan shows that the U.N. can play an important role in the settlement of Third World conflicts. In conjunction with that role it should work to restrict arms sales to Third World countries. It is also important, he maintains, for the U.N. to "find its role in the economic sphere."   To achieve these objectives the U.N. system must be de-ideologized so that it can focus on practical solutions to international problems.

In summary, the author sees an "international consensus taking shape" that is "opening up unprecedented vistas for the U.N." The task of the superpowers, as well as other nations, is to support the changes in the world body and seek diplomatic rather than military solutions to their disputes.

14

Moscow's U.N. Policy

Thomas G. Weiss and Meryl A. Kessler

At the height of the Vietnam War, some disillusioned Americans called for a greater United Nations role in Indochina and in the management of conflicts elsewhere. Hubert Humphrey, during his 1968 presidential campaign, attempted to build upon this mood. He called for a more activist U.N., promising that under his presidency the United States would utilize the U.N. more fully as a tool for managing conflicts. Thus, out of despair over the failure of American unilateralism emerged a desire for a more multilateral approach to foreign policy.

If history repeats itself, it does so with a sense if irony. Two decades later, the U.N. is again being invoked as a remedy for the ills of unilateralism. This time, however, the sentiment emanates not from a dissatisfied American electorate, but rather from a frustrated Soviet leadership. Much as did the American experience in Vietnam, Moscow's counterinsurgency in Afghanistan revealed the pitfalls of unilateral superpower intervention. The Soviet Union has learned firsthand the dangers of military overextension, particularly because of serious economic crises at home and in Eastern Europe. As a result, the Kremlin has become perhaps the most active and vocal advocate for a more dynamic United Nations.

This new Soviet attitude departs radically from previous Soviet positions. From the 1960s until the mid-1980s, Moscow viewed the world body as little more than a convenient platform from which to take rhetorical shots at American and Western policy, thereby forging a convenient solidarity with the Third World. In contrast, the Soviets are now treating the U.N. as a workable and desirable mechanism for combating difficult global problems. Recent Soviet public statements have proposed a wide array of measures to increase U.N. activities in international peace and security and also in the economic, social, and environmental spheres.

For Americans accustomed to a far less cooperative USSR, the problem has now become how to interpret this multilateral "new thinking." The question is whether Moscow's recent statements can be taken seriously, or whether they are simply empty slogans aimed at generating favorable world opinion. Even if one assumes a genuine Soviet commitment toward strengthening the U.N., other questions remain: What is the extent of that commitment? After so many years of emphasizing the sovereign rights of states, how much of its own sovereignty is the USSR actually prepared to cede to world organizations? To what extent does Moscow's new approach to the U.N. signal a retreat from unilateralism, and possibly even from the world political stage? Ultimately, how should Washington respond to Moscow's new love affair with the U.N.?

When Humphrey advocated a larger role for the United Nations two decades ago, he clearly did not believe that it should occur at the expense of U.S. power and prestige. A stronger and more active U.N. was not related to an American retreat from the world stage. Rather, Humphrey was suggesting that the United States would be able to extend its influence through a strengthened United Nations.

In much the same way, recent Soviet statements and actions indicate that while Moscow appears committed to reenergizing the U.N., it does not intend to relinquish power and retreat into isolationism. Rather, Moscow has sent clear signals that it hopes to remain an important force in international politics through its participation in a reinvigorated United Nations. For the Soviets today, as for Humphrey two decades ago, the U.N. is emerging as a less costly and more legitimate way to influence world events.

A central question for the West is whether Moscow's recent statements are credible. One way to distinguish a state's genuine policy goals from empty rhetoric is to compare what it says and what it actually does. A comparison of Soviet words and deeds at the United Nations during the 1960s, 1970s, and early 1980s reveals an enormous discrepancy. Although Soviet diplomats referred to themselves as "the leading force" or most "dynamic factor" at the U.N., they actually tended to resist most measures that would have given the organization any real independence or authority. While paying lip service to multi-

national ideals and lobbying regularly for disarmament and development, the Soviets attempted to limit the scope of the U.N.'s activities
by advocating strict limits on the growth of its budget. Although the
Soviets routinely scored rhetorical points against such international
pariahs as Israel and South Africa, they conveniently refused to provide significant aid or trade benefits to developing countries through
the U.N., arguing that socialist countries were not responsible for the
aftermath of colonialism.

In addition, Moscow's personnel policies discouraged Soviets from
developing any sense of loyalty to the organization. According to most
observers, including Arkady Shevchenko, who defected to the United
States in 1978 while serving as U.N. undersecretary general for political and Security Council affairs, Soviets assigned to the U.N. Secretariat and other U.N. bodies during this period acted primarily as Moscow's agents, not as international civil servants. The Kremlin had
always systematically rejected the principles of independence and
objectivity developed for employees of the League of Nations and
reincarnated in the U.N. Charter and personnel statutes. Soviets were
not supposed to serve the international community, but rather to maintain close ties to both the Soviet Ministry of Foreign Affairs and the
local Soviet mission. They mostly lived within Soviet compounds in
U.N. cities and were obliged to sign over a hefty portion of the dollars
from their U.N. paychecks to their government. For the most part,
Soviet personnel were restricted to limited-term assignments within
U.N. organizations before returning to the Soviet bureaucracy. In contrast to about two-thirds of U.N. employees generally, very few of the
Soviets working within the U.N. system had permanent contracts.
These policies were designed to prevent the development of any strong
nonnational ties and to keep Soviet citizens on a short leash.

In addition to the highly questionable commitment of staff to the
United Nations, the Soviet leadership was unwilling to participate in
and endorse a wide variety of U.N. activities. Perhaps most notable
was Moscow's almost systematic resistance to peacekeeping and its
repeated refusal either to pay its obligatory assessments or to offer
voluntary contributions. Although the Soviet Union's financial record
was somewhat better in terms of the U.S.'s social and economic activities, most of its contributions were made in nonconvertible rubles. It is
also worth noting that during this period the Soviets belonged to
relatively few of the U.N.'s specialized agencies, which deal with
scientific, technical, and economic issues. By the early 1980s Britain,
France, the United States, and China belonged to all 15 of the U.N.'s
specialized agencies; the Soviet Union belonged to only 9. Even compared to communist countries of Eastern Europe the Soviets belonged to

few of these organizations: Only East Germany and Albania belonged to fewer.

New Soviet Response

In contrast to the earlier discrepancies between Soviet words and deeds at the United Nations, the years since Mikhail Gorbachev's rise to power have witnessed a gradual but undeniable narrowing of the gap. Under the guidance of Deputy Foreign Minister Vladimir Petrovsky— who earlier served in the U.N. Secretariat and as head of the International Organization Department in the Ministry of Foreign Affairs— Moscow has supplemented many of its lofty platitudes about the U.N. with concrete action. Particularly over the past two years, this new approach to the U.N. has resulted in important changes in the Soviet government's stance on personnel policy, peacekeeping, economic activities, and a wide variety of other U.N.-related issues.

In terms of personnel policy, Moscow has taken significant steps to increase the independence of Soviets employed by the U.N. The first gesture in this direction occurred in 1987 when, for the first time, the Kremlin allowed large numbers of Soviet nationals in U.N. service to live in their own apartments outside the central Soviet diplomatic complex. Petrovsky announced the following year that Moscow would also allow Soviet nationals to sign long-term contracts with the U.N., thereby enabling them to function more effectively as international civil servants. This change in policy met at least one of the Reagan administration's prerequisites for resumption of U.S. funding for the U.N., which Washington began withholding in 1986 in an attempt to force organizational and budgetary changes.

While these alterations in Soviet personnel policy are important, they have been largely overshadowed by even more significant developments in Moscow's approach to U.N. peacekeeping. Since 1987 the Soviet leadership has both said and done a number of things to suggest that it is treating this issue with seriousness and commitment. The Soviets have put aside their earlier vague statements about a "comprehensive system of international security" and have instead put forward a number of specific proposals. Beginning with Gorbachev's highly publicized September 1987 *Pravda* article (reportedly drafted by Petrovsky), the Soviet leadership began to focus on peacekeeping as a worthwhile mechanism for "disengaging the troops of warring sides and observing ceasefires and armistice agreements."

Starting with the 43rd session of the U.N. General Assembly, the Soviets fleshed out this position, putting forward a wide range of proposals aimed at making the existing peacekeeping regime more solvent, more politically active, and geared toward preventive diplomacy. Moscow, for example, has expressed its willingness to consider a variety of financing schemes in order to rectify the U.N.'s chronic funding difficulties. The Soviets have been pressing vigorously for an expanded U.N. role in conflict resolution and mediation among belligerents. Finally, the Soviet delegation has put forward a number of proposals for both preventing and settling conflicts. Moscow has advocated some of these ideas in the past, such as the revival of the moribund Military Staff Committee and the establishment of a U.N. military reserve. But Soviet proposals also include some provocative new ones, including the establishment of U.N. observation posts in explosive areas, the deployment of a U.N. naval force to patrol the Persian Gulf, and the stationing of U.N. forces along the border of any country that seeks to protect itself from outside interference.

The Soviets have also taken significant steps to reinforce these words with deeds. In 1988-89 they actively supported the establishment of five new peacekeeping operations in various troubled regions, including U.N. military observers to oversee the withdrawal of the Red Army from Afghanistan and Cuban combat troops from Angola, U.N. truce monitors astride the Iran-Iraq border, and the military forces and civilians in both the U.N. Transition Assistance Group in Namibia and the U.N. Observer Group in Central America. In addition, Moscow has actively engaged in behind-the-scenes diplomacy in southern Africa and Southeast Asia. Vladillen Vasev, head of the East and southern Africa section of the Ministry of Foreign Affairs, played a critical role in preventing Angolan and Cuban walkouts during the 1988 negotiations. The Soviets persuaded Cambodia and Vietnam to move closer to the negotiating table and recently joined with other permanent Security Council members in a plan to end the twenty-year Cambodian conflict by having the United Nations administer the country and supervise elections, while U.N. peacekeepers ensure security.

As an apparent sign of their goodwill and in an effort to appease Western skeptics, the Soviets have reduced, with scarce hard currency, their outstanding debts for ongoing peacekeeping operations from about $200 million to $125 million and have committed themselves to repaying the remainder over the next three years. These payments contrast with Moscow's earlier practice of using a narrow conception of Soviet interests to determine whether to fund such activities. As such, these payments are particularly noteworthy because they symbolize the Kremlin's recent across-the-board endorsement of peacekeeping.

As for the U.N.'s technical and economic activities, the last few years have also witnessed important changes in Moscow's behavior. Whereas Soviet officials previously referred to technical organizations of the U.N. system as "arenas of conflict," Soviets now appear to view them as useful means of international regulation and coordination. Not only has Moscow considerably toned down its anti-Western rhetoric within these organizations, it has also demonstrated a far more forthcoming attitude. In the wake of two international public relations disasters—the shooting down of Korean Airlines flight 007 and the fire in the Chernobyl reactor—the Soviets cooperated extensively with the International Civil Aviation Organization and the International Atomic Energy Agency. Also, in yet another policy reversal, Moscow has ratified and paid its assessment to support the Common Fund of the United Nations Conference on Trade and Development to help stabilize world commodity prices.

In sum, the Soviet Union appears to have passed this somewhat crude credibility test: Not only has Moscow recently seized the high ground at the U.N. with some very forward-looking and provocative statements, but it has also followed up with meaningful actions. The Soviets now appear willing to say and do much of what is necessary to enable the United Nations to address pressing global problems.

By reading recent Soviet literature and speeches on the United Nations, one could easily come away with the impression that Soviet leaders and their senior advisers have been converted to world federalism. For example, in March 1988 Gorbachev adviser Georgi Shakhnazarov wrote a striking article optimistically appraising the possibility of "world government." Gorbachev and Foreign Minister Eduard Shevardnadze themselves liberally pepper their speeches with references to "interdependence"—a prominent concept in Western social science since the 1970s but until only recently anathema in the Soviet Union. Rather than stressing inevitable clashes between systems, Moscow now emphasizes the "balance of interests." Along these same lines, both Gorbachev and Shevardnadze have called repeatedly for a larger role for "the rule of law" in international affairs as well as an expansion of the compulsory jurisdiction of the International Court of Justice.

Given the Kremlin's long-standing antipathy toward the concepts of international law, world government, and interdependence, such statements are certainly surprising. Although globalist tendencies were present in the writings of such dissidents as the late Andrei Sakharov and some members of the Soviet scientific and scholarly community as early as the 1970s, these recent statements represent the first time such ideas have emerged in official parlance. They seem to reflect a new preoccupation with global interests, perhaps even at the expense of national interests. Indeed, one wonders whether Soviet foreign policy is being increasingly crafted by individuals schooled in *globalistika*, Russian for the study of world problems.

Contrary to the impression created by such statements, however, Moscow's new-found support for the United Nations is not based solely on idealism. As the Soviets themselves have made clear, this new attitude has not been derived from vague principles, but rather from concrete lessons of the last several years. Indeed, the central motivation for rethinking the U.N.'s role in global affairs appears to be a reassessment of the USSR's own interests and capabilities in a world in which power is increasingly diffuse. It is no coincidence that the Soviets' enthusiasm for U.N. peacekeeping has coincided with their search for a dignified means of disengagement from regional conflicts—most notably for their own troops in Afghanistan, but also for Soviet allies in southern Africa and Southeast Asia. Moscow is faced, on the one hand, with serious economic stagnation at home and, on the other, with the enormous costs and doubtful benefits of counterinsurgency in and military assistance to the Third World. The Kremlin appears anxious to reduce foreign commitments without creating a power vacuum. While this retrenchment is unlikely to entail the wholesale abandonment of such allies as Cuba and Vietnam, it does signal a new Soviet desire to avoid unpredictable and costly future entanglements in other parts of the Third World.

Greater reliance on U.N. institutions appears calculated to achieve these aims. The Soviets are able to extricate themselves abroad and cut the costs of military assistance elsewhere while using multilateral diplomacy to prevent the United States from taking advantage of this retreat. The strategy has the added benefit of preventing injury to the Soviet Union's status. In fact, increased support for and participation in U.N. peacekeeping can ultimately enhance Moscow's role as a responsible member of the international community. Such legitimacy represents an important first step toward an increased diplomatic role in Central America and the Middle East, where the United States has traditionally prevented the Soviet Union from playing a role commensurate with its superpower status.

The USSR thus is not relinquishing its ability to influence events in the Third World and has no intention of being sidelined there. Rather, judging from the content of many recent proposals, the Soviets clearly intend to remain an important force in world politics through their role in and contributions to an improved and expanded peacekeeping regime. In a 1988 aide-mémoire, Petrovsky suggested that Moscow would be willing to provide logistic support and assistance in training U.N. peacekeepers as well as volunteering its own troops for operations. Given that the superpowers have been routinely excluded from contributing troops to U.N. missions, such measures would certainly provide

Moscow with a far greater say in the scope and mission of peacekeeping operations.

Another indication of Moscow's intentions to remain a key international player is the emphasis it has placed on expanding the Security Council's role in the prevention and containment of regional conflicts. Gorbachev, Shevardnadze, and Petrovsky all have touched on this theme in major policy statements. Although the Soviets also supported augmented roles for the General Assembly and the U.N. Secretariat, they have stressed the primacy of the Security Council. For example, during his appearance before the General Assembly in September 1988, Shevardnadze proposed that the five permanent council members hold periodic meetings to review conflicts, and that the entire council (including its 10 rotating members) convene periodically for special meetings at the foreign-minister level and in "regions of tension." As a permanent member, the Soviet Union has a vested interest in such measures which, by enlarging the Security Council's authority, also ensure a larger Soviet voice in international conflict management.

In much the same way, the Soviets have also signaled their desire to play a larger role in the U.N.'s economic, social, and environmental spheres. One of the most striking aspects of Moscow's recent pronouncements is the repeated emphasis on joining the important U.N.-related economic and scientific organizations from which it is currently excluded. As Shevardnadze repeated in his opening address to the General Assembly in September 1989, and as Gorbachev reiterated to President George Bush at the Malta summit meeting, the Soviet Union is now interested in joining the General Agreement on Tariffs and Trade (GATT), the International Monetary Fund (IMF), and the World Bank. This marks an important departure from previous Soviet policy, which vociferously denounced these organizations—and in particular the Washington-based financial institutions—as nefarious capitalist instruments.

If on the security side the Soviets are now indicating that they want to help lead, on the economic and humanitarian side they are letting it be known that they at least want to get into the game. As Shevardnadze noted in September 1989, "the Soviet Union has programs for speeding up the integration of its economy, on an equal and mutually beneficial basis, into the world economy." While waiting for this integration, however, the Soviets have been actively trying to shape the U.N.'s agenda. Both Gorbachev and Shevardnadze repeatedly made Third World debt central to their discussion of world economic problems and have been quick to propose such far-reaching solutions as debt moratoria and forgiveness. While these are safe proposals given the

Soviet Union's insignificant role as a creditor, their implementation would nonetheless require the USSR to forgive its loans to clients like Cuba, whose indebtedness to the Soviet Union is estimated to be at least $10 billion.

At the same time, the USSR has taken the lead in advocating greater U.N. attention to environmental issues. Prodded by their own serious domestic problems (such as the fouling of Siberia's Lake Baikal) and by the Chernobyl catastrophe, Moscow has been actively underscoring the importance of what Gorbachev has called "ecological security." For instance, Gorbachev suggested last year that the United Nations establish an emergency ecological assistance center and made proposals for the creation of an international space laboratory devoted exclusively to monitoring the environment. Despite the vagueness of such suggestions, the main point is that the Soviets are now identified as leading proponents of multilateral environmental cooperation.

Clearly, the Soviet Union is carving out a niche as a leader in multilateral thinking, which contrasts sharply with the previous practice of slavishly following the Third World in an attempt to gain its favor. Although the Soviets still have not completely renounced this earlier tendency, and on certain issues continue to vote with the majority, Moscow has begun to identify itself more closely with the concerns of the industrialized world; in fact, it has taken the lead in shaping the U.N. agenda for the 1990s.

Isolated America

Ironically, during much of the period that Moscow was busy discovering the United Nations, Washington was abandoning it. During President Ronald Reagan's two terms, official American support for the U.N. reached an all-time low. Believing—at times correctly—that U.N. goals contradicted its own, the Reagan administration withdrew or threatened to withdraw from a number of U.N. agencies, stepped up the use of its veto in the Security Council, and refused to pay its dues. After more than three decades of legitimately reprimanding the USSR for its lack of cooperation and fiscal responsibility, the United States became the U.N.'s leading foot-dragger and debtor. Instead of paying at least 20 percent of the regular budget and 30 percent of the peacekeeping bills as it had previously, Washington has yet to make good on Reagan's promise to reimburse what now amounts to more than $500 million in back or overdue payments, more than half of the total arrears owed to the U.N.

During most of the Reagan years, Washington seldom endorsed multilateral approaches to security, and only when it supposedly served U.S. interests. It resisted U.N. involvement in regions considered to be part of the American sphere of influence and where it would conflict with U.S. goals. Therefore, the Reagan administration welcomed U.N. mediation of the Soviet embarrassment in Afghanistan, at the end of the Iran-Iraq conflict, and also in Namibia, where the process had been underway since 1978. But the United States systematically resisted greater U.N. involvement in Central America and in the Arab-Israeli conflict, except for peacekeeping operations in the latter. At the same time, Washington practiced aggressive unilateralism, intervening in Grenada and bombing Libya as well as financing insurgents in Afghanistan, Angola, Cambodia, and Nicaragua.

This highly selective approach contrasted sharply with growing Soviet acceptance of U.N. peacekeeping in Third World hot spots. While it was inconceivable that the United States would have asked the U.N.to help extricate U.S. forces from Vietnam, the USSR actively sought U.N. involvement in settling conflicts in Afghanistan and Angola and pressed its Vietnamese client to negotiate an end to the war in Cambodia. Such practices demonstrate the Soviets' willingness to allow the U.N.to play a major role in settling not only peripheral disputes but also those in which they and their allies are directly involved.

The new Soviet approach to the United Nations has posed an unexpected challenge to Washington. Having relinquished its leadership role, the United States must now come to terms with the Soviet Union's far-reaching initiatives. For the Bush administration, which views the U.N. in a more favorable light than did its predecessor, this challenge may actually represent a much-needed opportunity to examine its own approach to multilateralism.

As a first step, Washington should recognize that Moscow's desire for a leading role in an enhanced United Nations is not a threat; rather, it represents an opportunity to work together on difficult global problems. While the USSR is certainly seeking a more prominent role in the organization, evidence suggests that it does not wish to achieve this goal at the expense of the United States. In fact, many Soviet initiatives reflect a belated return to the original logic behind the U.N. Charter, namely great-power solidarity. By all indications, the new Soviet approach seems to be premised on the assumption that the U.N.'s machinery can be revitalized only if both superpowers throw their weight behind it—and Moscow's recent proposals are clearly designed to entice Washington to cooperate.

Some of Moscow's new ideas about peacekeeping, such as those concerning training and finance, bear a striking resemblance to earlier U.S. suggestions. Others, such as a proposal to enlarge the scope of the secretary-general's autonomy, clearly reflect constructive shifts in earlier Soviet positions. Such conciliatory gestures—combined with the positive mediating role the Soviets have already played—should help convince the Bush administration that the Soviets are not embracing peacekeeping as a means to pursue unilateral advantages in the Third World. Rather the USSR seeks to contain and prevent conflicts there, to pare military expenditures, and to prevent a negative spillover of regional conflicts into the East-West relationship.

While recognizing the opportunity for Soviet collaboration on mutually shared problems, the Bush administration at the same time should base its response on a critical evaluation of the recent Soviet proposals as well as on the strengths and weaknesses of the U.N. itself. With the enthusiasm of a recent convert, Moscow has produced an enormous number of proposals for reviving the United Nations. While a good many of these—such as improving the financial mechanism for peacekeeping and creating an elite, reserve peacekeeping force—are worthy of serious consideration, others reflect a certain political naivety by seeming to ignore some of the U.N.'s inherent limitations. The proposal to station peacekeeping teams on the border of any country that requests them, for example, violates the principle of neutrality underlying peacekeeping by placing the "blue helmets" in a position where they might be drawn into fighting. The immediate task for the Bush administration is therefore to sort through the dizzying array of Soviet proposals, identifying those areas in which Soviet-American collaboration under the auspices of the U.N. would be both feasible and desirable.

Members of the Bush administration first have to overcome many of their underlying prejudices about international organizations. As the first U.S. president with direct experience as U.N. ambassador (1971-1973), Bush knows firsthand about the organization's weaknesses. Secretary of State James Baker, from his experience as Treasury secretary during the last administration, is also familiar with the shortcomings of international economic institutions operating under U.N. auspices. To what extent they will be able to put aside these preconceptions and think creatively about the potential strengths of multilateralism in a dramatically altered East-West context remains to be seen.

Thus far, the administration's record, though better than its predecessor's, is mixed. On the one hand, aside form some warm words about the U.N. from U.S. Ambassador Thomas Pickering and a White House dinner invitation to U.N. Secretary-General Javier Pérez de Cuéllar after the Bush inauguration, the administration offered no substantive responses to the Soviets' U.N. initiatives in its first 15 months. Significantly, the president missed a historic occasion in his September 1989 keynote address to the General Assembly either to react to Moscow's proposals or to put forward a vision of his own. And despite U.N. compliance with Washington's request that it trim its bloated bureaucracy, the administration also has been unsuccessful in persuading Congress to release funds for repayment of outstanding debts owed to the organization. In fact, in 1989 the Senate voted to cut $123 million from the president's request for funding repayment of these debts. In addition, the administration has opposed a U.S. return to the United Nations Educational, Cultural and Scientific Organization, from which the Reagan administration withdrew.

On the other hand, as recent developments suggest, the administration seems to have begun to recognize some of the opportunities for superpower cooperation created by the Soviets' new thinking about the U.N. Reversing previous policy, the United States joined the Soviet Union and all other members of the Security Council in November 1989 in authorizing unarmed military observers for Central America. Their initial mission was to monitor the commitment by Central American governments to stop aiding insurgents, while civilians from the U.N. and the Organization of American States (OAS) monitored February's Nicaraguan elections. Violeta Chamorro's election victory over the Sandinistas set the stage for the Security Council's March 1990 endorsement of the second stage of the operation. Some 800 lightly armed U.N. soldiers are to collect the weapons of the *contras* in Honduras or in enclaves inside Nicaragua, while another U.N. and OAS civilian group supervises the eventual repatriation and relocation of the rebels. These first U.N. peacekeepers in the Western Hemisphere are a concrete illustration of how the superpowers can work together in regional security matters.

These decisions were preceded by two other firsts in U.N. history. In November 1989, for the first time in forty-four years, the superpowers cosponsored a General Assembly resolution aimed at reinforcing the work of the organization; then they held a joint press conference to introduce their text. This cooperation was consistent with the Soviet Union's growing openness to multilateralism and was a visible and encouraging indication of the Bush administration's realization of the U.N.'s role in global problem solving.

However, it is still too early to tell whether these latest developments are harbingers of a new era of superpower collaboration at the United Nations. As demonstrated by Washington's December 1989 threat to cut off future funding during the General Assembly dispute over the status of the Palestine Liberation Organization, U.S. domestic politics could still derail the administration from a more multilateral track. Moreover, "Operation Just Cause" in Panama indicated subsequently that Washington still sees unilateral armed intervention as a viable tool of U.S. foreign policy. Indeed, Washington's continued use of financial intimidation at the U.N. and of military force in Panama suggest that it still has not fully recognized the critical contributions international institutions can make as the Cold War ends and gives way to a more multipolar world.

A Multilateral Peace Dividend

The waning of the Cold War provides an unparalleled opportunity for superpower cooperation at the U.N. During the U.N.'s first four decades, the stark differences between the superpowers closely circumscribed the scope of its action in regional conflicts and contributed to the invective that characterized many activities and discussions in the economic, social, and environmental fields. Many U.N. activities amounted to, in former U.N. Undersecretary General Sir Brian Urquhart's words, "tiptoeing around the Cold War." In contrast, the Cold War's thawing allows the superpowers to address common, pressing problems in a less-politicized atmosphere. Diminished tensions raise the possibility that the U.N. may be able to function more along the lines that its founders intended—a point that even some of the U.N.'s most trenchant critics have conceded. As former U.S. ambassador to the United Nations Jeane Kirkpatrick wrote in December 1988, "One peace dividend of the Cold War's end may be a more effective United Nations."

Now is the most propitious time since the end of World War II to expand multilateralism. Both international and domestic support for multilateral activities appears to be running high. The Nobel Committee's decision to award its 1988 Peace Prize to forty years of peacekeeping efforts by some 500,000 U.N. soldiers symbolizes the high regard of the international community. As for U.S. public opinion, recent surveys indicate that by a three-to-one margin Americans would prefer U.N. troops, not U.S. forces, to intervene in Third World conflicts: by a four-to-one margin they believe that all U.N. member states, including the United States, should provide more tax money for U.N. efforts to keep the peace.

But more than just providing an opportunity, the impending end of the Cold War provides a reason for Washington to consider more seriously joining with the Soviets to strengthen the U.N. As the postwar bipolar coalitions break down and the world moves toward greater multipolarity, the United States is likely to see its ability to control events unilaterally eroded substantially. At the same time, this diffusion of power is likely to stimulate the emergence of regional superpowers whose interests may differ from those of Washington. Accordingly, U.S. national interests now may be better served by giving up some prerogatives to act unilaterally in order to secure the commitment of emerging powers to participate in future multilateral approaches to international relations.

In this context, it is crucial for the Bush administration to build immediately upon the momentum from recent successes in the realm of what is usually labeled the "high politics" of international security (such as peacekeeping and peacemaking) and then to proceed to work for similar success in the realm of "low politics" (such as development and the environment). During the Cold War, functionalists argued the contrary—namely, that in order to foster multilateralism it was better to avoid actions in the security area and concentrate on the U.N.'s relatively noncontroversial humanitarian and development activities. Now that bilateral superpower relations are improving and the U.N. is earning praise worldwide as a mechanism for mitigating violence, it is essential to consolidate and expand the peacekeeping regime so that this success can then spill into the economic, social, and environmental agencies.

Whether or not this happens depends in large part on Washington's response to Moscow's "new thinking" at the U.N. Although it is true that the United Nations cannot operate supported solely by an entente between the United States and the USSR, it is equally true that the U.N. cannot realize its potential, or even function effectively, without U.S.-Soviet cooperation. If Washington is to seize the full potential of this opportunity, it will have to overcome its traditional antipathy toward proposals originating from Moscow and begin to treat the Soviet Union as a real partner.

In the security realm, the Bush administration should think more carefully about possible areas in which coordinated superpower activities might help implement peacekeeping operations. For example, as noted earlier, the USSR is now prepared to assist in training peacekeepers. A U.S. offer to join in such activities would make a good deal of sense, particularly since Washington itself has stressed the necessity of improving the quality of U.N. soldiers. Superpower cooperation also would be both feasible and desirable in expanding the provision of logistics and intelligence to U.N. peacekeeping and accompanying humanitarian relief operations. While the superpowers' direct military involvement in such activities must for a time necessarily be curtailed, Soviets and Americans can nonetheless play an important supporting role, which would serve well their respective national interests. For the United States, a more visible supporting role would go a long way toward reversing the international community's perception of

American antagonism toward the United Nations. For the Soviet Union, which has a limited capacity to contribute funds for U.N. activities, such efforts would afford an opportunity for contributions in kind.

The late U.N. Secretary-General Dag Hammarskjold aptly described the invention of peacekeeping as "Chapter six-and-a-half." While described nowhere in the U.N. Charter, it falls between the chapters dealing with the peaceful settlement of disputes and with enforcement. Now, with a decrease in Cold War tensions, Washington could collaborate with Moscow in moving toward "Chapter six-and-three-quarters." Increased superpower cooperation would mean a more effective and dynamic U.N. presence in stopping and helping to resolve Third World disputes. It also could mean that at the turn of the century, the U.N. would be in a position to extend its activities to combating illicit drugs and terrorism, delivering humanitarian assistance in civil wars, and verifying more arms control agreements and domestic elections.

As for the economic realm, there is little hope for cooperation between the superpowers until the United States allows the Soviet Union to become a full-fledged actor in global economic affairs. Bush took a notable first step in this direction at the Malta summit when he agreed to support Soviet observer status in GATT. Another important development at Malta involved steps toward ending trade restrictions against the Soviet Union. Since the 1950s, the Soviet Union has been denied most-favored-nation status by the United States. And since 1974, the Jackson-Vanik amendment has linked Moscow's tariff status to the elimination of its restrictions on emigration. Washington now has offered to eliminate punitively high tariffs (up to 10 times the normal rates) after the Supreme Soviet adopts more liberal emigration laws. The United States should follow up by supporting immediate Soviet observer status in the IMF and the World Bank, leading toward full membership once the Soviets have undertaken necessary economic reforms.

At their joint November 1989 press conference, the U.S. and Soviet government representatives declared: "Perhaps the most important thing about this resolution is not its specific language but what it symbolizes as a new beginning at the United Nations." If a new era is really on its way, it can only arrive with the help of the United States. American interests and the credibility of the United States as a leader in world affairs would be enhanced by joining the Soviet Union in taking the lead at the United Nations.

15

The USSR's New Approach to the U.N.

Andrei Kozyrev

People are talking about a "renaissance" in the USSR's approach to the U.N. Perhaps there really is one. The USSR's reassessment of the role and place of the U.N. and of the possibilities of multifaceted diplomacy on the whole is a logical consequence of the course it has plotted for breaking down within the country the authoritarian system that generated introversion, economic autarchy and political uncivilness, for the formation of a civil society and a law-governed state, and for the enactment of economic reforms. The needs of the country's economic and scientific and technological development are making its participation in world economic ties imperative.

The U.N., whose activities reflect the processes of renewal, has for its part become an active participant in and catalyst to positive changes in the world and is facilitating solutions to the problems that arise.

However, the U.N. is having difficulty becoming a mechanism for exerting real political and economic influence on a new nonconfrontational and de-ideologized basis. Much effort will still be required for trust and mutual understanding to extend beyond the bounds of the accustomed view of the world, which simplistically divided it into two opposing military-political blocs. The certain inertia in the stands of some states, including the developed ones, which are used to living in the context of global confrontation and are experiencing considerable difficulties in adapting to the rapidly changing political environment, is taking its effect.

It is quite natural that under the circumstances, what is of particular interest for the Soviet Union is how its membership in the U.N. can promote the implementation of its domestic and foreign policies in the spirit of new thinking.

The U.N. is a sort of focal point for the concerns, worries and hopes for a more integral world today. It is here that each country has a possibility to define in a generalized form its attitude to its partners in the global community. The U.N. makes it possible to see a rather realistic picture of the world in all the diversity of its problems, contradictions and positive and negative tendencies.

It is fair to assume that the U.N. is and will remain for a long time to come what it was designed to become the moment it was founded—the most representative and universal intergovernment organization, the center coordinating countries' actions, a center as effective as the member states want and are capable of cooperating for the purpose. Clearly, the U.N.'s viability depends above all on how successfully the member states will be able, for all their diverse and at times contradictory interests, to attain the goals which they set themselves through multifaceted cooperation within the U.N. framework.

In this context I would like to call attention to the special importance of the U.N. in the conception of the balance of interests advanced by the USSR within the framework of new political thinking, a concept which is indissolubly linked with recognition of the fundamental significance of each nation's freedom to choose its own socio-political system.

With due account for all the diversity, contradictoriness and at times conflicts of interests represented in the U.N., its main purpose is to explore points of convergence through painstaking and persistent coordinating of different stands and to find ways leading to a consensus on topical problems of world development. It is not fortuitous that it is called the United Nations Organization.

Of course, there can be no balance of interests in the context of a world divided into conflicting, ideologically irreconcilable, military-political blocs engaged in boosting their conventional and nuclear weaponry. The East used to talk of the "aggressive nature" of imperialism, and the West, of communism, leaving to the U.N. the role of an arena where polemical swords clashed.

The anti-Western frenzy and anti-communist rhetoric of the two opposing blocs greatly whipped up extremism in the Third World. Having become victims of global confrontation to a certain extent, some Third World countries learned to adapt to these conditions and even to derive certain short-term benefits for themselves by playing on the readiness of each of the opposing sides to provide considerable political, economic and military aid in exchange for support of its line in the U.N.

However, the reason the U.N. Charter was of great importance was that it provided for levers which were supposed to effectively ensure the compatibility of states. It is not fortuitous that the Charter begins with the words: "to reaffirm faith in fundamental human rights, in the dignity and worth of the human person."

These rights are uniform and indivisible. Through the prism of the U.N. documents it is obvious that, as a rule, assertions of the existence of a "Western," "socialist" or "Eastern" concept of human rights and civil freedoms are nothing but an attempt to justify the existing incongruities with universal international standards, and frequently, simply an outright violation of them.

The struggle around the U.N. throughout its history cannot be explained solely by the rivalry between East and West, socialism and capitalism, the rich North and the poor South, by religious or ethnic conflicts or a combination thereof, although all these factors have definitely been present to one extent or another. I believe that the key contradictions, nevertheless, lie in the struggle between democracy and adherence to universal values, on the one hand, and totalitarianism and nationalism, on the other.

The entire course of the historical process required sweeping changes in the social life of the peoples in accordance with the U.N. ideals. If we cite a Biblical metaphor, we can say that having foreseen the truth of universal values and having expressed it at the moment the U.N. was created in the form of a revelation of sorts, the peoples returned for a time to the idols of nationalism, violence and fear. However, the very weight of their sins is returning them to the true faith, the symbol of which is the United Nations. And we can be proud it was from our country, from Russia, that voices calling for a spiritual perception of this universal need were heard. The following words by Andrei Sakharov on 3 April 1974 sounded as the voice of the prophet crying in the wilderness: "I consider the democratic path of development the only favorable one for any country."[1]

What can without exaggeration be called enthusiasm with which the international community and the U.N. circles responded to the signals for renewal or, as U.N. Secretary General Javier Pérez de Cuéllar put it, for the "rebirth" of the U.N., and of international relations, on the whole, which began coming from Moscow in April 1985 is logical under the circumstances.

In the spirit of the development of the postulates of new political thinking on security in an interdependent world, the U.N. is being assigned for the first time the extremely important function of being the main universal body of security, with its maintenance to be ensured on a reliable level. The U.N.'s regulating role is discerned above all in strengthening the organization as a mechanism of joint search for a balance of the rivaling interests of different states, and in turning the

U.N. into a true center of coordinated actions by states in accordance with the U.N. Charter. "The United Nations embodies, as it were, the interests of different states," Mikhail Gorbachev said in his U.N. address. "It is the only organization which can channel their efforts—bilateral, regional, and comprehensive—in one and the same direction. Fresh opportunities are opening before it in all the spheres within its competence: military-political, economic, scientific and technical, ecological and humanitarian."[2]

All these issues were included in the joint U.N. initiative of the USSR and the East European group of countries regarding a comprehensive approach to international security. One of the main goals of this initiative was the launching of extensive international dialogue in the U.N. about ways and means of ensuring security in the modern age, dialogue that would make it possible to inaugurate practical actions and map out concrete steps to attain it. The task of resolving the security problem in the world in one fell swoop, simultaneously and once and for all, was not posed. The point at issue was elaboration of common approaches, long-term efforts that would make it possible to advance gradually, but purposefully, step by step.

It is necessary to note the depth and inner harmony of the ideals of the U.N. and the principles of new political thinking. To begin with, the Charter and the most important decisions of the U.N. reject artificial attempts to reduce the problems of international peace and security chiefly to any one sphere, be it disarmament or any other. The joint initiative of the East European countries in the U.N. proposed a reasonable decision that envisaged efforts in all areas on a mutually complementary and equal priority basis fully in accordance with the letter and spirit of the Charter.

The decisions of the First Congress of People's Deputies of the USSR were a fresh milestone in the development of the Soviet approach to the U.N. Figuring foremost among the principles of the USSR's foreign political course that were endorsed at the Congress was the principle in which ensuring the nation's security above all by political means as a component part of general and complete security is linked with drawing on the prestige and possibilities of the U.N. That the universal international organization was assigned such an important role in effect symbolized the end of our being distanced from the outside world and evidenced not only a substantial shift in terms of our conceptual perception of the U.N.'s role in the modern world but also our resolve to become a full-fledged member of the international community.

The tabling at the 44th session of the General Assembly of a joint Soviet-American initiative to promote international peace, security and cooperation and the subsequent passing of a resolution to the effect by a consensus was a mighty impetus to the revitalization of the U.N. Even though many formidable barriers are still to be surmounted on this path, one can speak of a search for a new quality of international dialogue in the U.N., a dialogue characterized not by "intoxication from phraseology" but by a businesslike discussion of urgent problems.

I would like to make particular mention in this connection of the fact that the joint initiative in the U.N. was the result of the new quality of relations between the USSR and the United States. Having traveled the long and hard road of bilateral dialogue, the two great powers have reached the point of a "transition from mutual understanding to mutual action." The positive changes in Soviet-American relations have not spelled a lessening of attention to the U.N., as was sometimes the case in the past during "thaws" in relations between our two powers. Quite the contrary, multilateral cooperation and matters pertaining to heightening the U.N.'s effectiveness are becoming an important element of their dialogue. On the whole, discussion of "transnational" problems, i.e. problems of the fight against terrorism and narcotics, and cooperation in the ecology, which are closely linked with the U.N., have become firmly entrenched on the agenda of Soviet-American contacts.

No less important is the fact that over 40 states, which extensively represent the main political forces of the modern world, were the co-authors of the Soviet-American resolution. This eloquently attests to the difficult turnabout of international political practice of late toward the fruitful complementing of bilateral and multilateral efforts.

Thus, hopes for peaceful democratic transformations in the world community are again being linked with the U.N. This in and of itself attests to the fact that forces are operating in states and their mutual relations which are making for the onset of a peaceful period in historical development. The United Nations is called upon to play an important role in this process.

It is not fortuitous that of late many countries are more and more energetically raising the issue of enhancing the effectiveness of the U.N. and its contribution to the efforts to solve world problems.

It is a known fact that the Soviet Union has also advanced a series of specific proposals to strengthen the U.N., improve the performance of its Security Council and other major bodies, support the peace efforts of the U.N. Secretary General, and use the U.N. Armed Forces and its observers for settling regional conflicts and preventing the emergence of new hotbeds of tensions in the world. It can be stated with satisfaction that serious work has begun in all these areas in the U.N.; they are being studied in depth and debates on them are unfolding.

The practical involvement of the U.N. in strengthening the positive processes in the world has enhanced dramatically. The U.N. has begun paying serious attention precisely to problems which require the direct involvement of virtually all states and affect their interests. Obviously, advancement to a more secure world, one which accords with the U.N. ideals, cannot be a one-way street: it requires boldness and a re-examination of many stands on the part of our counterparts as well.

I am speaking, above all, of the Western countries that are the most developed economically and closest to the category of law-governed states. Hence their potential capacity for cooperation in the U.N. Its realization, however, depends on the readiness of other countries to follow the U.N. principles in practice. It is for this reason that it is so important to preserve and build on the impetuses of new thinking. Of course, it is impossible here to understate the complexity and at times the painfulness of the adaptation of countries of the West, as well as other groups of countries, to the new conditions. Whereas the European Community and Canada are agreeing more readily to cooperation and a search for compromises, the United States is having difficulty in overcoming both the skepticism it has amassed with regard to the U.N. and the habit of viewing the small countries of the Third World with haughtiness.

However, if the Western states are to learn to respect the legitimate interests of the less-developed countries, the latter for their part will have to overcome their "inferiority syndrome" with regard to the West, which is developing either into heightened aggressiveness and suspicion or into ingratiation or a loss of their own identity. Only through cooperation, not rivalry with the most industrialized countries, and through a repudiation of violence and terrorism, can the Third World countries surmount their underdevelopment. And many of them will be exploring such paths more persistently in the spirit of new thinking, which is evidenced by the decisions taken by the countries of the Non-Aligned Movement at their conference in Belgrade in 1989.

However, one cannot underestimate the danger of extremism and the great amount of "inflammable matter" in the Third World. All this is directly linked with the backwardness of many societies, the existence of long-standing ethnic and other conflicts, the inclination to coercive methods of settling them, and the lack or weakness of democratic traditions. We think that the U.N.'s authority will be all the greater if it gives more cogently a principled assessment to such situations and offers realistic and democratic solutions, above all in the interests of free self-determination of the peoples.

The peaceful revolution unfolding in the USSR, a revolution consonant with the U.N. ideals and enthusiastically received by the U.N. member countries, is of foremost importance for strengthening the positive tendencies and enhancing the U.N.'s role. The notions of *glasnost* and *perestroika* have become firmly entrenched in U.N. parlance. If these processes come to a standstill and mutate solely into a selection of slogans without legal safeguards, international cooperation could find itself back at the level of fruitless rhetoric. Perestroika not only provides us a moral and psychological right to and unprecedented possibilities for full-fledged participation in U.N. activities, but also prompts other states to review their stands in a positive vein.

What, then, are the guidelines and possibilities for practical utilization of the U.N.? Above all, the further enhancement of its peacemaking potential. The withdrawal of Soviet troops from Afghanistan was a sort of point of departure for the U.N.'s renewal, a major foreign policy step of perestroika which has made it possible to revitalize faith in the U.N. principles. The U.N. had been demanding this measure for many years. It promoted the attainment of the Geneva accords on Afghanistan, and now it is unanimously urging that they be observed by all sides, and that a broad-based government be formed; it itself is playing a useful role in the settlement of the Afghan problem.

The shift in the efforts to resolve the Afghan problem was the detonator of a sort of peaceful chain reaction of the settlement of other conflict situations with the participation of the U.N. The liberation of Namibia, the negotiations between Iran and Iraq, and the search for a settlement in the Middle East are based on Security Council decisions. U.N. observers are playing a useful role in Angola. The plans of the Central American states for a settlement in their part of the world provide for utilization of possibilities including those of the U.N. personnel. The presence of the U.N. "blue helmets" with the aim of keeping peace in these and several other regions symbolizes the transition from a duel of cannon to a search for national reconciliation and diplomatic solutions.

It is important to underscore the fact that as the experience of cooperation in the Security Council shows, the major powers, above all the permanent members of the Council, are capable on the whole of striking a balance of interests with regard to regional conflicts. The status of permanent member of the Security Council makes this type of action obligatory. At the same time an opportunity is being created for the Soviet Union to preserve and strengthen its status and influence as a great power in the world community through political means at less expense. The point at issue is not concessions to someone or compromises in matters of principle. Quite the contrary, effective cooperation in the U.N. can be based only on firm commitment to the principles enshrined in the Charter and on repudiation of double standards in applying them.

Alongside the enhancement of the U.N.'s peacemaking functions, the curve of this organization's expenses on peacekeeping operations is crawling upward. The USSR has also steered a course to liquidate its debt on the special account of the U.N.'s past peacekeeping operations, and for strict fulfillment of its obligations to finance current operations of this type.

By and large, the USSR's line proceeds from the belief that one has to pay for peace as, for that matter, all programs of constructive international cooperation. However, these expenses, which are reckoned in several tens of millions of dollars, cannot compare to the enormous political, moral and material, for that matter, expenses incurred by the course for autarchic development and unilateral involvement in regional conflicts.

In connection with the problem of settling conflicts I would like to call attention to still another important element. The freedom of nations to choose their own model of socio-political development presupposes non-interference and non-use of force in relations between states. The U.N. has repeatedly underscored the imperative nature of universal compliance with this norm, without exception. Here however, the point at issue is not an I-don't-care attitude, indifference of the world community to what is taking place within a state. The principle of freedom of choice blends organically in the U.N. with the entire set of democratic ideals which it upholds.

This is especially important today, when the category "within the country" is often closely linked with the category "outside." It is becoming quite obvious that internal rivalry in a number of countries spreads the process of their destabilization to vast areas. And at times it is far easier to find solutions to external aspects of a settlement than to elaborate its internal terms.

Here it is important to find the only correct path which, on the one hand, will help us avoid the Scylla of interference in domestic affairs and, on the other, the Charybdis of complete indifference and permissiveness. Evidently, the approach to these matters lies in unselective compliance with the U.N. Charter and the obtaining obligations, many of which were impeded and did not function during the Cold War period. Richard Gardner, a professor of law and international organization at Columbia University, writes very convincingly about this. For a long time, when states could not get along at all, they placed the emphasis, in their reading of the U.N. Charter, on the principle of "non-interference." Today, however, the situation has changed.

Nowadays it is commonly acknowledged that compliance with the main humanitarian norms is just as fundamental to international law and order as observance of the non-interference principle. In other words, unselective interpretation of the Charter presupposes a formula for settling conflicts which, if the principle of non-interference stands in its numerator, it has in the denominator the principle of respect for and ensuring of the basic human rights and freedoms.

This formula is already proving its viability. In this connection, such a new area of U.N. activity as monitoring honest elections in Namibia, Nicaragua and, over the long term, in Cambodia and Afghanistan is a sign of the times. Indeed, peoples' freedom to choose their destiny is above all free elections of their bodies of power by them.

The new attitude to human rights that is taking shape is patently evident on the example of the proceedings of the Third Committee of the U.N. General Assembly (social, humanitarian and cultural issues), in which a transition from exchange of mutual reproaches and accusations to an equitable, businesslike and pointed discussion of problems took place over a relatively short period of time. For all the specifics of countries and regions, elimination of these problems, like the polemics around them, is possible precisely through compliance with universal norms.

Of course, much still has to be done if a pointed dialogue on a search for and elaboration of fresh approaches and norms is to begin to make solid headway in practical terms. This evidently involves difficulties linked not only with the inevitable growing pains, but also with due account for the painful perception of this problem by a number of countries, specifically, in the Third World. At the same time it is unquestionable that this is a big and promising area where the international community can bend efforts.

In the disarmament sphere it is important that the U.N. is rendering moral and political support to bilateral Soviet-American talks and is declaring for the involvement of all the nuclear powers in these efforts. It is no less important that the U.N. become more energetically involved in measures to prevent the spread of nuclear and chemical weapons and missiles and promote openness in the military sphere.

This entails difficulties, too. In particular, the long-standing habit of some diplomats to speak with pleasure of the weapons which others have but of resisting in every way even mentioning anything that applies to their own country is having its effect. However, positive shifts are in evidence. For example, a group of government experts has been formed at the U.N. to prepare research on the problems of openness in the sphere of international weapons sales and deliveries.

The complexities of this new endeavor are already bespoken by the fact that the United States, alluding to the difficulties in financing research (although with regard to the volumes of weapons trade, the amount which is at issue is simply ridiculous), did not support the U.N.

General Assembly resolution to the effect in 1988, and only a year later did it vote in favor. Nor was it enthusiastically received by a number of Third World countries, which alleged that the specifics of their regions do not make it possible to set about a realistic restriction on arms import, although it would evidently be worthwhile to explore paths to reasonable minimal sufficiency in this sphere, especially with due account for economic and social problems.

Lastly, we have room for improvement in developing our stand on this issue, above all in ensuring openness of our own arms exports to a level at least comparable to that of the United States. On the whole, however, control of the sale of weapons does not brook delay; we have to tackle it in earnest and through common efforts.

The U.N.'s potential is also considerable in coordinating the principles and priority areas of global cooperation in environmental protection. The 1992 U.N. conference on the environment and development is of particular importance in this sense. It is important above all to utilize in full the pertinent U.N. agreements and programs on the environment. The fact that the USSR does not take part in many of them is still another legacy of the epoch of stagnation.

The USSR has steered a course for broadening its participation in international economic organizations and for phased joining of GATT, IMF, IBRD, and FAO. Establishment of coordination of the economic policy of the USSR with the development of the world economy on a market basis and upgrading of the economic levers for regulating it are becoming a vital issue.

As far as the U.N. is concerned, it is important for it to find its role in the economic sphere, proceeding from the concept of stable and sustained development for all. The struggle of the poor to divide up the property of the rich and, conversely, the fight of the rich against the poor serves no one's interests. Results of the April special session of the U.N. General Assembly on economic issues provided a good starting point for new economic thinking.

Of particular importance is the sphere of U.N. activity which provides for monitoring of efforts to protect human rights. The Soviet Union intends to broaden its participation in the control mechanism for human rights at the U.N. and within the framework of the European process, and it has proposed making the jurisdiction of the International Court regarding interpretation and application of the human rights agreements binding upon all states. For us, it is of principal importance to fully bring domestic legislation and practice in the USSR in line with international commitments in this sphere. I believe that the USSR Constitution could enshrine a general provision regarding the primacy of international law and the direct validity of its norms within the country, as is the case in a number of other countries, including the United States. At the same time, the United States is frequently criticized, with due cause, for its non-involvement in international human rights covenants.

Use of a U.N. expert commission and international experience in the economic and social spheres, with due account for our specifics, of course, could in many instances save people from mistakes and improvization and help resolve, by civilized methods, complex social problems, including those of young people, women, the disabled and the aged.

It is obvious in this connection that truly constructive participation in international organizations and drawing benefit from them are impossible if we do not break down the stereotypes of secrecy, if we do not reach a level, comparable with the industrialized countries, of providing information—military-political, scientific and technological, ecological, economic—to these organizations, and do not ensure the spread within the country of information about their work and the standards and recommendations they elaborate.

Lastly, more energetic involvement in U.N.-sponsored events and programs on the part of all the Soviet constituent republics with due account for their potential, cultural traditions and experience appears promising. It is essential to note that the republics have been invariably represented in the leadership of Soviet delegations to the U.N. and often have direct ties with regional and other international organizations. Evidently, all this deserves to be further developed. The main thing, however, is to find optimal forms of self-determination and integration by legal democratic methods, since coercive solutions, as the Stalinist period showed, place everyone who does resort to them outside the circle of civilized states and peoples.

The integrity of the world is ever more persistently raising the issue of a mechanism of cooperation among states and their voluntary subordination to universally recognized norms of civilized behavior. The international consensus taking shape on the need to follow the U.N. ideals is indicating the only reasonable alternative of world development. All this is opening up unprecedented vistas for the U.N. If this challenge of the times is to be met worthily, it is necessary to continue to deepen the overhaul that has begun in the U.N. and other international organizations. It is important that the activity of the U.N. system be more de-ideologized and coordinated, and focus on practical matters.

It is also obvious that the path from overcoming the paralysis into which the Cold War plunged the U.N. to what it was originally planned to be will be more complicated than was imagined and dreamed; it cannot be covered overnight. However, this path, and the stages comprising it, can and should be traversed, by combining enthusiasm and persistence with realism and imagination, and commitment to the U.N.'s democratic ideals with practical work to embody them in international relations.

Notes

1. *Znamya*, No. 2, 1990, p. 18.
2. *Pravda*, 8 December 1988.

PART FIVE

Economic Rivalry and Cooperation

Economic Rivalry and Geopolitics

Few areas of the superpower struggle during the Cold War have had such an ambivalent, yet potentially important role, as the economic relationship. United States trade policy toward the Soviet Union since World War II has tended to reflect in a more extreme manner the general trend of Soviet-American relations. When political relations were good and bilateral tensions low, the United States took a more liberal stance on economic and trade relations. When political relations were poor and bilateral tensions high, American policy effectively severed economic relations. The U.S. position on trade with the Soviet Union has usually been that there cannot be trade without prior political accommodation. The Soviet Union, on the other hand, has generally argued that trade should precede political accommodation and that economic relations would actually facilitate political and military accommodation.

The major factor restraining normal trade between the two countries has been national security concerns. The American perspective has been that an unrestrained flow of goods and services between the two countries would affect the military balance to the detriment of the United States.

Now that Soviet-American relations have entered a new, less confrontational phase, steps are being taken to improve the economic relationship. The severe economic problems in the Soviet Union have forced that country to turn to the West for trade and economic assistance, and because of the reduced military threat, the United States is more amenable to trade relations.

In their assessment of the United States' trade policy toward the Soviet Union, Adlai Stevenson and Alton Frye argue that policies formulated to deal with "an expansionist imperial state" are not appropriate for a nation being reshaped by pere-

213

stroika and *glasnost. During the Cold War the United States might have been justified in not helping an "enemy" state integrate itself into the world's capital and trading system. However, they maintain it is a different matter with regard to the economic and political system Mikhail Gorbachev envisages. A Soviet economy that has undergone the transformation contemplated by the Soviet leadership should be allowed full participation in the international economic system. For one reason, a Soviet Union engaged in the global economy would be less prone to backslide in its efforts to change its economic and political systems. This does not mean that the United States should pay for perestroika, even though it welcomes the move to the market economy in the Soviet Union, but it does mean that normalized trade relations should be encouraged.*

Not surprisingly, the authors recommend a shift in U.S. trade policy toward the USSR. First and foremost, the Jackson-Vanik Amendment to the 1977 Trade Act (which linked emigration from Communist countries to the normalization of trade relations) should be repealed. The two nations should have the opportunity to explore mutually advantageous trade relations and let the citizens of each country strike bargains that they consider profitable.

To facilitate trade relations the United States should support the USSR's efforts to join international trade and monetary systems. Some form of Soviet association with GATT (General Agreement on Tariffs and Trade) should be supported. Membership in the IMF (International Monetary Fund) is also to be encouraged, because few measures would contribute more to the predictability of transactions with the Soviet Union than its shift to a currency readily traded on world markets. It is unlikely that the Soviets will see a "fully" convertible ruble by the end of the century, but this is a worthwhile goal.

According to Valeri Karavayev, in "The Soviet Union is Opening Itself to the World," the socialist countries must revamp their social and economic systems if they are not to be pushed to the sidelines of world technological and economic progress. Extensive international cooperation and integration into the world economy is required to avoid becoming "a back-

yard of the world economy in the twenty-first century." No progress can be made while the old command economy exists, the author states, because the system is inherently incompatible with the capitalist mixed economies upon which the world economic system is based. Rapid integration into the world economy is a "locomotive" that can shunt the Soviet economy onto a market track. This is indispensable, because "driving forces" in the existing Soviet economy are simply inadequate for the transition to a market economy. This, he says, can only be achieved with external support and   cooperation.

The main channel for integration of the socialist countries into the world ·economy is to develop extensive economic ties with the West. The Soviet Union needs to attract not only material and financial resources, but also Western experience in management and marketing. To achieve these goals means that the Soviet Union will have to "open" its economy to the world. However, Karavayev realizes that such a huge economy will not be able to make this transition completely or all at once. It will have to be accomplished gradually, by establishing an "open sector" in the Soviet economic system encompassing only those regions and industries that are most prepared for economic integration.

The author admits that some progress has been made in foreign economic perestroika, for example the creation of joint ventures and free economic zones. However, actual progress in improving foreign trade is minimal, because the country has not yet made the structural changes that are necessary. Of the joint ventures registered to date, only about a quarter are actually operating. The development of free economic zones is being hindered by bureaucratic hurdles and the "centralist tendencies" of governmental departments. Furthermore, Soviet foreign debt is mounting.

The author stresses that integration into the world economy is not possible without a convertible ruble. The most promising approach, suggested by American economists, is to introduce a gold standard for the ruble. This would give the ruble direct access to the international money market as a full-fledged currency.

*The author concludes with the admonition: "The world is
not going to adapt to our economy; it is for our economy to
become a structural component of it, to find a place in the
world division of labor at the threshold of the twenty-first
century."*

16

Trading with the Communists

Adlai E. Stevenson and Alton Frye

In Moscow bold minds are asking where Marxism-Leninism went
wrong. Were its premises flawed? Was the execution inept? Communist governments are experimenting with the answers. Americans would
do well to pose similar questions about U.S. economic policy toward
these nations. Are the premises correct? Do changes in their policies
require new assumptions and changes in our policy?

The candor of Soviet self-criticism demands a comparable dose of
introspection on our part. We have never expected mea culpas from the
Soviets, and we have always prided ourselves on a capacity for self-
correction. Yet the United States has been slow to acknowledge evident
shortcomings in its economic policy toward the Soviet Union and other
communist countries.

Policies framed to deal with an expansionist imperial state driven
by authoritarian ideology and marked by the sacrifice of its citizens'
well-being to the appetites of its military establishment are not appropriate for a state being reshaped in the image projected by the archi-
tects of *perestroika* and *glasnost*. As evidence mounts that the reforms
of Mikhail Gorbachev are real, the West is challenged to rethink its
approach to the Soviet Union. If the international aggrandizement of
Stalin and Brezhnev gives way to genuine restraint abroad and gradual
democratization at home, it would ill serve the interests of the United
States to play the implacable antagonist, blinded by preconceptions
and paralyzed by inertia and timidity. The United States would
begrudge the revolutionary changes in Soviet behavior which it had
long demanded.

Even without such dramatic departures by Moscow, there is ample
reason to reexamine Washington's policy. The United States could

scarcely have blundered more often if it had followed a slapstick script. Over the past fifteen years American policy has continually undercut its political objectives, harmed its economic interests and eroded its leadership in the Western alliance.

This pattern is partly attributable to the difficulties of dealing rationally with a state perceived as a powerful, atheistic enemy seeking world domination. Suspicious of Moscow's motives, Washington has not been inclined to give the Soviets the benefit of any doubt on important questions. U.S. laws still reflect an assumption that the Soviet Union reigns over a monolithic bloc of communist countries in a world divided by ideology and geography into two hostile camps. A fear of the worst—not always unrealistic—has blinded the United States to changes already made and failures self-inflicted.

The Jackson-Vanik Amendment to the 1974 Trade Act is the prototype of self-defeating policies. America's reverence for human rights led Congress to impose a link between free emigration from communist countries and the normalization of trade with them. Passed after protracted but unsuccessful bargaining between the late Senator Henry Jackson and Secretary of State Henry Kissinger, this measure effectively denied Moscow nondiscriminatory access to U.S. markets through the most-favored-nation status and access to credit facilities that a 1972 trade agreement pledged President Richard Nixon to seek. The law conditioned MFN, as well as government loans and guarantees for communist countries, on free emigration, subject to one-year waivers approved by Congress after the president reported a country's "assurances" of such emigration.

Jackson-Vanik was conceptually flawed, and it proved counterproductive in operation....

Sour experience makes a powerful case for change. That change should begin with repeal of the Jackson-Vanik Amendment. It has not only poisoned the atmosphere for economic relations with the Soviet Union and other communist countries but it has blocked a reasoned debate about those relations. Despite the fledgling progress in Soviet-American relations during the late 1980s, Jackson-Vanik still hovers like a predator, devouring economic possibilities before they can emerge from the nest....

Many factors impinge on U.S. relations with each of the communist countries. Congress and the president need to weigh them all in order to reach a rounded judgment of the national interest. The singular preoccupation of the Jackson-Vanik standard prevents them from doing so. Repealing it would help to clear away the incoherencies obstructing trade and finance. It would enable the United States to shape a fresh assessment of East-West relations and to pursue its security interests with useful political flexibility. It would signal American recognition of meaningful change in the Soviet Union's behavior, both within and outside its boundaries. It would also comport with the nascent pluralism among communist nations now treated as a Soviet bloc....

The Reagan administration began a gradual movement toward more normal economic relations with the Soviet Union. Led by the late secretary of commerce, Malcolm Baldrige, the U.S.-Soviet Joint Commercial Commission in 1985 resumed sessions that had been suspended indefinitely in 1978. Various trade promotion activities have ensued, with hundreds of American businessmen visiting Moscow. Reagan lifted a ban on sales of some oil and gas equipment to the Soviets, a sanction tightened at the time of the Afghanistan invasion. He also allowed imports of Soviet nickel and furs to resume. Before leaving office Secretary Shultz recommended that COCOM end the "no exception" ban on high-technology exports after the Soviets withdrew from Afghanistan. The European allies support this return to a case-by-case review of such sales. U.S. reticence on this point could revive European fears of more "light switch" diplomacy—and Soviet suspicions that concessions only invite demands for more concessions. The ban should be lifted.

Increased commerce with the Soviet Union has been slow, but some developments are potentially significant. Several major firms have formed an American Trade Consortium and negotiated arrangements to permit repatriation of profits from operations in the Soviet Union, perhaps a model arrangement that will permit more income and capital flows to and from joint venture there. In December 1988 the Soviets further adjusted their rules for joint ventures to permit foreign participants to hold equity majorities and to delay taxation until several years after initial profits are realized. They also increased the number of Soviet organizations authorized to deal directly with foreign partners and suppliers. These attempts to accelerate the pace of the Soviet economy's engagement with foreign investors and markets reveal an alertness to the weaknesses of Moscow's first steps in this direction. American firms were involved in only about 15 of some 200 joint ventures.

These Soviet reforms follow similar measures in China and Hungary. Perhaps the largest economic opportunities for the near future are in Eastern Europe, where capitalist, free market traditions are rooted. Natural trading partners are divided by artificial political demarcations, and the human and economic infrastructures run deeper than in the Soviet Union and China. These different economic potentials, reflecting the various political and economic contexts of the several countries, invite an East-West trade policy that itself is capable of differentiating. The present U.S. policy takes too little account of the liberalizing tendencies within communist countries and of the decentralizing tendencies within the communist "bloc."

This policy flaw bears on export controls. The United States pays a high price for the quaint notion that trade is a privilege. By some estimates export controls have cost U.S. firms between $7 billion and $9 billion in exports and 180,000 jobs annually. A National Academy of Sciences survey of almost 200 firms found that over half claimed to have lost sales because of these controls. Such controls also hurt U.S. sales with non-communist countries; 26 percent of the companies surveyed said they had lost deals with free world customers because of export controls, and over a third of the companies reported such customers preferred to shift to other suppliers outside the United States. In 1985 the control process handled proposals approaching $80 billion in value. This gives an idea of how far it ranges beyond direct trade with the Soviets.[1]

In a wide-ranging review of COCOM's record, the National Academy of Sciences studies have urged a new balance between national security export controls and commercial considerations. They called into question the feasibility of enforcing the extensive COCOM list of controlled items and pressed for stronger enforcement of more limited restraints—"higher fences around fewer items." These studies and consultations within COCOM have helped build a consensus to shrink the export control list. In addition, the verdict emerged that, however compressed the list, the executive branch had to pick up its own tempo to reach timely decisions on export applications. With that goal in mind, the 100th Congress trimmed the Department of Defense's authority to delay the process, limiting DOD export license evaluations to "national security" as distinct from "foreign policy" considerations. It remains questionable whether such exhortations will be more effective than those in the past.

In the end, there must be some recognition that technology is inherently difficult to control. It travels on paper and in the human mind, as well as in tangible products. It is usually available from many sources. Security requires control of exports with clear military applications to adversaries. But the West's technology supremacy depends upon its economic and intellectual environment, resources for the development of inventions and their rapid application to commercial and military uses. The United States must stay ahead through a nurtured process of basic research and technological innovation.

It is essential to state the issues confronting U.S. policy with some precision. Posing the question "Should we help Gorbachev?" tends to divert discussion into narrow byways. If all the change that is transpiring in the Soviet Union rests on a single individual, if it has no roots beyond Gorbachev's alluring rhetoric, then there is little ground for optimism about its durability—or his. If the innovations are tentative and perishable, one would not be wise to argue for shifting American policy onto sandy terrain.

The dawning consensus, however, is that the changes within the Soviet Union are erupting from sources too deep to permit their suppression even if Gorbachev's tenure turns out to be relatively brief. He is a creature of economic and strategic necessities already recognized in China and other communist countries. What is remarkable is that this historical inevitability has been so slow in coming—and that it has not yet appeared in many communist countries....

Some reform initiatives may prove abortive, but the United States can shape policy on the probability that the broad tides of change will continue to flow. That expectation rests not on naivety, but on the calculation that attempts to revert to Stalinism would guarantee economic failure and political decline—and that even the old guards in Moscow and Prague can perceive these hazards. It rests on some conviction that what we have been saying about the superiority of our self-governing, capitalist systems in the West is inescapably true.

For policy purposes, it is not necessary to predict an outcome with certainty in order to prefer it. Surely, from the Western standpoint, a Soviet system that must become more benign in order to become more powerful is preferable to one that joins excessive military capability with the malign impulses of totalitarianism in decline.

But to welcome perestroika is not to advocate paying for it. In truth, there is little likelihood of excessive American investment in the still-risky Soviet economy. The U.S. business community has long since discounted forecasts of easy or early profits in the Soviet market. There is impatience with the sluggish bargaining required to close deals with Soviet bureaucrats and enterprises. Permitting U.S. investment in the Soviet economy is not payment for perestroika. It merely means repealing provisions that hamper commerce and penalize American companies.

As far as Soviet exports to the United States are concerned, the range of candidates remains limited. Over 90 percent of Soviet hard currency exports consist of oil, gas, gold and arms, not manufactures that would displace major domestic sales by U.S. firms. It is conceivable that buried deep in Soviet archives and laboratories are ingenious developments waiting to be commercialized, but so far the examples are few, e.g., sales of electromagnetic casting technology and an ion-gun hardening system for industrial cutting tools.

Understandably Moscow hopes that the joint ventures it now encourages will concentrate on exports to generate hard currency revenues, but the projected scale of such enterprises remains relatively modest. The volume of trade with communist countries may be small, but these are nations with which the United States can run a needed trade surplus.

The apprehension that the United States might be lured into paying for perestroika seems to focus on official credit arrangements, perhaps reflecting concern about methods once employed to pursue détente. If Moscow were to become eligible for Export-Import Bank financing, as agreed in 1972, today it would face stiff competition for the bank's limited resources. There is no disposition in either Congress or the executive branch to allow Export-Import Bank guarantees to become surrogate for foreign aid, for example, underwriting development in Soviet Siberia. In the midst of U.S. budget stringencies and chronic trade imbalances the bank is obliged more than ever to husband its authority and to devote its efforts to improving American export performance.

We do not suggest lending money to finance perestroika or denying credits to achieve some political purpose. It is unlikely that Soviet policies will be influenced materially by proffering or withholding cash. The clearest justification for official export assistance is the competitive imperative. If assistance is necessary to put U.S. exporters on an equal footing, then the Export-Import Bank should be in position to help. If there is foreign competition that requires official financial participation in U.S. ventures, the solution is not to punish American exporters but to negotiate international terms that prohibit subsidies. Such negotiations are best pursued with leverage, not with a unilaterally disarmed Export-Import Bank.

To preclude Export-Import Bank participation in business with communist countries discourages exporters, investors and private lenders from exploring opportunities. In any case, the bank's primary function is not to do the whole job but to lubricate the larger process. To the extent that there develops a need for selective use of Export-Import Bank assistance in trade, the option should be open. Otherwise American traders and financiers carry a handicap that their counterparts in other Western countries do not.

There appears to be a good understanding at the highest levels in Moscow that one way to energize Soviet domestic enterprises is to subject them, albeit gradually, to the stresses of international competition.

The emphasis on opening the Soviet Union to foreign investment and on working toward convertibility of the ruble reflects this insight. More than nostalgia lies in the recollection that Lenin had a convertible currency. This opening is a farsighted appeal for a return to pragmatism, coupled with a straightforward acknowledgment that the transition from the current 6,000 variations ("currency coefficients") to a unitary ruble exchange rate will take a decade or more.

For the West the prospect of convertible currencies and an end to the Council for Mutual Economic Assistance poses interesting policy questions. Few measures would contribute more to the predictability of transactions with communist countries than the shift to currencies readily traded on world markets. Such a development could testify to the growing strength and independence of communist economies. It could help to stabilize East-West economic relations.

Yet Soviet reformers who foresee a "fully" convertible ruble by the end of the century are optimistic. The painful changes entailed in moving to convertibility are meeting both bureaucratic and grass-roots resistance. Retail price reforms are already behind schedule and worries about inflation are mounting. Western imports needed for restructuring will be costly, while Soviet export potential (barring an oil price increase) appears rather low. Without a surge in hard currency earnings, Moscow's borrowing capacity will be limited, perhaps to another $20 billion or so. This calculus puts full convertibility of the ruble far into the future, although there may be intermediate stages centered on special economic zones, hard currency auctions and partial convertibility.

But do we want communist economies to be integrated into the world capital and trading system? Certainly not the Soviet economy we have learned to distrust. The economy Gorbachev envisages, however, would be a different matter. A Soviet economy that had undergone the transformations now contemplated could become a constructive participant in the international economic system arduously constructed by the free market countries.

With commitments to change being advertised by Moscow and other communist regimes, the United States and its allies cannot avoid a considered judgment about how to respond to these innovations as they unfold. The speed of reform will vary from one country to another, but the direction seems clear. Hungary is leaning West, and Czechoslovakia ... could restructure sooner than the Soviet Union, if [it] were so disposed. The prudent case-by-case engagement of these nations with the Western economy is a looming opportunity. It poses a particular challenge for the European Economic Community. It might as well involve a reformed Hungary as a remote Turkey.

The rejection of a Soviet request for observer status at the 1986 GATT meetings in Punta del Este conveyed reasonable doubts about whether a state-run economy could mesh with the market-oriented universe to which that organization is dedicated. But a number of American analysts incline more positively toward some form of Soviet association with GATT, on the theory that it could provide a window on Soviet economic activity and enable outsiders to encourage genuine price reform and the decentralization of markets.

Looking ahead, there has been speculation regarding future Soviet involvement in the International Monetary Fund. Leaders in Moscow have pointed out that an IMF relationship could expedite the country's graduation to currency convertibility. They note that a place in IMF would not give a veto to the Soviet Union and that, given the IMF structure, Moscow would hardly have enough leverage to disrupt its functions. Hungary and Poland are already members and the prospect of an eventual Soviet connection to IMF warrants examination.

As we evaluate these issues, it is reasonable to argue that a Soviet Union more engaged in the global economy would be less prone to backsliding in its economic and political evolution. In the phrase of one close observer, Brezhnev wanted foreign investment to avoid reform. Gorbachev wants it to foster reform.

Another development demands consideration by U.S. policymakers. While the Soviet or communist "bloc" is fragmenting, other nations, bound by a commitment to capitalism and by geographical proximity, are forming economic blocs in Western Europe, the Persian Gulf and North America. Where will the colossi of the communist world fit in this emerging, regional shape of things? It is too glib to say that they do not fit. In a new age of regional cooperation the free countries of the Pacific will be dealing with two communist mammoths, Russia and China, both hungry for trade and capital.

Does the communist countries' pursuit of foreign investment threaten U.S. interests? One can imagine scenarios in which it might do so. Gullible Western investors, shown the green light by changes in public policy, might divert so many resources to Soviet projects and joint ventures that they deprive other needy nations of capital. That redirection of capital flows could drive up the cost of funds to everyone, including the United States. Reverse leverage could come into play, with the American government and its allies under pressure to do nothing that might prompt the Soviets to default. These concerns are valid, but not conclusive. Western banks' painful over-exposure in Latin America and Eastern Europe, especially Poland, has bred a healthy caution about concentrating too many eggs in the Soviet basket. Most lenders have relearned the old banker's adage that "if a man owes you a hundred dollars, he's got a problem; if he owes you a million dollars, you've got a problem."

Present evidence makes worst-case anticipations implausible. The Soviets ... historically have been prudent, cautious, even reluctant borrowers. Sovereign borrowers, no less than others, cannot afford to antagonize the big players in Western capital markets. Besides, the West always has its assets to sequester, as Iran discovered. The risks are not exorbitant.

An interagency study done late in the Reagan administration found that rumors of massive Soviet borrowing in the mid-1980s were exaggerated. Dependable data are difficult to come by, but it appears that, adjusting for exchange rate shifts, total hard currency debt in the Soviet bloc grew by only about 14 percent from 1981 to 1986, and in fact declined if measured in constant dollars. Net Soviet debt to lenders reporting to the Bank for International Settlements, i.e., gross debt minus deposits in BIS banks, was actually less in 1986 than at the start of the decade. The study concluded that the Soviet capacity to service its debt is quite adequate.

To be sure Moscow has begun to dabble with bond issues underwritten in the West, and during 1988 Western lenders extended lines of credit amounting to several billion dollars, most of which are thought to be tied to purchases of consumer goods and equipment. The U.S. government believes that the majority of these credits are officially guaranteed, export-related borrowings permissible under OECD guidelines. This contrasts with the pattern of Soviet loans earlier in the 1980s, which appeared to be generally untied. Two-way trade with nonsocialist countries slackened somewhat, but Wharton Associates projects volume reaching $95 billion in the early 1990s. In the estimate of Soviet economist Abel Aganbegyan, removal of trade barriers could bring bilateral U.S.-Soviet trade levels up to a range of $10 billion to $20 billion within five to seven years.

Some analysts foresee Soviet hard currency debt rising from less than $30 billion in 1985 to over $50 billion in the near future.[2] The Soviets themselves are quite chary about this trend, and Gorbachev's advisers seem determined to hold debt service below 25 percent of export earnings. They look instead to joint venture to attract perhaps $20 billion in the near future, noting that China already has foreign investment commitments of that magnitude.

All things considered, alarm over Soviet penetration of Western capital markets is premature. From a policy standpoint the important objective in the near term is to improve the means of monitoring Moscow's activities in those markets. That task is part of the more general need to develop adequate information about capital flows—now so rapid and dominant an element in the global economy—as a building block for intelligent policy and for government interventions, when necessary to maintain stability. The United States will have more clout in extracting that information from the Soviets if it is a player, rather than a bystander, in Gorbachev's enterprise.

The shift in policy emphasis recommended here does not prejudge whether American firms will discover enticing and large-scale opportunities in the Soviet Union. Our contention is simply that the government should not strangle their search for such opportunities by policies that preempt consideration of mutually acceptable economic possibilities. The message is: let businessmen strike bargains they deem profitable—and keep enough steerage over U.S. policy to hold a safe and steady course in our overall relationship with communist states.

It is often the essence of political decision-making that governments must choose before there is a confident basis for judgment. So it is in shaping the next phase of U.S. economic relations with communist countries. The mistakes of the past fifteen years are clearer than the path into the next century. But, while remaining alert to the dangers, American policy should lift the impediments barring its citizens from exploring that path actively. In today's world economy, inertia is a recipe for neither prosperity nor security. There is no standing still.

Notes

1. Carol Rae Hansen, *U.S.-Soviet Trade Policy*, Washington, D.C.: The Johns Hopkins Foreign Policy Institute, 1988, pp. 10-11.

2. See "Report of the Special Interagency Task Force on Western Lending to the Soviet Bloc, Vietnam, Libya, Cuba and Nicaragua," 1988; also Hansen, *U.S.-Soviet Trade Policy, p. 32.*

17

The Soviet Union Is Opening Itself to the World

Valeri Karavayev

The socialist community countries are living through a challenging period of social and economic transition. This reality is recognized universally in East and West alike and, indeed, almost sounds trivial now. True, it is interpreted variously. Some predict the failure of world socialism, the disintegration of the "last world empire" and the miscarriage of the socialist experiment initiated in 1917. What is more, these forecasts come not only from the West but from socialist countries as well, including ours. Others speak of a crisis not of the socialist idea but of its Stalinist distortion, the obsolete, bureaucratic command system. They expect this system to give way to a new—humanist and democratic—model of socialism based on contemporary scientific and technological achievements and the common values of civilization. However, they describe this new model in rather vague terms giving the impression of something very abstract.

While these views are subjective, it is certain that the socialist community countries require deep-going social and economic changes if they are to end a crisis situation or a situation marked by stagnancy and fraught with crisis. Otherwise they are bound to be pushed to the sidelines of world technological and economic progress and may become a backyard of the world economy in the twenty-first century.

Current transformations in the socialist world are the object of bitter ideological struggles inside the countries involved, with opponents using negative experience as a trump card. Our conservatives readily accuse reformers of heading for a market economy. "Hungary, Yugoslavia and Poland are already following this road," they argue, "but look at their economic plight. What are you trying to achieve?" There is no doubt that those countries are burdened with debts and beset by inflation. Even so, the ordinary consumer there is incomparably better off than in our country because he is not suffering from shortages of sugar, soap, detergents or other necessities, and inflation is alleviated—at least partly—by adjusting wages, student grants, pensions....

As for the positive idea of building a socialist mixed multistructural market economy, we are making extremely slow headway in this direction, stumbling over ideological dogmas every now and then. Fortunately, the phrase "market socialism" no longer sounds like a terrible profanity, and we hear it uttered by our leaders. By contrast, the phrase "mixed economy" still causes a sort of allergy. Yet we have not only a state sector but a cooperative sector as well as an individual one: farmer households are springing up. The two last forms are private property however we may argue over terms, nor is it anything terrible, for it exists in the majority of socialist countries, where it has not shaken the foundations of the system in the least. As for mixed ventures with foreign participation, they are state capitalism. All this adds up to a socialist mixed multisectoral economy whose socialist character is determined by the absolute predominance of social forms of property.

Now isn't this very like the Swedish and other social democratic models comprising a state sector, a cooperative sector and a private sector and, at the same time, an elaborate system of social security and income regulation? Yes, nor is it anything bad at all. We should recognize at long last that the social democratic ramification of the labor movement has benefited working people more in the way of living standards and social guarantees than ours has. But the two ramifications have common roots, for our origins go back to social democracy. Borrowing its positive experience would both give fresh life to our ramification, which is patently out of breath, and return us to our origins.

To recognize the concept of a socialist mixed multisectoral market economy means clearing the decks for the most extensive international cooperation, economic cooperation included, and this is highly important to us. Economic openness, close association with the world market and integration into the world economy are inseparable from this concept. It is a meaningless slogan where the old command system persists, for such a system is inherently incompatible with the capitalist mixed economy and so cannot integrate into it. Not so the new, mixed socialist multistructural economy sharing common market relations with the West and therefore perfectly capable of integrating into the world economy.

Overall, speedy integration into the world economy is a locomotive which can shunt the Soviet economy onto a market track. Our own driving forces are still insufficient for us to accomplish this. Integration into the world economy makes for the development of market ties based on world prices, interest rates and other credit terms accepted in international capital markets, realistic currency rates and other objective economic indices. In step with our involvement in the world economy, these indices are forcing out our deformed, arbitrarily fixed internal prices, artificially lowered interest rates and absurdly unrealistic foreign exchange rates, thereby laying a basis for normal market relations.

The main channel for the integration of socialist countries into the world economy is economic ties with industrial nations of the West. Western countries are bound to retain a dominant position in the world economy, trade and technological progress, to remain a region of the greatest stability in economic growth and the main source of sophisticated commodities and capital. For socialist countries, it is particularly important to attract material and financial resources from the West at the early, most difficult stage of restructuring for the purpose of, among other things, saturating the home market with consumer goods in short supply. It would be hard for them to restructure and modernize their economies in isolation from the main centers of world technological and economic progress. The Western experience of management and marketing is gaining sharply in importance as a factor for the transition to an open market economy.

The point is that none but an open economy can really integrate into the world economy. It is an economy developing with due regard to the international division of labor, its participation in the latter fitting in organically with the reproduction process, an economy oriented to the world market, having an economic mechanism adjusted to international cooperation, receptive to whatever is positive in the world economy and equal to protecting itself from negative processes. This is what the economies of industrial countries of the West are like today. Socialist countries have taken the road to an open economy, except that they are very late.

Needless to say, so vast an economy cannot open itself to the world completely or all at once. This is still impossible due to our economic mechanism, which has still not been reformed in sufficient measure, nor our technological and even cultural level and ideological stereotypes inherited from the past: class chauvinism, xenophobia, excessive fear of espionage. We must open ourselves to the world gradually, by establishing an open sector encompassing all the regions and industries that are more prepared than others for foreign economic activity.

A radical economic reform was bound to include a restructuring of the foreign economic sphere. The number of decisions made and organizational changes effected to date as well as the radical character of some of them invite the conclusion, as some believe, that foreign economic perestroika is ahead of the economic reform as a whole. Indeed, production combines, enterprises, cooperatives have been granted the right to seek direct access to foreign markets and authorized to use part of their export earnings in hard currency as they see fit. This has made it possible not only to end departmental monopoly on foreign trade but to pull down the barrier dividing production and foreign economic activity for decades. The procedure of setting up joint ventures in the country has been substantially liberalized, and there is a decision to create free economic zones.

Nevertheless, the time for rejoicing is not yet. Our foreign trade is making no progress, its structure remains unfavorable, and so do imbalances in exchanges with the West. Our foreign debt is mounting. Of the more than 1000 joint ventures registered to date, only about a quarter are actually operating, with the production sphere accounting for a small fraction of them. The creation of free economic zones is being retarded. There is no clarity about the pattern of managing foreign economic activity, the functions of the State Foreign Economic Commission (SFEC) and the Ministry of Foreign Economic Relations have not been separated clearly enough, and then it is hard to understand why one and the same field of activity should be controlled by two administrative bodies.

Perestroika in the foreign economic sphere, like radical reform generally, is following an intricate and contradictory course, one step forward being offset by two steps or at least half a step back. Thus, the undeniably progressive decision by which the USSR Council of Ministers on 2 December 1988 authorized in principle all combines, enterprises and cooperatives to do business with foreign partners directly was supplemented with another decision of 7 March 1989. This one raised bureaucratic hurdles in the form of registration, licensing, quota fixing, declaration and other rules that seriously complicate the exercise of the rights granted by the original decision. And in December 1989 there came further restrictive decisions.

These instruments are said to be universally accepted in the world, which is true. The point at issue is the extent and manner of using them. It is unlikely that any other country in the world has banned the export of discarded electric motors because it considers them a strategic commodity. Nor can the rule by which all enterprises and cooperatives must seek export licenses from the ministry producing the output concerned even if they are not subordinated to that ministry be described as wise. This is as unreasonable as having American companies making cars seek export licenses from, say, Ford. Nothing good would come of it—if anything, it would produce a further instance of departmental monopoly....

What tends to delay the creation of free economic zones in our country is the centralist tendencies of our government departments. The point is not only that the SFEC is dragging its feet over drafting an all-Union decision on free economic zones and has monopolized the selection of places where they are to be set up first. It intends not only to appoint its own representatives but to impose on the projected zones departmental subordination of the enterprises to be situated there, state orders, rationed distribution of resources and complex bureaucratic management structures. Now who wants these command system enclaves at a time of transition to republican economic accountability and economic autonomy? The bureaucratic velleities of the SFEC have understandably come under fire at local levels and raised fears that free economic zones are going to be regarded as zones of the Soviet Union controlled by Moscow. Commenting on a relevant document prepared by the SFEC, Latvian economists note that it "faithfully follows the traditions of the old system and is aimed not only at preserving and strengthening it but at providing basic conditions for the future prosperity of the elite."[1] The reference is to the administrative, bureaucratic elite.

In his article "The Question of Nationalities or 'Autonomization'," Lenin wrote: "It is said that a united apparatus was needed. Where did that assurance come from? Did it not come from that same Russian apparatus which ... we took over from tsarism and slightly anointed with Soviet oil?"[2] Our present-day bureaucratic apparatus in charge of foreign economic relations was taken over largely from the period of stagnation, and slightly "anointed" with perestroika.

It is only fair to say that centralist excesses over the issue of establishing free economic zones are coupled with another extreme, localism. For instance, the early project of the concept of republican economic accountability in the Estonian SSR envisaged rather considerable isolation from the Union economy. "In implementing economic accountability," proponents of the concept write, "the Estonian SSR shall have jurisdiction over the organization of banking and money circulation, including the introduction of its own currency and the establishment of the procedure of exchanging it and the rate of exchange between it and other currencies, including the ruble as the common currency of the USSR. The currency of the Estonian SSR shall be the only currency circulating in the domestic market of the Estonian SSR."[3] Suggestions were made for the creation of free economic zones encompassing whole republics, and they did not come from Estonia alone.

However, these extreme views running counter to objective trends toward internationalizing production failed to gain ground and were described accordingly by Baltic economists themselves. "I think a republican currency would make sense in the context of full economic autonomy," said I.K. Kirtovsky, Director of the Latvian SSR Academy of Sciences Institute of Economics. "It would be unrealistic to search for ways to adopt a republican currency within the framework of the federation. That would hardly help protect the market in our conditions."[4] "The republic is one juridical person and the zone another," said one of his colleagues. "This is why the whole republic cannot be a zone at the initial stage."[5]...

As concerns specific problems of creating zones within the general framework established by decision of the Union government, republics should be allowed proper scope for initiative. Not every decision on creating a zone need be made by the USSR Council of Ministers. Such a procedure was originally decreed for joint ventures as well but afterwards it was renounced as inadvisable. Decision-making on setting up zones could apparently be left to the Union republics' Councils of Ministers, which should only agree with central departments the conformity of zone projects to the general framework set by decision of the Union government. If this were done, zoning could be taken out of the narrow framework established by the SFEC. All three zones selected by it— Vyborg, Nakhodka and Novgorod—lie in the RSFSR.

The adoption of universally accepted instruments of regulating demonopolized foreign economic activity and the creation of free economic zones, while important, are not the only lines of opening the Soviet economy to the world, of integrating it into the world economy. We ought to heed the view of the American economist Wassily Leontief and his colleagues, who advise against limiting the open sector of our economy to definite regions and propose including in it some industries in which we are adopting a management structure used by firms and market conditions of functioning. These American economists consider that the Soviet Union's light and food industries, which directly supply the consumer market, could become part of the sector. To this end they would have to be modernized by drawing extensively on Western credits and switching to the firm system and market conditions of management, including direct ties with subpurveyors and consumers and market prices. We would be expected to effect this transition stage by stage so as not to provoke an upsurge in inflation. We could benefit in the process from the experience of Western managers, who are used to operating in a market economy, and from managerial services, which should be paid for in hard currency to be derived from Western credits as one source.

The open sector of the economy could apparently encompass some other fields of activity, including partly agriculture, some of whose output the state pays for in foreign exchange even now as well as non-industrial construction. It is important that the entire open sector, regions and industries included, should consistently apply market principles of free enterprise and prevent any recurrence of methods of the command system.

Lastly, integration into the world economy is unthinkable without active effort to advance to a convertible ruble. The inconvertibility of our currency is the chief obstacle to joint business and to more extensive ties with the West generally. Also, it explains the increasing role of the dollar in our internal economic activity. True, there are signs of progress toward convertibility: we have decided to hold foreign exchange auctions, establish a more realistic exchange rate for the ruble in relation to the dollar in the case of non-commercial transactions, and so on. Still, the most promising approach to this problem seems to consist in the American economists' idea of introducing a gold standard for the ruble, of freely exchanging it for gold. There is a certain similarity between this and the reform of the early 1920s, when we acquired a hard currency by introducing the gold chervonets.

Leading officials of the USSR Foreign Economic Bank and some economists overhastily express the fear that the result may be a flight of our gold reserve into private hands, including foreign hands. But then Americans propose fixing a sufficiently high price for gold to limit its purchase and introducing a gold standard for the ruble stage by stage and sphere by sphere at home and abroad, which would do away with all cause for fear. As for the advantages of this measure, they are beyond question, for it would give the gold ruble direct access to the international money market as a full-fledged currency. Free conversion to gold of rubles circulating in the sphere of joint ventures would undoubtedly provide fresh impetus for this promising form of cooperation. Besides, it would be more convenient for the state to pay producers of grain and other farm products in short supply in gold rubles instead of in dollars. In short, the idea calls for both a serious analysis and a careful formulation.

The integration of socialist countries into the world economy presupposes a fundamental reappraisal of the role of the foreign economic factor in their social and economic development. What is an important yet supplementary factor or instrument needed for the solution of inner economic problems is becoming a major factor for world economic specialization. The world economy is not going to adapt to our economy; it is for our economy to become a structural component of it, to find a fitting place in the world division of labor at the threshold of the twenty-first century. The socialist community countries recognized this at the 45th CMEA Session (January 1990), which led off a radical restructuring of the Council with a view to accelerating the integration of member countries into the world economy.

Not that an organization for multilateral economic cooperation like the CMEA is becoming less necessary let alone redundant. With the internationalization of economic activity going deeper, organizations for regional economic cooperation exist everywhere, even in Tropical Africa. Hence it would be utterly illogical to renounce organized cooperation in so relatively developed a region as Eastern Europe and countries associated with it. But the need now is for a new CMEA, for a compact and dynamic organization and not just for a 30-story skyscraper where highly paid officials turn out an incredible quantity of papers against the background of virtual stagnation and diminishing cooperation between member countries. The task facing the CMEA is to advance fast toward greater openness to the outside world and higher efficiency.

Perestroika in the Soviet Union and the revolutionary changes coming about in Eastern Europe are objectively drawing us closer to the civilized world, removing all that had separated us. "The world," says the CPSU CC Platform for the 28th Party Congress, *Toward a Humane, Democratic Socialism,* "is freeing itself from the fetters of confrontation. The oneness of contemporary civilization, which needs a new world policy, has become more evident. The Cold War has been stopped." The renunciation of the barren, outdated policy of confrontation has opened the road to a rapprochement between countries with different social, economic and political systems. Collapsing under our very eyes after the "Iron Curtain" of the Cold War period are the concrete walls and barbed-wire fences which for long decades isolated peoples from each other and even divided one nation into two states in the heart of Europe. Ample opportunities are being provided for the really free movement of people and ideas across borders. The road to a common European home is open, nor is that home going to be what EC Commission Chairman Jacques Delors described earlier as a European village of separate cottages carefully locked against poor neighbors.

Far-reaching changes are also taking place in Europe-wide economic cooperation. There is a decision to establish a European Bank for Reconstruction and Development with the participation of West and East European countries. It will create a financial basis for multilateral economic cooperation. Trade agreements have been signed between the majority of European CMEA countries, including the Soviet Union, and the EC Commission. Thereby a real groundwork has been laid for the subsequent creation of an all-European economic area as the material foundation for a common European home.

Viewed against the background of qualitative changes in international economic cooperation, the COCOM [Coordinating Committee] ban on exporting technology to socialist countries and the Jackson-Vanik amendment, now rejected by one of its authors (the other is no more), are an obvious anachronism. "It is only by removing obstacles to scientific and technological exchange and by really making the work economy a world system that a material foundation can be provided for peaceful development," to quote the CC Platform.

Incidentally, this is the first time that an official party document of ours has used the concept of world economy in the sense of a single whole, thereby overcoming a concept that for years had distinguished between a "world capitalist" and a "world socialist" economy. Life itself and the realities of today's world have disproved this scholastic formula.

The CC Platform reflects and carries forward the idea of forming one world comprising increasingly interdependent countries, with the Soviet economy joining organically in world economic relations. It states that creating a single, full-scale and regulated Union market is a prerequisite for this as well as for moving on to a convertible ruble. The Platform stresses the importance of competition on the home market by producers, foreign firms included. It directly sets urgent tasks in foreign economic activity: making Soviet goods and services more competitive, steadily reinforcing the foreign economic independence of enterprises and hence their independence as to hard currency, and ending the raw-material trend of exports and restructuring imports....

Notes

1. Rigas Balss, 24 October 1989.
2. V.I. Lenin, Collected Works, vol. 36, Moscow, Progress Publishers, 1966, p. 605.
3. Sovelskuya Estonia, 30 September 1988.
4. Rigas Balss, 26 October 1989.
5. Rigas Balss, 25 October 1989.

PART SIX

Europe After the Cold War

Section 1
SUPERPOWER
DISENGAGEMENT
IN EUROPE

Several years have passed since the Berlin Wall and the Communist regimes came crumbling down in the revolutions of 1989. The euphoria that resulted from these momentous events is now being replaced by a sober contemplation of the realities and challenges of the new Europe. For all its drawbacks, the division of Europe into two rival blocs after the Second World War kept the peace for forty-five years. Now this order has been radically transformed, and superpower relations in Europe have changed just as dramatically. Soviet forces will be gone from Germany by 1994, and Soviet leaders have declared their readiness to withdraw all Soviet troops from Eastern Europe by 1995. U.S. forces have already been reduced in Europe and further reductions are likely. Germany has been unified, the Warsaw Pact no longer exists, and NATO is de-emphasizing its military functions because of the reduced Soviet threat. These dramatic changes have caused debate on the opportunities and dangers facing the new Europe and on the best way to preserve peace. Although it is generally accepted that both superpowers will continue to play a significant role in European affairs, the nature of these changed roles is far from clear.

F. Stephen Larrabee, in his article "The New Soviet Approach to Europe," points out that the collapse of communism and the unification of Germany has shattered the foundations of the USSR's postwar policy toward Europe. This policy had three key elements: (1) Soviet hegemony in Eastern Europe, (2) the division of Germany, and (3) the bipolar division of Europe. None of these apply in the new Europe. As a result the Soviet Union has had to construct a new policy not only toward Eastern Europe, but for Europe as a whole.

According to the author, President Mikhail Gorbachev's new policy does not appear to have been based on a "grand design" for Europe, at least initially, but emerged incrementally as the Soviet Union adjusted to the rapid turn of events. Although he did not ignore the United States, Gorbachev's early pronouncements indicated that he intended to place greater importance on Western Europe in his new foreign policy. However, this is not to suggest that he was adopting a "Europe first" strategy. Clearly his highest priority was to obtain an accommodation with the United States. Furthermore, Gorbachev does not wish to see the United States withdraw from Europe. He sees the presence of American troops in Europe as a factor of stability, and has stressed that the United States has an important place in the "European home." A reunified Germany is one reason why the Soviets want to keep the United States involved in Europe; the United States would remain an important constraint on Germany's freedom of action, especially regarding nuclear weapons.

In his article, "The Problems of the USSR's European Policy," Sergei Karaganov maintains that the developments in Eastern Europe in late 1989 and early 1990 "consolidated and carried forward some trends generally favorable to the Soviet Union." This is because the Cold War in Europe had a negative impact on the Soviet Union and its East European allies, primarily because the confrontation restricted their access to scientific and technological developments. As a result, the Soviet Union lagged behind the capitalist nations in economic growth and scientific/technological achievements. This, along with the enormous defense expenditures required to defend against the opposing alliance, were the primary reasons for economic stagnation in the Soviet Union and its long overdue reform.

Although the Soviet Union had allowed itself to be drawn into the European arms race during the Cold War, this trend can now be reversed, since the opposing alliance has cut back on military spending in response to the reduced "threat from the East."   Recently concluded European arms control agreements have also enabled the superpowers to reduce military expenditures in Europe.

Despite these "favorable" developments, the Soviet Union is concerned about the changes in Europe.   The disintegration of the bloc system is hardly welcome because the result will be greater instability in Eastern and Western Europe.   Karaganov does argue that NATO will prove to be more durable than the WTO "in the short term," and of course he was correct in this assumption.   Seemingly anticipating the demise of the Warsaw Pact, he points out that Eastern Europe will remain a military "buffer" for the USSR whether the alliance exists or not.   The newly independent states in Eastern Europe are unlikely to allow an invading army to cross their territory without putting up a fight.   But the dissolution of the WTO does mean a loss of conventional armament strength; therefore, the Soviet Union will have to rely on nuclear weapons for the foreseeable future to defend itself against attack.

Karaganov's comments on the impact that the changes in Europe have had on the Soviet Union's status as a superpower are particularly interesting.   It is true, he states, that the Soviet Union's ability to influence international events has decreased.   However, in his view, the USSR will inevitably have to abandon its status as a global superpower, which is not necessarily negative.   In fact, this development will probably be "useful."   Why?   Because it is exceedingly "expensive" to maintain such status, and doing so has brought economic ruin to the country.   He recommends that the Soviet Union "renounce this status to reassign our country its natural Russian role, the role of a great European power having interests in ... Asia."

In summary, the author contends that the USSR, from its perspective as a European power, needs to develop a new policy towards the continent suitable to the "post-confrontation period" which is on the horizon.   The thrust of such a policy, he says, will be the call for "accelerated construction of a new security system."

18

The New Soviet Approach to Europe

F. Stephen Larrabee

Under Mikhail S. Gorbachev, Soviet policy toward Europe has undergone the most dramatic changes since the end of World War II. Soon after coming to power, Gorbachev embarked on a policy designed to strengthen ties with Western Europe and exploit transatlantic differences. At the same time, he tried to redefine relations with Eastern Europe, putting greater emphasis on "freedom of choice" and economic efficiency.

Gorbachev's policy was predicated on a gradual evolution of the bipolar security system in Europe and the continued existence of two German states. His initiatives, however, unleashed forces that took on a dynamic of their own and resulted in the collapse of communism in Eastern Europe and the destruction of the bipolar security order based on the division of Europe into two opposing political-ideological blocs. As a result, the Soviet leadership is now faced with the need to construct a new policy not only toward Eastern Europe but toward Europe as a whole. Moreover, it must do so at a time when the Soviet Union faces major internal difficulties that could severely limit its capacity to pursue a vigorous and coherent European policy.

Brezhnev's Legacy

Soviet policy in Europe under Gorbachev must be seen against the background of the policy that he inherited from his predecessors, especially Leonid I. Brezhnev. Brezhnev's policy during his latter years was characterized by two principal features. The first was the USSR's isolation in Western Europe. Brezhnev's military buildup, especially the development of the SS-20 medium-range missile, proved to be a major strategic blunder and had a negative impact on Soviet relations with Western Europe. Rather than weakening Western cohesion and providing the USSR with important military advantages—as was its apparent intention—the buildup had the opposite effect, strengthening the cohesion of the North Atlantic Treaty Organization (NATO) and leading to a counterdeployment of United States missiles on European soil.

This miscalculation was compounded by a serious tactical error: the decision to walk out of the intermediate-range nuclear forces (INF) talks in Geneva in November 1983. This walkout made the Soviet Union appear to be the main obstacle to arms control, further tarnishing its image in Western Europe. As a result, by the time Gorbachev assumed power in March 1985 the Soviet Union had become seriously isolated.

The second feature of Brezhnev's policy was a visible erosion of Soviet hegemony in Eastern Europe. On the economic side, progress toward integration within a Council for Mutual Economic Assistance (CMEA) had virtually ground to a halt. On the political side, the Soviet effort to freeze East-West relations after the collapse of the INF talks upset the USSR's East European allies and accentuated differences within the Warsaw Pact, particularly with Hungary and East Germany, both of which had developed a strong vested stake in East-West détente. These problems were compounded by the impact of the succession issue, which increasingly preoccupied the Soviet leadership, deflecting attention away from pressing international problems, including those in Eastern Europe. As a result, Soviet policy toward Eastern Europe was increasingly characterized by drift and stagnation.

In short, by the mid-1980s the Soviet empire, as Charles Gati aptly put it, was "alive but not well."[1] The once monolithic bloc has become not only more diverse but also more fragmented. Stability had been bought at the price of stagnation, and ideological corrosion had replaced ideological cohesion as the hallmark of Soviet policy toward Eastern Europe.

New Thinking and Western Europe

When Gorbachev assumed power in March 1985, he inherited a European policy in deep crisis. In Western Europe, the Soviet Union was isolated, its policy stalled as a result of the INF debacle. In Eastern Europe, the USSR found itself at odds with its allies, many of which increasingly sought to exploit the Soviet preoccupation with internal problems—particularly the succession issue—to expand their room for maneuver. At the same time, Gorbachev was confronted with a mounting economic crisis that threatened to undermine the Soviet Union's ability to remain a major military and political power.

These developments required changes in Soviet policy toward

Europe. Moreover, they coincided with a shift in Soviet perspectives on Western Europe and NATO. In the 1950s and 1960s the Soviet Union had seen Western Europe (with the exception of France) largely as a pliant tool in the United States' global strategy. While the Soviets realized that West European interests were not always identical with those of the United States, they thought that American economic and military power ensured that American interests would largely prevail.

In the 1970s and 1980s, however, there was a growing recognition of the importance of Western Europe as an independent "power center" within the capitalist world. As Alexander Yakovlev, one of Gorbachev's closest advisers, noted in 1985:

> The distancing of Western Europe, Japan, and other capitalist countries from U.S. strategic military plans in the near future is neither an excessively rash fantasy nor a nebulous prospect. It is dictated by objective factors having to do with the rational guarantee of all of their political and economic interests, including security.[2]

Gorbachev's report to the 27th Party Congress reflected some of these insights. He noted that the economic, financial, and technological superiority that the United States had exercised in the past had been "put to a serious test" and that Western Europe and Japan were challenging the United States even in areas where it had traditionally exerted undisputed hegemony, such as high technology. Many sectors of West European public opinion, he claimed, "had begun to openly discuss whether U.S. policy coincides with Western Europe's notions about its own security and whether the U.S. was going too far in its claims to leadership." While admitting that the economic, political, military, and other common interests of the three centers of power (the United States, Japan, and Western Europe) could not be expected to break up in the near future, he warned that the United States "should not expect unquestioning obedience of its allies" and predicted that "contradictions" within the capitalist camp were likely to increase as a result of the emergence of new centers of power.[3]

Gorbachev's early statements clearly suggested that he intended to take a more differentiated approach to relations with the West, according greater importance to Western Europe. Soon after coming to power, for instance, he acknowledged the importance of relations with the United States but noted: "We do not view the world solely through the prism of these relationships. We understand the importance of other countries."[4] In effect, this represented an upgrading of the role of other areas, especially Western Europe, in Soviet policy....

This is not to argue, as some observers have, that Gorbachev has adopted a "Europe first" strategy.[5] Indeed, one of the striking features of Gorbachev's first years in power was his high priority on obtaining an accommodation with the United States. Relations with Western Europe, though accorded a higher priority than in the past, were still regarded as secondary to the improvement of relations with the United States.

Some Soviet officials, in fact, openly complained that this preoccupation with the United States had blinded the USSR to trends toward greater political and military self-assertion on the part of Western Europe:

> U.S. monopoly on engaging in dialogue with the USSR consolidates American leadership in the West, leaving Western Europe a secondary role in world politics. In our view, we largely facilitated this ourselves. Bewitched by the industrial and military might of the United States, we failed to notice, or—to be more precise—did not take fully into account, the fact that Pax Americana was shaking and had begun to crumble, while other imperialist centers, including Western Europe, were becoming more active in world affairs.[6]

Soviet policy, they charged, had failed to pay sufficient attention to these changes. They pointed in particular to the intensification of European military integration, which "had picked up speed since Reykjavik," warning that "passivity" and attempts to ignore the creation of a European defense "will inescapably lead to a situation where this defense will be fashioned according to American formulas, to the prejudice of the USSR." As a result, the Soviet Union would be forced to deal with a joint NATO position, in this case a United States position, just as it was increasingly forced to deal with a joint European position of the European Community (EC). These officials called for "new approaches" that would take due account of the European desire for greater independence in security matters.

These remarks, though hardly typical, reflected a growing debate about the implications of European defense. On this issue, as on others, there was no consensus. One school of thought saw the prospects for serious cooperation as largely ephemeral; a second, taking the trend more seriously, argued that the intensification of economic integration was providing the basis for much closer security and military cooperation.

The key issue, in Moscow's view, was the impact of these developments on East-West relations. Were they an effort to develop Western Europe into a truly independent power center or simply an attempt to strengthen the European pillar of NATO and influence Western Europe's voice in the shaping of NATO military policy? Again, there were different views. However, the dominant one—at least within the

Soviet Foreign Ministry—tended to regard the trend toward closer
military cooperation as a potential threat to East-West détente and an
effort to strengthen the European pillar of NATO. Writing in *International
Affairs*, the journal of the Soviet Foreign Ministry, V. Stupishin,
a high-ranking Foreign ministry official, concluded:

> The growth of military integration in Western Europe and creation of
> some new organizational forms of a "European buttress" of NATO may
> provide Western Europe with yet another instrument for influencing the
> U.S.A. But a far more essential and really negative result of this will be
> that the split of Europe into opposed blocs will be consolidated and new
> obstacles will be put up in the general European process and the con-
> struction of a common European home will be impeded, to the detri-
> ment of our interests as well. That is why we are so concerned over the
> military-integration tendencies in Western Europe.[7]

The debate over European defense reflected a broader shift in Soviet
attitudes in the late 1980s regarding developments in Western Europe.
In the 1970s and early 1980s the greater self-confidence and assertiveness of Western Europe had generally been welcomed and seen as undermining United States influence within NATO. Gorbachev's remarks at
the 27th Party Congress had largely reflected this perspective. By the
late 1980s, however, Soviet officials and analysts were beginning to
take a more differentiated view of these developments. The critical
West European reaction to the Reykjavik summit and the fears of
"denuclearization" prompted by the INF treaty, especially in France
and Great Britain, contributed to growing recognition that this new
West European self-assertiveness might not always work to Soviet
advantage....

The European Community

Concern with the implications of West European military integration has been one aspect of the broader Soviet concern with the process
of West European integration generally. For many years the USSR
regarded the EC as little more than an instrument to strengthen the
European pillar of NATO. Soviet attitudes toward the EC, however,
have undergone a significant evolution under Gorbachev. Since the
mid-1980s, Soviet analysts have shown an increasing appreciation of
the growing role of the EC as an economic and political actor in international affairs. In particular, analysts have pointed to a marked
evolution toward formulating common EC positions on foreign policy.[8]
Soviet analysts see the EC decision to create a single internal market
by 1992 as "a qualitatively new stage" in the integration process,

which will have major implications for East-West relations.[9] This, they argue, will accelerate integration—including foreign policy and military—and encourage closer cooperation in other areas. In the 1990s the United States (and, by implication, the Soviet Union) will have to deal with a Western Europe that is economically and technologically stronger as well as politically and militarily more cohesive.

The emergence of the EC as a new power center has required the Soviet Union to adopt a new approach toward the organization. This new approach began to manifest itself soon after Gorbachev assumed power. During Italian Prime Minister Bettino Craxi's visit to Moscow in May 1985, the new Soviet leader announced the USSR's willingness to recognize the EC as a "political entity" and to resume negotiations regulating relations between the EC and the CMEA, which had been broken off in the spring of 1980.[10] These negotiations led to the signing of a "Common Declaration" between the EC and the CMEA on 25 June 1988, which provided the framework for the establishment of diplomatic relations and the conclusion of trade agreements between the EC and individual members of the CMEA.

The 1988 Common Declaration was primarily motivated by economic concerns, particularly the USSR's desire for access to West European trade and technology. But it also reflected the Soviet leadership's growing appreciation of the important political role that the EC had begun to play in East-West relations. Soviet officials and analysts have increasingly pointed to the long-term political implications of accelerated integration, which is seen as laying the groundwork for closer cooperation in other areas, including foreign policy and the military.

From the Soviet Union's perspective, the main danger is that West European integration will solidify the division of Europe into blocs, erecting new barriers to East-West trade, and deepening the economic and technological gap between the two parts of Europe. Gorbachev's emphasis on the "common European home" has thus partly been aimed at preventing the creation of new impediments to Soviet access to West European research and development programs and ensuring that the USSR will benefit from new technology as West European integration intensifies.

Eastern Europe

Gorbachev does not appear to have had a "grand design" for Eastern Europe. Rather, his policy emerged gradually as a result of incremental changes and adjustments. The cumulative effect of these changes, however, has been seriously to erode Soviet influence in Eastern Europe.

Initially, Gorbachev's policy differed little from that of his predecessors. Its emphasis was on increasing political, economic and military integration—albeit on a more consultative basis. In effect, Gorbachev tried to strike a balance between the legitimization of "national interests" and the promotion of "international obligations" and between the demands of diversity and the desire for unity. The greater weight, however, was clearly on the side of closer unity.

Gorbachev's statements during 1986 and 1987 continued to reflect this uneasy balance between the demands of diversity and the desire for unity. The sense of continuity in Soviet policy in this period was reinforced by the appearance of authoritative articles by top Soviet officials in the Soviet press stressing the importance of "proletarian internationalism" (a code word for Soviet hegemony) and attacking market-oriented policies and other steps that violated "general laws of socialist construction."[11] Such articles were counterbalanced, however, by others representing a more open and flexible policy, suggesting the lack of a firm line on Soviet policy toward Eastern Europe.[12]

During late 1987 and early 1988, however, the outlines of a new policy toward Eastern Europe—a "Gorbachev doctrine" began to emerge. In essence, this doctrine represented an effort to extend the principles of perestroika and "new thinking" to relations with the USSR's East European allies. It was designed to eliminate "distortions" that had inhibited socioeconomic development of the bloc countries in the past— many of them rooted in the Stalinist system imposed on these countries in the late 1940s and early 1950s—and to create a more balanced relationship based on true partnership and mutual respect for national differences.

In the political arena, Gorbachev showed a willingness to grant East European leaders greater flexibility and freedom to decide their own affairs—as long as their efforts did not directly contradict or undercut Soviet interests. Allies were allowed greater initiative, especially in disarmament matters and relations with Western Europe. Consultation between the Soviet Union and its allies became more regularized and more genuine. While the Soviet Union continued to set the agenda for bloc relations, especially on military matters, the views of the East European allies were more frequently solicited.

There was also greater recognition—and tolerance—of diversity within the bloc. As Gorbachev stressed in a speech in Prague in April 1987:

> We are far from calling on anyone to copy us. Every socialist country
> has its specific features, and the fraternal parties determine their politi
> cal line with a view to the national conditions.... No one has the right to

claim a special status in the socialist world. The independence of every party, its responsibility to its people, and its right to resolve problems of the country's development in a sovereign way—these are indisputable principles for us.[13]

He reiterated this point in his speech commemorating the seventieth anniversary of the Bolshevik Revolution on 2 November 1987, noting: "Unity does not mean identity or uniformity."[14] In short, the Soviet Union no longer claimed that there was a single path to socialism or that only one model is universally valid. Each national party had the right to decide how socialism should best be developed in its own country, taking into account its own circumstances as well as its obligations to the socialist community as a whole.

The most important shift, however, was Gorbachev's willingness to repudiate the Brezhnev doctrine. Initially, Gorbachev showed a reluctance to face the issue squarely, in part because he did not want to destabilize the Gustáv Husák/Milos Jakes regime in Prague, which was closely associated with the period of "normalization" following the Soviet-led invasion of 1968. Soviet domestic considerations—above all, resistance from the conservatives within the Communist Party of the Soviet Union (CPSU)—also probably played a role.

Beginning in 1988, however, Gorbachev began step by step to move closer to repudiating the doctrine. The communiqué issued at the end of the Gorbachev trip to Yugoslavia in March 1988, for example, expressed "respect for different paths to socialism and stressed the right of all countries to unimpeded independence and equal rights" regardless of their sociopolitical system.[15] In his speech to the Council of Europe in Strasbourg in July 1989 Gorbachev was even more explicit, stating that "any interference in internal affairs, any attempts to limit the sovereignty of states—both friends and allies or anyone else—is inadmissible."[16]

Finally, during his visit to Finland in October 1989, Gorbachev openly repudiated the Brezhnev doctrine. The doctrine, Soviet Foreign Ministry spokesman Gennadi Gerasimov stressed, was "dead." It had been replaced by what he termed the "Sinatra doctrine," referring to Frank Sinatra's popular song entitled "My Way." This implied, as Gerasimov put it, that each East European country was free to carry out political and social changes "their way" without interference from the USSR. At the Warsaw Pact meeting in Moscow in December 1989 the 1968 invasion of Czechoslovakia was formally condemned as "illegal," and the member states committed themselves to following a policy of strict noninterference in each other's internal affairs.

These measures were accompanied by a strong emphasis on the need for economic reform. While Gorbachev did not force the Soviet model of reform on his East European allies, he made it clear that the East European economies had to be restructured to make them more efficient and competitive. On the one hand, he stepped up the pressure on his East European allies to increase the quality of their manufactured goods exported to the Soviet Union; on the other, he indicated that the USSR was no longer willing to provide Eastern Europe with raw materials and energy at previous levels.

Rather than creating greater cohesion within the bloc, however, Gorbachev's emphasis on reform accentuated the divisions among the Soviet Union's East European allies. Within Hungary and Poland, his calls for reform legitimized the reformers' calls for more radical, more rapid change. At the same time, these calls indirectly increased the pressure on the remaining bloc members to embrace reform more seriously.

By 1988 the bloc had in effect split into two camps. On one side was a reformist group composed of the USSR, Hungary, and Poland. On the other was a "rejectionist front" consisting of Czechoslovakia, East Germany, and Romania, which either rejected reforms outright or were less than enthusiastic about implementing them. Bulgaria was somewhere in between: General Secretary Todor Zhivkov paid lip service to reforms, but he dragged his feet in actually implementing them.

To be sure, Gorbachev did not directly demand that his allies adopt the Soviet model of reform. However, by way of example and word he indirectly increased the pressure on the orthodox members of the bloc to embrace reform more seriously. Perhaps most important, he increased popular expectations and pressures for change from below. In many East European countries, such as East Germany and Bulgaria, Gorbachev became a symbol of reform and a rallying point for discontent, especially among intellectuals.

In several instances, moreover, Gorbachev directly intervened to accelerate the process of change. In Poland, for example, Mieczyslaw Rakowski, the party leader, reportedly agreed to the creation of a Solidarity-led government in August 1989 after a telephone call from Gorbachev. In Bulgaria, Foreign Minister Petar Mladenov apparently received a green light to oust Zhivkov during a stopover in Moscow just before the critical Central Committee meeting that led to Zhivkov's removal on 10 November 1989. And, in Czechoslovakia, Soviet officials reportedly worked behind the scenes in November 1989 to undermine the Jakes government.

Gorbachev's role in initiating the transition in East Germany was also critical. He did not stop Hungary from opening its borders and allowing the East German refugees camped in Budapest to emigrate to

West Germany—the move that touched off the crisis in East Germany—and he intervened to press the East German leadership to allow the East German refugees in the West German embassy in Prague to emigrate to the Federal Republic. Moreover, in the crucial period in August and September 1989 the Soviets appear to have encouraged the efforts by Egon Krenz and some of his close associates to depose Erich Honecker.[17]

Finally, during his visit to East Berlin in early October 1989, Gorbachev made it clear to the East German leadership that in case of any turmoil the Soviet troops in East Germany would stay in their barracks. Thus, effectively withdrawing his support of Honecker, Gorbachev accelerated the crisis in East Germany (and indirectly the entire bloc). In the past the East German leaders had assumed that in case of major unrest they could count on Soviet "fraternal assistance." Gorbachev's remarks, however, made it clear that the East German leaders could no longer count on Moscow to intervene to save them if things got out of hand.

The unrest in East Germany had an important "demonstration effect" throughout Eastern Europe: it provided concrete proof that the Brezhnev doctrine was really dead. Once this became clear, the other regimes fell in rapid succession. Bulgarian leader Todor Zhivkov was ousted on 10 November 1989; Czechoslovak leader Milos Jakes stepped down in early December; and Nicolae Ceausescu was forced to flee on 22 December and was executed a few days later. By Christmas the spasm of revolt was over and the transition process had begun in all the former Communist countries of the Soviet bloc.

This is not to argue that Gorbachev consciously sought to introduce Western-style democracy in Eastern Europe. Clearly, he did not. What he hoped for was to replace orthodox Communists with more reform-minded ones. However, the legitimacy of the Communist parties in Eastern Europe was so weak that the process of change, once initiated, was impossible to control from above. Even in Hungary, where the party had begun the transition and carefully sought to stage-manage the process, the changes soon took on a momentum of their own, eroding support for the party and eventually sweeping it from power in the March 1990 elections....

The USSR and the Future
European Security Order

The collapse of communism and the unification of Germany have shattered the foundations of the USSR's postwar policy toward Europe. This policy was based on three pillars: (1) Soviet hegemony in Eastern

Europe; (2) the division of Germany; and (3) the bipolar political division of Europe. All three pillars are now destroyed beyond repair. The USSR is thus faced with the task of constructing a new policy not only toward Eastern Europe but toward Europe as a whole.

Originally, Gorbachev appears to have envisaged a gradual process of change in Europe during which both alliances would continue to exist but would lose their predominantly military character and take on increasingly political functions. The alliances, including the Warsaw Pact, were seen as stabilizing mechanisms. Soviet analysts argued, for instance, that the Warsaw Pact could play a useful role as an instrument for the "controlled and orderly transition" of the two blocs to a lower level of military confrontation and as a means for conducting arms-control negotiations.[18] Others argued that the pact should be maintained, but that it should be transformed into a "mature political partnership" in which all parties enjoyed equal rights.[19] They suggested that the East European role be expanded and that a permanent secretariat be set up in one of the East European countries.

The idea of a prolonged transition based on the continued existence of the two alliances, however, seems increasingly unrealistic. As a result of the rapid changes in Eastern Europe, the Warsaw Pact has become a hollow shell. It may continue to exist for several more years but as an effective military alliance it is clinically dead. The unification of Germany deprives the pact of its most important military asset. At the same time, the withdrawal of Soviet forces from Hungary and Czechoslovakia—scheduled to be completed by the end of 1991—severely weakens the USSR's ability to conduct coalitional warfare. Hungary, moreover, has announced that it will formally withdraw from the pact in 1991, which could lead to the formal disbanding of the Warsaw Pact.

As the pact has disintegrated, the Soviet Union has begun to push more forcefully for strengthening pan-European structures as an alternative to the two alliances. Some Soviet analysts, for instance, have suggested a two-phase approach. The first phase (1990-1991) would begin with the creation of all-European centers for the prevention of crisis and arms-control verification. This phase would be followed by a second stage in which a permanent secretariat and agencies on ecology, migration, and economic cooperation would be set up.[20] Soviet analysts have also suggested that the Council of Europe could be expanded to take on a pan-European character.

There have also been hints that the USSR may favor setting up a two-tier security structure with a permanent council, composed of the USSR, the United States, France, Britain, and Germany, which would become the core of a new security system and report back to the 35. Such ideas, moreover, dovetail closely with those put forward by Moscow's former East European allies. The foreign minister of Czechoslovakia, Jiri Dienstbier, for example, has proposed that a European Security Commission be formed with headquarters in Prague. This commission would act as an executive organ of a pan-European system of collective security.

In the future the Soviets can be expected to push such pan-European schemes more vigorously. They are one of the few ways that the USSR can be assured of exerting influence in Europe. In addition, such schemes could contain the growth of instability and nationalism in Eastern Europe, which many Soviet analysts see as a growing threat to European security. To counteract this danger, some Soviet analysts have called for the intensification of ties to Western countries and the "accelerated construction of a new security system, particularly the creation of permanent institutions for all-European control of political processes.[21] Such a system is also seen as providing a "corset" to ensure that German unification evolves peacefully and does not pose a threat to the general trend toward increased East-West cooperation.

The Soviets recognize, of course, that NATO is unlikely to fade away immediately, but they hope that the general political climate of East-West détente will make it increasingly less relevant and that its military functions will gradually atrophy. Thus they can be expected to put intensified emphasis on disarmament proposals that will weaken NATO's military potential, especially its nuclear capability.... [O]ne of the USSR's prime goals will probably be eliminating land-based missiles and nuclear artillery and preventing any modernization of NATO's air-delivered nuclear component. Soviet negotiators are also likely to press for significant reductions of United States combat aircraft and troop levels in any follow-on negotiation to CFE [Conventional Forces in Europe].

This does not mean, however, that the Soviet Union wishes to see the United States withdraw from Europe. The USSR recognizes that it will take some time to create a new security order in Europe and that the transition period could be destabilizing. Thus, it has come to see the presence of American troops—albeit at significantly reduced levels—as a factor of stability, at least for the short to medium term.[22] In addition, it seems willing temporarily to accept some stationing of American nuclear weapons on European soil.

This shift has been part of a general evolution of the Soviet attitude toward the American role in the construction of the "common European home." Initially, the concept had a strongly anti-United States edge and Soviet officials were ambiguous about the American role. Recently, however, Soviet officials and analysts have stressed that the United States has an important place in the European home. In his speech before the Council of Europe in Strasbourg, for instance, Gorbachev noted that the United States and the Soviet Union were a "natural part of the European international-political structure" and that their participation was "not only justified but historically qualified."[23] Soviet analysts, echoing this line, have argued that without the participation of the United States, construction of the common European home would be more difficult.

The process of German unification, moreover, is likely to reinforce the Soviets' predisposition to keep the United States involved in Europe. Although Gorbachev has accepted German unification as well as German membership in NATO, the USSR cannot be sure about the long-term direction of political developments in Germany. The United States remains an important constraint on German freedom of action, especially regarding nuclear weapons. A total withdrawal of American forces might reopen the nuclear question in Germany—something the Soviet Union strongly wishes to avoid. This concern gives the USSR an added incentive to keep the United States engaged in Europe rather than to encourage its total withdrawal.

At the same time, Germany's importance in the Soviet Union's European policy is likely to increase. Germany is the USSR's largest Western trading partner and its main source of technology and credits, which will be important for the modernization of the Soviet economy. Moreover, Germany will be the most important political actor in Europe. Thus, if the Soviet Union wishes to pursue an active policy toward Europe, it will have little choice but to strengthen its ties with Germany. Indeed, Gorbachev's invitation to Kohl to visit his hometown of Stavropol during the chancellor's visit to the USSR in July 1990—an honor accorded no other Western leader to date—seemed designed to initiate a new era of more cooperative relations with a united Germany.

The unification of Germany, moreover, is likely to give a new push to the process of European unification. Over the long term, unification may lead to a weakening of Atlanticism and United States influence in Western Europe, but it will also pose serious dilemmas for the USSR. For one thing, it will increase the attractiveness of the EC to the countries of Eastern Europe, making any efforts by the Soviet Union to transform the CMEA or keep it alive more difficult. For another, it will make the export of Soviet industrial products and other commercial transactions to Western Europe more difficult.

On the political level, the process of integration is likely to foster a more cohesive foreign policy on the part of Western Europe, allowing EC members to speak more forcefully with one voice on international issues. Internally, moreover, it will accelerate a shift in the locus of decision-making power on many issues from national capitals to Brussels and Strasbourg. Thus, if the Soviet Union wishes to pursue an active European policy, it will have to develop stronger ties to the EC and its associated institutions rather than simply concentrating on expanding ties to individual West European countries.

The CMEA, however, is not likely to disappear, at least not immediately. The countries of Eastern Europe conduct 40 to 80 percent of their trade within the CMEA. If it were to be disbanded, they would have to redirect their trade toward new markets. Replacing the Soviet market quickly would be difficult—and costly—since many East European goods are not internationally competitive. Thus the CMEA will probably continue to exist in some form for the next few years, at least as a means of facilitating bilateral trade. It is likely, however, to become much more of an "information gathering agency" like the Organization for Economic Cooperation and Development (OECD) in Paris than a mechanism for promoting close economic cooperation between the Soviet Union and its former East-European allies. Moreover, given the Soviet Union's own growing economic difficulties, the USSR is likely to reduce its delivery of energy and raw materials to Eastern Europe. This will exacerbate these countries' economic problems as they attempt to transform their economies along market lines.

Conclusion

The Soviet Union will face a substantially changed security environment in Europe in the 1990s. In order to adapt to this environment, major adjustments in Soviet policy will be necessary. These adjustments will have to be made at a time when the Soviet Union is undergoing profound change. How this process evolves will have a major influence on the Soviet Union's role in Europe in the coming decade.

Indeed, the disintegration of the Soviet internal empire is likely to be one of the most important factors affecting the future of Europe in the 1990s. It is highly questionable whether the Soviet Union will remain an integral multinational state. As centrifugal pressures increase, some of the republics, such as the Russian Federation and the Ukraine, are likely to seek greater autonomy—even independence—and may begin to pursue their own "European" policies, especially in the economic area. The growing political fragmentation of the USSR could be a major source of instability in Europe and make the integration of the Soviet Union—or major remnants of it—into a broader European framework more difficult.

It would be short-sighted, however, for the West to exploit this period of convulsion and weakness to exclude the Soviet Union from

Europe. That would only strengthen the more radical nationalist and exclusionist forces in Soviet society. Rather, Western policy should encourage a gradual evolution toward greater internal democracy, a greater reform of the Soviet economy, and its integration into the world economy. A less inward-looking, more democratic Soviet Union integrated into a broader European security order in which it has a strong but not dominant voice is more likely to guarantee peace and stability than a frustrated but still militarily powerful empire that feels isolated and excluded from Europe.

Notes

1. Charles Gati, "Soviet Empire: Alive But Not Well," *Problems of Communism*, March-April 1985, pp. 73-86.

2. Interview in *La Repubblica*, 21 May 1985 (reprinted in Foreign Broadcast Information Service, *Daily Report: Soviet Union*, 24 May 1985, CCI).

3. *Pravda*, 26 February 1986.

4. *Pravda*, 8 April 1985.

5. Jerry Hough, "Gorbachev's Strategy," *Foreign Affairs* 63, Fall 1985, pp. 33-55.

6. S. Vybornov, A. Gusenkov and V. Leontiev, "Nothing is Simple in Europe," International Affairs, no. 3, March 1988, p. 35.

7. V. Stupishin, "Indeed, Nothing in Europe is Simple," *International Affairs*, no. 5, May 1988, p. 73. This article was essentially a reply to the Vybornov, Gusenkov and Leontief article cited in note 6.

8. See the report on the EC prepared by the Institute of World Economy and International Relations (IMEMO), in Moscow, "Europeiskoe soobshchestvo segodnia. Tezisy Instituty mirovoi ekonomiki i mezhdunarodnykh otnoshenii AN SSSR," *Mirovaia ekonomika i mezhdunarodnye otnosheniia*, no. 12, April 1988, pp. 8-9.

9. See the material prepared by the West European Research Department of IMEMO on the implications of the formation of the internal market of the EC, "Posledstviia formiro-vaniia edinogo rynka Evropeiskogo soobshchestva material podgotovien otdelom zapadnoevropeiskikh issledovanii IMEMO," *Mirovaia ekonomika i mezhdunarodnye otnosheniia*, no. 4, April 1989, p. 40.

10. On the background to the Gorbachev Initiative and the development of relations between the EC and the CMEA before 1985, see Christian Meier, "Die Gorbachev-Initiative vom 29 Mai 1985-vor neuen Verhandlungen zwischen RGW und EG," *Aktuelle Analysen*, Bundesinstitut fuer ostwissenschaftliche und internationale Studien, 20 August 1985; and Bernhard May, Normalizierung der Beziehungen zwischen der EG und den RGW," *Aus Politik und Zeitgeschichte* B 3/89, 13 January 1989, pp. 44-54.

11. See in particular O. Vladimirov, "Vedushchii faktor mirovogo revolyutsionnogo protsessa," *Pravda*, 21 June 1985. The article was reportedly written by Oleg Rakhmanin, the hard-line deputy in chief of the Department for the

Liaison with Socialist Countries within the International Department of the Central Committee. In the fall of 1986, Rakhmanin was replaced by Georgi Shakhnazarov, a prominent supporter of reform. Rakhmanin's removal and Shakhnazarov's ascendency were important signs that the reformist line was beginning to gain ground.

12. See in particular Oleg T. Bogomolov, "Soglasovanie ekonomicheskikh interesovi i politiki pri sotsialisme," *Kommunist,* no. 10, July 1985, pp. 82-95.

13. *Pravda,* 11 April 1987.

14. *Pravda,* 3 November 1989.

15. *Pravda,* 19 March 1988.

16. *Pravda,* 7 July 1989.

17. David B. Ottoway, *Washington Post,* 11 November 1989.

18. Andrei Kokoshin, "Konturi peremen," *SShA: Ekonomika, Politika, Ideologiya,* no. 2, February 1990, pp. 31-33.

19. Mikhail Bezrukov and Andrei Kortunov, "What Kind of an Alliance Do We Need?" *New Times,* no. 41, 10-16 October 1989, pp. 7-9; and idem, "Nuzhna Reforma OVD," *New Times,* no. 3, March 1990, pp. 30-35.

20. Sergei Karaganov, "Architecture for Europe to Ensure the Transition Periods Safely," *Moscow News,* 21-27 May, 1990, p. 12.

21. Sergei Karaganov, Problemi evropeiskoy politiki SSSR," *Mezhdunarodnaya Zhizn,* July 1990, p. 93.

22. As the study *Tactical Nuclear Weapons in Europe* by Bayev et al. noted, "Despite all its negative features, the U.S. military presence is a major stabilizing element in relations among Western nations, and to some degree, in the entire system of East-West relations," p. 12.

23. *Pravda,* 7 July 1989.

19

The Problems of the USSR's European Policy

Sergei Karaganov

Developments in Eastern Europe in late 1989 and early 1990 consolidated and carried forward some trends generally favorable for the Soviet Union. The European security system imposed by the Cold War and based on confrontation between the two military blocs and putting the Soviet Union at a disadvantage began to give way. It had compelled our country with its relatively weak allies to hold its own against an alliance greatly surpassing it in economic power. Confrontation had cut us off to a considerable extent from the achievements of the most advanced part of world civilization in science, technology, culture and thought and resulted in reproducing conservative approaches and social structures in our society. A factor preventing long-overdue reform and democratization, it had led society to stagnation and crisis.

The trend toward slower growth and then also toward a reduction in the military effort and military spending of the opposing alliance—a trend on the rise for two or three years—has become more marked in recent months. The "disappearance" of the enemy and of targets for attack and hence the impossibility of claiming that the "threat from the East" is real has buried the program for "modernizing" land-based NATO missiles and nuclear artillery ammunition.

The threat of aggression from the West and of using military power as a means of pressure has practically been eliminated. We owe this not only to a new, bold foreign policy and internal changes. The war menace has diminished appreciably also because in earlier years the Soviet Union did away with nearly all of the West's military advantages. Power politics have become pointless. We have a definite reserve of strength but in building it up, we regrettably spent more than was necessary by allowing ourselves to be drawn into the arms race in some sectors....

The fact that the Soviet Union is seen as a motor of democratization has enhanced the already unprecedented international prestige of the country's leadership.

Consensus among the main political forces, if not directly in support of *perestroika*, then at least in favor of creating a proper external environment for it, of stabilizing the process of change, has grown. It emerged in Western Europe two years ago and was backed in May 1989 by the United States. This fully expressed itself in the reserved, civilized reaction of Western governments to nationalist outbreaks and the overall situation in Lithuania.

The changes in the GDR, Czechoslovakia, Bulgaria, and Romania, like those that preceded them in Poland and Hungary, are further evidence that the only road is democratization and an economy restructured on market principles and that the slower the changes, the higher their cost. Today a slow pace of change, to say nothing of any reverse movement, would bear the threat not only of international political, but social class isolation, in fact, of confrontation with the rest of the world.

Among the achievements scored by Soviet European policy in late years are the beginning of real disarmament and a new approach to the human dimension of the European process offering our people ample opportunities for spiritual and just human contact with neighbors in Europe.

The outside world has accumulated a positive inertia and a reserve of goodwill toward our country. But while there are changes, our European policy is still faced with many old and new problems. Progress was made primarily by removing conceptual, ideological and political roadblocks left from the past. To use a metaphor, we are only just beginning to build the house we need, having cleared the building site and added some new foundations to those laid earlier. What is required now is not only an idea of the general trend of this construction, such as the concept of a common European home, but blueprints.

But before starting work on these blueprints, we must ascertain the external environment in which a new security system is to be built and the problems and realities which our country is likely to encounter in Europe.

Old and New Problems

Let us first look at some effects of the revolutionary changes in East European countries. We know from history that such changes have a potential not only for renewal and the removal of long-standing contradictions but for negation and instability. Our country is paying dearly for Stalinism, for past mistakes, for 1968. Surfacing in countries that are our friends and neighbors are both anti-communist and anti-Soviet sentiments. [But] for all that, today most nations take a more positive view of the Soviet Union than ever since liberation from fascism, regarding it as a country which contributed or raised no obstacles to deliverance from a hateful order.

The inadequate development of new political structures at a time when earlier structures have been discredited, plus a difficult economic situation in the majority of East European countries, will most probably make for mounting tension that may even cross borders. There is no guarantee, said Eduard Shevardnadze in his address to the Political Commission of Europarliament on 19 December 1989, "that the danger of the emergence of dictatorships, of transformation into totalitarianism, of the rise of crisis situations at European or even world level is out of the question."

The period of instability is going to carry into at least the middle of this decade. It will in all likelihood be characterized by unstable governments and rapid changes in public opinion on problems of both home and foreign policy. Nor can destructive outbursts of nationalism or conflicts on that basis between countries be ruled out.

Today's European security system is unsuited for controlling and absorbing such processes. Its original purpose was to control durable confrontation between two camps, not a process of peaceful change fraught, however, with instability. There is not even a permanent diplomatic mechanism to meet new requirements. A system of permanent multilateral consultations is also needed as an instrument of exerting multilateral influence on new political forces coming to power in Eastern Europe.

The drastic acceleration of the process of dismantling the existing security system calls for new structures, procedures and institutions to avert an expansion of the political vacuum created by the fact that the erosion of old security structures is ahead of the formation of new ones.

Institutionalizing the European process and hastening the creation of new security systems are also necessary for blunting the edge of the German question and settling it on a common European basis. German unification in the middle term is apparently not at variance with Soviet interests, meaning primarily an end to the division of Europe brought on by, among other things, the division of Germany. The Soviet Union, which has an enormous nuclear capability and will remain militarily powerful in the foreseeable future, has less reason than weaker neighbors of Germany to worry about the military political implications of unification. Even so, there remains some concern which may grow especially against the background of the painful processes taking place in the USSR. This may happen if German unification results in seriously upsetting the military political balance without the compensation of a really decisive cut in the strength and offensive power of the Bundeswehr, by the new state assuming explicit obligations that would rule out the very possibility of its posing a threat to neighbors, to their territorial integrity, and by a set of accords establishing institutional political and military political foundations for a new security system. Without such measures a situation might arise which many in the Soviet Union would find unfavorable and very similar to the one in which Germany found itself after World War I, by the terms of the Versailles Treaty.

It is to be hoped that the Germans ... will arrive at a reasonable solution, taking into account the interests of the Soviet Union and other European countries. Like others, if not more than others, they have a stake in continued stability and perestroika in the Soviet Union and in a further decline in the role of the military in European politics. Lastly, they are interested in ensuring that unification, which will give rise to complications and frictions anyway, proceeds as peacefully as possible, without any external impediments.

But the Soviet Union must define its policy toward the new great power in the making, which is bound to take up a central place in European politics and economy. Our earlier refusal even to discuss the German question—a refusal largely due to pressure from the former leadership of the GDR and those who echoed it in our country—left us largely unprepared for the current course of events and possibly robbed us of many political and other advantages.

What makes it necessary to get rid of vestiges of an ideological approach and adopt a policy based on an adequately conceived, enlightened national interest, is also the circumstance that developments in Eastern Europe have brought out more clearly than before—a trend toward a change in the balance of European and, indeed, world forces. This trend, which started more than twenty years ago, is unfavorable for the Soviet Union. Its roots lie in the fact that the socio-economic model we are now trying to get away from proved inherently incapable of adapting to the STR and made for an increasing lag in science, technology and economic growth. The current decade is unlikely to see the end of this lag in comparison with leading capitalist and many developing countries. To catch up with them, we must thoroughly restructure our economy and production relations.

The trend toward a relative decrease in the international leverage of our country is due to the erosion of the bipolarity of the world, on which it was based to a considerable degree, and to the relative decline in the role of the military factor in East-West relations. The United States, too, has lost some of its influence for the same reasons. A further reason for our diminished possibilities, which is also typical of the United States if less than of us, is excessive spending on arms and excessive global involvement, which merely created an illusion of might but was and still is very costly.

The trend toward a change in the power balance was already at work in the 1970s but was disguised by a temporary weakening of the foreign political positions of the United States, which we emulated, and by a change in the military power balance in our favor. Our assuring ourselves that the world balance of power had changed in favor of socialism also played a role. The trend manifested itself in full measure in the early 1980s. The military balance had never been so favorable as in that period, and at the same time the Soviet Union found itself in international political semi-isolation, the majority of countries in the world rejecting its policy and social system.

A further circumstance to be borne in mind is that while we have renounced our previous socio-economic and political model, we have not yet created and it will take time to create a new, attractive and viable model. This will continue seriously limiting our influence in the sphere of ideas and politics.

Perestroika and new thinking in foreign policy, our new policy as a whole, make up to a degree for the diminished appeal of our model. At present our policy enjoys much higher prestige and greater political influence than, say, ten years ago, but this compensation is limited. Taken as a whole, our possibilities for influencing the outside world show a relative decrease.

These limitations are accentuated by our apparently having exhausted a major instrument for influencing the outside world: our home policy. It is perestroika and the concomitant processes of democratizing and humanizing our society that have delivered a stronger blow to distrust and hostility toward our country than even disarmament measures. For the "Soviet threat" was feared not only because we were overarmed but because people could not understand our society, our socio-political system, which was closed....

The current shift in the power balance of the world (including Europe, where it is favorable for the EC countries) will not imperil our security if accompanied by a continued policy of reducing armaments and demilitarizing European politics. On the contrary, the military threat from the West will go on diminishing.

Indeed, abandoning the status of a global superpower imposed upon us by history, the Cold War and partly by our own unwise policy is ultimately inevitable and would be useful as I see it. This status is very expensive, nor did it bring our people anything but further enormous expenditures and a prolongation of the existence of command socialism due to illusory, generally very short-lived achievements on the world scene.

Renouncing this status to reassign our country its natural Russian role, the role of a great European power having interests in Asia and preserving for a time its present status solely at the nuclear level, would release vast resources. Furthermore, it would reduce the number of potential sources of conflict with other countries, give us a freer hand and greater flexibility in foreign policy and enable us to concentrate on really decisive lines, above all on restructuring our economy and socio-political system. Attaining all this would reverse the trend I have described. I am certainly not calling on our country to isolate itself, to stop working for the solution of global problems or desist from active diplomacy. But it is time we revised our excessive military, political and economic commitments. Strictly speaking, we have already begun revising them.

In planning our policy toward Europe, we should bear in mind that due to the dramatic changes which recent months have seen in East European countries, the Soviet Union today arouses somewhat less interest among the world public, politicians and businessmen. This is largely a passing phenomenon. A political drama is more fascinating than an intricate political process but sooner or later the former transforms into the latter.

There is no deliberate policy of isolating the Soviet Union. But we need to realize the dangers. By lagging behind what are now all-European political and social changes, our country may find itself outside the new European community that is shaping up.

A reversal of perestroika, even a temporary one, would very likely also reverse the process of reducing military political and economic pressure from without. The main confrontational structures in the West have been weakened but are still there and may be revived. In view of such developments, the erosion of the WTO may accelerate, with some East European countries adopting an anti-Soviet position and seeking military political support from the West.

The intensification of the long-running process of the majority of East European countries reorienting themselves in a measure toward the West is somewhat reducing the possibilities of exerting influence through them as well....

At the same time, there are obvious limits to the westward drift of East European countries. The WTO countries have deep-going common interests. These include the need for reformist forces to lean on each other for support, the importance of having a stable external environment at a time of swift internal changes, dependence on arms deliveries, and just economic interdependence, which goes deep and will persist in the foreseeable future. Lastly, East European countries, which are much weaker politically and economically than their leading Western neighbors, need political support to have room to maneuver in the dialog with the West. From this point of view, they are probably more in need of alliance with the Soviet Union than vice versa, although interest is mutual and deep-going. The political basis of the alliance is also strengthened by no longer tying its members' hands in the foreign policy sphere. The Soviet Union itself is pursuing the most active policy of rapprochement with the West.

But this is no reason for complacency. Now that the possibilities of exerting influence through Eastern Europe are dwindling, we must compensate by stepping up our diplomatic effort in the Western, pan-European sector to draw our country into world and European economic institutions and links, to adjust our economy to them by adopting market principles and effecting decentralization....

Basically, even a serious weakening of the WTO, which may be expected to come about sooner or later, is unlikely to increase the military threat to our country. The military significance of the WTO has already decreased noticeably. Our allies' troops account for only a fraction of the strength of the coalition. Their contribution is being reduced still further by political instability, which will probably characterize many allied countries in the years immediately ahead.

With today's highly mobile armed forces, greatly increased firepower and nuclear weapons, a territorial buffer is far less valuable than forty or fifty years ago. The main thing, however, is that the West has no such interests prompting it to commit aggression with an eye to territorial conquest, nor is it likely to have such interests in the future. The reason for this is not only the powerful curbs imposed by democratic institutions but the fact that in this age of STR, capitalism no longer needs to control population and territory directly. This kind of control may become a mere burden.

Further, it is common knowledge that any major war on the continent would spell the end of European civilization and cause incalculable loss of life as well as environmental, economic and social damage in all European countries. This is not to say that there is no war menace whatever. Overarmament is still there. Programs for developing new weapons are being slowed down but have not been abolished. Lastly, there may be nationalist excesses. Both the whole of European history and recent years of our own history dictate prudence and foresight. Of course, a complete dissolution of the WTO in the next few years is not a preference. While the alliance's military significance is waning on the evidence, its political value is not. The Warsaw Treaty is needed, if in new forms, as a means of preventing a "Balkanization" of Eastern Europe. But above all else it is important as an instrument of reshaping European politics, drawing East and West closer together, regulating arms cuts and disarmament and settling the German question. The WTO is necessary as a source of confidence for leading quarters in many countries, not least in our own country. This writer specializes in international problems, and so can analyze the prospect of a weaker WTO with a measure of equanimity. But many population groups and politicians in our country, being still deeply concerned for historical reasons about the danger of attack from the West as well as being used to the existence of a protective buffer, are unlikely to react to such changes with the same equanimity. Some may be prompted to make unfair use of current changes as arguments against perestroika and arms cuts.

The difficulties facing the WTO are largely typical of NATO as well. But the latter has a much more developed political infrastructure. It influences more strongly the thinking of a sizable portion of public opinion and leading quarters in the member countries and will apparently prove more durable in the short term than the former although one bloc would hardly live on for long after the other had ceased to exist.

However, the prospect of a rapid disintegration of the bloc system is hardly welcome. The alliances not only serve as instruments of confrontation but are among the few levers of regulating European politics. If they weakened faster than new structures and guarantees of security were created, the result could be greater instability in both Eastern and Western Europe due to a revival of fears and distrust. A practically inevitable increase in the feeling of uncertainty and unpredictability might slow down the process of all-European rapprochement.

New political realities are posing certain military problems in a new way. Thus, the concept of the Vienna accords [regarding conventional weapons] proceeded largely from a different political and military strategic situation in Europe. The level of political confrontation was higher at the time and so was, at least theoretically, the level of unity in the WTO. There was no question of the possibility of the GDR withdrawing from the alliance. A pullout of Soviet troops from East European countries was discussed mostly in theoretical terms.

Changes in East European countries, primarily the likely dissolution of the National People's Army of the GDR and a further weakening of the WTO, are certain to alter the military balance to a degree and to produce new military political realities. How serious are these changes? Can they affect the accords being drafted at Vienna? From what a tentative analysis suggests, they are not qualitative. The territory of East European countries remains a buffer which any invading army would have to cross. (The likelihood of such an invasion is now seen as almost non-existent.) Be that as it may, the armies of East European countries, primarily Czechoslovakia and Poland, would resist aggression.

The limited advantages which the West may win as a result of transformations in Eastern Europe will be very similar to those that we had until recently and largely retain in Europe. They can be neither converted into military dividends nor used as a means of political pressure but will provide the West with a definite "margin of safety."

This inconvertibility of advantages is due not only to the political intentions of the two sides or the general situation but to the fact that the Soviet Union commands a huge nuclear capability which makes any threat virtually improbable even in case of a serious superiority in conventional forces.

But the absence of the usual "margin" in the sphere of conventional forces, the changes taking place in Europe and the unification of Germany may cause concern among some sections of our population and military. We ought to offset this concern by temporarily increasing psychological—certainly not military—reliance on the nuclear factor for our security. Owing to anti-nuclear rhetoric and calls for the elimination of nuclear weapons, this factor is plainly underestimated from the psychological point of view.

I believe we need to continue relying for a time on nuclear arms due to the inadequate economic, scientific and technological development of our country, a difficult domestic situation and a weakening of the system of alliances. The existence of a nuclear capability, even one falling far short of today's abnormally excessive capability, deprives the other side of the hope of winning by exploiting its technological advantages and the race in conventional armaments. But there can be no question of giving up the long-term goal of eliminating nuclear weapons. Also, the orientation to a general reduction in the role of the military factor in European politics should be maintained....

Lastly, there is a further powerful trend, one determining the environment in which European politics will develop. It is the trend toward an increase in the relative strength and influence of Western Europe both in the Atlantic community and on the continent. The EC Twelve are not only becoming an economic superpower but committing themselves more and more manifestly to a common foreign policy.

The indisputable gains made in West European integration require something more than the obvious: their recognition and an extension of our economic and political cooperation with the EC. The Soviet Union recognizes them and is extending cooperation. But against the background of the difficulties which our country is experiencing, those gains pose a question hard to answer. How is Europe to achieve economic unity? Should it try to breathe new life into our economic integration and then to unite integrational alignments? Or is the task to seek directly a rapprochement with the EC, using a renewed CMEA as an instrument regulating trade and economic links between the Soviet Union and East European countries?

What Is to Be Done?

The above description of the situation in Europe is incomplete and may probably be disputed in part. Nevertheless, it indicates, in my opinion, that while European politics have left the period of confrontation behind they have not yet entered the post-confrontational period. They are in a transitional phase where history is being made and the groundwork laid for decisions that will determine them for decades to come. The new era calls for a new version of Soviet policy toward Europe, one based on the positive inertia accumulated to date yet adapting to the complex realities shaping up. The unpredictability of changes clearly makes it necessary to anticipate or forestall them. We need to work out a forecast of the evolution of Europe, doing it as realistically as possible even though it may be unpleasant in some respects. We must do our best to forestall or control events, never allowing ourselves to be pulled along by them. We must be well aware of our limits and refuse to cling to what we are bound to miss anyway, except that the price will be forfeiting additional political assets and resources. We must soberly recognize realities and compensate for the loss of influence in some spheres by building it up in others through an active policy and stepped-up multilateral diplomacy.

Growing elements of instability and unpredictability in Eastern Europe and a relative decrease in the Soviet Union's possibilities call for emphasis on intensified political interaction with Western countries and all participating states of the CSCE, on accelerated construction of a new security system and the setting up in the near future of permanent institutions for all-European control of political processes, if only at the level of consultations as a start. There is an undeniable need to set up agencies that would control the environment and the situation in regard to human rights (or to adapt the agencies already there). The Soviet Union has already advanced many specific ideas, including the ones presented by Foreign Minister Eduard Shevardnadze in his December 19, 1989 Brussels address. Apart from consultative functions, a standing pan-European forum could draft a supplement to the Helsinki Final Act in the form of a universally acceptable phased plan to establish a security system for a common European home or the confederation or union of states proposed by François Mitterrand.

Such institutions would function at a political level as a kind of "corset" for German unification's external aspects to prevent its dissociation from the overall trends of relations between Eastern and Western Europe and stave off a revival of fears.

Settling the German question and preserving factors for stability while at the same time continuing to demilitarize the continent could benefit from an agreement on reducing tactical nuclear weapons and foreign military presence all over Europe to the lowest possible symbolic levels in the next few years.

The existing security system cannot meet the challenges of the period of transition: growing nationalism in Central and East European countries, instability, the emergence of a political vacuum in the region, German unification, and misgivings which these developments may generate in many countries, including the Soviet Union. Indeed, it is doubtful whether even an institutionalized CSCE process can fully meet them in view of its inevitably slow course. There is a need to go further by setting up a system of both political and military political agencies of a pan-European character and by making military political integration throughout Europe the order of the day as speedily as possible. Integration could be brought about either by merging existing organizations or—more realistically—by setting up new agencies to merge them and help them interact. Worth pondering, specifically, is an interconnected system of agencies comprising control and verification centers serving to avert crises, remove all danger of war, and combat terrorism. So is an all-European military committee that would coordinate their activity. Also multilateral forces seem to be called for which would be responsible for maintaining peace and combating terrorism.

One could propose a whole series of other purely foreign political measures. But while they are necessary, they are not what matter most. It is more and more evident that success in building a peaceful and prosperous common European home and Soviet participation in its construction will depend primarily on whether the peoples of our country succeed in overcoming ethnic discord and conservative opposition, setting out on the road of European civilization and building an effective model of production and a socially equitable model of distributing benefits as well as an efficient democratic political system. If this is done, a common European home will be built together with and hence also for us. If not, the wishes of our worst enemies, who would like to force the Soviet Union out of the world and European history, will be fulfilled. Obviously, we can neither accept such an alternative nor allow it to materialize.

Section 2
STABILITY AND SECURITY
IN THE NEW EUROPE

While Larrabee and Karaganov focus on Soviet policy in the new Europe, Stanley Sloan considers the American perspective on a new European security system. Sloan observes that U.S. policymakers and NATO will probably have to accommodate two very different scenarios depending on whether reform in the Soviet Union continues. If reform comes to a halt, the West will need to retain mutual defense arrangements, modified to reflect the changes in Europe in order to balance the continued Soviet threat. On the other hand, if political and economic reform in the Soviet Union continues, it may be possible to move from the NATO alliance toward greater reliance on all-European security structures. Sloan suggests that the CSCE (Conference on Security and Cooperation in Europe) framework could be extended and developed into the basis of a cooperative security system.

The United States, therefore, should develop a parallel policy structure that provides for continued reliance on NATO to balance Soviet power, while at the same time preparing for transition to some form of collective security system in which the Soviet Union could share responsibility with all other European states, the United States, and Canada. During this period of adjustment, NATO would play an important role, but eventually it would be dissolved because its functions would be redundant to the new security system.

Mikhail Bezrukov and Yuriy Davydov discuss the prospects for European stability and security in their article entitled "The Common European Home and Mutual Security." The authors argue that now is the time for a gradual dismantling of the European system inherited from the past. The conditions are right to create a new European political order based upon Mikhail Gorbachev's idea of a "common European home." Integral to this new order would be the principle of "mutual security." The advantages of the new system would be the elimination of the arms race in Europe, increased stability through all-European institutions, and expansion of economic ties.

The construction of the common European home could be achieved in several stages. In the first phase, existing institutions (such as NATO and the Council for Mutual Economic Assistance) would be used to promote improved relations. Better economic relations would be a major component of this first stage. As they put it, "the mutual security idea ... has an economic dimension." In subsequent stages, all-European institutions would be created to promote "European integration."

The authors make it clear that the United States and Canada should be involved in the new European mutual security system. For one reason, their inclusion would increase both countries' stake in European stability. Also, Europe has basically had a positive influence on U.S. behavior and it is important for this relationship to continue. Any effort to exclude the Soviet Union should be resisted as well; to attempt to do so would renew Cold War fears and destabilize the entire region. This would not make sense, since stability is the ultimate goal of the "common European home" proposal.

Although few would mourn the demise of the Cold War, John J. Mearsheimer makes some post-Cold War predictions regarding Europe's future that are disquieting. In fact, he argues that we may soon lament the loss of order that the Cold War gave to "the anarchy of international relations." He believes that the prospects of major crises, even wars, in Europe is likely to increase markedly now that the Cold War has ended. The reason is that the new Europe will have a multipolar distribution of power—a state system that created incentives for aggression in the past.

After outlining various scenarios for the nuclear future in Europe, Mearsheimer contends that nuclear proliferation is probably inevitable but could provide for stability on the continent if it were well managed. The problem is that it is extremely unlikely that it will be well managed.

His argument that the end of the Cold War is actually dangerous and means, paradoxically, that the superpowers have an interest in continuing the bipolar confrontation. And because there is little the United States or the West Europeans can do to perpetuate the Cold War, the task of maintaining it is mainly in the hands of the Soviet Union. The United States might assist its rival to do so, he says, but the American public is unlikely to support the idea of propping up a rival power.

20

NATO's Future in a New Europe: An American Perspective

Stanley R. Sloan

Early in 1984, when I was drafting a volume on *NATO's Future*, readers suggested that I insert a preface summarizing my assumptions about the future of the Warsaw Pact and the Soviet Union before launching into my discussion of NATO.[1] Responding to their helpful comments, I concocted a little story, set in the year 2005. In my fictional tale, the Berlin Wall had come down. Germany was united, democracy and market economies were established in Eastern Europe, and the Conference on Security and Cooperation in Europe had concluded a review conference with a summit establishing a European Peace Order. Nuclear weapons had been removed from Central Europe, U.S. and Soviet strategic forces had been cut to minimal levels, and European armed forces were at historic lows.[2]

This bit of story-telling was not an attempt at prophecy, but rather my interpretation of how Europe might look if the stated objectives of Western policies were achieved. After trying to describe such an ideal outcome, I observed that if we could count on such change, "we perhaps could also plan to dissolve NATO and withdraw U.S. forces from Western Europe."[3]

We are, however, some distance from fully realizing the conditions described in this optimistic scenario, and major uncertainties remain concerning some key factors, particularly the role of the Soviet Union in all of this. It is no surprise, therefore, that the issues provoked by the East European revolution and the process of German unification have stirred a fundamental policy debate in the United States, as well as in Europe, about how European security arrangements should be shaped to reflect the new political and military circumstances.

Revolutionary Changes

It has become commonplace to describe the last year as a period of revolutionary change. One of the most obvious structural and political consequences of the East European revolution and the process of German unification has been the disintegration of the Warsaw Pact. The Soviet Union's perception of its security requirements has over the past four decades been the main source of Warsaw Pact cohesion. Once Mikhail Gorbachev decided that the Soviet Union no longer needed, or could no longer afford, such an expensive security blanket on its Western borders, the tightly stitched quilt began to come apart. In the wake of the democratic revolution in Eastern Europe, the new governments of Hungary and Czechoslovakia have negotiated terms for the removal of all stationed Soviet forces by mid-1991. The Poles would like the Soviets out too, as long as they can be assured that a united Germany would not try to change its borders with Poland. The government of a unified Germany will eventually want Soviet troops to go. This raises the possibility that, irrespective of East-West arms control negotiations, all Soviet military forces could be withdrawn from Central Europe in the next few years.

The Soviet leadership recently spoke of the Warsaw Pact as having a future as a political consultative organization. Skeptics question, however, whether there is sufficient common purpose to hold the Pact together, even in this minimal way, against the centrifugal forces currently pulling it apart. Late in 1989 many analysts (including the author) continued to believe that the Warsaw Pact might have some role to play as part of some transitional security architecture for Europe. But early in 1990 it has become increasingly undesirable to contemplate any meaningful future role for the Pact unless European political trends diverge sharply from their current directions. [The Warsaw Pact was disbanded during 1991—Eds.]

Perhaps the most important wild-card in the pack is the great uncertainty about the future of the Soviet Union and its role in Europe. The Soviet Union's East European allies are moving toward the West and away from Soviet economic, political and military dominance, and the independence movement has spread even to the Soviet republics. Even if Lithuania, Estonia, Latvia and other republics with separatist tendencies do not become fully independent, the Soviet empire is rapidly becoming more diverse, with a variety of more decentralized relationships emerging between Moscow and several republics.

The related but more important question is the future of reform in the Soviet Union itself. Of all the uncertainties now characterizing European politics, the future of the Soviet Union is most central to the potential for change in the European security environment. The Soviet factor is key to the development of American thinking about future European security arrangements. If the Soviet Union should over the next decade move progressively toward becoming a true parliamentary democracy and a participant in the international economic system, with all the internal reforms that those two processes would require, then it is difficult to imagine a European security system premised primarily on coping with an antagonistic Soviet Union. On the other hand, it would be virtually impossible to move toward any sort of collective security system in Europe if the Soviet Union should retrench both politically and economically. We may not be able to determine for several years to come whether the "reforming" or "retrenching" Soviet model is the one on which plans for a future European security system can be based, and Western policies will probably have to prepare for both contingencies.

Policy Challenges

These revolutionary developments certainly constitute a "victory" for the democratic principles and economic philosophies pursued by Western countries since the Second World War. It will be a lasting victory for the West, however, only if the results are translated into new European relationships and institutions that can preserve the fruits of the victory for all, including the Soviet Union. In other words, we must ensure that, having won the war, we do not lose the peace.

At the end of the Second World War the allied powers faced immense political, economic, and institutional challenges in rebuilding the international order. The war had wiped much of the slate clean, and postwar planners had a virtual *tabula rasa* on which to draw up new treaties and international organizations. The postwar security structure in Europe was built largely on the foundation established in April 1949 with the signature of the North Atlantic Treaty. The Treaty became the main vehicle for the defense of U.S. security interests and the political justification of most U.S. international security policies. It also provided the umbrella under which European recovery could proceed, democracy could be established in the western part of Germany, and West European economic and political cooperation could develop.

Today, at the end of the Cold War, we face a different sort of challenge. The countries of Eastern Europe have been crippled by fatally flawed economic and political systems, not devastated by military conflict. This suggests that the recovery process can start from a higher economic base than was possible after the War. On the other hand, the slate is far from clean, and the task of establishing new institutions and relationships to suit new political realities will run into many obstacles placed there by history that have not been removed by the end of the Cold War. Some institutions may no longer have a constructive place in the future, the most dramatic case in point being the Warsaw Pact. Some international relationships, such as the Four-Power status in Germany, no longer seem appropriate to the new political conditions.

Perhaps most troublesome will be the plethora of perceptions and attitudes based on old political realities that will block progress toward new structures and institutions until the process of political consensus-building sorts out and disposes of obsolescent ideas. Does the term "East" have any meaning when much of the East wants to join the West both politically and economically? If we still formulate policies based on traditional concepts of "East-West" relations, are we forcing countries into an international structure that they have worked so hard to escape? What meaning will neutrality have if there are no fundamental ideological differences structuring the international system? These are just some of the questions that the changes in Europe will force us to examine.

U.S. policy ... will thus be called upon to shape an approach that both adjusts to the changes that have occurred, and yet leaves open some flexibility for the future—a political and diplomatic challenge almost as daunting as those following the Second World War.

NATO and the Dynamics of Change

NATO's Supreme Allied Commander, U.S. General John Galvin, even before the dramatic events of 1989, often faced skeptical questions about NATO's continued relevance. He had a standard reply that is worth repeating here. General Galvin would refer to the "wing-walker rule." The rule was supposedly a basic truth for those fearless flyers who performed stunts on the wings of aircraft in exhibitions across the United States earlier this century. The rule is quite simple: Don't let go of one support until you have a firm grasp on another. This is good advice. We should not let go of NATO until we find another reliable support to grasp. But after the events of [1989] there is a relevant corollary to General Galvin's wing-walker rule. The corollary is that when the pressure of events starts weakening one support, you had better start looking for another.

The apparent disintegration of the Warsaw Pact and the political and economic weakness of the Soviet Union have naturally raised serious questions about NATO's future. U.S. Secretary of State James Baker and other Western officials have proposed that the alliance, now losing much of its military rationale, become a more political alliance in the future. Secretary Baker's essential premise, the focus of an important speech delivered late in 1989 in West Berlin, was that a new European security architecture "should reflect that America's security—politically, militarily, and economically—remains linked to Europe's security."[4] The Secretary of State argued that NATO's future role could focus on coordinating verification efforts required to implement the treaty expected to be produced in the Vienna CFE negotiations on conventional armed forces in Europe. In addition, according to Secretary Baker's approach, NATO could help develop common Western approaches to regional conflicts and weapons proliferation outside Europe, and shape initiatives to build economic and political ties to the East.

Many observers, however, doubt whether NATO can continue as an effective organization without a Warsaw Pact threat as its raison d'être. Even those who agree that NATO can be sustained as a Western political caucus do not agree on the main purposes the caucus should serve. Secretary Baker's suggestion for coordination of CFE verification efforts probably attracts more support than any other part of his package. There is wide agreement that sharing of verification information in a timely and efficient manner makes sense. But beyond this one practical proposal, the other concepts fail to arouse much enthusiasm or support. The NATO countries have always found it difficult to coordinate approaches to Third World regional security issues, and even more difficult to use NATO to do so. Why should this become easier in the future, particularly without a Soviet threat to provide even minimal cohesion for such efforts? The coordination of policies toward the East fits conceptually with NATO's past role, particularly as it was defined in the 1967 Harmel Report, but this role appears less and less relevant as much of the East becomes part of the West.

NATO's Secretary-General, Germany's Manfred Wörner, has been doing his best to keep his public posture synchronized with political developments; but it is hard for the organization to do the same. With all the uncertainty about the future, the 16 NATO governments have not yet been able to give new direction to the institutional bureaucracy. The bureaucracy therefore has no choice but to sit on its hands, stuck with old doctrines that are undermining the public perception of its importance rather than projecting an image of future relevance.

The question of what future European security "architecture" would be in the interest of the United States has provoked a debate both within and outside the U.S. government. There is a broadly based consensus in Washington that the United States should remain "involved" in future European security arrangements, even if the U.S. role is less prominent than in the past; there is less consensus on how the United States can most effectively implement this consensus.

The debate has focused on the question whether the United States should emphasize the need to preserve NATO while adapting it to the new European circumstances or whether it should begin to prepare a shift toward greater reliance on all-European security structures linked to the Conference on Security and Cooperation in Europe (CSCE)....

The outcome of this somewhat artificially focused "NATO versus the CSCE" debate could well determine the nature and extent of U.S. influence in future European developments. Should the United States take an approach that is not politically viable with its European friends or with the U.S. congress, its influence over developments will be severely handicapped. On the other hand, if the outcome produces a U.S. policy that resonates with the European countries and attracts domestic U.S. public and congressional support, the United States could play a major role in the construction of the European security system of the future.

Short-term Policy Imperatives

The current policy debate includes a mixture of long-term preferences for future European security architecture and shorter-term policy decisions. The long-term architectural choices are important, but it may not be possible to sort out those choices for several years. While the debate on architecture continues, a variety of policy decisions will be required in the short term, and those decisions must respond to criteria reflecting the blend of continuity and change that now characterizes the European landscape.

First, even though the changes that have already occurred and those that are in process have virtually eliminated the threat of any Soviet-led attack on Western Europe, the West will have to ensure that remaining Soviet power is effectively balanced by Western military capabilities. This element of continuity with the past should not be difficult to manage in terms of resources, but could be challenging politically. Determining what level and types of nuclear and conventional forces will be sufficient to accomplish this task will be controversial both within the United States and among the Western allies.

Second, it will be in the interest of the United States and the other NATO countries to ensure that legitimate Soviet security interests are respected in the settlement of the Cold War that is now being arranged. The Soviet Union's negotiating position is weak, and not likely to strengthen substantially any time soon. In the interest of future stability, the Cold War settlement need not necessarily accommodate every Soviet wish, but should try to ensure that the Soviet Union is not so dissatisfied that it would seek at some point in the future to undo the "wrongs" that it felt were done to it at the end of the Cold War.

Third, if the United States wants to maintain a close and constructive relationship with Germany in the future, U.S. policy will be called on to continue to support the right of a unified Germany to full sovereignty in the international community of nations. No country in a period of growing international interdependence enjoys total sovereignty, and Germany undoubtedly will be constructive in placing limits on its own military potential in order to contribute to a stable European security order. But harsh expressions of concern about Germany's future reliability by the United States could, by producing a defensive reaction in Germany, become a self-fulfilling prophecy.

Fourth, at a time when the main non-Soviet members of the [former] Warsaw Pact are seeking to join the West both politically and economically, it presumably is not in the interest of the United States or the Western countries to take any actions that tend to force those countries back into the embrace either of the Warsaw Pact or of the Soviet Union....

Finally, U.S. policy will have to respond to expectations in Europe and in the United States that a reduced Soviet threat will be translated into a real "peace dividend." Policies designed without taking this requirement into account would not attract public enthusiasm or parliamentary support. In particular, the strong interest in the U.S. Congress in the defense burden-sharing issue in previous years is likely to be translated into Congressional desires that future European security arrangements be shaped in ways that significantly reduce the burden of the U.S. contribution to defense in Europe....

National Perspectives

The Soviet Union, in spite of its political and military retreat from Central Europe, remains a military superpower, albeit with an uncertain political future. Its strategic nuclear forces remain the most serious potential threat to European as well as U.S. security. But Soviet economic troubles and internal political turmoil have fundamentally weakened the Soviet negotiating position in Europe. Ideally, the Soviets would like to keep Germany out of NATO but wrapped securely in a web of internationally binding commitments to reduce its military forces, remain a non-nuclear power, and renounce any future change in European borders. Realistically, Moscow may have to accept less, even though most governments will be sympathetic to Soviet concerns, preferring to avoid an outcome that the Soviet Union would regard as inequitable and therefore attempt to undo at some point in the future....

Trying to deal with the complexities presented by the positions of its allies, the Soviet Union and the emerging democracies in Eastern Europe, the Bush administration has said that it supports a Europe "whole and free" with a continued role for NATO and the United States. The United States has also advocated establishing some institutional linkage between North America and the members of the European Community as part of the new transatlantic "architecture." The administration played a central role in arranging the "Two-plus-Four" formula for discussing the international aspects of unification between the Germans and the "Four Powers" but, beyond advocating a continuing role for NATO, it has been cautious about articulating clear preferences for future European security arrangements. Administration officials have supported a reunified Germany with membership in NATO, arguing that such an approach would secure everyone's interests, including those of the Soviet Union.

The Bush administration's approach, however, has added to the impression that NATO is too firmly anchored in the past. The President's philosophy, as described privately by his advisers, is that unless we know where we want to go we are better off doing nothing. This cautious concept certainly has its merits—if the administration had articulated a vision for the future of Europe in early autumn 1989, it might have looked rather silly just a few months later; on the other hand, in the coming months there probably will be a stage in the process of shaping Europe's future at which the most compelling image or political framework will begin to capture an international consensus. If the United States does not have politically attractive ideas to contribute in advance of that critical juncture, then the outcome will be dictated largely by others.

Institutions: What Framework for the Future?

The transition to a new European security system and closer all-European economic ties may require creation of some new institutions that reflect new political realities. Some key potential elements of a more cooperative European security are already in place or in the making. Given the great variety of interests and perspectives that will have to be accommodated, how can a new European security system be constructed, and how does NATO fit in?

European governments are moving toward a consensus that the Conference on Security and Cooperation in Europe, which includes 35 NATO, [former] Warsaw Pact and European neutral and Non-Aligned countries, should become the over-arching framework for discussion and decisions on the future of Europe. All the main players participate in the CSCE, and most governments have already identified the CSCE process as a key part of future European security arrangements.

But skeptics, some prominently placed in the Bush administration and supported by prominent observers outside the government,[6] point out that the 35-nation group is so diverse that it would not be an effective decision-making body. They argue that traditional antagonisms, for example those between Greece and Turkey, would frequently block consensus and that even small peripheral countries like Malta could exercise a veto. They also note that the basis for the CSCE—the 1975 Helsinki Final Act—is not a treaty and therefore is not legally binding on the members.

There are reasonable criticisms of, but not necessarily fatal flaws in, the CSCE route. The question is how to overcome these shortcomings in the CSCE framework. The skeptics' critique may in fact hold the key to the solution. The first step may be to envision transforming the CSCE Final Act into a treaty, amending the Final Act to add features necessitated by German unification and to establish a practical relationship between the CSCE framework and the other European organizations and arrangements. This process would help deal with the concerns of countries that are not directly involved in the Two-plus-Four discussions. Transforming the Final Act into a treaty would beneficially bypass the process of drafting a peace treaty, thereby dealing with German sensitivities on this point. Finally, the treaty mechanism would allow the U.S. Congress to play a direct role in establishing future security arrangements, strengthening American political support for those arrangements.

The CSCE Final Act lays out a set of guidelines for cooperation among states in promoting peace, economic cooperation, and human rights in Europe. This "declaration on principles guiding relations between participating states," which would be the heart of a new treaty, usefully precludes any changes in European borders except through peaceful means. A critical step would be to amend the Final Act to reflect the outcome of the Two-plus-Four talks—the conditions under which German unity [took] place. These terms might include, for example, promises not to station NATO forces on Germany's eastern territory, and German reaffirmation of its commitment not to become a nuclear power.

It will also be important to link the CSCE political commitments to the process of conventional arms control. This linkage could help provide the reassurance required by the Soviet Union concerning ceilings on future German military forces. The CFE negotiations on conventional forces, already under the CSCE umbrella, provide a mechanism for monitoring reductions in military force levels throughout Europe and for regulating future military relations between current NATO and [former] Warsaw Pact countries. The verification and compliance provisions ... of [the] first-stage CFE accord could serve as the core for a future management system for European military forces.

A second-stage CFE could produce substantial conventional reductions for all participants, and a restructuring of forces to limit the potential and incentives to initiate hostilities between or among any of the participants. The neutral and Non-Aligned countries which now participate in the CSCE could be affiliated with the CFE process through participation in the compliance and confidence-building procedures, if not in the reductions themselves. The process of conventional arms control within the CSCE framework will in any case have to be restructured away from its current East-West foundations to encourage stable and peaceful military relations among all participants viewed on a bilateral and regional basis, and not just on the East-West level as originally intended.

It would be logical, given the blurring of bloc-to-bloc distinctions that is taking place, for CFE-II reductions to be taken on a national basis, with all participants reducing forces on an agreed percentage basis. National limits could serve as the cap on German military forces desired by the Soviet Union, without singling out Germany, by surrounding those limits with a multilateral context in which all countries accepted limitations on their forces.

New negotiations on United States and Soviet short-range nuclear weapons seem likely to join the international agenda by 1991. While such negotiations are a necessary ingredient in the process of adjusting military force structures to accommodate new political realities, the negotiations themselves will probably be conducted outside the CSCE framework. The outcome of the negotiations, however, could be fed into the CSCE framework as part of the outline for an evolving, more cooperative European security system.

In addition, the provision in the Final Act that acknowledges the sovereign right of states to enter into treaties and other international agreements could be strengthened to acknowledge clearly the legitimacy of all treaties, bilateral accords, and organizations in Europe that contribute to the goals articulated in the Final Act. This "grandfather clause" would spread the CSCE umbrella over a wide range of present institutions, as well as over new institutions deemed necessary in the future. The clause would also make it clear that it will not be necessary or even desirable to do everything "at 35" in the future, and that practical cooperation consistent with the goals of the CSCE can take place at a variety of bilateral, regional, and transatlantic levels. This approach would also provide the basis for continued adherence of current NATO members to the North Atlantic Treaty, whose principles should be preserved even if the organization itself becomes less relevant to new political realities in Europe....

Giving the CSCE process legal standing could provide an institutional way for the U.S. and the Soviet Union to remain constructively involved in future European developments—an important consideration—while at the same time supplying the international framework for German reunification. Such a framework could make it easier for the Soviet Union to swallow the membership of a united Germany in NATO, and in other arrangements that have been suggested for a European defense pillar to integrate German military forces with those of its neighbors.

For several years into the future, many practical areas of cooperation in defense may be coordinated through existing NATO mechanisms. Further down the road, the European Community or the Western European Union (of France, Great Britain, West Germany, Italy, Belgium, the Netherlands, Luxembourg, Portugal and Spain) might assume many of these functions, particularly if the U.S. military presence on the ground in Europe is reduced to token levels.

As noted above, a CSCE Treaty would also allow the U.S. Congress to participate, through the ratification process, in the creation of a new European order. This would help establish a strong domestic foundation for a leading U.S. role in the process of strengthening democratic institutions across Europe and in the construction of a more cooperative European security system. This is not just a parochial American concern. Those with good historical recall will reflect on the refusal of the Congress to go along with President Woodrow Wilson's League of Nations plan following the First World War. U.S. abstention from participation in the League seriously limited its potential. Following the Second World War, the Truman administration was sufficiently wise to enmesh the Congress in the treaty commitments and institution-building of the early postwar period; and the involvement of the Congress in building the system helped ensure support for its continuation. A new

European security order likewise would benefit from an American commitment shared equally by the Republican presidency and the Democratic-controlled Congress.

Implications for the Role of the United States

These potential developments raise a series of important issues for U.S. foreign and defense policy. President Bush has frequently stated his resolve to see that the United States remains an active participant in Europe. However, a Europe in which NATO's role is less prominent would also make dealing with our European friends more complex. The United States has just begun to explore questions about what the full range of its means of influence are beyond its military strength within NATO, about which of these is likely to be most important in the years ahead, and about which may require additional resources or new impetus. Such changes may also create subtle or overt alterations in ongoing U.S. bilateral relations. The Bush administration has tried to assure Britain that our "special relationship" will not suffer in the context of a new European mosaic, especially one in which Germany plays a more dominant role; but it is hard to imagine any existing U.S.-European relationships that will be untouched by the process of change now under way.

West European economic and political cooperation has progressed to the point where the European Community countries can achieve consensus on a wide range of issues and now act in a coordinated way in many circumstances. There are still, however, many issues on which the major European powers disagree. This is particularly true when it comes to the "big" issues such as future monetary cooperation, Third World issues and defense organization, to name a few. Recent events have raised questions about whether the United States still has a useful role to play in shaping Europe's future. Such splits as exist among our allies, however, suggest that the United States probably still has a potentially constructive "leadership" role to play, at least in suggesting approaches to future pan-European issues.

Perhaps the key argument for the United States remaining actively involved in European security arrangements is the fact that twice in this century already the United States has had to send soldiers to fight and die in Europe to help restore international order. The postwar U.S. investment in European security arrangements has paid large dividends in terms of war avoidance and has played an important political role in supporting democratic forces and ideas on the European continent.

It appears certain now that the United States will be able to reduce its military involvement in Europe substantially below current levels.

Even conservative estimates expect at least a 50 percent reduction in U.S. force levels in Europe over the next several years down to 150,000 military personnel; other estimates project a token force of no more than 50,000 by the end of the 1990s. Some observers advocate a total U.S. pullout in order to get all Soviet forces out of Eastern Europe.[7]

As the prominence of the U.S. military role in Europe recedes, it is generally thought that U.S. political influence will recede as well. On the other hand, as the importance of military instruments of power diminishes in relations between the European countries, influence may depend much more on political and economic instruments of power. Under such circumstances, future U.S. influence in Europe may depend much more on the political and economic roles that it plays than on the strength of its immediate military presence. U.S. influence may decline, but not just because it no longer has a leading military role in Europe.

The most fundamental issue for the United States in 1990 is what role it wants to play in the new European architecture. It will be difficult for the United States to formulate coherent and politically supportable policies toward the process of change in Europe until there is more consensus on the goals that we seek and the outcomes we prefer. Members of Congress as well as the administration will necessarily confront this basic question as they attempt to establish new defense spending, arms control and foreign aid priorities in the coming months and years.

Many observers are asking whether the Congress would support a continued military presence in Europe if the U.S. nuclear presence were removed, and whether the United States would be willing to deploy any troops in Europe if it no longer had such a dominant voice in European security decision-making. Another question that might be asked is whether the United States would deploy troops in Europe if NATO, for all intents and purposes, ceased to exist. These are good questions, and they cannot be answered definitively today.

A key ingredient might be whether or not the Congress has been involved in the process of creating the new order. If it has been, and there is general support for the outcome, senators and representatives will be inclined to do what is necessary to make the system work. The cost of a token U.S. presence in Europe would be minor compared to the costs sustained by the United States throughout the postwar period, and should not be a major political issue.

Another ingredient will be the American public opinion. Early in 1990, while public opinion polls show that a majority of Americans want to reduce U.S. forces in Europe below the current U.S. goal of around 200,000, a large majority (in one poll by a 76 percent to 18 percent margin)[8] believes that the U.S. should maintain at least some troops on the continent. Such polling data reflects a fundamental continuity in U.S. public support for the U.S. commitment to peace in Europe. In previous years that support has been demonstrated by a willingness to deploy substantial numbers of forces in Europe in spite of resentment about equitable burden-sharing with the allies. Current polls suggest a willingness in the future to deploy some forces in Europe even without an imminent Soviet threat to European security.

Some European experts and officials are talking about establishing a collective security system within the CSCE framework.[9] Such a system would require that all the major participants have military forces available for collective action against any country that attempted to use force against a member of the system. The evolution of such a collective security system under the CSCE umbrella would provide an additional rationale that might be compelling with both the Congress and with U.S. public opinion in support of a continued U.S. military presence in Europe as a U.S. contribution to the peacekeeping effort.

The U.S. Congress and the American people would probably be prepared to support a continued U.S. military presence in Europe at significantly lower levels provided that two basic conditions were fulfilled. First, the European countries would have to indicate clearly their desire to have American forces stationed in Europe, either in a revised NATO framework, or in the context of new bilateral or multilateral arrangements with NATO countries, or in the framework of a new collective security system. If an American force presence in Germany becomes politically unacceptable (or withdrawal becomes the price for a complete pullout of Soviet forces from Germany), then the question would be whether other European countries would be willing to host this token presence. France comes most immediately to mind as the country most appropriately located to host U.S. forces. Belgium and the Netherlands are also candidates because of their proximity to Central Europe, but they have less available space for hosting U.S. forces than France. Clearly, France would not host "NATO" forces, but would the French government be willing to host U.S. forces on a bilateral basis within the framework of a new European security system? We do not know the answer to this question, but it is clear that without a strong European desire for a continued U.S. presence and a willing host, U.S. forces will surely leave.

Second, the continued presence of U.S. forces would be conditioned on a stable military as well as political situation for their presence. American politicians in the past have argued that U.S. forces would not stay if nuclear weapons were banned because, given the previous conventional force imbalance in face of the Warsaw Pact, U.S. forces would have been exposed to unacceptable risks of attack and defeat by Pact forces. Under the new circumstances—the Pact's political and military disintegration and the creation of a conventional balance through the CFE negotiations in the early 1990s, presumably followed by deep cuts and defensive restructuring later in the 1990s—U.S. forces would not need to possess nuclear weapons on the ground in Europe to be secure.

Perhaps the most difficult obstacles to overcome in creating a new European security system are the psychological hurdles that have to be cleared. The Russians have been forced to pass many of those hurdles early in the process, losing both the Warsaw Pact and their East German ally within a matter of months. Accepting those changes was quite easy for the United States—part of the Cold War "victory." But the next stages will probably require the United States, remembering General Galvin's "wing-walker" rule, to contemplate moving from one source of support to another. After 40 years of justifying much of our role in the world in terms of the North Atlantic Treaty Organization, it will not be easy to develop new rationales. Even when political leadership in the United States reaches a consensus on which to base the U.S. role in the world, it may take years of conditioning and positive experience before we feel totally comfortable with the new framework.

As the decade of the 1990s begins, it is still unclear whether the Soviet Union will continue down the path to reform or will retrench. Under such circumstances the United States might be foolish to give up on security arrangements that have worked in the past; it should strive to adapt them to new political circumstances. But the United States would be equally ill advised not to prepare for the new possibilities that would emerge should the Soviet Union continue to move toward democracy and a mixed economy. Under such circumstances, adaptation might be insufficient, as continuation of NATO as a military alliance might block the realization of a cooperative European security system. The United States therefore might be best prepared for the future if it developed a parallel policy structure that keeps open the potential for continued reliance on a mutual security arrangement (NATO) still intended largely to balance Soviet power, while at the same time preparing for transition to some form of collective security system in which the Soviet Union could share the responsibility with all other European nations, with the United States and with Canada for discouraging the threat or use of military force in relations between participants in the system.

During this period of adjustments and uncertainty, NATO will continue to play an important role. NATO still provides the best framework for consultation between the United States and its European allies. The main task of those consultations over the next several years should be finding ways to arrange orderly construction of new cooperative venues to replace the old. The goal would be to seek:

- to preserve the North Atlantic Treaty Organization as an essential safety net until the future course of Soviet reform becomes much clearer than it is today;
- agreement on a strengthened CSCE framework as the umbrella over a more cooperative European security system that could under the right circumstances evolve into a true collective security framework in the future, but which in the meantime would help to resolve security dilemmas surrounding German unification, the protection of legitimate Soviet security concerns and the Westernization of Eastern Europe;
- an effectively functioning process to monitor force levels and activities throughout Europe, and to arrange further reductions and restructuring of forces after completion of the CFE accord now being negotiated; and finally,
- a routine and institutionalized relationship between the United States and the European Community, to serve as an open channel for the resolution of trade and economic issues and for consultation on foreign policy issues.

In this process, consultations in NATO could make a key contribution to the construction of a new Europe. Those consultations might eventually lead to the dissolution of much of the NATO structure of the past. On the other hand, the fact that NATO faced itself toward the future and became instrumental in helping to shape it might validate some continuing political role in a new European security system. Ironically, perhaps the only way NATO can be assured of some continuing relevance is if it urgently contemplates and prepares for its own demise.

Notes

1. The views expressed in this article are the author's own and not those of any government agency.

2. Stanley R. Sloan, *NATO's Future: Toward a New Transatlantic Bargain*, Washington, D.C.: National Defense University Press, 1984, p. xvii.

3. Sloan, *NATO's Future*, p. xviii.

4. "Excerpts from Baker's Speech on Berlin and U.S. Role in Europe's Future," *New York Times*, 13 December 1989, p. A18.

5. Thomas L. Friedman, "A Baltic Chill on Relations," *New York Times*, 8 April 1990, p. 15.

6. For example, see Henry A. Kissinger, "Germany, Neutrality and the Security 'System' Trap," *Washington Post*, 15 April 1990, p. D7. Kissinger acknowledges that Western policy is in need of "a coherent concept" for Europe's security future but argues against trying to substitute a collective defense system under the auspices of the CSCE for the mutual defense arrangements in NATO. According to Kissinger, in a collective security arrangement, "a major rogue country would be secure in the knowledge that it would have a de facto veto over the actions of the so-called security system." Kissinger did not offer his own "coherent concept," but rather suggested that a new NATO study, modeled on the 1967 Harmel Report, might be required to produce such a concept.

7. For example, see Jenonne Walker, "U.S., Soviet Troops: Pull Them All Out," *New York Times*, 18 March 1990, p. E19.

8. David Shribman, "Americans, while voicing some deep concerns, widely favor German reunification, poll shows," *Wall Street Journal*, 16 March 1990, p. A16.

9. See, for example, Michael Z. Wise, "Warsaw Pact Ministers Hear Call for New Order," *Washington Post*, 18 March 1990, p. 33. The story quotes Czechoslovak Foreign Minister Jiri Dienstbier, hosting a Warsaw Pact foreign ministerial meeting, as saying "The core of any collective system of European security must be a treaty committing every party to provide assistance, including military assistance, in the event of an attack against any participant in the system. This requires a mechanism enabling the implementation of this commitment."

21

The Common European Home and Mutual Security

Mikhail Bezrukov and Yuriy Davydov

The problem of mutual security in Europe should not be reduced to that of stability inside different European regions or countries. It is in fact much wider. The future of the European continent depends to a great extent on the general evolution of East-West relations.

Stability in Europe, divided into two blocs opposing each other, was assured in the past several decades by three interrelated factors:

- The existence of external threats for each bloc (whether they were real or imagined is another question);
- Military mutual deterrence based on a growing capacity of the sides to destroy each other;
- The predominance of the superpowers—the Soviet Union and the United States—in their respective blocs.

This kind of stability proved to be strongly built though it had three important shortcomings: a) it was very expensive; b) it distorted the perception of real problems and needs of the region; and c) it was potentially dangerous, for its collapse could have brought about a nuclear catastrophe. In other words, the situation was stable but not sufficiently secure. In the past that was perhaps the only possible kind of stability given the realities of the international situation, and it survived the crises of the Cold War era.

The end of the 1980s will, beyond doubt, enter the history of international relations as a period of rapid erosion of the walls that have been separating East and West.

The break through the dividing lines is due primarily to the reform movement that is gathering strength in the East. Mounting reforms of economies and political structures in some of these countries here are accompanied by a radical revision of their foreign policy concepts. Rejected or substantially weakened are many "idols" of the past; many basic ideas about the outside world are reconsidered. Parallel steps are visible in the West: The "image of the enemy" has faded; the division of the world into "us" and "them" is being replaced by a more promising idea of unity of humanity. The consensus achieved in the Vienna follow-up meeting of the CSCE reflects this new reality.

There are other signs indicating that we are in a process of fundamental changes in East-West relations on European soil. Following the INF Treaty, we witness sincere efforts of the East and the West to lower the balance of conventional forces in Europe. Both in the West and in the East the superpowers are losing their dominant Cold War style positions. It is quite understandable why Mikhail Gorbachev's appeals for "new political thinking" are echoed by President George Bush's calls to move "beyond containment."

It is now more and more widely recognized both in the East and in the West that relations between the European states could surpass the limits set up by the Cold War confrontation. Mutual fears and enmity can and should be replaced by a growing East-West cooperation and dialogue. Already several generations of politicians on both sides have tried to lead their countries to victory in our "historical dispute." In doing so they were convinced of the validity of a black-and-white formula, "we or they." Now it is clear more than ever that this approach has been *erroneous*. "We *and* they, together" is the principle that should guide our efforts in East-West relations.

The evolution of the situation in Europe gives rise to discussions about its future and about a new European political order. At the core of these discussions is a striving for a European identity. Among many ideas that have emerged is Mikhail Gorbachev's idea of a "common European home." In Prague on 10 April 1987, he said: "We now turn ourselves resolutely against the division of the continent ... we have introduced the idea of a 'common European home'." In this connection at least four questions arise: Are there any preconditions for building this common European home? What can every side gain from it? What serves as a basis for the edifice? What difficulties may the process of constructing it face?

The idea of a unified, peaceful Europe is an old one. In the past many of the best minds of the continent embraced it in one form or another—Kant, Voltaire, Rousseau, Saint-Simon, Mazzini, Garibaldi and even Metternich, among many others. The main reason for the present surge of interest in the idea is simply that now the time is ripe for it. A set of preconditions now exists, making it possible to move beyond the postwar European system of relations.

The most general of these preconditions are: the historical memory of the European people with its deep understanding of inadmissibility of a new war; a high level of mutual understanding among the nations of the continent (higher than in any other region); a uniquely diversified system of bilateral and multilateral interactions, especially the Helsinki process; and a common cultural and historical heritage. These are good starting ground for building a system of relations in Europe based on the principle of mutual security.

The present situation gives us some additional reasons to believe that Europe is ready for a gradual dismantling of the system it has inherited from the past.

First, it is evident that Europe has already been living for many years under circumstances where the Cold War has exhausted itself. The states of the East and the West have reached most of the goals they had been aiming at when participating in it. At the same time some goals, which proved to be unattainable, were dropped. By now many of the social and political differences that once had been the main reason for confrontation have eroded or even disappeared totally. Some of the differences are, of course, still present, but they are much less acute than they were forty years ago. Today, the high level of military preparations do not correspond to the level of social and political differences existing between the countries of Europe.

Second, representatives of a new generation are entering active political life in European countries and in the United States. They are free from the stereotypes of the 1940s and 1950s; they fear less; and they believe more in the peaceful development of East-West relations. They do not share some of the allegiances of the generation of their fathers and above all they refuse to accept the system of political-military division of Europe.

Third, the perception of a threat to survival is changing. Traditionally both sides were obsessed with the specter of nuclear and conventional wars. But as it turned out there are other important sources of danger as well. And they are common both to the East and to the West: deterioration of environment, international terrorism, drugs, and so forth. Global problems cannot be solved by one state, one alliance or even one social system. This means that besides national and regional interests there are also those of the European and global communities.

Fourth, both in the East and in the West we observe more tolerance toward other belief systems and more readiness to listen with patience to the arguments of the other side. The age of uncompromising "theological disputes" between advocates of capitalism and adherents to the socialist idea is clearly becoming a thing of the past.

Fifth, democratic institutions are gaining strength in both parts of the European continent. And as we know from our historical experience, democratic societies have convincingly demonstrated their preference for non-military solutions of any disputes that arise between them.

One can draw the conclusion that the process of change in Europe has reached a critical point. The area of shared interests in East-West relations has considerably grown while their confrontation has drastically diminished. This process gave a powerful impulse to the idea of mutual security. Let us hope that both the East and the West will take advantage of the current situation.

Possible Positive Outcomes

Overcoming of the division of Europe and construction of the common European home based on mutual security principles can be successful only if both the East and the West perceive the advantages of a new system of relations in comparison with the old ones. What are these advantages?

- The emergence of a system of mutual security, eliminating fears and suspicions, would allow both sides to use huge resources that are now spent on the arms race for solution of other problems;

- The enlargement of a European network of economic ties—a big European economic market could provide dynamic economic development for the whole region;
- Strengthening of political stability on the European continent, by the creation of all-European institutions, could help to solve political, economic and other problems;
- Organic ties between East and West European states can be created;
- An all-European consciousness can emerge, as opposed to national and group egoisms.

Principles and Stages

It is possible to overcome the division of Europe only on the basis of common approaches to such fundamental issues as mutual security; trust between peoples and states; non-interference into internal affairs of the other nations; human rights; democracy; legal foundation of the functioning of the international, state and public life; role of the market forces in the economy; etc.

The desire expressed by the Soviet Union to join some of the international agreements worked out by the Council of Europe reflects a readiness of the Soviet side to reach common understanding with the West on these issues. The final document signed in the Vienna follow-up CSCE conference demonstrates that the values of the East and the West are closer to each other than many skeptics might have expected. This document is a very important step toward the common European home.

The construction of the common European home could be divided into several stages.

In the initial stage, dramatic changes in the existing European structures are undesirable. NATO, the Warsaw Treaty Organization, the European Community and the Council for Mutual Economic Assistance could play a role in a positive transformation of relations among the European countries, especially if their functioning undergoes appropriate reforms. At the same time the emergence of new forms of regional cooperation should not be excluded, first of all in the East.

The Warsaw Treaty Organization and NATO should in any case stop performing their traditional functions, determined by the East-West confrontation of the Cold War years....

During this initial stage, both the East and the West, having in mind mutual security principles, should concentrate their efforts on the following three goals:

- Levels of military confrontation on the European continent should be lowered.

- National laws and foreign policies of the European states should be brought in line with international agreements, especially those worked out through the Helsinki process.
- Both sides should encourage development of transnational economic ties between independent producers and agencies (that is, those whose activity is not directly guided by government bodies and is based on market principles).

The last goal will not be easy to reach, given the current economic difficulties being experienced by East European countries and the Soviet Union, and also the incompatibility of the Western market economies and the highly centralized ones that are still largely in place in the East European countries and the Soviet Union. But it should be kept in mind that without such ties it is hardly possible to move toward the creation of what could be termed organic ties between the countries of the East and the West, and therefore towards the common European home.

Thus the mutual security idea has also an economic dimension.

In later stages, emerging common or comparable features in the national structures and foreign policies of European states would create the necessary preconditions for intensive cooperation between them. Formation of transnational economic complexes would make them more interdependent economically and would facilitate economic integration. Similarities in political structures and legal regulations would make it much easier to establish all-European institutions.

In these later stages, all-European institutions would be increasingly relied on in regulating relations in different spheres: security problems, economic exchanges, foreign policy, culture and education, etc. They would be moving forces behind European integration. The precise forms of their activity will be determined by the process of construction of the common European home.

The common European home would include, first, all the territory from the Atlantic to the Urals. But this in no way means the exclusion of the United States and Canada, for they are linked to Europe by extensive historical, political, economic and cultural ties. Any attempts to erect artificial barriers between North America and Europe will inevitably fail. They contradict the very goal of forming a new system of relations in Europe based on mutual security principles. It will never be possible to create the common European home at the expense of the United States and Canada, who have played an important role in the Helsinki process.

Politically and economically, North America is even more a part of Europe than even some European nations presently are. Modern technology has drastically shrunk the Atlantic, and the United States and Canada (especially in security terms) are as close to Europe as Great Britain was at the beginning of the present century, or even closer.

The United States and Canada should in some form be involved in the European mutual security system. Their dependence on and their involvement in it will increase the stake of both countries in European stability. One also has to take into consideration the possibility that if the United States withdraws politically from Europe, that could create fears and feelings of insecurity in some of the West European nations, which could be highly destabilizing in the long run. It should also be kept in mind, as history shows us, that there is a certain positive and healthy European influence on the behavior of the United States in the political-military sphere, an influence one would like to keep.

It is often said that the Soviet Union is too big and has too many problems to be part of a stable European system. This argument in favor of exclusion of the Soviet Union from all-European cooperation may look a weighty one. But other considerations should also be taken into account. First, historically and culturally, the Soviet Union belongs to Europe. For many centuries we have influenced European developments and have felt in turn their impact. European countries are our traditional and natural partners and though the Soviet Union (Russia) differed in the past and still differs from our European neighbors, our mutual attraction should not be overlooked. Second, the Soviet Union and other European countries are interdependent in many respects. Soviet problems would inevitably knock at the doors of other European nations. Third, the USSR may not be so big after all. The United Europe that would surface after 1992 would be large and powerful by any standards. Fourth, any attempt to exclude the Soviet Union from the common European home would renew Cold War fears and suspicions and would destabilize the situation in the whole region. In other words, it will be impossible to create a viable system of relations in Europe based on the mutual security principle without the Soviet Union.

Transitional Period

Transitional periods are usually difficult ones and the present course of events in Europe is no exception. Any transitional period is marked by the coexistence—and the conflict of—the old system of relations that has outlived its time, and the gradually emerging new approaches and structures. This very conflict by itself may be a significant destabilizing factor. For the moment the legacy of the Cold War is still with us and a new era of East-West cooperation free from military threats is making but its first steps.

Cold War symptoms are still numerous, unfortunately. Large armies face each other. Many institutions brought to life by the East-West confrontation continue to function. The temptation to gain one-sided concessions has not disappeared, nor has the habit to rejoice at misfortunes of the other side. We still hear "fatherly" advice in speeches as to what is to be done in this or that part of Europe.

Sprouts of a new type of relations on the European continent have to grow through stones of enmity and estrangement inherited from the past decades. But they do grow. Both in the East and the West, understanding is growing that Europe now has an unprecedented opportunity to draw a final line between its future, and its past marked by confrontations and wars. The "new political thinking" calls precisely to remove all political obstacles that bar the road toward unity of Europe and to open a new page in the history of this continent.

The main problem facing Europe today is to ensure the stable (and peaceful!) evolution of Europe toward a new political order. Where could possible threats to this evolution come from? There are several potential sources of instability:

- There could be attempts from both the East and the West to exploit contradictions and problems inherent to the processes of change in both parts of Europe to obtain one-sided advantages.
- There could be failure or unsatisfactory results of negotiations on conventional and nuclear weapons or confidence-building measures, or violations of the already existing agreements.
- Technological innovations could arise in the military sphere that could complicate negotiations between East and West and upset the military balance in Europe....
- Reforms in the Soviet Union and East European countries could fail or "skid"; there could be a failure to create a common (market) base for economic interactions between East and West.
- Hazards could arise from the difference in the levels and characters of economic and political integration in the East and in the West; and the gap could deepen between integrating Western Europe and transforming the East.
- Attempts could be made to exclude the Soviet Union or the United States—or both of them—from the new political order in Europe.
- The process of military integration in Western Europe could pose a hazard if it led to a rapid growth of West European military capabilities....

Most of these sources of instability could undermine the foundations of the mutual security system in Europe.

Both East and West have an interest in a peaceful transition to a more stable political order in Europe. They should do everything in their power to reduce these and any other threats to the present positive developments on the continent. The common European home and European political stability are not identical ideas. But they are interrelated ones. It is hardly possible to build a common European home in an unstable international environment. On the other hand, only gradually overcoming the division of Europe can ultimately assure a more stable European political order.

22

Why We Will Soon Miss the Cold War

John J. Mearsheimer

Peace: It's wonderful. I like it as much as the next man, and have no wish to be willfully gloomy at a moment when optimism about the future shape of the world abounds. Nevertheless, my thesis in this essay is that we are likely soon to regret the passing of the Cold War.

To be sure, no one will miss such by-products of the Cold War as the Korean and Vietnam conflicts. No one will want to replay the U-2 affair, the Cuban missile crisis, or the building of the Berlin Wall. And no one will want to revisit the domestic Cold War, with its purges and loyalty oaths, its xenophobia and stifling of dissent. We will not wake up one day to discover fresh wisdom in the collected fulminations of John Foster Dulles.

We may, however, wake up one day lamenting the loss of the order that the Cold War gave to the anarchy of international relations. For untamed anarchy is what Europe knew in the forty-five years of this century before the Cold War, and untamed anarchy—Hobbe's war of all against all—is a prime cause of armed conflict. Those who think that armed conflicts among the European states are now out of the question, that the two world wars burned all the war out of Europe, are projecting unwarranted optimism onto the future. The theories of peace that implicitly undergird this optimism are notably shallow constructs. They stand up to neither logical nor historical analysis. You would not want to bet the farm on their prophetic accuracy.

The world is about to conduct a vast test of the theories of war and peace put forward by social scientists, who never dreamed that their ideas would be tested by the world-historic events announced almost daily in newspaper headlines. This social scientist is willing to put his theoretical cards on the table as he ventures predictions about the future of Europe. In the process, I hope to put alternative theories of war and peace under as much intellectual pressure as I can muster. My argument is that the prospect of major crises, even wars, in Europe is likely to increase dramatically now that the Cold War is receding into history. The next forty-five years in Europe are not likely to be so violent as the forty-five years before the Cold War, but they are likely to be substantially more violent than the past forty-five years, the era that we may someday look back upon not as the Cold War but as the Long Peace, in John Lewis Gaddis's phrase.

This pessimistic conclusion rests on the general argument that the distribution and character of military power among states are the root causes of war and peace. Specifically, the peace in Europe since 1945—precarious at first, but increasingly robust over time—has flowed from three factors: the bipolar distribution of military power on the Continent; the rough military equality between the polar powers, the United States and the Soviet Union; and the ritualistically deplored fact that each of these superpowers is armed with a large nuclear arsenal.

We don't yet know the entire shape of the new Europe. But we do know some things. We know, for example, that the new Europe will involve a return to the multipolar distribution of power that characterized the European state system from its founding, with the Peace of Westphalia, in 1648, until 1945. We know that this multipolar European state system was plagued by war from first to last. We know that from 1900 to 1945 some 50 million Europeans were killed in wars that were caused in great part by the instability of this state system. We also know that since 1945 only some 15,000 Europeans have been killed in wars: roughly 10,000 Hungarians and Russians, in what we might call the Russo-Hungarian War of October and November, 1956, and somewhere between 1500 and 5000 Greeks and Turks, in the July and August, 1974, war on Cyprus.

The point is clear: Europe is reverting to a state system that created powerful incentives for aggression in the past. If you believe (as the Realist school of international-relations theory, to which I belong, believes) that the prospects for international peace are not markedly influenced by the domestic political character of states—that it is the character of the state system, not the character of the individual units composing it, that drives states toward war—then it is difficult to share in the widespread elation of the moment about the future of Europe. Last year was repeatedly compared to 1789, the year the French Revolution began, as the Year of Freedom, and so it was. Forgotten in the general exaltation was that the hope-filled events of 1789 signaled the start of an era of war and conquest.

A "Hard" Theory of Peace

What caused the era of violence in Europe before 1945, and why has the postwar era, the period of the Cold War, been so much more peaceful? The two world wars before 1945 had myriad particular and unrepeatable causes, but to the student of international relations seeking to establish generalizations about the behavior of states in the past which might illuminate their behavior in the future, two fundamental causes stand out. These are the multipolar distribution of power in Europe, and the imbalances of strength that often developed among the great powers as they jostled for supremacy or advantage.

There is something elementary about the geometry of power in international relations, and so its importance is easy to overlook. "Bipolarity" and "multipolarity" are ungainly but necessary coinages. The Cold War, with two superpowers serving to anchor rival alliances of clearly inferior powers, is our model of bipolarity. Europe in 1914, with France, Germany, Great Britain, Austria-Hungary, and Russia positioned as great powers, is our model of multipolarity.

If the example of 1914 is convincing enough evidence that multipolar systems are the more dangerous geometry of power, then perhaps I should rest my case. Alas for theoretical elegance, there are no empirical studies providing conclusive support for this proposition. From its beginnings until 1945 the European state system was multipolar, so this history is barren of comparisons that would reveal the different effects of the two systems. Earlier history, to be sure, does furnish scattered examples of bipolar systems, including some—Athens and Sparta, Rome and Carthage—that were warlike. But this history is inconclusive, because it is incomplete. Lacking a comprehensive survey of history, we can't do much more than offer examples—now on this, now on that side of the debate. As a result, the case made here rests chiefly on deduction.

Deductively, a bipolar system is more peaceful for the simple reason that under it only two major powers are in contention. Moreover, those great powers generally demand allegiance from minor powers in the system, which is likely to produce rigid alliance structures. The smaller states are then secure from each other as well as from attack by the rival great power. Consequently (to make a Dick-and-Jane point with a well-worn social-science term), a bipolar system has only one dyad across which war might break out. A multipolar system is much more fluid and has many such dyads. Therefore, other things being equal, war is statistically more likely in a multipolar system than it is in a bipolar one. Admittedly, wars in a multipolar world that involve only minor powers or only one major power are not likely to be as devastating as a conflict between two major powers. But small wars always have the potential to widen into big wars.

Also, deterrence is difficult to maintain in a multipolar state system, because power imbalances are commonplace, and when power asymmetries develop, the strong become hard to deter. Two great powers can join together to attack a third state, as Germany and the Soviet Union did in 1939, when they ganged up on Poland. Furthermore, a major power might simply bully a weaker power in a one-on-one encounter, using its superior strength to coerce or defeat the minor state. Germany's actions against Czechoslovakia in the late 1930s provide a good example of this sort of behavior. Ganging up and bullying are largely unknown in a bipolar system, since with only two great powers dominating center stage, it is impossible to produce the power asymmetries that result in ganging up and bullying.

There is a second reason that deterrence is more problematic under multipolarity. The resolve of opposing states and also the size and strength of opposing coalitions are hard to calculate in this geometry of power, because the shape of the international order tends to remain in flux, owing to the tendency of coalitions to gain and lose partners. This can lead aggressors to conclude falsely that they can coerce others by bluffing war, or even achieve outright victory on the battlefield. For example, Germany was not certain before 1914 that Britain would oppose it if it reached for Continental hegemony, and Germany completely failed to foresee that the United States would eventually move to contain it. In 1939 Germany hoped that France and Britain would stand aside as it conquered Poland, and again failed to foresee the eventual American entry into the war. As a result, Germany exaggerated its prospects for success, which undermined deterrence by encouraging German adventurism.

The prospects for peace, however, are not simply a function of the number of great powers in the system. They are also affected by the relative military strength of those major states. Bipolar and multipolar systems both are likely to be more peaceful when power is distributed equally in them. Power inequalities invite war, because they increase an aggressor's prospects for victory on the battlefield. Most of the general wars that have tormented Europe over the past five centuries have involved one particularly powerful state against the other major powers in the system. This pattern characterized the wars that grew from the attempts at hegemony by Charles V, Philip II, Louis XIV, Revolutionary and Napoleonic France, Wilhelmine Germany, and Nazi Germany. Hence the size of the gap in military power between the two leading states in the system is a key determinant of stability. Small gaps foster peace; larger gaps promote war.

Nuclear weapons seem to be in almost everybody's bad book, but the fact is that they are a powerful force for peace. Deterrence is most likely to hold when the costs and risks of going to war are unambiguously stark. The more horrible the prospect of war, the less likely war is. Deterrence is also more robust when conquest is more difficult. Potential aggressor states are given pause by the patent futility of attempts at expansion.

Nuclear weapons favor peace on both counts. They are weapons of mass destruction, and would produce horrendous devastation if used in any numbers. Moreover, they are more useful for self-defense than for aggression. If both sides' nuclear arsenals are secure from attack, creating an arrangement of mutual assured destruction, neither side can employ these weapons to gain a meaningful military advantage. International conflicts then become tests of pure will. Who would dare to use these weapons of unimaginable destructive power? Defenders have the advantage here, because defenders usually value their freedom more than aggressors value new conquests.

Nuclear weapons further bolster peace by moving power relations among states toward equality. States that possess nuclear deterrents can stance up to one another, even if their nuclear arsenals vary greatly in size, as long as both sides have an assured destruction capability. In addition, mutual assured destruction helps alleviate the vexed problem of miscalculation by leaving little doubt about the relative power of states.

No discussion of the causes of peace in the twentieth century would be complete without a word on nationalism. With "nationalism" as a synonym for "love of country" I have no quarrel. But hypernationalism, the belief that other nations or nation-states are both inferior and threatening, is perhaps the single greatest domestic threat to peace, although it is still not a leading force in world politics. Hypernationalism arose in the past among European states because most of them were nation-states—states composed mainly of people from a single ethnic group—that existed in an anarchic world, under constant threat from other states. In such a system people who love their own nation can easily come to be contemptuous of the nationalities inhabiting opposing states. The problem is worsened when domestic elites demonize a rival nation to drum up support for national-security policy.

Hypernationalism finds its most fertile soil under military systems relying on mass armies. These require sacrifices to sustain, and the state is tempted to appeal to nationalist sentiments to mobilize its citizens to make them. The quickening of hypernationalism is least likely when states can rely on small professional armies, or on complex high-technology military organizations that operate without vast manpower. For this reason, nuclear weapons work to dampen nationalism, because they shift the basis of military power away from mass armies and toward smaller, high-technology organizations.

Hypernationalism declined sharply in Europe after 1945, not only because of the nuclear revolution but also because the postwar occupation forces kept it down. Moreover, the European states, no longer providing their own security, lacked an incentive to whip up nationalism to bolster public support for national defense. But the decisive change came in the shift of the prime locus of European politics to the United States and the Soviet Union—two states made up of peoples of many different ethnic origins which had not exhibited nationalism of the virulent type found in Europe. This welcome absence of hypernationalism has been further helped by the greater stability of the postwar order. With less expectation of war, neither superpower felt compelled to mobilize its citizens for war.

Bipolarity, an equal balance of military power, and nuclear weapons—these, then, are the key elements of my explanation for the Long Peace.

Many thoughtful people have found the bipolar system in Europe odious and have sought to end it by dismantling the Soviet empire in Eastern Europe and diminishing Soviet military power. Many have also lamented the military equality obtaining between the superpowers; some have decried the indecisive stalemate it produced, recommending instead a search for military superiority; others have lamented the investment of hundreds of billions of dollars to deter a war that never happened, proving not that the investment, though expensive, paid off, but rather that it was wasted. As for nuclear weapons, well, they are a certifiable Bad Thing. The odium attached to these props of the postwar order has kept many in the West from recognizing a hard truth: they have kept the peace.

But so much for the past. What will keep the peace in the future? Specifically, what new order is likely to emerge if NATO and the Warsaw Pact dissolve, which they will do if the Cold War is really over, and the Soviets withdraw from Eastern Europe and the Americans quit Western Europe, taking their nuclear weapons with them—and should we welcome or fear it?

One dimension of the new European order is certain: it will be multi-polar. Germany, France, Britain, and perhaps Italy will assume major-power status. The Soviet Union will decline from superpower status, not only because its military is sure to shrink in size but also because moving forces out of Eastern Europe will make it more difficult for the Soviets to project power onto the Continent. They will, of course, re-main a major European power. The resulting four- or five-power system will suffer the problems endemic to multipolar systems—and will therefore be prone to instability. The other two dimensions—the distribution of power among the major states and the distribution of nuclear weapons—are less certain. Indeed, who gets nuclear weapons is likely to be the most problematic question facing the new Europe. Three scenarios of the nuclear future in Europe are possible.

The "Europe Without Nuclear Weapons" Scenario

Many Europeans (and some Americans) seek to eliminate nuclear weapons from Europe altogether. Fashioning this nuclear-free Europe would require that Britain, France, and the Soviet Union rid them-selves of these talismans of their sovereignty—an improbable eventu-ality, to say the least. Those who wish for it nevertheless believe that it would be the most peaceful arrangement possible. In fact a nuclear-free Europe has the distinction of being the most dangerous among the envisionable post-Cold War orders. The pacifying effects of nuclear weapons—the caution they generate, the security they provide, the rough equality they impose, and the clarity of the relative power they create—would be lost. Peace would then depend on the other dimen-sions of the new order—the number of poles and the distribution of power among them. The geometry of power in Europe would look much as it did between the world wars—a design for tension, crisis, and possibly even war.

The Soviet Union and a unified Germany would likely be the most powerful states in a nuclear-free Europe. A band of small independent states in Eastern Europe would lie between them. These minor Eastern European powers would be likely to fear the Soviets as much as the Germans, and thus would probably not be disposed to cooperate with the Soviets to deter possible German aggression. In fact, this very prob-lem arose in the 1930s, and the past forty-five years of Soviet occupa-tion have surely done little to mitigate Eastern European fears of a Soviet military presence. Thus scenarios in which Germany uses force against Poland, Czechoslovakia, or even Austria enter the realm of the possible in a nuclear-free Europe.

Then, too, the Soviet withdrawal from Eastern Europe hardly guarantees a permanent exit. Indeed, the Russian presence in Eastern Europe has surged and ebbed repeatedly over the past few centuries. In a grave warning, a member of President Mikhail Gorbachev's negotiating team at the recent Washington summit said, "You have the same explosive mixture you had in Germany in the 1930s. The humiliation of a great power. Economic troubles. The rise of nationalism. You should not underestimate the danger."

Conflicts between Eastern European states might also threaten the stability of the new European order. Serious tensions already exist between Hungary and Romania over Romania's treatment of the Hungarian minority in Transylvania, a formerly Hungarian region that still contains roughly two million ethnic Hungarians. Absent the Soviet occupation of Eastern Europe, Romania and Hungary might have gone to war over this issue by now, and it might bring them to war in the future. This is not the only potential danger spot in Eastern Europe as the Soviet empire crumbles. The Polish-German border could be a source of trouble. Poland and Czechoslovakia have a border dispute. If the Soviets allow some of their republics to achieve independence, the Poles and the Romanians may lay claim to territory now in Soviet hands which once belonged to them. Looking farther south, civil war in Yugoslavia is a distinct possibility. Yugoslavia and Albania might come to blows over Kosovo, a region of Yugoslavia harboring a nationalistic Albanian majority. Bulgaria has its own quarrel with Yugoslavia over Macedonia, while Turkey resents Bulgaria's treatment of its Turkish minority. The danger that these bitter ethnic and border disputes will erupt into war in a supposedly Edenic nuclear-free Europe is enough to make one nostalgic for the Cold War.

Warfare in Eastern Europe would cause great suffering to Eastern Europeans. It also might widen to include the major powers, especially if disorder created fluid politics that offered opportunities for expanded influence, or threatened defeat for states friendly to one or another of the major powers. During the Cold War both superpowers were drawn into Third World conflicts across the globe, often in distant areas of little strategic importance. Eastern Europe is directly adjacent to both the Soviet Union and Germany, and it has considerable economic and strategic importance. Thus trouble in Eastern Europe would offer even greater temptations to these powers than past conflicts in the Third World offered to the superpowers. Furthermore, Eastern European states would have a strong incentive to drag the major powers into their local conflicts, because the results of such conflicts would be largely determined by the relative success of each party in finding external allies.

It is difficult to predict the precise balance of conventional military power that will emerge in post-Cold War Europe. The Soviet Union might recover its strength soon after withdrawing from Eastern Europe. In that case Soviet power would outmatch German power. But centrifugal national forces might pull the Soviet Union apart, leaving no remnant state that is the equal of a unified Germany. Finally, and probably most likely, Germany and the Soviet Union might emerge as powers of roughly equal strength. The first two geometries of power, with their marked military inequality between the two leading countries, would be especially worrisome, although there would be cause for concern even if Soviet and German power were balanced.

A non-nuclear Europe, to round out this catalogue of dangers, would likely be especially disturbed by hypernationalism, since security in such an order would rest on mass armies, which, as we have seen, often cannot be maintained without a mobilized public. The problem would probably be most acute in Eastern Europe, with its uncertain borders and irredentist minority groups. But there is also potential for trouble in Germany. The Germans have generally done an admirable job of combating hypernationalism over the past forty-five years, and of confronting the dark side of their past. Nevertheless, a portent like the recent call of some prominent Germans for a return to greater nationalism in historical education is disquieting.

For all these reasons, it is perhaps just as well that a nuclear-free Europe, much as it may be longed for by so many Europeans, does not appear to be in the cards.

The "Current Ownership" Scenario

Under this scenario Britain, France, and the Soviet Union retain their nuclear weapons, but no new nuclear powers emerge in Europe. This vision of a nuclear-free zone in Central Europe, with nuclear weapons remaining on the flanks of the Continent, is also popular in Europe, but it, too, has doubtful prospects.

Germany will prevent it over the long run. The Germans are not likely to be willing to rely on the Poles or the Czechs to provide their forward defense against a possible direct Soviet conventional attack on their homeland. Nor are the Germans likely to trust the Soviet Union to refrain for all time from nuclear blackmail against a non-nuclear Germany. Hence they will eventually look to nuclear weapons as the surest means of security, just as NATO has done.

The small states of Eastern Europe will also have strong incentives to acquire nuclear weapons. Without them they would be open to nuclear blackmail by the Soviet Union, or by Germany if proliferation stopped there. Even if those major powers did not have nuclear arsenals, no Eastern European state could match German or Soviet conventional strength. Clearly, then, a scenario in which current ownership continues, without proliferation, seems very unlikely.

The "Nuclear Proliferation" Scenario

The most probable scenario in the wake of the Cold War is further nuclear proliferation in Europe. This outcome is laden with dangers, but it also might just provide the best hope for maintaining stability on the Continent. Everything depends on how proliferation is managed. Mismanaged proliferation could produce disaster; well-managed proliferation could produce an order nearly as stable as that of the Long Peace.

The dangers that could arise from mismanaged proliferation are both profound and numerous. There is the danger that the proliferation process itself could give one of the existing nuclear powers a strong incentive to stop a non-nuclear neighbor from joining the club, much as Israel used force to stop Iraq from acquiring a nuclear capability. There is the danger that an unstable nuclear competition would emerge among the new nuclear states. They might lack the resources to make their nuclear forces invulnerable, which could create first-strike fears and incentives—a recipe for disaster in a crisis. Finally, there is the danger that by increasing the number of fingers on the nuclear trigger, proliferation would increase the risk that nuclear weapons would be fired by accident or captured by terrorists or used by madmen.

These and other dangers of proliferation can be lessened if the current nuclear powers take the right steps. To forestall preventive attacks, they can extend security guarantees. To help the new nuclear powers secure their deterrents, they can provide technical assistance. And they can help to socialize nascent nuclear societies to understand the lethal character of the forces they are acquiring. This kind of well-managed proliferation could help bolster peace.

Proliferation should ideally stop with Germany. It has a large economic base, and so could afford to sustain a secure nuclear force. Moreover, Germany would no doubt feel insecure without nuclear weapons, and if it felt insecure its impressive conventional strength would give it a significant capacity to disturb the tranquility of Europe. But if the broader spread of nuclear weapons proves impossible to prevent without taking extreme steps, the current nuclear powers should let proliferation occur in Eastern Europe while doing all they can to channel it in safe directions.

However, I am pessimistic that proliferation can be well managed. The members of the nuclear club are likely to resist proliferation, but they cannot easily manage this tricky process while at the same time resisting it—and they will have several motives to resist. The established nuclear powers will be exceedingly chary of helping the new nuclear powers build secure deterrents, simply because it goes against the grain of state behavior to share military secrets with other states. After all, knowledge of sensitive military technology could be turned against the donor state if that technology were passed on to adversaries. Furthermore, proliferation in Europe will undermine the legitimacy of the 1968 Nuclear Non-Proliferation Treaty, and this could open the floodgates of proliferation worldwide. The current nuclear powers will not want that to happen, and so they will probably spend their energy trying to thwart proliferation, rather than seeking to manage it.

The best time for proliferation to occur would be during a period of relative international calm. Proliferation in the midst of a crisis would obviously be dangerous, since states in conflict with an emerging nuclear power would then have a powerful incentive to interrupt the process by force. However, the opposition to proliferation by citizens of the potential nuclear powers would be so vociferous, and the external resistance from the nuclear club would be so great, that it might take a crisis to make those powers willing to pay the domestic and international costs of building a nuclear force. All of which means that proliferation is likely to occur under international conditions that virtually ensure it will be mismanaged....

Missing the Cold War

The implications of my analysis are straightforward, if paradoxical. Developments that threaten to end the Cold War are dangerous. The West has an interest in maintaining peace in Europe. It therefore has an interest in maintaining the Cold War order, and hence has an interest in continuing the Cold War confrontation. The Cold War antagonism could be continued at lower levels of East-West tension than have prevailed in the past, but a complete end to the Cold War would create more problems than it would solve.

The fate of the Cold War is mainly in the hands of the Soviet Union. The Soviet Union is the only superpower that can seriously threaten to overrun Europe, and the Soviet threat provides the glue that holds NATO together. Take away that offensive threat and the

United States is likely to abandon the Continent; the defensive alliance it has headed for forty years may well then disintegrate, bringing an end to the bipolar order that has kept the peace of Europe for the past forty-five years.

There is little the Americans or the West Europeans can do to perpetuate the Cold War.

For one thing, domestic politics preclude it. Western leaders obviously cannot base national-security policy on the need to maintain forces in Central Europe simply to keep the Soviets there. The idea of deploying large numbers of troops in order to bait the Soviets into an order-keeping competition would be dismissed as bizarre, and contrary to the general belief that ending the Cold War and removing the Soviet yoke from Eastern Europe would make the world safer and better.

For another, the idea of propping up a declining rival runs counter to the basic behavior of states. States are principally concerned about their relative power in the system—hence they look for opportunities to take advantage of one another. If anything, they prefer to see adversaries decline, and invariably do whatever they can to sped up the process and maximize the distance of the fall. States, in other words, do not ask which distribution of power best facilitates stability and then do everything possible to build or maintain such an order. Instead, each pursues the narrower aim of maximizing its power advantage over potential adversaries. The particular international order that results is simply a by-product of that competition.

Consider, for example, the origins of the Cold War order in Europe. No state intended to create it. In fact the United States and the Soviet Union each worked hard in the early years of the Cold War to undermine the other's position in Europe, which would have ended the bipolar order on the Continent. The remarkably stable system that emerged in Europe in the late 1940s was the unintended consequence of an intense competition between the superpowers.

Moreover, even if the Americans and the West Europeans wanted to help the Soviets maintain their status as a superpower, it is not apparent that they could do so. The Soviet Union is leaving Eastern Europe and cutting its military forces largely because its economy is floundering badly. The Soviets don't know how to fix their economy themselves, and there is little that Western governments can do to help them. The West can and should avoid doing malicious mischief to the Soviet economy, but at this juncture it is difficult to see how the West can have a significant positive influence.

The fact that the West cannot sustain the Cold War does not mean that the United States should make no attempt to preserve the current order. It should do what it can to avert a complete mutual withdrawal from Europe. For instance, the American negotiating position at the conventional-arms-control talks should aim toward large mutual force reductions but should not contemplate complete mutual withdrawal. The Soviets may opt to withdraw all their forces unilaterally anyway; if so, there is little the United States can do to stop them.

Should complete Soviet withdrawal from Eastern Europe prove unavoidable, the West would confront the question of how to maintain peace in a multipolar Europe. Three policy prescriptions are in order.

First, the United States should encourage the limited and carefully managed proliferation of nuclear weapons in Europe. The best hope for avoiding war in post-Cold War Europe is nuclear deterrence; hence some nuclear proliferation is necessary, to compensate for the withdrawal of the Soviet and American nuclear arsenals from Central Europe. Ideally, as I have argued, nuclear weapons would spread to Germany but to no other state.

Second, Britain and the United States, as well as the Continental states, will have to counter any emerging aggressor actively and efficiently, in order to offset the ganging up and bullying that are sure to arise in post-Cold War Europe. Balancing in a multipolar system, however, is usually a problem-ridden enterprise, because of either geography or the problems of coordination. Britain and the United States, physically separated from the Continent, may conclude that they have little interest in what happens there. That would be abandoning their responsibilities and, more important, their interests. Both states failed to counter Germany before the two world wars, making war more likely. It is essential for peace in Europe that they not repeat their past mistakes.

Both states must maintain military forces that can be deployed against Continental states that threaten to start a war. To do this they must persuade their citizens to support a policy of continued Continental commitment. This will be more difficult than it once was, because its principal purpose will be to preserve peace, rather than to prevent an imminent hegemony, and the prevention of hegemony is a simpler goal to explain publicly. Furthermore, this prescription asks both countries to take on an unaccustomed task, given that it is the basic nature of states to focus on maximizing relative power, not on bolstering stability. Nevertheless, the British and the Americans have a real stake in peace, especially since there is the risk that a European war might involve the large-scale use of nuclear weapons. Therefore, it should be possible for their governments to lead their publics to recognize this interest and support policies that protect it.

The Soviet Union may eventually return to its past expansionism and threaten to upset the status quo. If so, we are back to the Cold War. However, if the Soviets adhere to status-quo policies, Soviet power could play a key role in countering Germany and in maintaining order in Eastern Europe. It is important in those cases where the Soviets are acting in a balancing capacity that the United States cooperate with its former adversary and not let residual distrust from the Cold War obtrude.

Third, a concerted effort should be made to keep hypernationalism at bay, especially in Eastern Europe. Nationalism has been contained during the Cold War, but it is likely to re-emerge once Soviet and American forces leave the heart of Europe. It will be a force for trouble unless curbed. The teaching of honest national history is especially important, since the teaching of false, chauvinist history is the main vehicle for spreading hypernationalism. States that teach a dishonestly self-exculpating or self-glorifying history should be publicly criticized and sanctioned.

None of these tasks will be easy. In fact, I expect that the bulk of my prescriptions will not be followed; most run contrary to important strains of domestic American and European opinion, and to the basic nature of state behavior. And even if they are followed, peace in Europe will not be guaranteed. If the Cold War is truly behind us, therefore, the stability of the past forty-five years is not likely to be seen again in the coming decades.

Section 3
ARMS CONTROL
IN EUROPE

In a discussion we have entitled "Soviet Arms Control Objectives in Europe," his second contribution to this volume, F. Stephen Larrabee agrees with the view that Mikhail Gorbachev has seen arms control as the primary means of enhancing Soviet security and reducing East-West confrontation. The best example of this was the recent breakthrough in European arms control agreements. During the 1987 Washington summit the two superpowers made a historic agreement to eliminate INF (Intermediate-Range Nuclear Forces) from Europe. This accord was unprecedented for a number of reasons, including the commitment of the United States and USSR to eliminate a complete class of weapons from their respective arsenals. Gorbachev's motive for agreeing to the so-called "zero option" (eliminating all INF systems including those the Soviet Union had deployed in Asia) was that he apparently hoped that the INF agreement would break the logjam in other negotiations, especially the Strategic Arms Reduction Talks (START).

It has been in the field of conventional arms control, Larrabee maintains, that Gorbachev has shown the greatest willingness to depart from past Soviet policy. He seems to believe that Soviet political and economic reform would be enhanced by reductions in conventional weapons more so than by reductions in nuclear arsenals. In other words, reductions in conventional weapons promise substantial economic savings over the long run. To achieve this goal, there has been a shift in Soviet doctrine toward an increased emphasis on defense and war prevention. Furthermore, the concept of "reasonable sufficiency" is now being applied to conventional as well as strategic weapons. The most important indication of Gorbachev's commitment to conventional arms reductions has been his promise to unilaterally withdraw troops from Eastern Europe and reduce the Soviet armed forces by 500,000.

Larrabee is convinced that the CFE (Conventional Arms Forces Europe) treaty, signed in November 1990, is the most important arms control treaty signed in the postwar period. In establishing equal ceilings on major categories of weapon systems, the treaty affirms the fundamental change in the balance of power in Europe. Furthermore, the signing of the CFE treaty should lead to negotiations on short-range nuclear forces (SNF). Such talks have been a Soviet goal since 1987, when Gorbachev proposed that not only intermediate-range, but also short-range nuclear weapons should be completely eliminated. NATO was less than responsive to this proposal to "denuclearize" Europe, however, because tactical nuclear weapons were considered necessary to counterbalance Soviet and Warsaw Pact conventional superiority. Now that the CFE talks have been successfully concluded, the attitudes of both sides have changed. The Bush administration is now more supportive of the negotiations but has argued that there should be a "partial reduction" in SNF, not a total elimination. For its part, the Soviet Union is now proposing a "minimum nuclear deterrent" and seems likely to accept the continued presence of some nuclear weapons in Europe for a limited period. The ultimate Soviet goal, however, is to have them eliminated entirely. Actually, because the United States is likely to unilaterally withdraw most of its ground-based tactical nuclear weapons from Europe, the SNF talks have lost their sense of urgency. Nevertheless, Larrabee expects the Soviets to continue to press for such talks because in agreeing to consider the issue the superpowers confirm that "Europe is entering an era of reduced confrontation."

In their essay "Is a 'Third Zero' Attainable?" Pavel Bayev and his associates discuss the prospects for a nuclear-free Europe and the impact this would have on superpower relations. The issue is whether short-range nuclear forces should be eliminated in Europe, as the Soviets have called for, or whether *there will be continued reliance on nuclear weapons in the European theater.*

Initially, the Soviets were adamant about the need to totally eliminate these weapons, but in 1989 they changed their stance by agreeing that such weapons could be reduced to a level that achieved "minimum containment." The authors explain that one reason for this change was the recognition that the elimination of nuclear weapons in Europe would "inevitably" result in the United States withdrawing its forces from Germany. The USSR is opposed to this because the U.S. presence, "all its negative aspects notwithstanding," is a stabilizing component of both intra-Western and East-West relations. Moreover, the relative significance of the U.S. presence as a stabilizing factor is likely to increase rather than decline.

Another reason for changing their stance on short-range nuclear weapons is that the Soviets, for economic reasons, are giving priority to the reduction of conventional weapons. If they achieve this goal, they will rely temporarily on nuclear weapons for their deterrence value while Europe makes a transition to a new system of regional security.

The authors make it clear that the total elimination of nuclear weapons in Europe is still in the long-term interests of the Soviet Union. However, to attempt this now would be "rushing events unless preceded by a consolidation and restructuring of the European security system." Nevertheless, political and military arguments for preserving nuclear weapons are eroding fast, and unilateral reductions are a definite possibility. The best approach, they conclude, is for the United States and the USSR to work out a process of "parallel" unilateral reductions.

23

Soviet Arms Control Objectives in Europe

F. Stephen Larrabee

... In contrast to his predecessors, especially Leonid I. Brezhnev, Gorbachev has seen arms control as the primary means of enhancing Soviet security and reducing East-West confrontation. Moreover, he has been willing to adopt more flexible positions than his predecessors, especially regarding verification, in order to obtain agreements. He has also shown a much greater appreciation of the political impact of such agreements.

This change is well illustrated by Gorbachev's approach to limitations on intermediate-range nuclear forces (INF). Leonid I. Brezhnev and Yuri V. Andropov had consistently rejected President Ronald Reagan's proposal to eliminate all INF systems (the "zero option"). Instead, they tried to maintain Soviet superiority in this category of weapons, arguing that they wanted only "equal security," which in reality meant that the USSR should be allowed to maintain intermediate-range weapons equal to all those possessed by the United States and its European allies. This refusal led to the breakup of the negotiations and the American counter-deployment of American cruise and Pershing II missiles in later 1983.

In contrast to Brezhnev and Andropov, however, Gorbachev—after some hesitation—agreed to the total elimination of all Soviet medium-range missiles, including those based in Asia. Moreover, during United States Secretary of State George Schultz's visit to Moscow in April 1987, Gorbachev proposed eliminating not only all intermediate-range missiles but also all shorter-range missiles (with ranges from 500 to 1000 km)—the "double zero" option. This proposal caused considerable consternation within NATO, especially in West Germany, because it meant that the West would be left with only short-range missiles and nuclear artillery with ranges below 500 km for defense against a Soviet conventional attack. Many Europeans thought the proposal was a dangerous step toward the "denuclearization" of Europe. Once the United

States had signaled its willingness to accept the offer, however, the West European countries, especially West Germany, had little choice but to accept the decision and put the best face on it.

Gorbachev's willingness to agree to eliminate all intermediate- and shorter-range missiles appears to have had several motives. First, in contrast to his predecessors, Gorbachev thought that Soviet security could be better ensured by "political means"—i.e., arms control—than through a continued military buildup. Second, Gorbachev needed to break the general deadlock in arms control in the wake of the collapse of the Reykjavik summit in October 1988. The West saw the INF issue as the main obstacle to improved East-West relations. Thus, Gorbachev apparently hoped that the INF agreement would have a positive impact on East-West relations and break the logjam in other areas, especially the Strategic Arms Reduction Talks (START).

Third, there were sound military reasons for agreeing to the zero option. While the accord required the Soviet Union to scrap its entire SS-20 force as well as its remaining SS-4s and SS-5s, it eliminated an important nuclear threat to Soviet territory—particularly from the Pershing II, which has a short flight time of twelve to fourteen minutes. Moreover, the Soviet Union could still cover many of the same targets in Europe by redirecting some of its strategic forces—a fact that may well have helped convince the Soviet military to go along with the decision.

Finally, the agreement threatened further to erode the credibility of the American nuclear deterrent and to increase fissures within NATO. As Western analysts and officials pointed out, the elimination of all INF and shorter-range nuclear missiles in Europe would make the strategy of flexible response much more difficult and probably require some changes in Western strategy. The pressure for further reductions was bound to increase, especially from West Germany, where most of the remaining short-range nuclear systems were deployed. Thus the long-term political benefits may have seemed worth the short-term military costs.

The INF accord also had important advantages for the West. First, it eliminated an important military threat to Western Europe. Second, it required the Soviet Union to make large asymmetrical reductions and set an important precedent for other negotiations, especially those related to conventional arms. Third, the agreement contained stringent verification provisions, including on-site inspection. This represented a significant shift in the Soviet position and set another important precedent for other negotiations.

In the field of conventional arms control, however, Gorbachev has shown the greatest inclination to depart from past Soviet policy. Gorbachev's predecessors, especially Brezhnev, showed little inclination to take conventional arms control seriously. Brezhnev gave top priority to strategic nuclear arms control. Moreover, he feared the consequences of any large-scale withdrawal of Soviet forces on the political stability within the bloc.

Gorbachev, by contrast, seems to believe that Soviet political and military objectives can be furthered by progress in conventional arms control. His interest in conventional arms control has probably been influenced by several factors. First, on the broadest political level, it had become increasingly clear that a major improvement in Soviet relations with Western Europe was impossible without seriously addressing West European concerns about Soviet conventional preponderance. This was the main source of West European insecurity and the main rationale for NATO's existence and its reliance on nuclear weapons for defense. Second, a major reduction of conventional forces promised substantial economic savings over the long run. Third, on the military level, there was increasing concern that Western advances in high-tech conventional weapons, especially precision-guided missiles, would erode traditional Soviet advantages in tanks and manpower.

Gorbachev's "new thinking" provided an important framework for the shift in the Soviet approach to conventional arms control. The concept of "reasonable sufficiency" was applied not only to strategic weapons but also to conventional arms. This meant, in effect, that the USSR could afford to reduce some conventional forces, since it only needed enough forces to repel an aggressor rather than to conduct an offensive on his territory.

Similarly, the shift in Soviet doctrine toward an increasing emphasis on defense and war prevention pointed in the same direction.[1] In the past, Soviet conventional forces had been configured and trained to conduct a rapid offensive designed to seize and hold Western territory if a conflict in Europe broke out. This required large-scale conventional superiority in order to overrun Western defenses. Under the new doctrine, however, Soviet forces were to be trained to fight defensively in the initial period of a conflict and then to reestablish the status quo ante rather than seek to carry the war immediately over to Western territory.

This new doctrine permitted a gradual reduction and restructuring of Soviet conventional forces in a less offensive and threatening posture. Under the new doctrine the Soviet Union no longer needed great numerical superiority in tanks and manpower. Nor did it need large quantities of offensively oriented materials, such as bridge-building equipment, which was primarily designed to enhance its capacity to conduct large-scale offensives. Long-range offensive aircraft could also be reduced.

Gorbachev's approach to conventional arms control reflected these new realities. Beginning in 1986 the Soviet Union began to adopt a more flexible approach to conventional arms control. The most important shifts in the Soviet position included: Gorbachev's willingness to extend the negotiating zone to admit Soviet territory up to the Ural Mountains, a long-standing Western demand; his open acknowledgment that asymmetries existed—which his predecessors had implicitly denied—and his commitment to eliminate them; the adoption of a more flexible position on verification, especially on-site inspection; a more forthcoming attitude toward the release of data; and a shift, noted above, in Soviet doctrine, putting greater emphasis on defense.

The latter shift was codified in a new Warsaw Pact Doctrine, announced at the meeting of the Warsaw Treaty Organization (WTO) Political Consultative Committee in East Berlin at the end of May 1987. The communiqué issued at the end of the meeting specifically stated that the doctrine of the WTO was defensive.[2] In addition, it asserted that the goals of the Vienna negotiations on Conventional Forces in Europe (CFE) should be guided by the principle of "reasonable sufficiency" and that the negotiations should seek to eliminate the capability for surprise attack and large-scale offensive action. These goals had long been espoused by the West, and the public commitment to them by the Warsaw Pact implied a significant rapprochement between the two alliances.

The most important indication of Gorbachev's seriousness about conventional arms control, however, came in his speech to the United Nations General Assembly in December 1988. Gorbachev promised unilaterally to withdraw 50,000 Soviet troops and 5000 Soviet tanks from Hungary, Czechoslovakia, and East Germany; reduce the Soviet armed forces by 500,000 men by 1990; withdraw from Eastern Europe assault-landing troops and other offensively oriented accessories, such as bridge-crossing equipment; cut Soviet forces in the Atlantic-to-the-Urals area by 10,000 tanks, 8500 artillery systems, and 800 combat aircraft; and restructure Soviet forces in Eastern Europe along "clearly defensive" lines. Although the initiative still left the Soviet Union with substantial advantages in a number of important areas, it significantly undercut the Soviet capability to launch a short-warning attack—a long-standing Western concern.

Few Western officials or analysts had expected Gorbachev to make such a dramatic gesture. Moreover, in taking the initiative, Gorbachev seems to have overridden objections by the military, including those of the chief of the General Staff, Marshal Sergei Akhromeyev, whose removal was announced the same day. Indeed, the initiative was evidently the result of a prolonged debate between those favoring unilateral measures (located primarily in several Soviet think-tanks and in key positions in the Foreign Ministry) and those opposed (located mostly in the Ministry of Defense and General Staff).[3] In the end, Gorbachev was apparently persuaded that a dramatic political gesture was needed to convince the West of his seriousness and to give new momentum to the conventional arms control talks in Vienna due to begin a few months hence. Gorbachev may have also hoped that the unilateral cuts would have a favorable impact on Western public opinion and stimulate pressure in the West to make a reciprocal gesture.

While the West did not respond with a reciprocal reduction, the initiative did have an important political impact on the general climate surrounding the opening of the CFE negotiations in Vienna in March 1989. In fact, by the time that negotiations opened, the Western and Soviet approaches were relatively close. The Soviet proposal presented at the opening round of the talks on 6 March by Foreign Minister Eduard A. Shevardnadze provided for a three-stage process:

- Both NATO and the WTO would reduce their armed forces and conventional armaments 10 to 15 percent below their current levels.
- Troop levels and armaments would be reduced by 25 percent.
- Each side's armed forces would be reduced in all categories of arms, including naval forces.

Shevardnadze also called for strict verification provisions and the immediate initiation of separate negotiations on short-range nuclear systems.

The Soviet proposal was in broad accord with NATO's proposal on several important points: equal limits on important weapons systems; the general magnitude of reductions (the WTO proposed cuts 10 to 15 percent below current levels, the West 5 to 10 percent), and the need for extensive verification measures. Moreover, both sides agreed that the overall goal of the talks should be to eliminate the capacity for surprise attack and large-scale offensive action.

Important differences, however, remained on whether to include aircraft and troops—the United States wanted to focus solely on tanks and offensive armor—and on short-range nuclear weapons. These differences were narrowed by the USSR's proposal at the end of May, which suggested geographic ceilings on weapons and essentially accepted the basic Western framework for cutting tanks, artillery, and armored troop carriers. The differences were further reduced by President George Bush's proposals at the NATO summit a few days later. The president agreed to include combat aircraft and attack helicopters in the negotiations. He also proposed that each side reduce its armed forces to 275,000 soldiers—a move that would require the United States to withdraw 30,000 and the Soviets 350,000 soldiers. Finally, he agreed that talks on short-range nuclear forces (SNF) could be initiated once the CFE negotiations had been concluded. Bush insisted, however, that the SNF talks should be designed to lead to a "partial reduction" of SNF, not their total elimination. And in deference to West German concerns, a decision regarding the modernization of 88 Lance short-range missiles (FOTL) was postponed.[4]

These two moves significantly reduced the gap between the two sides and contributed to rapid progress in the talks. The negotiations were given new impetus in March by the agreement in Ottawa to limit each side to 195,000 soldiers in the central zone. The United States, however, was allowed to maintain 225,000 overall in Europe. The latter agreement marked an important compromise by Gorbachev in that it codified unequal ceilings—a major American goal.[5] The Soviets, by contrast, were given no right to deploy troops outside the central zone.

However, Soviet interest in a rapid conclusion of the talks waned visibly in the spring of 1989, slowing their momentum. The deadlock appears to have been related to Soviet concerns about the process of German unification. The Soviet Union was apparently unwilling to move forward in Vienna to reduce its own forces substantially until there was greater clarity about the size and configuration of the military forces of a united Germany, as well as the future of NATO strategy. The changes in NATO nuclear strategy announced at the NATO summit in July, together with Chancellor Helmut Kohl's public assurances shortly thereafter that the forces of a united Germany would be reduced to around 370,000 men (less than half the current total of the two armies combined), appear to have allayed the most important Soviet concerns. Thereafter, rapid progress was made in resolving the remaining major outstanding issues—limits on weapon holdings by individual nations (the "sufficiency rule"), limitations on naval aircraft, and limitations on weapons in specific subzones. In early October the two sides agreed in principle on the outlines of a draft treaty. The final breakthrough in the negotiations was the result of an important Soviet concession: Moscow agreed to include land-based naval aircraft in the final agreement—a long-standing United States goal—without insisting that the same apply to carrier-based aircraft, which the United States wanted excluded. This concession removed the last major obstacle to an agreement.

The CFE treaty, which was officially signed at the thirty-four-nation CSCE Summit in Paris in November 1990, is the most important arms-control treaty signed in the postwar period. The treaty codifies a fundamental change in the balance of power in Europe by establishing equal ceilings on major categories of equipment, including tanks, artillery, and personnel carriers, thereby eliminating major Soviet advantages in these weapons systems. As a result of the treaty, the Warsaw Pact will have to destroy about 19,000 tanks, while NATO will have to destroy only about 4000 tanks. The treaty will require no substantial cuts in NATO's armored troop carriers and no cuts in its artillery or combat aircraft. The Warsaw Pact, by contrast, will have to destroy thousands of these weapons.

The signing of the CFE treaty is likely to be followed by a new set of negotiations (CFE-IB) designed to establish national ceilings on the forces of individual countries. In these talks the Soviet Union's main goal will probably be low ceilings on the military forces of a united Germany. It is also likely to try to obtain treaty-related restrictions on NATO and German forces stationed in the former territory of East Germany.

The conclusion of a CFE I agreement will also open the way for negotiations on short-range nuclear forces (SNF). Such talks have long been a Soviet goal, but there has been a visible shift in the Soviet position on SNF negotiations since mid-1989. Originally, the Soviets seemed intent on pressing for total elimination of all short-range systems (the "third zero"). However, Gorbachev spoke of the creation of a "minimum nuclear deterrent" in his speech in Strasbourg in July 1989.[6] Similarly, during a visit to NATO headquarters in Brussels, Soviet Foreign Minister Shevardnadze suggested a two-stage process for SNF negotiations. In the first stage, SNF would be reduced to low common ceilings, and in the second stage they would be eliminated entirely. Leading Soviet analysts have also referred to such a two-stage process.[7]

The shift in the Soviet position appears to have several motivations. First, the Soviet Union seems to recognize that there is strong resistance in Western Europe, especially in France and Britain, to the total denuclearization of Western Europe and that pressing for such a goal at this point would be counterproductive, stiffening Western resistance to reductions and possibly inhibiting further progress in conventional arms control. Second, with the loss of Soviet conventional superiority, which will be codified in a CFE I agreement, the Soviets may feel a greater need to retain some nuclear weapons as a hedge against NATO's technological superiority. Finally, eliminating all tactical nuclear weapons could precipitate a withdrawal of American troops from Western Europe, thereby increasing instability during the transition period.

Thus, unless the West European countries, particularly Germany, press for a total elimination of short-range systems, the USSR is likely to accept the continued presence of some nuclear weapons on West European soil at least for an interim period. The first phase of the SNF negotiations will probably be directed at establishing equal but lower ceilings on land-based nuclear systems. Nevertheless, despite what appears to be an emerging consensus on the basic goals of the negotiations, substantial technical problems remain. There is no agreement, for instance, on the "unit of account"—warheads, launchers, or delivery vehicles—or the geographic scope of the negotiations. Moreover, the verification problems are formidable. Finally, the question of whether to include French and British nuclear systems remains unresolved.

The political evolution in Europe, however, may make the resolution of some of these problems easier. It is increasingly likely that the United States will unilaterally withdraw most, if not all, ground-based tactical nuclear weapons from Europe, leaving air- and sea-based nuclear weapons as the backbone of its deterrent strategy. Moreover, from the Soviets' perspective, the change in NATO strategy announced at the NATO summit in London in July 1990—whereby nuclear weapons will only be used as a "last resort"—diminishes the threat posed by the remaining weapons on European soil. At the same time, the withdrawal of Soviet troops and military equipment from Eastern Europe will significantly reduce the Soviet short-range nuclear threat to Western Europe.

These developments have somewhat diminished the importance of the SNF negotiations. Nevertheless, since such weapons can be easily moved back into the negotiating zone, it will be useful to have agreed, verifiable constraints on them. For political reasons, moreover, the Soviet Union is likely to press for the rapid commencement of negotiations. They strengthen the impression, both at home and in Europe, that Europe is entering a new era of reduced confrontation, thereby legitimizing the Soviet push for a greater reliance on pan-European security structures. In addition, negotiations offer an important means to try to block the modernization of NATO's air-based component, particularly plans to develop a new tactical air-to-surface missile (TASM). Thus, in future talks, the Soviets are likely to press for deep cuts in nuclear-capable aircraft as well as restrictive provisions on air-to-surface missiles. Initially, the USSR may also try to link the negotiations to the question of tactical nuclear weapons at sea, though it seems likely that this issue will be dealt with in separate talks on naval arms control.

Notes

1. For a detailed discussion of the shift in Soviet doctrine, see William Odom, "Soviet Military Doctrine," *Foreign Affairs* 67 (Fall 1988), pp. 114-134; and Edward L. Warner III, "Soviet Military Doctrine: New Thinking and Old

Realities in Soviet Defense Policy," *Survival* 30 (January-February 1989), pp. 13-33.

2. See *Pravda*, 30 May 1987.

3. See Roy Allison, "Gorbachev's New Program for Conventional Arms Control in Europe," in *Gorbachev's Agenda Changes in Domestic and Foreign Policy*, edited by Susan L. Clark (Boulder: Westview Press, 1989), pp. 5-13.

4. In May 1990 the Bush administration quietly shelved the idea of Lance modernization altogether after it became apparent that there was no support for the program in Europe. For a good discussion of the Lance modernization issue, see Hans Binnendijk, "NATO's Nuclear Modernization Dilemma," *Survival* 30 (March-April 1989), pp. 137-155.

5. The United States was eager to avoid equating American troops in Europe with Soviet troops. Hence, it pressed for unequal ceilings in order to avoid the appearance of parity. See R. Jeffrey Smith, "U.S., Soviets Reach Troops Cut Accord," *Washington Post*, 14 February 1990.

6. *Pravda*, 7 July 1989.

7. See Paval Bayev et al., *Tactical Nuclear Weapons in Europe* (Moscow: Novosti Press Agency Publishing House, 1990), 14, pp. 40-46.

24

Is a "Third Zero" Attainable?

Pavel Bayev, Sergei Karaganov,
Victor Shein, and Vitali Zhurkin

The breath-taking pace of the political processes going on in Europe has turned aside military political issues that were traditionally in the focus of debates on European security. This is a welcome sign of demilitarization of thinking on the European security system if not yet of the system itself. On the other hand, realities plainly lag behind thinking, and the mountain-high stockpiles of weapons which were produced in the years of political confrontation, now becoming a thing of the past, are still there. So is the military skeleton of European confrontation propped up by a system of military financing. The problem of dismantling it remains difficult both conceptually and from the practical point of view.

Specifically, the situation with regard to reducing and eliminating the nuclear component of the confrontation—tactical nuclear weapons

(TNWs)—is far from clear. The debate centering on this issue in recent years has not been exactly constructive. The Soviet Union insisted on eliminating all TNWs in the foreseeable future. But the majority of the political forces in power in the West took a stand for continued reliance on nuclear arms, refusing even to discuss any reductions in them in Europe because they feared a "trap"—a proposal for a "third zero" to support the INF treaty that it would have been politically impossible to reject. Things were made worse by many Westerners' advocacy of "modernizing" TNWs, a posture which the other side was bound to interpret as aimed at building up military capability and obtaining specific advantages. In these circumstances, Soviet experts saw a "third zero" as the most effective means of preventing "modernization."

The situation has largely eased off by now. On making a sober appraisal of its balance of interest, NATO postponed modernization of its land-based missiles, a move seen by many experts as "burying" it. The demolition of the Berlin Wall, the spurt toward democracy in the GDR, Czechoslovakia, Bulgaria and Romania and the quickened process of rapprochement between the two German states apparently went beyond dropping modernization from the agenda of realpolitik. The prospect of eliminating all systems of land-based TNWs—missiles and nuclear artillery alike—in the foreseeable future seemed to become very likely. Both political and military arguments in favor of preserving them are being eroded fast. A further component of the NATO TNW modernization program, namely, the key concept of replacing nuclear bombs by air-to-surface missiles, appears to be much more vulnerable than before.

In 1989, the Soviet Union, for its part, adopted a realistic stand. (Needless to say, it did not renounce the idea of ultimately abolishing all nuclear arms, an objective justified politically and morally.) First we proposed talks not only on eliminating but on reducing and eliminating nuclear weapons. Subsequently Mikhail Gorbachev stated in his Strasbourg address that we were willing to constructively discuss the concept of minimum containment. Lastly, Eduard Shevardnadze proposed in his December [1989] speech to the Political Commission of the European Parliament that the first stage of talks should concern itself with reducing deterrents to the minimum, whereupon the sides could move to the next stage, that is, begin discussing nuclear arms reductions first and not their elimination.

The road to fruitful talks is open. The political situation now shaping up gives promise of rapid progress. But before taking this road, we should reappraise our own interests and the interests of the other side and try to envisage both the ultimate goal and intermediate ones, which can only be done through political and scientific discussion. This article, like these writers' reports on whose conclusions it is largely based, are intended to encourage this kind of discussion.

One of the patent shortcomings of Soviet political theory is the absence of an integral concept of national interests. Most long-term tasks were therefore set on ideological principles, with foreign political practice geared to these tasks in insignificant measure. The problem of Soviet interests in connection with nuclear weapons is among those requiring analysis whose lack makes all attempts to define our national interests vulnerable from the outset. Yet such attempts are necessary, if only as a means of stimulating discussion.

In what sense does the line of eliminating nuclear weapons definitely meet our interests? The nuclear arms race initiated by the United States was one of the reasons for the division of Europe, giving rise to military confrontation structures and the consolidation of the West in opposing the Soviet Union. The movement in favor of eliminating nuclear weapons should help in principle to demilitarize security systems, something in which the Soviet Union has an unquestionable stake.

The proposal for doing away with all nuclear weapons (among them tactical ones)—a proposal indicative of our readiness to renounce our nuclear superpower status—drew attention in Europe to our new foreign policy. It helped and goes on helping to improve the image of the Soviet Union.

Our country is interested in a continued policy for the elimination of TNWs also because it needs to respond to mounting anti-nuclear sentiments in Europe, its eastern part included.

The elimination of TNWs would reduce the likelihood of any conflict rising fast to a nuclear level and then to the level of a global nuclear conflict. Thus it would meet the interests of our country and the whole of humanity.

The presence of large quantities of ammunition and TNW delivery vehicles in an area of potential hostilities makes it possible to immediately escalate any armed conflict, a move which might be prompted by, among other things, fear of losing these weapons. Their massive deployment in the combat order of troops adds to the probability of a non-nuclear conflict becoming nuclear also because the very first gun salvos and air strikes would hit control and communication systems, nuclear arms delivery vehicles and nuclear ammunition depots. This could have consequences hard to predict as regards escalation of the conflict (unsanctioned use), to say nothing of nuclear pollution of the environment.

All such hypothetical scenarios concern the possibility of a war already on growing into a nuclear one. Yet war is most unlikely, and this is also recognized by Western experts. Besides, Soviet policy and military strategy are increasingly directed toward averting any war. The growing defensive trend of doctrines and the changing structure of the armed forces of both alliances will reduce the possibilities of conducting offensive operations deep in enemy territory. In this situation, the destabilizing effect of TNWs evidently tends to diminish.

As for other interests involved in the elimination of tactical nuclear forces, they are less obvious.

According to an opinion that has struck deep root in the West, the existence of these forces curbs the buildup of conventional ones. West European politicians often referred to NATO's superiority in nuclear weapons to resist U.S. pressure in favor of building up conventional forces. Soviet armed forces reductions in the second half of the 1950s and the early 1960s were largely a result of increased nuclear potentialities, such as of the creation of a TNW arsenal (lagging roughly five years after NATO's). At the same time, the nuclear arms race occasionally urged on the buildup of non-nuclear forces. For instance, as well, the Soviet Union apparently regarded growing armored power as a means of neutralizing the nuclear superiority of the West.

By and large, however, there seems to be no strict correlation of trends in the conventional and the nuclear arms race; in any case, it has not been conceptualized. This is demonstrated by the trend of our military buildup in the 1970s, when the consolidation of strategic parity and the abolition of NATO's advantages in nuclear arms in Europe were accompanied not only by a qualitative improvement but by a serious quantitative increase in our non-nuclear capability. There is hardly a rationale for so wide-ranging a military buildup, which went hand in hand with a process of easing tensions, and as for removing its direct and indirect effects, this still calls for serious foreign policy efforts.

There is sufficient reason on the whole to presume that whereas in the past TNWs were chiefly an incentive for the conventional arms race, today they generally restrain it. Militarists cannot but realize that with nuclear arms still there, it is practically impossible to win this race by reaping political or military dividends. Nor does the impact of the nuclear factor leave any room for hope should the arms race be extended to further areas in which NATO's technological superiority could be put to effective use, according to Western experts.

The connection between nuclear and conventional armaments in the context of the disarmament process is a complex phenomenon. It is obvious enough that cuts in conventional forces and armaments at the first stage of the Vienna talks could provide a favorable political atmosphere for nuclear arms reductions (NATO even insists on this as a necessary condition). At subsequent stages, the parties to the talks would find it hard to agree on really far-reaching cuts without serious reductions in TNWs. However, this does not imply their complete elimination, which the main ruling groups in the West find absolutely unacceptable. Fear of reductions in conventional armaments paving the way for the elimination of all nuclear weapons in Europe was one reason for the resistance put up during the drafting of the mandate for the Vienna talks, above all on the part of France and Britain. At present this consideration toughens the stance of NATO on tactical aircraft and the alliance's categorical refusal to define strike aircraft as well as both European nuclear powers' bid to exempt their carrier aircraft from reduction.

The Soviet Union could in principle have a stake in the elimination of tactical and all other types of nuclear weapons in Europe even from the orthodox military political point of view that is renounced today (but is taken into account by Western experts). By virtue of a somewhat more favorable geographic location, the accumulated advantages in conventional forces and the possibility of relying on strategic forces, some of which can be targeted on installations situated in Europe, the elimination of TNWs could place the USSR in a relatively preferable strategic position.

However, the Soviet Union cannot really be interested in the elimination of TNWs for this reason. The West, which commands substantial economic superiority over the WTO, would allow no reasonably serious change in the military balance and would restore the balance at a higher level should it be upset. No advantages can be secured also because there is very little likelihood of a scenario leaving the balance of conventional forces roughly on their present level should TNWs be reduced or even eliminated altogether.

What is likely is a different course of development in which the Soviet Union is strongly interested for political and economic reasons: an end to the main imbalances in conventional forces and major cuts in SOWs along with cuts in TNWs. If these cuts were made, the Soviet Union and the WTO would be left with an only irremovable advantage, their geographic location. They owe this advantage to the transoceanic situation of the United States and the absence of strategic depth in the system of the combined armed forces of NATO, but NATO's advantages in the qualitative parameters of armaments would evidently make up for it. In such a context, it could become necessary for the WTO to offset possible advantages of the West for the period of transition to entirely defensive structures (a process that will take a decade at the least).

A further conceivable interest of the Soviet Union could consist in loosening the unity of NATO and in trying to hasten the withdrawal of U.S. troops. The West accuses us of such designs, proceeding from a widespread assumption that is not questioned there (we wonder how reasonably). According to it the elimination of nuclear arms in Europe would inevitably result in the United States withdrawing its forces from West Germany.

The counter-arguments are obvious: attempts to stimulate crisis developments in NATO would be at variance with the Soviet Union's real interests and might prove counterproductive in the end. The important thing, however, is that our country is not interested at all in such developments in view of the contemporary political situation. Furthermore, thanks to the changing power balance between the United States and Western Europe and to the erosion of the notion of the existing threat, Western unity as opposed to the East is loosening in any case.

The Soviet Union can have no stake in adding further factors for instability to what is a more and more unstable situation anyway. The U.S. presence, all its negative aspects notwithstanding, is a visible stabilizing component of intra-Western relations and, to a degree, of East-West relations as well. At a time when the military balance in Europe shows a steady downward trend, the negative aspects of the U.S. presence are losing in impact while its relative significance as a stabilizing factor may increase.

Besides, it is in the interest of both the Soviet Union and Western Europe that the United States remain tied to Europe militarily. Such a dependence in a wide area of security discourages Washington from large-scale and dangerous recourse to force and makes it keener on European stability.

We do not mean to say that we think the Soviet Union has a stake in perpetuating the American and Soviet presence on the territory of their allies. What we do mean is that there should be a continued presence reduced to a symbolic level as a stabilizing factor for the period of transition from the present to the future system of European security, to be based in much greater measure on political guarantees and European institutions.

One of the Soviet Union's fundamental interests lies undoubtedly in a substantial lowering of the level of military confrontation in Europe. Cuts in military spending coupled with conversion of military production and science are indispensable to perestroika. Economically, priority should be given to reductions in conventional armaments, which swallow a sizable proportion of military resources. These writers therefore believe that in the period of transition, with the role of the military component of Soviet policy steadily decreasing, the Soviet Union could be interested in first reducing conventional armaments and armed forces while continuing to rely in a measure on the nuclear factor.

This interest will endure as Europe is unlikely to succeed before the end of this century in setting up a highly dependable security system based mainly on political guarantees. The period of transition is made more complex by the fact that the East European countries have embarked on inevitable and necessary changes involving elements of instability. The evolution of the political situation has already spelled an end to our military, primarily nuclear presence in some countries. In this situation the role of TNWs may come to play a bigger role also as a means of reassuring those sections of our public opinion that may be concerned about the effects of these changes in terms of the security and prestige of our country as well as some of our allies.

In appraising Soviet interests concerning the problem of eliminating TNWs in Europe, it is necessary to remember that fear of their elimination in Europe and, as a result, of a weakening of U.S. guarantees and the possibility of a major or even a complete U.S. troop withdrawal is one of the main reasons for the trend toward the military political integration in Western Europe that has intensified over the past two or three years.

The above brief analysis does not warrant explicit conclusions about how far the elimination of TNWs in the foreseeable future meets or contradicts Soviet interests. On the strength of an analysis of the balance of these interests, we are inclined to consider that basically the line of doing away with this nuclear weapon meets in the long run the interests of the Soviet Union. At the same time, we feel that to eliminate it completely could mean rushing events unless preceded by a substantial consolidation and restructuring of the European security system and if effected before the Soviet economic reform bears tangible fruit and the pace of the country's scientific and technological progress is greatly quickened.

Besides, the majority of Western leaders regard such "crash" elimination of all TNWs as absolutely unacceptable for the time being. Washington considers that the provision of nuclear guarantees to its allies is a key prerequisite for maintaining the stability of NATO and preserving U.S. positions in it.

The leaderships of West European countries are against renouncing TNWs, for they fear that this would erode the unity of the alliance, loosen U.S. strategic ties to Western Europe and undermine their countries' largely restraining influence on the United States. Alarmist sentiments due to the changing role of West Germany and the evolution of relations between the two German states are particularly widespread now. The preservation of TNWs on West German soil and its modernization are listed among measures that can slow down the advance to the unification of the two Germanies and prevent the FRG from becoming a nuclear power.

Paris and London are opposed to the elimination of Soviet and American TNWs, fearing that it would put the abolition of the tactical and then the strategic arsenals of France and Britain on the agenda.[1]

One reason why the NATO countries reject the idea of a nuclear-free Europe, of the elimination of TNWs, is the widespread conviction of historical origin that a non-nuclear balance, even at a lower level, would be unreliable as a means of preventing war even if the political foundations of security were to be strengthened.

Western conservative centrist leaders are particularly uneasy about calls for the elimination of nuclear arms in Europe who know that in addition to a large body of Western opinion, it is sought even by influential right wing conservatives. Among these are American military political leaders who want to give the United States greater freedom of action by disengaging it from European security, as well as many West German politicians who see TNWs as an obstacle to German unification.

As for NATO's nuclear strategy, two trends coexist in it. The trend toward integrating nuclear and non-nuclear weapons into a common strategy goes on developing. The material basis for the close compatibility and "interoperability" of nuclear and conventional armaments is provided by ever stronger emphasis on double-purpose systems as well as by the use of a single system of reconnaissance, targeting, communications and control.

However, the evolution of NATO military strategy in this direction is hampered by serious realities. These include a growing awareness even among the military that any use of nuclear weapons even only occasionally or with "demonstrational" intent is unacceptable because it would threaten an uncontrollable escalation, as would recourse to any large-scale, non-nuclear war because it could not only have disastrous ecological consequences but lead almost inevitably to the disintegration of society in European countries and the destruction of existing political systems.

Coming increasingly to the fore as a result is another trend in the evolution of NATO strategy.

It consists in consolidating the role of TNWs as the most important means of deterring war and in ruling out in effect the possibility of using them in military operations. Advocates of this trend, who include liberals and many centrists in the United States and a wide spectrum of forces ranging from the Social Democrats to center-oriented conservatives in Western Europe, declare for continued reliance on nuclear deterrence. But they single out a definite aspect of it, which is aimed at deterring war, at averting it, through the threat of retaliating for a conventional attack with nuclear weapons and escalating the conflict to a strategic level, which would automatically result in unsustainable damage. Exception is taken to the views of those partisans of deterrence who consider that to make it effective, one has to have a capability for a diversified warfare using nuclear weapons, a capability for "escalational domination," and so forth.[2] To put it plainly, there are differences between the advocates of politicized "deterrence through prevention" and militarized "deterrence through intimidation."

The concepts of the advocates of "containment/prevention" and "nonfirst use of nuclear weapons" have many negative aspects. They reject the idea of ridding Europe of nuclear arms, whose preservation means preserving the possibility of nuclear catastrophe and stimulates the race in nuclear arms and missile technologies. It also means preserving the role of nuclear weapons as a pillar of the military-bloc structure of European security, a structure resting to a considerable extent on military confrontation. Besides, there remain some possibilities for using TNWs as a means of deterrence and pressure.

But these concepts also have important positive aspects. They offer opportunities for drastic cuts in this weapon synchronized with large-scale reductions in conventional forces and for a notable reinforcement of military strategic stability on the continent. Hence the promise of ending or restricting certain potentially destabilizing trends in the conventional arms race relating primarily to missile technologies.

Before discussing the possible parameters of the balance of "minimum means of containment" which may result from future agreements, these authors wish to state some conclusions reached by us on the basis of an analysis of the evolution of the European nuclear balance between the 1950s and the 1980s.

The buildup of both sides' TNWs was determined not so much by their notions of threats or by the military strategic concepts worked out by them but by military bureaucratic logic, by military technological inertia, by the "life cycles" of weapons systems. It became independent to a degree even of changes in military strategic guidelines, preceding them in many cases and going beyond rational requirements. Before the early 1980s, political factors played no visible role in the trend of TNWs buildup. This politically and strategically irrational buildup was exemplified most strikingly by the increase in the American TNW arsenal in Europe in the 1960s and by the scale on which the Soviet Union deployed its RSD-10s [known to the West as the SS-20s—Ed.] in the 1970s and 1980s.

The buildup of the two TNW arsenals went on along lines that were mutually independent to a considerable extent. It is hard to say whether the concept of balance played a real and not a propaganda role. The development trend itself was isolated in a measure from changes in the balance of SOWs and conventional forces in Europe. This discrepancy obviously imposed additional expenditures on the Soviet Union in the 1970s and early 1980s, when our country strove simultaneously to alter in its favor the balance in SOWs, TNWs and conventional forces alike. This buildup did not win and was not intended to win "superiority" but played a role in complicating the political situation.

The attempts which both sides made time and again to reckon up balances between various weapons, such as IRMs, were basically mistaken although much depended without doubt on the actual purpose of the operation. The nuclear balance in Europe is determined by the totality of the nuclear forces sited on the continent: those differing in range and supplementing or off-setting each other, as well as strategic forces intended for or seen as intended for use in Europe.

For all the importance of assessing the balance from the military point of view, it is greater from the political point of view, especially for NATO countries. For the West European members of this bloc, the problem of nuclear guarantees is more acute than it ever was for the WTO countries due chiefly to the geopolitical factor.

Both militarily and politically, the nuclear balance in Europe is linked most intimately with the balance of conventional forces. Specifically, the West regards NATO's nuclear weapons as a means compensating for the advantages of the WTO in conventional forces and armaments.[3] In turn, the Soviet military leadership saw these advantages, to the best of our knowledge, as a necessary means of countervailing the nuclear superiority of NATO, primarily in the air component of TNWs.

For these reasons, a verified parity in TNWs conceived as quantitative equality in means of delivery and ammunition or even as equality in combat potentialities is less necessary for achieving stability and security in Europe than a similar parity at strategic level.

Parity in this sense has practically never existed. However, there is no ruling out the likelihood of quantitative evaluations of TNWs during preparations for talks acquiring decisive significance and giving rise to deep-seated differences, as was the case at the talks on Euromissiles. Negotiated solutions will probably be based on a particular version of quantitative balance although the two sides may depart from absolutizing parity as they seek such solutions.

The main criteria which an optimum balance of nuclear forces in Europe should meet (until they are completely eliminated) may be listed as follows. The nuclear forces of both sides should:

- be seen as aimed not at flexibly exchanging nuclear strikes or carrying on military operations, but merely at preventing war;
- be viable enough, especially in the event of a non-nuclear strike, and have a reliable and lasting control system precluding unsanctioned use;
- be of a size and have a structure adequate to maintain confidence in the dependability of the existing security system, including the maintenance of a measure of "linkage" between Western Europe and the United States;
- conform in qualitative and quantitative makeup to the task of stabilizing the military balance in reducing conventional armaments as well as TNWs themselves.

Following are several options of reduction based on the assumption that the early phase of talks will be aimed at effecting drastic cuts in TNWs but not at eliminating them as yet.

The method of unilateral reductions, including reductions prompted by the example of the other side, may prove very fruitful. (Both sides virtually apply it already.) Accordingly, the sides could work out as an option parallel unilateral reductions to jointly specified intermediate levels (meaning also very low ones). In that case, the only subject of talks would be to come to terms on the pace of reduction, the quantitative and qualitative parameters of residual levels, control and verification procedures and confidence-building measures in the nuclear sphere.

Seeing, however, that fairly influential political forces in the United States, Britain and France are still reluctant to accept far-reaching reductions in TNW arsenals, reliance on chiefly unilateral steps may prove ineffective from the point of view of a drastic lowering of the level of the nuclear balance. The method that will in all probability remain preferable is that of traditional talks based on mutual understanding reached beforehand and backed by unilateral moves speeding progress toward accords.

Talks should be preceded by the settlement of some complicated issues concerning their object.

First, should the sides only discuss means of delivering nuclear weapons or nuclear ammunition as well? The possibility of repeated use of all tactical means of delivering nuclear weapons makes it important in principle to take account of the quantity of ammunition, which determines, strictly speaking, the extent to which the European theater is saturated with nuclear arms. On the other hand, the extreme complexity of the technical aspects of verification and control and the need to achieve real results at an early date impose accepting at the initial stage of the talks an agenda aimed at limiting reductions to means of delivery. The readiness for unilateral cuts in nuclear ammunition shown by both sides creates favorable conditions for writing these cuts into a treaty at the next stage of talks.

Another issue is including the TNWs of France and Britain in the object of talks. The special position declared by the two countries at Vienna on reductions in tactical aircraft, which they say must not include their aircraft carrying nuclear weapons, suggests that building an initial nuclear balance may run into a traditional logjam. This situation being unacceptable, it is advisable to discount at the early stage of talks the TNW arsenals of France and Britain on the understanding that they are to be taken into account without fail in working out decisions on the ultimate quantitative TNW levels in Europe.

The third question, the most difficult of all, is how far restricting the object of talks to land-based systems, that is, artillery and tactical missiles, is acceptable to the Soviet Union and the WTO. The answer to this question can be linked directly to the results of the first stage of the Vienna talks, since the share of the aircraft component of TNWs may change substantially. The problem of ending imbalances in tactical aircraft is still one of the most challenging ones at Vienna, and the sides' positions did not show signs of drawing closer together until the WTO took steps in favor of a compromise which it set out in proposals submitted at Vienna on 28 September 1989.

In the event of the WTO approach being accepted—it calls for either alliance reducing its frontline air force to 4700 aircraft (except for anti-aircraft units)—NATO superiority in aircraft carrying nuclear weapons is likely to be decreased by a considerable margin. It could apparently be eliminated altogether if strike aircraft were limited to a ceiling of 1500 aircraft, as proposed by the WTO for a start. The situation would be more complicated were NATO to get its way by having the whole tactical air force reduced by 15 percent against the NATO level. In addition, the quantitative ceiling, 5700 combat aircraft, formally proposed at Vienna, turns out to be much higher than was called for previously.[4] If this proposal were accepted, NATO's relative superiority in aircraft for the delivery of nuclear weapons could even go up, since the Soviet Union would have to effect greater reductions.[5]

Thus there emerge at least two main alternatives of the likely object of talks on radical reductions in TNWs: broad and narrow. The former alternative would set limits to all delivery vehicles at once and a ceiling on nuclear ammunition. Presuming that the sides agreed on the latter alternative, they would first reduce land-based nuclear weapons only, limiting the quantity of ammunition mounted on aircraft and preventing its qualitative modernization. In the former case, which is doubtless more preferable, the sides could arrive at more extensive accords while in the latter they could advance more rapidly to concrete results, except that this would not completely block the race in TNWs.

The initial purpose of TNW talks could be to extend reductions achieved at the first stage of the talks on armed forces and conventional armaments to TNWs. The talks should be aimed at bringing about large-scale stabilizing cuts, which would be a spur for rapid progress at them. It is necessary, however, to proceed from the visible limits of the sides' flexibility, for they restrict the possibilities of compromise solutions.

In view of these limiting factors, the problem of eliminating nuclear artillery and reducing the number of control posts for land-based tactical missiles (not only of the Soviet Union and WTO but of NATO as well) without modernizing them in any way could be settled in a short time at the early stage of the talks on TNW reductions.

The elimination of nuclear artillery is being made possible by both the increasing obviousness of its military inefficiency and the West's reassessment of it as a deterrent. The fact that by the early 1980s the Soviet Union and WTO had attained rough parity in nuclear artillery capability is said to have convinced the majority of Western specialists more strongly than ever that this weapons system holds out no promise as a means of delivering nuclear arms.[6] At the early stage of the Vienna talks the sides will in all likelihood set reasonably low quantitative ceilings on artillery systems not only throughout the European theater (16,500 pieces of a caliber exceeding 100 mm) but in Central Europe (4500 pieces). This means that further quantitative cuts within the framework of TNW talks will hardly be possible. Still, the elimination of all nuclear shells could be an attainable goal, and it would be preferable to extend such a "zero option" to the whole territory of the Soviet Union and the United States. Such an accord would be verifiable not only through inspections of ammunition depots and permanent monitoring at the plants concerned but through supervision of combat training within the framework of confidence-building measures.

Guidelines for further cuts in TNWs can only be formulated in general terms in view of the uncertainty surrounding the pace and scale of the disarmament process in the area of conventional armaments and SOWs.

In the event of the initial stage of talks only dealing with land-based nuclear weapons, the content of the second stage, which would presumably be synchronized more or less strictly with progress at the talks on further cuts in armed forces and conventional armaments, would apparently consist in extending the object and including the key issue of aircraft. The level already proposed by the WTO—1500 strike, or in other words, carrier aircraft—could serve as a general guideline for settling it.

In accordance with this guideline, the sides would solve another major problem of this stage of TNW talks, the problem of setting a common ceiling on tactical nuclear ammunition. The third problem would be to evolve an effective system of control and verification. The preservation of a reasonably powerful strike air force would presumably necessitate a certain nuclear security reserve that could comprise both forward-based systems and flexible, viable weapons deployed in the second strategic echelons. A combination of land-based missiles and aircraft weapons could be the optimum alternative structure of tactical nuclear forces meeting these requirements. But in view of developments in Central European countries, the elimination of all land-based TNW systems could become politically preferable. With due regard to the possible unilateral reductions considered above, the nuclear ammunition of either side could be limited to 1000 rounds.

Such a potential could not be regarded as minimal or symbolic, for it would not in principle rule out the possibility of a flexible exchange of nuclear strikes in the course of hostilities. A qualitative reduction of this possibility could be achieved at the next stage of talks on a radical cut in TNWs that would lower the nuclear balance to the minimum level, and curb the race in military technologies. The transition to a symbolic nuclear potential would apparently require a twofold or threefold cut in ammunition against the previous stage (that is, to between 300 and 400 rounds), meaning ammunition mounted on aircraft that might be assigned for the purpose to facilitate control and verification.

We believe an important characteristic of this minimal or symbolic TNW potential should be the global dimension of limitation, that is, inclusion of the whole Soviet and U.S. territory, which would make it impossible to build up a nuclear arsenal fast in a crisis situation. Besides, a decision would apparently have to be made at that stage on sea-based nuclear weapons intended for use in Europe. The parameters of this decision could include the elimination of the nuclear possibilities of carrier aviation and the establishment of a low ceiling on long-range SBCMs [sea-based cruise missiles].

A reduction of TNWs to symbolic levels coupled with a reduction in conventional arsenals would make for a qualitative change in the political and military strategic situation on the continent. The simultaneous restructuring and stabilization of the European security system by politicizing it and building confidence would sooner or later create a situation where nuclear arms become unnecessary even for those who now consider them indispensable. The way would be paved for the elimination of all TNWs, and this, in turn, would constitute a most important stage in the transition to a nuclear-free world.

Notes

1. See F. Heisbourg, "The British and French Nuclear Forces. Current Roles and New Challenges." *Survival*, July-August 1989.

2. See L. Freedman, "I Exist: Therefore I Deter." *International Security*, Summer 1988.

3. See H. Binnendijk, "NATO's Nuclear Modernization Dilemma." *Survival*, March-April 1989.

4. This figure appeared in the proposals submitted by NATO at Vienna last June and concretizing President George Bush's "Brussels Initiative." We wish to underline that the figures cited in data published in January 1989 were 4000 combat aircraft as well as 530 aircraft laid by and 530 training planes. See *Conventional Forces in Europe: The Facts*, 1989, p. 27.

5. According to Soviet official sources, the WTO has 7184 combat aircraft for the frontline and anti-aircraft defense and NATO, 5500 combat aircraft. See *Pravda*, 30 January 1989.

6. See, for instance, Ph. Karber, *The Soviet Threat: Comparative Assessments*, 1988, p. 22.

PART SEVEN

Third World Issues

PART TWO

Third World Issue

We now turn to the role of the United States and the Soviet Union in the Third World and their attitudes toward regional conflicts. This topic may seem peripheral to some of the major issues between the two countries, particularly the military balance and their respective roles in Europe. However, developments in the Third World are a critical part of the U.S.-Soviet relationship. Political relations between the two powers have frequently been marred by differences and developments in the Third World. Because of the "balance of terror," superpower bilateral behavior in areas of direct confrontation (such as in Europe) have been extremely prudent. Therefore, the ideological and political struggle between the two giants has tended to take place among their "client" states or neutral countries in the Third World. Superpower relations there have been played as a "zero-sum" game in which any "gain" by one power automatically meant a "loss" for the other. Furthermore, terms such as the "domino theory" suggested that entire regions would come under the control of one superpower if the opposition did not respond.

According to S. Neil MacFarlane, in his essay entitled "Superpower Rivalry in the 1990s," Soviet and American objectives in the Third World have changed dramatically in recent years. As a result, the relevance of Third World policies to their competition as superpowers has declined. They no longer see their activities in these areas as a zero-sum game in which a gain for one side automatically equaled a loss for the other. Indeed, because of their new relationship they are more apt to see opportunities for cooperation rather than inevitable conflict in regional disputes.

According to MacFarlane, Soviet analysts are now critical of past Soviet policies that sought to promote socialism in the Third World. Increasingly they attribute conflict in the Third World to indigenous factors rather than imperialism. The Soviets have less interest in revolutionary insurgency and have shown a preference for political rather than military solutions to such conflict. Furthermore, there is an ever-increasing tendency to avoid situations that risk confrontation with the United States. Regional conflicts should not be allowed to have a destructive impact on the evolving superpower accommodation on issues perceived to be more critical. These developments have led to a growing Soviet interest in multilateral political settlement of regional and internal conflicts and a renewed appreciation for the role that the United Nations can play in resolving such conflicts.

With regard to the United States, the author says the trend is for the United States also to promote superpower cooperation in limiting and/or resolving Third World disputes that aggravate the new bilateral Soviet-U.S. relationship. Another similarity in the superpower perspective is that American analysts increasingly suggest that the past U.S. "over-attention" to Third World conflicts and the role of the USSR in these conflicts has diverted resources from more important tasks. The emerging American stance on Third World concerns is to consider U.S. interests less in terms of the East-West conflict and more from the perspective of resolving North-South issues.

MacFarlane concludes his essay with a word of caution. "Those who argue that we are in the midst of a qualitative transformation of the nature of Soviet and U.S. approaches to the Third World would do well to remember that we have seen many of these changes before." Nevertheless, he argues that the prospects for actual change are greater than before because both superpowers have learned that their past Third World competition had little impact on the balance between them, and efforts to manipulate the balance have carried great political costs for both countries.

In his exposition entitled "Reappraisal of USSR Third World Policy," Andrei Kolosov explains that the withdrawal of Soviet troops from Afghanistan was a turning point in the USSR's relations with the Third World. Even more important than the troop withdrawal, he suggests, is that Moscow admitted that the war was a mistake and saw it as a major impediment to the USSR's normalization of relations with the rest of the developing world. Actually the Soviet move toward reducing its involvement in the developing world has developed gradually, but increasingly the Soviet preference for using multilateral mechanisms to solve regional issues has become evident.

Moscow's "confrontational approach," which divided countries into "ours" and "not ours," has been abandoned. The new Soviet policy is to seek pragmatic solutions to problems based on national interests rather than ideological goals. One practical goal is to lessen the economic burden of Soviet involvement in these areas.

There has been criticism of the Soviet policy change, the author concedes, but he argues that it makes no sense to honor commitments made when "the entire logic of the vision of the world was different," and when the results have been counterproductive and have contributed to the deterioration of the Soviet economy.

Kolosov is particularly critical of the military aspects of past Soviet relations with Third World countries. He argues that although the USSR does have security interests in the developing areas, they are "extremely limited." Although arms sales have played a key role in the USSR's relations with these countries, he doubts that his nation has vital interests in these areas that need to be protected with weapons. He also questions the claim that arms deliveries have produced enormous hard-currency profits for the USSR. Actually, most of the weapons have been given away for political reasons or the bills have remained unpaid. He admits that for economic reasons it would be a mistake to stop arms sales entirely, but they should not be delivered to "explosive areas," nor should their delivery "violate the principle of reasonable sufficiency at the regional level."

In sum, economic expediency, not ideological and political preferences, should determine the Soviet Union's relations with the Third World. Some aid should be given, but only if it promotes the economic development of both the giver and receiver. Most importantly, it is time to stop dividing the world into camps. When Soviet interests clash with U.S. inter-

ests, *the two powers should seek solutions based on compromise. In any other case, U.S. actions should be of no concern to
the Soviet Union. "The quicker the legacy of confrontation is
surmounted in the Third World, the quicker we will move
forward."*

25

Superpower Rivalry in the 1990s

S. Neil MacFarlane

Two factors stand out as determinants of the post-war history of the
Third World: the eclipse of the European colonial powers by the two
superpowers as dominant actors in world politics; and the rejection in
much of the colonial world of external domination. The withdrawal of
the colonial powers from their possessions is, in part, a result of their
exhaustion and loss of will during the two world wars. The spread of
nationalist ideas, of the liberal principle of self-determination and of
Marxian ideas of anti-imperialism, and the actions of subject peoples
inspired by these ideas also contributed decisively to the eclipse of the
great colonial empires. The nature of the geopolitical and ideological
rivalry between the two superpowers, in conjunction with the stasis
imposed on their competition in Europe by nuclear weapons and the
emergence of a perceived vacuum in the decolonizing and post-colonial
Third World, compelled the U.S.A. and the USSR to compete for influence and position in the Third World. At the same time, the revolt of
the Third World against external domination made this a far more
difficult terrain than before in which to pursue such objectives. The
environment they sought to control could not be controlled. Gains made
at the expense of the other were limited and ephemeral. The history
of the superpower rivalry in the Third World is that of the gradual
recognition of the limits on superpower initiative there, its potentially
high costs and historically insignificant benefits.

In assessing the historical development of and current trends in
superpower competition in the Third World, I shall begin with a discussion of the superpowers' objectives in the Third World and of the
interpretive prisms through which they have viewed it. An examina-

tion of the historical development of their relationship in the Third World follows, leading to an analysis of the current stage of Soviet and U.S. approaches to the Third World. I shall conclude with some comments on learning and on the prospects for competition and superpower behavior in the Third World.

The topic is necessarily centered on the superpowers themselves, but this gives insufficient play to indigenous factors in Third World politics. The Third World is not a passive terrain on which the great powers can exercise their aspirations, a fact which historically has been insufficiently appreciated in U.S. and Soviet analyses, which have tended toward ethnocentricity and excessive globalism. I suggest that the superpowers are coming to the conclusion that this distortion of perspective, this insensitivity to realities on the ground, accounts in part for their frustrations in dealing with the Third World. This may lead to a realization that their competition is not strictly a zero-sum game in which Third World states are objects rather than subjects of history, to a reduction in superpower expectations of durable long-term gains emanating from their competition there, and to more realistic, regionally oriented approaches to Third World politics.

Superpower Objectives in the Third World

Before examining continuities and changes in the historical record of Soviet and U.S. policies in the Third World, it is useful to examine in a more abstract sense the objectives that are being pursued there. Historically, the formulation of superpower policies in the Third World has been dominated by objectives relating to their bipolar rivalry. The two states have traditionally perceived processes of change in the Third World to be significant largely in terms of the effort either to contain or to roll back Soviet-sponsored communist revolution on the one hand, or as a component of a global revolutionary process directed against imperialism on the other. Even issues which are not derived directly from the central rivalry, such as the rise of a Chinese challenge in the USSR or the question of Islamic fundamentalism, have tended to be perceived in Moscow and Washington in terms of their impact on the competition between them.

However, not all the objectives of the superpowers in the Third World are directly related to this rivalry. And as shall become clearer later, the salience in both countries of objectives related directly to superpower competition appears to be diminishing. So too does their interest in Third World revolution, due to a change in the character of the central relationship between them, reassessment on both sides of the merits of zero-sum competition in the Third World, and the growing comparative significance of Third World imperatives essentially unrelated to the policies of the other superpower.

The distribution of power in the international system is such that only the USSR is sufficiently powerful to threaten the U.S.A., and vice versa. Moreover, each subscribes to a universalizable system of beliefs antithetical to that of the other. This ideological contradiction strengthens the perceived threat from the other: each side has perceived the other's efforts to be directed not only at the erosion of its own power but at the destruction of its principles of political, economic and social organization.

These concerns have fostered great sensitivity to border security. Hence, for example, in commenting in 1980 on the significance to U.S. security of developments in Central America, Ambassador Kirkpatrick noted that:

> the deterioration of the U.S. position in the hemisphere has already created serious vulnerabilities where none previously existed and threatens now to confront the country with the unprecedented need to defend itself against a ring of Soviet bases on its southern flanks from Cuba to Central America.[1]

One can cite analogous statements made by Leonid Brezhnev in 1979 to the effect that, since Soviet security was at stake, the USSR could not view with indifference intervention in the internal affairs of Iran by other powers (presumably the U.S.A. in particular). One can question the sincerity of the stated Soviet belief that the threat in Afghanistan was one of imperialist destabilization of a pro-Soviet regime of socialist orientation,[2] but such questioning need not draw into doubt either the significance of the security objective in Soviet behavior in Afghanistan, or its link to considerations of bipolarity. The loss of Afghanistan to anti-Soviet forces—whether or not these were the creatures of the U.S.A.—would constitute a net loss in the overall correlation of forces with the West. It would also render a sensitive and exposed sector of the Soviet periphery less secure.

The obverse of each superpower's interest in control over contiguous Third World areas is an interest in competing for influence in areas bordering the other superpower. Military positions throughout much of the Third World have been considered by each to be useful in the attempt to threaten and contain the other. In the case of the U.S.A., military facilities in proximity to the USSR (for example in the Indian Ocean and the Gulf) and along sea lines of communication linking the U.S.A. to the periphery of the Eurasian land mass are deemed necessary for the U.S. capacity to resist Soviet expansion. Likewise, for the USSR, positions in Cuba facilitate intelligence collection and allow those lines of communication to be threatened while diverting U.S. attention away from Europe and on to matters closer to home.

Even where the desire for military facilities may not be a significant direct policy concern, to the extent that each side thinks the other is so motivated, it may act upon that perception. Hence, although it is eminently questionable whether the USSR has ever seriously entertained the prospect of establishing bases on the Central American mainland, it appears that a U.S. concern about such an objective has informed the U.S. response to Soviet ties with the Sandinista regime.

Bipolarity has important political dimensions as well. In conditions where the world is seen to be reasonably equally divided between two major power centers, any slight shift in favor of one or the other, resulting for example from a change in allegiance of a third country, takes on considerable symbolic importance. Any such gain might encourage further efforts elsewhere on the part of the favored adversary. Other states with ties to the weaker power may conclude that such links are unwise and that they should make their peace with the rising actor. Each side fears a domino effect. Events inconsequential in themselves may unleash processes which cause significant damage to vital interests. Hence Secretary Kissinger argued, with reference to Soviet involvement in Angola in 1975, that if the U.S.A. limited its response to Soviet challenges to areas of vital interest, such Soviet actions would

> sooner or later create an international situation in which the overall balance is so shifted against us that it will either require the most massive exertions and turn us into a military garrison, or lead us into some sort of confrontation.[3]

It is plausible that the USSR recently combined increased military assistance to Nicaragua and Angola with its withdrawal from Afghanistan out of a similar concern about the domino effect of this latter measure (see below). If prestige is "a reputation for power,"[4] and acts as a deterrent to challenges to power, then the erosion of credibility and the failure of prestige may invite such challenges.

The question of prestige leads to that of status. The growth of the USSR as a military power in the post-war period and its emergence as one of the two most powerful actors in world politics led to expectations of U.S. recognition of its equality not only in central theaters but also in the Third World, and notably the legitimacy of the claim to a role in regional politics commensurate with that of the U.S.A.

The capacity and the aspiration of the USSR to actualize its claim to a role in regional politics and security varies from region to region. It is clearly lowest in the Western hemisphere due to the latter's proximity to the U.S.A., persistent deficiencies in Soviet force projection capa-

S. Neil MacFarlane

bilities, and the understandable sensitivity of the U.S.A. to security developments in this region. By contrast, Soviet status concerns appear to be a significant factor in Soviet policy in Asia, the Middle East and Africa.

The U.S.A., meanwhile, having grown accustomed to relative primacy among external actors in much of the Third World, and interpreting Soviet actions as a revisionist challenge to the international status quo, has at various times resisted Soviet attempts to establish its role as a political actor and arbiter in the Third World, and attempted to undermine Soviet successes in inserting itself into regional politics. U.S. policy toward the Arab-Israeli peace process appears to have been motivated in part by an effort to deny a role to the USSR.[5] This is related to considerations of the balance of power, since to the extent that the USSR can establish itself as a legitimate player in the politics of specific regions, it may use that status to impede U.S. diplomacy and to enhance further its own influence. Not only is such status potentially useful in diplomacy, but it also responds to the nationalist animus of much of the Soviet elite.

Beyond these considerations of power, status and prestige, there are those of ideology. Both sides have sought to extend the area in which their conceptions of political, social and economic order prevail, for three reasons. First, to some extent they considered their own worldview to be universally right. More importantly perhaps, there is a strong tendency on the part of both sides to assume that their security is enhanced through the proliferation of their ideologies. In the U.S. tradition such assumptions date back to Tom Paine, who considered that the spread of liberal revolution would allow the democracies to live in peace and security.[6] It is also found in the Wilsonian tradition of "making the world safe for democracy." "Marxist totalitarianism" is inherently subversive of international order and corrosive of U.S. power.[7]

In traditional Soviet theory, bourgeois democracies tend to cooperate with their confreres in the global class struggle between capitalism and socialism and can only be unreliable as allies of the USSR. Such assumptions underlay Stalin's thorough revamping of the internal social, economic and political arrangements of his Eastern European satellites along Soviet lines. More recently, disappointments with nationalist regimes in the late 1960s and 1970s may have convinced Soviet policymakers that only through the promotion of vanguard party regimes following a path of socialist orientation could a reliable position in the Third World be developed and sustained.

Third, both states appear to believe that the domestic legitimacy of government is to some degree preserved or strengthened by efforts (or at least the semblance of efforts) to spread the faith. The radicalization of Khrushchev's Third World policy in the early 1960s, in the face of challenges from the left wing of the communist movement, is perhaps demonstrative of this concern. Likewise, in the case of the U.S.A., the proclaimed fidelity to the *contras* and their freedom-fighting colleagues elsewhere in the Third World may be seen in part as an effort to preempt the potential opposition of true believers to the current thrust of U.S. policy toward the USSR.

Just as the imperatives of status and ideology were related to those of power and bipolarity, so too were concerns not directly attributable to the rivalry between the superpowers. The origins of the fundamentalist Islamic threat to the interests of both superpowers had little to do with East-West rivalry; but both the USSR and the U.S.A. focused on its impact on that rivalry. From the U.S. perspective, instability associated with fundamentalist challenges to conservative or secular nationalist regimes created opportunities for Soviet penetration into the Middle East. For the USSR also, Islamic fundamentalism was a threat largely in the context of the competition with the West. To the extent that it threatened to spill over into the USSR itself, it would weaken the power of the USSR and the socialist camp in its global struggle against imperialism.

Likewise, the essentially economic question of access to raw materials is interesting given the significance of these imports in sustaining a potential Western war effort. The loss of access to Gulf oil supplies would jeopardize the economic health of U.S. allies and their capacity to cooperate in joint efforts against the USSR in war and peace. Southern Africa is significant, because U.S. defense industries depend to a considerable degree on imports from that region.

Finally, the preoccupation of both superpowers with the PRC as a threat to their objectives in the Third World has been closely interwoven with the larger concerns of bipolarity and the correlation of forces. This was the case, from the U.S. point of view, in Vietnam in the mid-1960s. The Soviet rivalry with the Chinese grew out of the internal dynamics of the world communist movement. But in the face of the rapprochement between the U.S.A. and the PRC in the mid-1970s, Soviet concerns about competition with the PRC for influence in the Third World were linked to the relationship between the superpowers. Garthoff notes, for example, that the USSR's initial concerns in Angola revolved around what the Soviets perceived to be evidence of Sino-American collusion against the USSR in the Third World.[8] Both the Vietnamese and Angolan cases suggest, moreover, that in the bipolar context, entry by one superpower into a conflict in response to the purported actions of some third party has a tendency to result in competition between the superpowers.

Superpower Assessments of
Third World Politics

The two superpowers, in developing strategies and policies to address these objectives and concerns, did so through distinct though curiously similar interpretive prisms. The discussion of superpower interpretive prisms is problematic. There are dangers in anthropomorphizing states which encompass increasingly complex polities. Decisions are seldom the result of coherent rational calculation. Instead, they emerge for often obscure reasons from an interplay between a wide array of interested groups and coalitions. The actions purportedly based on these decisions are in turn strongly influenced by bureaucratic politics and standard operating procedures. The policies of both superpowers toward the Third World often show the influence of competing internal perspectives. The nature of their policies has shifted substantially over time. However, there are certain tendencies of interpretation in U.S. and Soviet responses to phenomena in the Third World which have been widely shared, quite durable, and which have considerably influenced the approaches of the two states to the South.

These interpretive prisms were seriously flawed in their underestimation of the indigenous roots of political process in the Third World, and of the capacity and desire of Third World political actors to expand their autonomy from external influence. Three examples suffice: attitudes toward the sources of Third World conflict; assessments of the significance of revolutionary movements; and perceptions of the applicability of the superpowers' own historical experiences in other countries.

Both sides have tended to underestimate the indigenous roots of conflict and to stress their own global rivalry in causal explanation. President Reagan typified this tendency some years ago in noting that, without Soviet meddling, there would be no hotspots in the Third World. On the Soviet side, there are a legion of examples of the attribution of Third World civil and regional conflict to imperialism.[9] In this instance, the problem seems to lie partly in Marxist ideology, and in particular the tendency to depreciate the significance of "subjective" factors such as ethnicity, nationalism and religion in politics. The tendency of both superpowers to underplay the role of indigenous factors as causes and sustainers of Third World conflicts encourages an underestimation of the autonomy of such conflicts and an overestimation of the degree to which they can be controlled.

With regard to revolutionary processes, on the Soviet side, from Khrushchev to Brezhnev, anti-Western national liberation revolutions were seen as components of a world revolutionary process directed against imperialism, as allies involved in a common struggle. Such perspectives have often extended to radical nationalist regimes produced by such struggles, particularly in instances where these regimes embraced some variant of "scientific" socialism. They were particularly strong in the mid and late 1970s *vis-à-vis* movements and regimes espousing Marxism-Leninism and "vanguard party" rule. These attitudes led to an overestimation of the degree to which such regimes are willing to subordinate themselves in a Soviet-led world revolutionary movement and of the staying power of such regimes, and consequently to commitments which have often brought little by way of concrete gain while embroiling the USSR in local disputes.

The U.S.A. essentially bought into the Soviet logic. Assuming that anti-Western left-wing movements were necessarily pro-Soviet, that once entrenched they were extremely difficult to remove (given the organizational advantages of the Leninist model), and that they were likely to damage Western economic interests and to impede Western access to needed raw materials, U.S. governments have tended to shun or oppose indigenous revolutionary processes. This perspective has an air of self-fulfilling prophecy, since such opposition can transform distaste for the West, the colonial and "neocolonial" legacy to dependence on the USSR.

Lastly, both sides have tended to project their own domestic experience as a model for Third World states and movements. On one side we saw the touting of Soviet political and economic forms as a panacea in Third World modernization; on the other, democracy and free enterprise. Both sides believed that their experience was relevant despite substantially different cultural, historical, economic and political conditions in "target" countries, and both underestimated the obstacles in the path of such replication. This also encourages activism in foreign policy. Basing policy significantly on the desire to propagate politico-economic models which embody deeply held values and are a source of legitimacy means also that it becomes difficult to abandon such policies when they do not work. Disentanglement becomes difficult not just because of prestige and credibility concerns, but because it constitutes a betrayal of the "values which made this country great."

Historical Background

The behavior of both superpowers in the Third World displays an apparently cyclical pattern. Both Soviet and U.S. policy have oscillated between activism and relative passivity from the early 1950s to the present day. In the Dulles period of U.S. diplomatic history, the effort to globalize containment dominated U.S. behavior in the Third World....

By contrast, the USSR was relatively quiescent. After the failure in Iran, Stalin turned his attention in foreign policy to the consolidation of Soviet gains in Eastern Europe. In conditions of a U.S. monopoly on atomic weapons and massive superiority in force projection capability, taking risks in the Third World did not seem a worthwhile option. Although willing to sanction communist insurrection in Southeast and South Asia, the USSR went little beyond rhetorical endorsement.[10]

The initial U.S. spate of activity slackened in the mid and late 1950s,[11] while Khrushchev rekindled Soviet interest in the Third World. A portent of things to come lay in the Soviet decision to transfer a small quantity of arms to Guatemala in 1954. But the real indicators of change were Khrushchev and Bulganin's visit to South Asia and the first arms deals with Egypt in 1955. There followed a rapid expansion in pro-Arab Soviet activity in the Middle East, and in economic and military assistance to India and later in the decade to emerging radical states in Africa such as Guinea and Ghana.[12] When Castro came to power in Cuba, this activism extended to Latin America.[13] In addition to the rapid expansion of diplomatic ties and the cultivation of close economic and security relations with a wide array of "progressive" Third World regimes, the USSR also displayed a more forward-looking military policy characterized by missile rattling on Middle Eastern and Caribbean issues, limited interventionism (as in the Congo in 1960), and isolated efforts to expand military assets in the Third World (such as the installation of medium-range and intermediate-range ballistic missiles in Cuba in 1962).[14] Khrushchev's decision to compete actively in this new arena was encouraged by a misreading of President Kennedy's resolve, and by the growing Chinese challenge to Soviet credentials as a revolutionary actor in world politics.[15] This kindled a growing Soviet interest in insurgent movements, evinced by assistance to the provisional government of Algeria and the Pathet Lao.

The result of this emergent Soviet activism and a number of other factors (to be discussed more fully below) was a U.S. return to Third World activism during and following the Kennedy administration, with rapid increases in economic and security assistance across the board and specific regional initiatives such as the Alliance for Progress. Simultaneous activism brought the two superpowers into collision in Cuba in 1962. Intervention in Vietnam and the Dominican Republic underlined the U.S. willingness to use force to deal with what it perceived to be communist threats to its interests in the Third World.

The Cuban crisis meanwhile brought a reconsideration in the USSR of the merits of competitive military behavior in the Third World in the face of overwhelming U.S. superiority in force projection. The Vietnam and Dominican affairs strengthened this constraint as the new post-Khruschev leadership took power. The rapid growth of U.S. economic assistance programs under Kennedy had also drawn into question the Soviet capacity to compete in economic terms, while much Soviet aid had been misapplied and misused. (This was of particular importance at a time of growing internal strain on Soviet resources.) The result was the beginning of a period of retrenchment in the Third World in the aftermath of the Cuban missile crisis, which gathered steam after Khrushchev was replaced in October of 1964 and a number of prominent Soviet friends (Sukarno, Nkrumah and Ben Bella) met their demise. A major permissive condition of this retrenchment was the cultural revolution in China and the demise of Chinese rivalry in Third World politics.

This was not, however, a period of full-scale retreat, but rather of the concentration of Soviet attention on a rather more limited number of venues (the Middle East and Vietnam), and a shift in the balance of instruments deployed in pursuit of Soviet objectives from the economic to the military.[16]...

Shifting budget priorities in the U.S.A., deepening economic difficulties and growing domestic opposition to the Vietnam War occasioned yet another downturn in U.S. policy. President Nixon responded to opposition to further forceful defense of U.S. interests in the Third World by articulating the doctrine that came to bear his name.[17] The U.S.A. withdrew from Vietnam in 1973. Two years later, the Ford administration looked on impotently as their erstwhile allies fell in the face of north Vietnamese violations of the Paris Accords. Congress rejected the Ford administration's efforts to assist the Frente Nacional de Libertacao de Angola (FNLA) and Uniao Nacional para a Independencia Total de Angola (UNITA) in Angola.

The U.S. government perceived détente as a means of managing retrenchment, by capturing the USSR in a web of interdependent relations which gave this erstwhile revolutionary actor a stake in the status quo.[18] Unfortunately, this U.S. reassessment coincided with, and was perhaps partly a cause of, a resurgence of Soviet activism in the Third World typified by the Soviet deployment of several thousand air defense personnel to Egypt in 1970, the resupply of Egypt and Syria during the October War in 1973, Soviet and Cuban assistance to the MPLA in 1974-1976 in its struggle to take and hold power in Angola, and to Ethiopia's military regime in its effort to repulse a Somali invasion in 1977-1978, and finally the Soviet invasion of Afghanistan.[19] This rekindling of Soviet activism was all the more disturbing since it came to focus

on self-styled vanguard party Marxist-Lenin regimes, ostensibly committed to deep internal socio-economic transformation and to a foreign
policy of solidarity with the USSR in its struggle against imperialism.
U.S. concern was heightened by the fact that two of these beasts
popped up in the Western hemisphere (Nicaragua and Grenada in
1979), and that the odds seemed good at the end of the decade that the
revolution would spread—with Soviet and Cuban assistance—to other
Central American countries.[20] Indeed, Soviet assistance to many insurgent movements increased at this time as well. Aid to long-term friends
in Southern Africa such as SWAPO and the ANC increased, reflecting
Soviet optimism about the likely course of events in that region after
the victory in Angola. There is also evidence that the USSR arranged
for (if it did not directly provide) military assistance to the Frente
Farabundo Marti para la Liberación Nacional (FMLN) in El Salvador
in 1980-1981 in the aftermath of the victory in Nicaragua.[21]

The renewal of Soviet activism presumably resulted from a number
of factors, among them concern about the potentially delegitimizing
effects of détente in the context of a renewal of the challenge from the
PRC, disappointment with the fruits of détente (namely the Stevenson
and Jackson-Vanik amendments), signals that the U.S. conception of
détente did not preclude the unilateral U.S. quest for advantage in the
Third World (namely Chile and the U.S. effort to cut the USSR out of
the Middle East),[22] the attainment of parity coupled with the expansion of Soviet force projection capabilities, which permitted activities
that had in earlier years been logistically impossible, and the reduction in the credibility of U.S. deterrence of Soviet political and military initiatives in the Third World resulting from the defeat in Vietnam and the "syndrome" which resulted.

Perceived Soviet gains and the growing Soviet threat to U.S. interests in the Third World, along with the sense of having been taken advantage of during a post-defeat period of weakness, were important
factors in the swing to the right in U.S. domestic politics which resulted in the Reagan administration. Perhaps the most salient aspect
of its Third World policy outside the Middle East was a return to anti-
Soviet activism. But it was activism with a difference, a pursuit of
U.S. interests through challenges to the status quo rather than efforts
to maintain it.

To sum up, periods of Soviet passivity tend to be ones of U.S. activism and vice versa. On the face of it, the record suggests a degree of
responsiveness of one superpower to the policies of the other. But the
responses appear to differ. While Soviet activism (as in the late 1950s
and late 1970s) appears to elicit an activist U.S. response, it is U.S.
passivity, by lowering the risks of opportunism, which elicits Soviet

militance. This asymmetry suggests that the prospects for the synchronization of Soviet and U.S. policies in the Third World are poor. Any reduction in U.S. activism, to judge from the historical record, is liable to evoke an opportunistic Soviet response.

Change in Superpower Perspectives
on the Third World

This brings me to an examination of the current Soviet and U.S. policy in the Third World. As one would expect from the cyclical pattern described above, U.S. militance in the early and mid-1980s apparently occasioned a Soviet reconsideration of late 1970s activism. In ideological terms, the literature prior to Gorbachev's accession to power evinced growing doubts about the prospects for the transition to socialism,[23] and about the Soviet capacity to hold on to recently acquired assets,[24] disillusionment with many of their ideological confreres in the Third World,[25] concern about the effects of Third World competition on the central relationship between the U.S.A. and the USSR,[26] unhappiness with the costs of "empire" and concern about the capacity of the USSR to bear it,[27] and an interest in the development of relations of mutual economic benefit with significant Third World actors (such as Brazil, Mexico and India) independent of ideological orientation.[28]

These trends have continued to develop under Gorbachev to the point where most analysts of Soviet Third World theory would consider them to be the dominant tendency of articulation.[29] Indeed, Soviet analysts now go considerably further, criticizing previous optimism concerning the trend in the correlation of forces in favor of world socialism in the Third World,[30] and the quality of prior Soviet analyses of Third World politics,[31] and indeed questioning the relevance in the Third World of "Eurocentric" class-based Marxist theories.[32] Analytical interest in factors such as ethnicity, clan and religion, whose significance Soviet analysts are said to have underestimated, has grown markedly.[33] Conflict in the Third World, for example, appears to be attributed increasingly to such factors, rather than to the influence of imperialism. These trends have been accompanied by a reduction in the level of Soviet enthusiasm for revolutionary insurgency in areas such as South Africa, Namibia and Central America, and a preference for political rather than military settlement of these insurgent conflicts.[34] This occurs in the context of growing stated skepticism about the use of force as a political instrument in the Third World.

This is related to an apparent reassessment of the relationship between local conflict and the superpower relationship. Denying the role of imperialism as a source of conflict in the Third World implicitly dissociates such conflict from the struggle between socialism and capitalism, and absolves the USSR of its revolutionary responsibility to participate in such altercations as part of its own crusade against the forces of darkness. The growing stress on the possibility of escalation and on the destructive role that regional conflicts play in the superpower relationship provides a positive incentive and/or justification for steering clear of situations in the Third World where there is a risk of confrontation with the U.S.A.

All of this is occurring under the umbrella of a dramatic reduction of emphasis on Third World issues (and in particular issues relating to revolutionary movements and regimes) in general statements about Soviet foreign policy.[35] Soviet comment on the Third World these days suggests a reduced interest in the Third World as a whole, in revolutionary process in the Third World (as opposed to state-to-state diplomatic and economic relations based on the intrinsic importance of the state in question rather than its ideological rectitude),[36] and interest in disengagement from conflicts which carry a significant risk of failure and significant burdens for the USSR, while troubling the waters of the Soviet-U.S. relationship. More broadly, the Soviets have redefined security in non-zero-sum terms, arguing that here, as on other "global issues," the interests of the superpowers converge rather than conflict.[37]

These developments have brought in their stead a growing Soviet stated interest in multilateral political settlement of regional and internal conflicts in which it has become involved, a reassessment of the merits of superpower consultation on this topic, and a renewed appreciation of the role which the U.N. can assume in these circumstances.[38] In South Africa, for example, Soviet commentators have replaced their qualified enthusiasm for insurgent struggle with an endorsement of negotiation leading to an orderly and peaceful transition to majority rule. To judge from recent interviews, this has brought them into a degree of conflict with elements of the ANC, including the South African Communist Party.[39]

That all of this is not just hot air is evident from the recent behavior of the USSR and its allies in the Third World. Perhaps the most obvious superficial indicator of change in Soviet perspectives on Third World security and on their relations with revolutionary regimes in the Third World is the withdrawal from Afghanistan.[40] One should be careful, however, about drawing generalizations from the Afghan case. The involvement in the Afghan conflict has carried much higher military and human costs for the USSR than their support for other states beset by civil and regional conflict. The intensity of Soviet involvement was also such as to make the Afghan question a particularly serious irritant in the superpower relationship. Also, it appears that they were having difficulty in maintaining more exposed positions in the face of growing guerrilla pressure, and were faced with the choice of maintaining existing force levels and accepting a gradual shrinkage in their zone of control, sizeable escalation in order to sustain existing positions, or withdrawal. None of these characteristics is shared to the same degree by the other regional conflicts where the USSR is supporting revolutionary regimes.

Nonetheless, there are widespread indications of substantial change in Soviet practice throughout the Third World. The focus of Soviet diplomacy appears to have shifted to states such as India, Mexico and Brazil, which are intrinsically important and have some potential for mutually beneficial trading relationships with the USSR. The Soviets have quite clearly been putting pressure on their Third World clients to improve their economic performance and reduce the burden they impose on the Soviet economy, through internal reforms to expand the sphere of opportunity open to private initiative and through the expansion of trading and investment ties to the developed Western economies.[41]

They have also been encouraging friends involved in civil and regional conflicts to resolve them through political settlements. In recent years the Soviets have supported efforts to negotiate settlements in Cambodia, Afghanistan, Angola, Ethiopia and Nicaragua, among others. Significant concessions and unilateral efforts to reduce involvement in conflict have frequently been made in these contexts by friends of the USSR and by the USSR itself. In the Angolan case, Angola and Cuba accepted (with encouragement from Soviet diplomats) linkage of the Cuban presence in Angola to that of South Africa in Namibia, a shortening of the timetable for Cuban withdrawal, and the closure of ANC bases in Angola. The Vietnamese—again apparently with Soviet encouragement—have carried out a unilateral withdrawal from Cambodia, without a political settlement. Cuban forces are now withdrawing unilaterally from Ethiopia. The Soviets themselves withdrew unilaterally from Afghanistan without any final settlement of the conflict.

In this search for political settlement of regional disputes, the Soviets have been counseling their allies to contemplate internal political reforms to improve prospects for settlement of regional disputes, even where these reforms ostensibly depart from the centralist prescriptions of orthodox Soviet theory on political organization. These include proposals for powersharing in a transitional government leading to free elections in Angola, support for the legalization of opposition activity in Nicaragua, support for regional autonomy in Eritrea, and so on. One may surmise that the opening of talks between the MPLA's Dos Santos and UNITA's Savimbi resulted in part from Soviet pressure on the

MPLA to compromise on the question of dealing with Savimbi.[42] Likewise, Mengistu's change of heart on negotiation with the Eritrean People's Liberation Front (EPLF) may have resulted in part from clear evidence of Soviet impatience with his intransigence and the incompetence of his military. This willingness to contemplate the partial deconstruction of vanguard party regimes reflects in part a Soviet realization that insurgency in such instances as those of Angola and Afghanistan has shifted from being an instrument in the promotion of Soviet objectives to constituting a threat to their realization.

Diplomatic statements have meanwhile expressed interest in the potential role of the U.N. as a mediator and executor of political settlement. The U.N.'s role during the Afghan negotiations may have been both a source and a confirmation of this reassessment. Changing Soviet perspectives on the U.S. are evident in the Soviet decision to pay its back dues on peacekeeping operations and in support of the U.N.'s supervisory role in Namibia's transition to independence under Resolution 435.[43]

The Soviets are also opening direct contact with the regional adversaries of their clients in order to improve channels of communication and their position as interlocutors and potential intermediaries involved in these processes of settlement. The gradual opening of Soviet-Israeli relations is one example. Another is the expansion of informal contacts with white South African academics typified by the London conference in June 1989. A third is the recent report of direct discussions being opened between Soviet diplomats and representatives of the EPLF.[44]

On the other hand, there seems to be little evidence of a complete write-off of previous investment in and commitment to the socialist-oriented states. Despite the rhetoric of peaceful settlement, military assistance to Angola, Nicaragua and Vietnam shows no sign of drying up. Indeed, in some instances (for example, Angola and Nicaragua), it increased after Gorbachev's accession to power.[45] In the meantime, Soviet military assistance to SWAPO continued until the Namibian settlement and persists to the ANC. The Soviets have maintained a massive resupply operation for the Afghan army and for the population of government-held areas since their withdrawal. This would appear to run in the face of the image created above of a USSR desirous of cutting its losses in regional conflicts by pursuing political settlements. The increase in arms transfers to select revolutionary regimes poses a problem for those arguing that the USSR is moderating its policy in the Third World and that it is shifting away from force as an instrument of policy.

On the other hand, the USSR may be seeking to enhance the negotiating position of its allies so that they will not have to settle from a position of weakness. Abandoning them wholesale would carry significant prestige costs while encouraging further challenges to such regimes. The USSR is itself resisting a domino effect. The Afghan withdrawal may have made the USSR more likely to underwrite the security of allies involved in conflicts where the costs to the USSR remain comparatively low. This does not suggest that their rhetoric and diplomacy of political settlement are insincere. A lack of enthusiasm for repeating the U.S. experience of departing from Third World outposts by helicopter from the embassy roof is understandable. It is also consistent with genuine efforts to minimize their prospects of such an outcome while limiting damage to credibility through negotiating political solutions in situations where military ones are not forthcoming.

This is perhaps demonstrated by the Angolan case, where dramatic increases in Soviet and Cuban assistance and a vigorous escalation of the war were accompanied by—and possibly facilitated—movement toward the political settlement of late 1988. Thus, the Cuban relief of Cuito Cuanavale at the end of 1987, and the advance of substantially reinforced Cuban forces into Southwestern Angola to engage the South Africans directly in 1988 coincided with agreement that Cuban forces should leave Angola rapidly in the context of a settlement of the Namibian question. This was accompanied by some Soviet pressure on the Angolan government to sit down with UNITA to discuss ways of ending Angola's civil war. The Soviet conception of the utility of force in practice has shifted from a focus on victory to a focus on the facilitation of political settlement.

There are several reasons for this general shift in Soviet thinking about and policy toward the Third World. I have already noted the role of U.S. activism or reactivism—the Reagan doctrine's challenge to what the administration perceived to be Soviet positions in the Third World—in producing Soviet reassessment. This was reinforced in a general sense by the U.S. defense build-up of the Reagan years and the strain it placed on Soviet military and economic resources.

But the matter goes deeper, causing one to question interpretation of this new phase in Soviet policy merely as a reflection of the traditional cyclical pattern. Several other factors are plausibly related to change in Soviet policy. In the first place, we have seen how Chinese activism has played a role in the determination of Soviet policy. By the early 1980s, this Chinese challenge had largely disappeared, removing an important source of Soviet activism. The Soviet economy deteriorated dramatically in the late 1970s and early 1980s, making the burdens of activism in the Third World harder to bear, and divert-

ing the attention of policy-makers to internal issues and to the development of foreign policies which would permit them to address their
domestic problems more effectively. Most prominent among such policies seems to be a reduction of tension with the West and the U.S.A., in
turn allowing a reduction of the pressure of military competition, as
well as enhanced access to Western technologies and expertise useful for
coping with the problems of economic restructuring.

This coincided with a generational change, not only in the leadership but also at the upper levels of the foreign policy bureaucracy (for
example, the appointment of foreign policy professionals such as
Dobrynin and Korniyenko to replace orthodox ideologues such as
Ponomarev and Ul'yanovsky in the international department of the
party central committee, and of diplomats with U.S. expertise to a
growing number of deputy ministerships in the ministry of foreign
affairs). Among those benefiting from this evolution were a number of
academics and party figures who had consistently advocated a moderate state-centric revision in Soviet policy in the Third World ... and
those who had focused on the growing salience of global issues in East-
West relations....

The other important source of change is disillusionment with the
returns of previous policy. The Soviets received less than they anticipated from their activism of the previous decade at a cost greater than
they had bargained for. The path of socialist orientation tended to
implant itself in very poor states whose economies had been damaged
by prior civil war. Economic performance subsequent to the victory of
the revolution was unimpressive. Chronic factionalism in many
socialist-oriented regimes (such as South Yemen and Angola) impeded
the stabilization of the vanguard party democratic centralist regimes.
Their ideological message was greeted with indifference or hostility
by large sectors of the traditional population. All of these factors were
exacerbated by widespread endemic civil conflict in countries such as
Angola, Mozambique, Ethiopia, Cambodia and Nicaragua. In turn,
they exacerbated these conflicts further. The utility of military force
as a means of stabilizing client regimes was repeatedly drawn into
question by the persistence and deepening of indigenous resistance.[46]
Insurgent movements supported by the USSR such as the ANC and
SWAPO made little headway in their efforts to topple incumbent
conservative regimes. The net result is a wasteful and growing Soviet
military and economic burden at a time when the USSR is increasingly
unable to bear it.

Soviet strategic gains from the expansion of its coterie of friends in
the Third World are on the whole marginal (with the qualified exception of the intelligence-gathering facilities in Cuba and the base at

Cam Ranh Bay), given the concerns of these states about sovereignty. Political influence with them was partial, given their tendency to pursue their own independent internal and external agendas and their capacity to exercise reverse leverage on the USSR. The Soviet foreign policy activism which produced these relationships, meanwhile, carried significant costs in relations with more moderate or conservative Third World states, and with the West. Finally, although the Afghan outcome suggests little about the Soviet willingness in any given instance simply to walk away from a troubled ally, the experience in Afghanistan has drawn into question in a hitherto unknown manner the capacity of the USSR to secure political objectives through the use of military force against an aroused and bellicose Third World population. In short, the record is not good from the Soviet perspective. Change in Soviet theory and practice reflects learning from this infelicitous experience.

Turning to the U.S.A., this period has been one of heightened activism in challenging Soviet positions and regimes allied to the USSR, as noted above. The U.S.A. has taken a leaf out of the Soviet book by assisting insurgent movements forcefully resisting regimes friendly to the USSR. In ideological terms, the period has been one of a return to vigorous universal advocacy of the U.S. model of democracy and free enterprise.

This cyclical pattern would suggest that, as Soviet policy moderates itself, the intensity of the U.S. challenge to Soviet interests and defense of its own will also diminish. There is already considerable evidence that this is happening. The Reagan administration seemed intrigued by the new Soviet reasonableness, and cooperated in several multilateral peace processes aimed at resolving regional issues which were complicating the central relationship.[47] ... [T]he U.S. (or at least the state department) has accepted the principle of a conference in the Middle East in which the USSR would play some role. In Afghanistan, the U.S.A. cooperated in an agreement on Soviet disengagement without a provision for a successor government. It is hard to conceive of the Bush administration pursuing the Reagan doctrine to the same degree, since one of the doctrine's major premises (the need to resist Soviet expansionism) is now in doubt. The budgetary emphasis of the early 1980s on the development of forces for "low intensity conflict" is unlikely to survive the current clamor for reduction in U.S. defense spending.

The trend, particularly since Afghanistan, appears to be toward an exploration of the prospects for superpower cooperation in limiting, and assisting the resolution of, Third World disputes troubling the bilateral Soviet-U.S. relationship. In the absence of truly salient Soviet-U.S. confrontation in the Third World, the attention of policy-makers seems to have drifted to matters only tangentially (if at all) related to Soviet-U.S. competition. The salient issue of the late 1980s, for example, appeared to be how to get rid of Noriega rather than how to get rid of the Sandinistas or how to contain Soviet expansion. The most salient issue in U.S. policy toward the Third World in the coming year is likely to be drugs. Debt will probably be a distant second, barring any major defaults or financial collapses.

Not surprisingly, one sees in the literature of the current period a growing chorus of opinion to the effect that Cold War competition in the Third World is receding, that conflicts in the Third World are rooted in local causes and that dominoes do not necessarily fall. Some analysts extend this further to argue that, given the insubstantial character of U.S. interests in the Third World, what happens there is just not that important to U.S. security, with specific identifiable exceptions. The U.S.A. has less need of facilities there in the missile and satellite age, and Soviet expansion in the past has not resulted in serious damage to the U.S. position.

In this context, it is argued, overattention to the Third World and the role of the USSR there diverts scarce resources from other more important tasks. Indeed, excessive concern about the effects of essentially local disputes on the Soviet-U.S. balance may have the pernicious effect of globalizing regional issues. The advent of Marxist regimes does not significantly affect U.S. economic interests, since they have no choice but to deal with the West. The USSR is not powerful enough to sustain a durable empire in the Third World at the expense of the West. If it attempted to do so, the costs to the USSR in terms of overextension of resources would probably exceed the benefits. To the extent that the Third World does impinge on U.S. interests, it does so largely in the North-South context of debt, trade, drugs and demography.[48]

Prospects and Conclusion

Those who would argue that we are in the midst of a qualitative transformation of the nature of Soviet and U.S. approaches to the Third World would do well to remember that we have seen many of these things before. In the period of comparative Soviet retrenchment in the mid-1960s, for example, Soviet writers expressed similar disillusionment with the course of political development in the Third World, similar discontent with the burden that Khrushchev's Third World adventures placed on the shoulders of the Soviet worker, and a similar preoccupation with the role of the USSR as an example of revolution rather than a promoter of it. On this basis, many predicted at the end of the 1960s that we were destined for a period of pragmatic

moderation of Soviet policy in the Third World. The advent of détente, meanwhile, convinced many that the Cold War competition in
the Third World was receding and that we could turn our attention,
therefore, to other problems affecting our relations with the South. By
the end of the 1970s, however, we had returned to intense competition.

Nonetheless, in assessing the likelihood that the cycle be repeated
once again, it is worthwhile noting that although many of the causes of
the current phase will not necessarily last, several contributing factors
appear durable and may consequently attenuate the cycle. On the
Soviet side, we have seen how reassessment is a product not merely of a
stronger U.S. posture, but of a gradually accumulating experience of
policy in the Third World, an experience which suggests that maximal
objectives are difficult to attain and carry considerable potential costs.

This has forced a reassessment of Soviet perspectives on Third
World competition which is far more substantial than any that has
occurred previously. Among major departures one can cite concerns about
the relevance of Marxist theory to Third World conditions, deep pessimism about prospects for political and economic development in the
Third World, and serious questioning of the relevance of class struggle
both within Third World societies and between capitalist and socialist
world systems.

Moreover, the Soviet treatment of its own economic problems differs
from that in previous periods of retrenchment. Comment on this subject
suggests a belief that the problem is structural, that its solution will
take a long time, and that stability in relations with the West is necessary in the long term. In other words, we are on new and uncharted
ground and the analogy to earlier periods of moderation may therefore
be misplaced.

Turning to the U.S.A., the earlier historical discussion suggests that
U.S. activism in the Third World is stimulated by an enhanced sense of
threat from the USSR. For as long as Soviet moderation endures, therefore, the cyclical pattern is unlikely to reemerge. More importantly, a
focus on the cyclical character of U.S. policy masks longer term trends in
U.S. attitudes and policy which reflect a similar experience of repeated disappointment in relations with Third World allies, of great
difficulty in stimulating economic and political development along
lines prescribed in U.S. ideology, and of great loss associated with
efforts to impose the U.S.A.'s will. The critical experience here is, of
course, that of Vietnam. One forgets the consensus between liberals and
conservatives on the need for intervention in Vietnam and on the legitimacy of the use of force there.... And the evolution of the debate on
Central America suggests that forging an elite and mass consensus on
such a policy is practically impossible. Relations with Marxist states

such as Angola and Mozambique, moreover, have provided concrete evidence that such regimes are not "irredeemable," that their emergence has no obviously detrimental impact on U.S. interests, and that Third World radicalism does not necessarily advantage the USSR in a concrete and significant sense.

The experience of both superpowers suggests not only that the Third World competition has little impact on the balance between them, and that efforts to manipulate the balance through initiatives in the Third World are risky and carry great political costs, but that they are becoming more risky and more costly. As Third World states accumulate the means for more effective political and military resistance to efforts by outsiders to manipulate them, these risks and costs have grown. Third World politics are not derivative of central ones. The Third World was never particularly susceptible to superpower control. It is increasingly less so. The evolution of the perspectives of both powers on the Third World suggests a growing understanding of these basic points. At the risk of subsequent refutation by events, therefore, I would suggest that the short and medium-term prospect for the competition in the Third World is one of attenuation.

In the longer term, there is good reason to believe that a return to the intensity of the late 1970s and early 1980s is unlikely. Neither side is likely to value Third World stakes and to assess their relevance to the central balance in the same way that they did during the Cold War and its renewal in the 1980s. Indeed, the danger from the Third World's perspective may well be not so much of renewed competition as of indifference.

Notes

This article is a shortened and revised version of a paper presented to the Defense Intelligence College Conference on Revolutionary Change in the Third World (27-29 June 1988). It is based in part on research conducted under the auspices of the Berkeley Stanford Program in Soviet International Behavior. My understanding of Soviet perspectives on this topic has been greatly enhanced by participation in a U.S.-Soviet exchange program funded by IREX.

1. J. Kirkpatrick, "U.S. security and Latin America," in H. Wiarda (ed.), *Rift and Revolution,* Washington, D.C.: American Enterprise Institute, 1984, p. 329. This essay appeared originally in *Commentary,* January 1980.

2. The clear underestimation of the local sources of resistance to the PDPA regime suggests, however, a mistaken Soviet perception that instability in the country was externally induced.

3. Testimony in hearings on U.S. involvement in the civil war in Angola, as cited in R. Johnson, "Exaggerating America's stakes in Third World conflicts," *International Security* 10(3), Winter 1985-86, p. 54.

4. R. Gilpin, *War and Change in World Politics*, Cambridge: Cambridge University Press, 1981, p. 31.

5. See Henry Kissinger's account of his attempt to exclude the Soviets from participation in the post-1973 peace negotiations, in H. Kissinger, *Years of Upheaval*, London: Weidenfeld & Nicolson, 1982, pp. 1033-1066.

6. See T. Paine, "The Rights of Man," in P. Foner (ed.), *The Complete Works of Thomas Paine 1*, New York: Citadel Press, 1945, p. 348.

7. For a critical appraisal of these perspectives, see S.N. MacFarlane, "The 'Marxist threat' to U.S. interests," forthcoming.

8. R. Garthoff, *Détente and Confrontation*, Washington, D.C.: Brookings, 1985, pp. 527-528. The amplitude and intensity of Soviet comment on Sino-U.S. collaboration in Southern Africa in journals such as *Narody Azii i Afriki, Mirovaya Ekonomika i Mezhdunarodnye Otnoshenia*, and *Kommunist* itself during this period support this interpretation.

9. Soviet writers frequently asserted, moreover, that explanation of Third World conflicts in terms of local factors was a bourgeois subterfuge designed to obscure the basic responsibility of imperialism. See S.N. MacFarlane, "The Soviet conception of regional security," *World Politics* 37(3), 1985, pp. 300-301.

10. See C. McLane, *Soviet Strategies in Southeast Asia*, Princeton, New Jersey: Princeton University Press, 1966, p. 361; and R. McVey, "The South East Asian insurrectionary movements," in C. Black and T.P. Thornton (eds.), *Communism and Revolution: The Strategic Uses of Political Violence*, Princeton, New Jersey: Princeton University Press, 1964, pp. 145-164.

11. S. Huntington, "Patterns of intervention: America and the Soviets in the Third World," *The National Interest*, Spring 1987, p. 42.

12. For a useful account of this stage of Soviet activism, see R. Kanet (ed.), *The Soviet Union and the Developing Nations*, Baltimore, Maryland: Johns Hopkins University Press, 1974, Chapter 2.

13. For the early evolution of the Soviet-Cuban relationship, see W.R. Duncan, *The Soviet Union and Cuba*, New York: Praeger, 1985, pp. 28-32; and J. Levesque, *L'URSS et la Révolution Cubaine*, Montreal, Quebec: Presses de l'Université de Montreal, 1976, pp. 25-106.

14. On the Cuban missile crisis, see G. Allison, *Essence of Decision*, Boston: Little Brown, 1971; and R. Garthoff, *Reflections on the Cuban Missile Crisis*, Washington, D.C.: Brookings, 1987.

15. For an account of the effects of the Sino-Soviet conflict on Soviet policy toward the Algerian war, see D. Zagoria, *The Sino-Soviet Conflict, 1956-61*, Princeton, New Jersey: Princeton University Press, 1962. For the effects of the conflict on Soviet policy toward West Africa, see R. Legvold's excellent account of the evolution of Soviet policy toward Ghana and Guinea in *Soviet Policy toward West Africa*, Cambridge, Massachusetts: Harvard University Press, 1970. See also D. Albright, "The Soviet Union, communist China, and Ghana," New York: Unpublished Columbia University Ph.D. dissertation, 1971.

16. On the shifting balance between military and economic instruments in Soviet policy, see Gu Guan-fu, "Soviet aid to the Third World: An analysis of its strategy," *Soviet Studies* 35(1), 1983, pp. 72-74; R. Laird, "The Latin American arms market: Soviet perceptions and arms transfers," *Soviet Union/Union Sovietique* 12(3), 1985, pp. 277-304.

17. On the Nixon doctrine, see R. Litwak's useful study *The Nixon Doctrine*, Cambridge: Cambridge University Press, 1984.

18. See R. Garthoff's characterization of détente in *Détente and Confrontation*, Washington, D.C.: Brookings, 1986, p. 20.

19. For discussions of these events and of the role of Soviet military power in them, See R. Menon, *Soviet Power and the Third World*, New Haven, Connecticut: Yale University Press, 1986; and, from a somewhat different perspective, B. Porter, *The USSR in Third World Conflicts*, Cambridge: Cambridge University Press, 1984.

20. J. Kirkpatrick, "U.S. security and Latin America."

21. See J. and V. Valenta, "Soviet strategy and policy in the Caribbean Basin," in H. Wiarda (ed.), *Rift and Revolution*, Washington, D.C.: AEI, 1984, p. 230.

22. R. Garthoff, *Détente and Confrontation*, p. 520, notes that Kissinger apparently felt that competition in places such as Angola was a normal aspect of the process of détente. But when it turned out that the U.S.A. was incapable of competing on this basis, his conception of détente changed and the question of linkage loomed large.

23. There was increasing comment on the difficulties of accomplishing the transition to socialism in the conditions obtaining in many of the "socialist - oriented countries."

24. The increasingly frequent comment concerning the reversibility of the non-capitalist approach to development and of the path of socialist orientation.

25. There was commentary on mismanagement of the economies and political organization of states of socialist orientation and the unscientific subjectivism of Third World allied leaders, which in turn led to excesses in the implementation of the transition from capitalism.

26. Comment on the prospects for escalation from Third World conflict to central confrontation increased considerably during the last years of the Brezhnev period and the Andropov and Chernenko interregna. In the Gorbachev period, there has been explicit recognition that Soviet behavior in the Third World during the 1970s significantly damaged the détente process.

27. See Andropov's famous remark of 1983 to the effect that the principal burden in non-capitalist development and the transition to socialism in the Third World had to be carried by the Third World states themselves, the USSR assisting as much as it could. The thrust of his remark appears to have been to underline that there were no blank checks. "Rech' General'nogo Sekretarya Ts K KPSS tovarishcha Yu V Andropova," *Kommunist* 9, 1983.

28. On this point see F. Fukuyama, *Moscow's Post-Brezhnev Reassessment of the Third World*, R-3337-USDP, Santa Monica: RAND, 1986.

29. See F. Fukuyama, "Patterns of Soviet Third World Policy," *Problems of Communism* 36(5), September-October 1987, pp. 1-2, 5-10; J. Hough, *The Struggle for the Third World*, Washington, D.C.: Brookings, 1986; E. Valkenier, *The USSR and the Third World: An Economic Bind*, New York: Praeger, 1983; Valkenier, "Revolutionary change in the Third World: Recent Soviet assessments," *World Politics* 37(3), April 1986, pp. 415-434; Valkenier, "New Soviet thinking about the Third World," *World Policy Journal* 4(4), Autumn 1987, pp. 651-674; and most recently G. Golan, *The Soviet Union and the National Liberation Movement*, London: Unwin Hyman, 1988.

30. G. Mirskii, "K voprosu o vybore puti i orientatsii razvivayushchikhsya stran," *Mirovaya Ekonomika i Mezhdunarodnye Otnoshenia* 5, 1987, pp. 72-73.

31. R. Avakov, "Novoe myshlenie i problema izuchenia razvivayushchikhsya stran," *Mirovaya Ekonomika i Mezhdunarodnye Otnoshenia* 11, 1987, pp. 49, 51-57.

32. G. Mirskii, "K voprosu o vybore puti i orientatsii razvivayushchikhsya stran," *Mirovaya Ekonomika i Mezhdunarodnye Otnoshenia* 5, 1987, p. 71.

33. For example, see G. Mirskii, "K voprosu o vybore puti i orientatsii razvivayushchikhsya stran," *Mirovaya Ekonomika i Mezhdunarodnye Otnoshenia* 5, 1987, p. 71.

34. The embrace of armed insurgency in Central America characteristic of the early 1980s has largely disappeared. Likewise, enthusiasm for insurgent struggle as a means of resolving the South African question has dampened.

35. Compare, for example, Brezhnev's comments on the Third World in his report to the 26th Party Congress (*Pravda*, 24 February 1981) with those of Gorbachev to the 27th (*Pravda*, 26 February 1986).

36. Soviet commentators now tout the Soviet-Indian relationship as a model for Soviet policy in the Third World. This is a far cry from the focus of the late 1970s on relations with vanguard party regimes.

37. See Gorbachev's 27th Party Congress report in *Pravda* (26 February 1986), pp. 2-10.

38. See, for example, Gleb Starushenko and Viktor Goncharov's comments on prospects for revolutionary success in South Africa and the desirability of a negotiated political settlement in that country. Starushenko went so far as to advocate guarantees of special group rights for the white population as part of this settlement. G. Starushenko, "Problems of struggle against racism, apartheid and colonialism in South Africa," Moscow: Institute of Africa, 1986; V. Goncharov, "Soviet Union and Southern Africa: The issues of ensuring regional security," as reprinted in *Southern Africa Record* 47-48, 1987, pp. 77-81.

39. See the account of an interview with Joe Slovo, *The Manchester Guardian*, 19 July 1989. I am indebted to Dr. Helen Kitchen for this reference.

40. Discussions with Soviet scholars prior to and during the withdrawal sug-

gested a widespread sense in the academic community that the regime could not survive. The PDPA's staying power—and the incapacity of the guerrillas to deliver the final punch—appear to have come as a surprise to many Soviet analysts.

41. A recent conference of African Marxists in Accra not surprisingly concluded that the South could not depend on the USSR for meaningful assistance in the transition to socialism.

42. This was obviously not the only, or necessarily the most important source of Dos Santos' change of heart. Other African leaders have mounted intense pressure on the MPLA to negotiate with UNITA. But he could not escape the conclusion that the Soviets were growing tired of their underwriting of this endless war.

43. The USSR originally opposed Resolution 435 as a basis for a Namibian settlement.

44. Private conversation.

45. The Angolan case is particularly interesting, as historically Angola has paid for weapons deliveries with oil revenues. Soviet assistance increased in 1985-1987 despite Angola's reduced capacity to pay (the result of a drop in world oil prices) with the implication that the USSR was here accepting a new and significant burden at a time when Soviet economic difficulties purportedly make the Soviets unwilling to do so.

46. The Ethiopian case was a particularly disastrous illustration. In April 1988 a full Ethiopian brigade was decimated at Afabet, thereby crippling the Asmara-based Second Army and allowing the EPLF to consolidate its hold on the great bulk of the Eritrean hinterland. One year later, in February 1989, a large Ethiopian force was trapped at Ende Selassie in Tigre in a joint operation mounted by the EPLF and the Tigrean People's Liberation Front (TPLF). State Department sources estimate that as many as 20,000 Ethiopian troops perished.

47. For example, the U.S.-sponsored talks between Angola, South Africa and Cuba. It is true, however, that there was little unanimity on Southern African issues in the administration, some apparently preferring to pursue the insurgency option of UNITA to victory rather than attempting through cooperation with the USSR to achieve a regional solution. On this topic, see M. Clough, "Southern Africa: Challenges and Choices," Foreign Affairs 66(5), Summer 1988, pp. 1066, 1069.

48. For a recent expression of this, see C. Maynes, "America's Third World hangups," Foreign Policy 71, Summer 1988, pp. 117-140. See also J. Slater, "Dominos in Central America: Will they fall? Does it matter?" International Security 12(2), Autumn 1987, pp. 105-134; R. Johnson, "Exaggerating America's stakes in Third World conflicts," International Security 10(3), Winter 1985-86; R. Feinberg, The Intemperate Zone: The Third World Challenge to U.S. Foreign Policy, New York: Norton, 1983; and L. Schoultz, National Security and

United States Policy toward Latin America, Princeton, New Jersey: Princeton University Press, 1987. For a dissenting view, see S. David's forthcoming article in *International Security*. It is not my purpose to assess the merits or demerits of this tendency of articulation in U.S. discourse about the Third World. But it would be hard to contest its domination of the current discussion, particularly in the context of growing Soviet moderation in the Third World.

26

Reappraisal of USSR Third World Policy

Andrei Kolosov

The course for perestroika was proclaimed five years ago. Its foreign policy aspect was based on new political thinking, which presumed a considerable reexamination of our view of the world and our country's place in this world. The chief element here is a repudiation of the vision of the world divided into two conflicting camps, and an explaining away of practically all the processes taking place in international affairs by the struggle between these camps. The priority of universal values and a realization of interdependence as a characteristic feature of today was declared.

Over the years of perestroika official foreign policy orientations have developed into the realization that in economics, politics and law there are universal achievements of civilization which ensure freedom and development and that, guided by them we can harmonize the interests of our nation with the interests of others. In Malta the difficult words that we do not consider the U.S.A. our enemy were pronounced at long last. A lowering of the level of military rivalry has become a reality. During the European process the proclaimed commitment to the common values of civilization has begun to materialize. People on both sides of what used to be called the "iron curtain" now breathe easier, they have begun to rid themselves of a fear of war, to come to know one another better and to cooperate. Real progress has just begun, but it is already obvious that living like this is easier and freer, that much less energy can be spent on weaponry and the struggle against the enemy, and much more on development.

This does not mean that today or tomorrow everything will be peaches and cream. There will still be conflicts of interest. At the first stage problems that were latent for a long time will surface. However, such a turbulent period, unlike the previous one, has prospects; there is progress from senselessly stubborn military rivalry and whipping up of tensions to a pragmatic search for a "balance of interests," to positive cooperation.

The correctness of this course is not obvious to everyone. Some evidently view it as a betrayal of the principles in which elements of Marxism-Leninism in the Stalinist understanding, of imperial monarchism and blind patriotism are united under the common denominator of a reluctance for change.

However, few people who espouse these views can explain intelligently where the material and cultural needs of our impoverished society clash with American interests to such a degree as to consider the U.S.A. the enemy and, sacrificing a great deal, bear the burden of confrontation with that country and its allies. Few can explain how the interests of our people are served by the foisting of our will or our model on other peoples, and what Soviet people have received for decades of such policies. It is just as difficult to show how, without fundamentally changing our foreign policy, we could hope to become a respectable part of the modern world on a par with others and use its achievements and overcome our growing lag behind the industrialized, and in very many parameters, behind what are not the most industrialized states. One cannot seriously continue to believe that today a country can be great only by stockpiling destructive weapons, not to mention that the economy, which does not measure up to advanced standards, will not be able sooner or later to produce modern weapons.

The people who are against the repudiation of confrontation and expansionism, and against the removal of barriers between the outside world and us are guided not by the interests of the people of the country but by a desire to preserve the pre-perestroika situation, the pre-perestroika political system and power structure. The division of the world into warring camps is a direct continuation of internal camps. Conversely, recognition of pluralism, and the liberation of society from the oppression of the state are indivisible from a renewal of foreign policy, from the repudiation of confrontation and secretiveness. The influence here is mutual. Insufficient resolve and consistency in altering foreign policy is simultaneously a sign of insufficient boldness of internal reforms and a continuing dangerous reserve of opponents of any reforms at all.

Foreign policy should be brought in line with the new principles on a comprehensive basis. It cannot be selective since it is called upon to promote the country's renewal in the interests of the people, and does not serve any more what we call the administer-by-command system. In the 1970s we were going through a period of relative normalization of relations with the West which went down in history as détente. It was not a product of the changes within our country; it was an effect of a time-serving nature and was doomed the moment the logic of changes in foreign policy began impelling us to work changes domestically. For all its innovativeness, the course for détente in foreign policy was not consistent and full either. Essentially it affected only political and trade and economic relations with the U.S.A. and the other Western countries and, in part, control over existing armaments, virtually without affecting military development and policies in the Third World. These areas in the foreign policy context became the levers that enabled the system to break down very easily the seemingly irreversible achievements of détente which began demanding true openness and democratization in society.

The depth of the current changes in foreign policy has, of course, greatly overshadowed what was done in the period of détente. But they are palpable once again above all in relations with the West in the political and economic areas, in the sphere of arms reductions and limitations, and in tolerance toward the changes in Eastern Europe. There were added the desire for broader people-to-people contacts and cooperation on a wide range of global problems and, what is of no small importance, a readiness to assume commitments in human rights. However, fulfillment of these commitments such as, say, the course of the discussion on the Law on the Press, is proceeding with great difficulty.

Military development and plans are still in the shadows. Even though it is linked much more now than in the past with disarmament agreements, virtually no safeguards against the unexpected appearance of new versions of the SS-20 or the Krasnoyarsk radar station have been created yet.

As to the policy in the Third World, it was believed that peaceful coexistence could not apply to that part of the globe, that it was there that the antagonistic contest between the two systems was being decided, that it was there that the center of the military rivalry with the United States was located. The focal point of policy in the Third World was the desire to put as many countries as possible under our control and do as much damage as possible to the other side's interests. On the other side, this was veiled by the philosophy of solidarity with progressive regimes and support for social transformations; in reality the ideological motives and all the more so a real assessment of the nature of the regime and its policy vis-à-vis its people did not have substantial meaning. Brazen anti-communism and anti-Sovietism, if

366   Andrei Kolosov

the situation fitted into the scheme of anti-Americanism, was forgiven. A typical example was the then-widespread assessment of the Iranian revolution, which essentially boiled down to the fact that all its specifics notwithstanding, it accorded with our interests as being strikingly anti-American.

The "Vietnamese syndrome" that the U.S. went through only whetted appetites. As a result, we waged an outright war in Afghanistan, we were deeply enmeshed in several acute regional conflicts (and we encouraged socialist developing countries to take part in them), and we promoted the creation of regimes in different parts of the world that tried, under the banner of anti-imperialism, to implement in their own conditions the administer-by-command model and therefore counted on us in everything. The specifics of these regimes, the militarist bent typical of our domestic and foreign policy, and the backwardness of the Soviet civilian economy that was strongly manifest even then made for the fact that military cooperation and arms deliveries were the heart of our relations with developing states "friendly" to us. Their militarization only pushed them even farther into participation in conflicts and into authoritarian rule and worsened the situation in the economy that was rapidly falling apart as it was, as a result of the application of our scheme. The "allies" demanded more and more resources, became more deeply involved in conflicts, and increasingly strengthened in everyone's eyes the association between Soviet policy and instability, authoritarianism and economic failures. Other developing states, above all the most prosperous ones economically, cooperation with which could have yielded us real benefit, came to have a stronger distrust in the Soviet Union and a reluctance to have anything to do with it, and even openly protested against its adventures in the Third World.

After 1985, the reassessment of our Third World policy did not begin right away. It took several years to set about the withdrawal of troops from Afghanistan and even more time to admit that the Afghanistan war was a mistake. Clearly, this decision was a difficult one and required great political courage; nevertheless, this was obviously the most urgent foreign policy problem. Soviet people continued to die in Afghanistan, and our participation in the war there remained the chief impediment to normalization of relations with the rest of the world. Our turn toward settling other regional conflicts and reducing our involvement in developments in different parts of the Third World also began very gradually. Dialogue on this topic was launched with the U.S.A., we began energetically using multilateral mechanisms, the United Nations above all, in the search for solutions to conflict situations, and we started urging our partners in the Third World to work for peaceful settlements of problems and to attain reconciliation within their countries.

The successes scored on this path are obvious: with U.N. participation, the framework for the withdrawal of troops from Afghanistan was devised, the process of provision of independence to Namibia drew to a close, the war between Iran and Iraq has been ended, progress toward a peaceful settlement in Central America has begun, and the outlines of a normalization of the situation in Cambodia and the Western Sahara are starting to take shape.

At the same time, many Third World countries' attitudes toward the Soviet Union have changed drastically; we have begun winning trust even among those which did not want to have anything to do with us at all. Many of these states are promising and quite solvent counterparts for developing trade and economic relations.

The changes in our foreign policy philosophy and in the nature of our actions in the Third World, and the development of extensive relations with different countries from this region have enabled us to take a fresh approach to many global problems on a multilateral basis as well. Our confrontational approach to the West and desire to involve the Third World in it and and divide the former into countries that were "ours" and "not ours" largely impeded a possibility for the U.N. and other organizations to solve international economic and many other problems. The removal of tensions and the realization that today's problems require cooperation from everyone who is prepared to tackle them have made it possible to normalize the situation there somewhat, and to begin exploring ways out of politicized dead ends and proceed toward pragmatic compromise solutions based on our practical interests, not ideological ambitions.

Nevertheless the changes in our relations with the Third World are less impressive than those in our relations with our former "enemy"— the West. Some of the most odious manifestations of the old policy have been eliminated, the elements that created the most difficulties for us in our relations with the U.S.A. and other Western and developing states not oriented to us have been removed, and attempts have been made to lessen the economic burden of our involvement in Third World affairs. However, a detailed assessment of the former policy is still at development stage, and the tenet on the repudiation of confrontation has not been brought to the logical conclusion that the system of priorities and the nature of the ties that have taken shape in the epoch of the support of the "anti-imperialist struggle" in the Third World should be reassessed. The latest of our official statements, especially those made during Foreign Minister Eduard Shevardnadze's tour of Africa, and the noticeable evolution in the positions of countries close to us inspire hope that there will be a faster progress toward a new policy in the Third World. For these changes to become more profound it is important that the old infrastructure be discarded, above all in the military sphere, which ensured and generated a confrontation policy.

All our partners in Eastern Europe, this region that is truly important for us, have been replaced over these years. There are now non-communist governments in power in some countries. Soviet military presence in Eastern Europe has been reduced considerably, and the withdrawal of troops from there continues. There is nothing wrong with this. Without such revolutionary breakthroughs, a new non-confrontational period cannot be ushered in, the splitting up of the world cannot be overcome, and its advanced achievements cannot be drawn on. As to the Third World virtually all our partners are in place. They continue to receive our political support and military and economic assistance, albeit perhaps to a slightly lesser extent. In most cases they are not the initiators of the settlement of conflicts into which they have been drawn. They are brought with great difficulty to stands which open at least somewhat the door to a settlement. More often than not these countries are in a catastrophic economic state and cannot ensure the elementary needs of their populations. More often than not they are far removed from democracy and respect for human rights, and many of them are waging war with part of their own people. Evidently, we just recently felt ashamed that just a few days before Ceausescu's fall we were not telling the truth about him and were even prepared to render him political support. I am certain that we can perhaps feel much more shame for many of our former and current partners in the Third World.

That this state of affairs goes on like this, is hardly harmless. Wars continue in Afghanistan, Angola, Ethiopia, and to a certain extent in Central America. The situation is explosive in Cambodia, Mozambique and elsewhere. We or our closest allies have been drawn into all of them in one form or another. People are dying in all of them. Our weapons are being used in all of them in one form or another. All of them are potentially fraught with a drastic worsening of the regional and overall international situation, a worsening that is capable of throwing the world far back. The arms race continues, also not without our participation, Southern Asia, the Near and Middle East, Northern Africa and the Caribbean Basin. Reports are still coming in of the appearance, now in one point, now in another, of new Soviet weapons, weapons that are likely more destructive and modern than those in other countries of this region.

The paradox is that we took an active part in the attempts to settle the situation in all these regions and, moreover, scored certain, but almost always limited success. Of course, we cannot settle conflicts, some of which are rather difficult, unilaterally or only together with the Americans. On the other hand, all these wars would have in effect been impossible if we had not supplied the weapons and resources for them, if we had honestly told the forces waging them that we would not be supporting them anymore. However, in order to do this, we need to scuttle our former categories of victory or defeat, we need to carry out the same revolutionary turnabout as in Europe, and overcome internally the confrontational logic of rivalry with the U.S.A., most of which spawned or perpetuated these conflicts. Thus far, this is not taking place, or it is taking place very slowly. The most vivid and difficult example for us is Afghanistan.

Just over a year ago our troops left Afghan territory; Soviet people have stopped dying there. This is an enormous and indisputable achievement. This does not mean, however, that we have left the war, that we have rid ourselves of its moral, political and material burden. The war in Afghanistan continues, and at times even more actively than during the period of our military presence there. Afghanis continue to die, and there is still a hotbed of tensions in direct proximity of our borders, at a most important point of Asia. Afghanistan continues to be a country that cannot ensure its development, or even feed its people, for that matter. Aside from arms deliveries, we are still shouldering the burden of extensive economic aid to Afghanistan, and not the aid that ensures independent development, since the war in effect rules out construction, but daily supplies of food and other essentials that are not in great supply in our country. Different expenditure figures are named. Regrettably, not in our press or in our official statements. Nor are our deputies taking a real interest in this. As far as weapons per se are concerned, Western sources are quoting between 250 and 400 million dollars a month. It is not hard to calculate how much this has cost since the troop withdrawal.

Of course, the conflict in Afghanistan and around it is a highly complicated problem where the inertia of hatred and irreconcilability is enormous. Many participants, above all a motley kaleidoscope of intra-Afghan forces, are involved there. It is difficult to settle this conflict, no matter how much we want to do so. It would be incorrect to maintain that throughout these years the Americans were consistent in their attempts to extinguish this fire. Their line exhibited a vacillation between a desire to truly settle this conflict and a desire to preserve it as a burdensome thorn for the Soviet Union. Pakistan's line is even more contradictory. On the other hand, it would be wrong to assert that the Americans are not giving, nor have ever given a chance for settlement. The U.S.A. is not interested in Afghanistan turning into another Iran, and is definitively declaring in favor of Afghanistan's not being hostile to the Soviet Union and of its legitimate interests being taken into consideration in a settlement. With all that it should not be forgotten that the mujaheddin are difficult interlocutors even for those who are supporting them.

The situation is also complicated by the fact that the mujaheddin are also more inclined to a settlement through force in hopes of winning a military victory over the Najibullah government. Nevertheless, our main task in Afghanistan should have been not only the troop withdrawal, but also efforts for solutions that would promote the establishment of such a structure against which the Afghan people would not fight and which would normalize political life in the country, when the struggle would not be waged by force of arms. There is no guarantee that this goal would have been reached, but the aspiration to it should be dictated by a sense of responsibility for the many years of armed intervention and by a sincere desire to put an end to the war and truly halt the interference in the affairs of another country. Otherwise, this is not a sweeping reexamination of the view of this conflict, and of all conflicts in general, but merely a change in the means of politics and no direct involvement of troops.

It is only today, when the strong-arm line is increasingly showing its futility, when at least a stalemated outcome of the war there has become even more obvious, that slow progress to other stands, stands aimed at settling the conflict, has begun. We ourselves are already talking about the necessity of negative symmetry, we recognize though in cautious expressions, our responsibility for finding settlement formulas, and we are voicing the readiness of the U.N. to take part in this process, and we understand that the path to normalization of the situation is a somewhat transitional, neutral state, not reconciliation with one of the belligerents remaining in power.

The same approach, in principle, not in detail, holds true for the other conflict situations in which we were involved most of all and which were linked above all with internal contradictions and struggle. In principle it should be obvious to everyone that we have no intentions of continuing to preserve a situation where such wars are waged with our weapons and our resources. The only aid we can render is to promote a rapid settlement formula that would enable the people to determine freely, with safeguards, and preferably, under international control, what form of administration and what government it prefers. Only in this way will talk of freedom of choice have real meaning, rather than serve as a vail for preserving the status quo. There can be different concrete schemes of action here—from preserving the government in power and simply holding fair elections, as in Nicaragua, to U.N. representatives more or less fully replacing the state structures, as seems to be taking shape in the Cambodian case. If this variant does not suit the government in power, there can be only one alternative—the cessation of our military, economic and other aid, and of political support in the international arena. We cannot force an end of the war, but we certainly should not fuel it.

Such an approach will not only yield us big political and economic dividends but also accord with norms of universal morality and solidarity. It cannot be seriously believed that, from the moral standpoint, it is more important to observe and extend commitments made to certain governments in earlier times, when the entire logic of a vision of the world was different, than to try to end the destruction of people and rid one's ruined country of additional burdens and prompt other countries to develop independently. What solidarity can we be talking about when in practice it develops above all into military aid to countries whose people are literally starving not as a result of natural calamities but largely as a result of war and political ambitions? True human solidarity is being manifested at this time by the other world, one which, despite political antipathies, helps with foodstuffs and other things required for people's survival. We, however, "helped" to such an extent that even without new deliveries of weapons so much of them had been stockpiled for hostilities to be actively carried on. This, incidentally, is taking place in many areas where both sides are fighting, ultimately, with our, essentially unpaid-for, weapons, which demonstrates once again the absurdities and immorality of such policy.

Military cooperation is the main element of the structure of relations with the Third World countries closest to us who are used to imitate us in basing their foreign and home policies on force. It is practically impossible to obtain our official data on arms deliveries, all the more so with regard to individual countries. It is also impossible to learn how much resources are being spent on all this. The claim that arms deliveries yield us enormous hard-currency profits seems, at this juncture, nothing more than a myth. Of course, individual transactions are profitable, but they have long been cancelled out by all sorts of debts and gratuitous deliveries. The theme of arms deliveries is becoming increasingly acute in our talk about the Third World. It is becoming a self-sufficing factor of our policies, one which prevents us from maneuvering freely.

Arms deliveries, which are uncontrolled and not linked with the strategy of new political thinking, to countries where the situation is relatively calm, are dangerous too. More often than not, our weapons are being stockpiled on a large scale which often tips the regional balance of power. Some of our steps to beef up the military potential in the Third World, including those that might, even indirectly, help the appearance of potentialities in the nuclear, chemical and missile sphere, will sooner or later inevitably complicate the global disarmament situation as well. Talk about any "strategic alliances" and defense needs can hardly be convincing in this case.

Evidently, we will have certain interests in the Third World linked with our security. However, they are extremely limited. The specifics of our geographical location and economic development level, and the nature of economic ties do not make it possible to seriously talk about our having vital interests in the developing world which need to be protected with the aid of weapons, if we do not consider as such interests the senseless race to establish our influence far away from our borders, a race dictated only by the logic of maintaining confrontation. Nor will we forget that even the most massive weapons deliveries do not guarantee stable influence at all, as was shown by the example of Egypt and other countries.

While remaining a nuclear power, we probably need certain military installations abroad to maintain communications with the submarine fleet and to carry out electronic surveillance. However, we need to weigh well, not only with the participation of the military department, the scope in which this is necessary, and if it is necessary, then to see whether it would be cheaper to meet these needs through the development of space-based facilities. The tenet of the need for the virtual omnipresence of our Navy and, by implication, bridgeheads for supplying it evokes still greater doubts. It would not be bad if the military clearly explained how and what vital interests of our country it protects in oceans far from our shores. If it turns out that its presence there is, after all, expedient, then it is worthwhile to weigh our possibilities and decide whether we can supply it there on a commercial basis. Incidentally, although the U.S.A. and other Western countries have interests in the Third World that are objectively somewhat different from ours, our restraint will inevitably lead to a substantial scaling down of military presence abroad, above all by dint of financial considerations. Demands for this are persistently being made in the West even today.

Evidently we are not prepared, like Czechoslovakia, to end weapons exports in principle. Economically, it is expedient not to stop this entirely; but they should be delivered on a completely different basis. For one thing, firm restrictions should be introduced that are linked with the undesirability of deliveries to explosive areas and of deliveries that would violate the principle of reasonable sufficiency at the regional level which change the balance of power there or introduce qualitatively new weaponry there. Such restrictions could be introduced on both a unilateral and a coordinated basis. In principle, the West is prepared for talks on this theme, if we do not attempt to make arbitrary exceptions for ourselves. For another, arms deliveries should be made on a purely commercial basis, one that would take account not only of current solvency but also of the prospects for economic development. We simply have no other option in our current state.

Economic expediency, not ideological and political preferences, should become the determinant for developing economic ties with the Third World as well. This will be ultimately profitable not only for us but also for the countries with which we cooperate. Other kinds of economic interaction corrupts more often than not. It is not fortuitous that virtually no country that counted above all on cooperation with us has been able to establish a mechanism of stable development, even though it has put up some major facilities and scored certain successes in individual areas. In our integral and interdependent world it is preferable for such a big and potentially rich country as ours not to fully stop rendering gratuitous aid. This is not only a moral obligation but also a certain contribution to the future, to its development and stability. However, the volume, nature and direction of this aid should be discussed publicly and promote what our country can do without detriment to its own development. In any event, the procedure for using it should be strictly controlled, including through multilateral mechanisms, and it should be aimed above all at the development of the economies of Third World countries, and, in extreme instances, at aid to the population directly. Otherwise this is both a waste of our resources and a disservice to the peoples of the developing countries. Our experience, and that of the West, too, for that matter, has amassed much proof of this.

Our approach to global, above all economic, problems and a discussion of them on a multilateral level should change accordingly as well. We should be guided not by considerations of "unification of forces in the struggle against imperialism" and not by abstract slogans of solidarity, but by calculations of expedience based on the objective laws governing the economy, and by our interests. Considering our "intermediate" position between the industrialized and developing worlds, our interests in different matters can coincide with the different groups of countries.

Such a turnabout in relations with so many states will evoke a host of questions. What about our friends and our moral commitments to them? What about the entire "three worlds" concept and the West's role in the developing countries? What should our criteria in assessing Third World governments be?

Of course, every state and every people have moral commitments. However, one should regard moral commitments above all to peoples, not governments or regimes. If we are talking about internationalism, we need to clearly visualize what internationalism the point at issue is—the internationalism of authoritarian regimes, the internationalism of the administer-by-command system which existed in the past and which has not died yet, or universal internationalism. If we are talking about the latter, free development and well-being of our people and other peoples should be our main concern. We cannot force regimes to leave, but we can honestly talk about changes in our policy, in our political morality. And if it is truly new, it cannot ignore such a criterion as democracy in assessing the situations in the Third World. Societies in the developing countries are different, and they cannot be made democratic overnight. But tolerance has its limits here as well. We must make it clear that our sympathies lie on the side of compliance with democratic norms and human rights as they are understood in international documents. Nor should we be afraid of insisting on international control, neither of determining our attitude to any regime depending on the results of such control.

It is important to depart once and for all from dividing the world into camps. There should be criteria of universal morality and human rights, a criterion of our national interests, and a criterion of the need to pragmatically tackle the development needs facing humanity. With whom we will be solving these or other problems depends on how close a country is to these criteria, not on whether this country is a member of our camp or another camp. An analysis, including a critical one, of the U.S. policies in the Third World is a separate subject. Unlike the earlier practice, we should determine our line not by the rule of contraries but by our interests realistically understood and openly discussed. Should they clash with the U.S. interests we shall have to seek solutions jointly. In any other case U.S. actions should be of no concern to us.

The term "Third World" has come from the times when there was a split into two hostile worlds. Today, when we are trying to overcome the split of the world into two hostile camps, the term "Third World" loses its former meaning, although, of course, there is still some commonality in the developing countries, which is linked with historical roots and the economic and political development levels. However, all of us are moving more and more rapidly to an integral world in which contradictions and problems will remain but which will be able to be solved only through concerted efforts. The quicker the legacy of confrontation is surmounted in the Third World, too, the quicker we will all move forward.

The Future of
Soviet-American Relations

PART EIGHT

The Future of
Soviet-American Relations

For the first time in almost half a century, both the United States and the Soviet Union have a chance to plan their foreign policy strategies without exclusive and obsessive reference to one another. The rigid bipolar international system prevalent during the Cold War placed a set of constraints on the foreign and defense policies of the superpowers that severely restricted their policy options. However, in the post-confrontational phase of their relationship the two nations will have a greater number of foreign policy alternatives. This complicates any predictions regarding their future relationship. Nevertheless, the purpose of these final chapters is to assess what probable trends and policies will shape Soviet-American relations up to the year 2000 and beyond.

The Chinese say it is very difficult to make predictions, particularly about the future. However, there is benefit to be derived from speculating about what might be and what needs to be done to bring about a possibly more secure tomorrow.

The two essays in this section venture to explain the future of Soviet-American relations by evaluating seemingly inexorable trends that will shape the behavior of the two powers as they move into the twenty-first century. Both selections highlight the similarities in the two countries' positions in world affairs, and the international goals that merit their policy support. The American author foresees a "global partnership" resting on the pillars of disarmament, development, and democracy. The Soviet commentator sees an analogous world, with demilitarization, globalization, and democratization serving as the agenda for superpower relations.

In his essay "Where Should We Go From Here?" Georgy Arbatov seeks to answer this specific question: Can the super-

powers cooperate?   Or, on the other hand, will the current warming in relations turn out to be "another fleeting episode to be replaced by the next attack of the Cold War?"

His answer to the first question is affirmative because he believes that changes in the international and domestic situation of the two nations give them little alternative but to cooperate. Contemporary problems demand the collaboration of the USSR and United States if resourceful and enduring solutions are to be found.   This is not to imply, he says, that even acting together they can expect to fully control international crises.   One reason is that their opportunities to influence world affairs is declining, and will likely continue to decline, rather than increase.   Nevertheless, the economic and military power of the Soviet Union and U.S. place a "special responsibility ... upon the two nations for preservation of peace, the strengthening of international security, and the provision of favorable conditions for the social and economic development of all humanity."

Arbatov does not go as far as Maynes in recommending a global partnership, but the two analyst's proposals are nevertheless very similar.   Arbatov contends that the superpowers have the opportunity, and probably the obligation, to assist in the evolution of three dominant trends in global affairs: the decline in the role of military power, the globalization of world society, and democratization of world politics.

Concerning the role of military force, he argues that the modern world has reached such a level of economic and scientific/technological development that none of the disputes that gave rise to war in the past justify such action in the contemporary era.   In other words, military force is no longer an appropriate instrument for achieving rational political goals.   With regard to the globalization of society, he sees humanity evolving into a "single community."   All nations are experiencing similar problems and as a result the border between foreign and domestic policies is being erased.   Economic interdependence is central to this concept, as is the unified front that states are forming in opposition to a possible nuclear conflict.   Another trend that Arbatov detects in the international sphere is the democratization of global politics.   The increased role of public opinion in the foreign policy formulation and implementation *process for almost all nations is but one example of this phenomenon. Also, public diplomacy in international interaction is becoming the norm, rather than the exception.*

To return to his original question, "Can the superpowers cooperate?" Arbatov's answer is that the prospects are good because they will need to for the purpose of "self-preservation." For this reason, he concludes, "there is perhaps a basis for looking to the future with growing optimism."

Charles William Maynes, in his essay "America Without the Cold War," contends that it is time for us to seriously ponder the profound influences that recent changes in the international arena have had on American foreign policy. An extended debate on the future of American foreign policy is inevitable, he says, because the Cold War's end has deprived the U.S. foreign policy establishment of its "main organizing principle: anticommunism."

Maynes maintains that the new American foreign policy might be built on one of three foundation stones. A foreign policy based strictly on national interest would allow the United States to withdraw its presence from throughout the world, but he doubts that public opinion in the nation would support what amounts to a return to isolationism. Another approach would have the "export of democracy" serve as the sextant of American foreign policy. This amounts to a crusade for political change, and therefore a large military capability would have to be maintained. Indeed, because military intervention would sometimes be necessary to implement this policy, U.S. foreign policy officials would have to persuade the American public that the ends (democracy) justified the means (military intervention). This approach does have its drawbacks, of course. Frequently international law would have to be ignored and this would put the United States at odds with other nations, particularly the Soviet Union. Furthermore, the United States could easily incur more obligations than it could fulfill. Ensuring that the United States supported only "real" democracies rather than "facade" democracies is still another problem.

It is the third alternative, global partnership, that Maynes finds most promising. This approach assumes that the two superpowers will find it mutually advantageous to cooperate in international affairs because both have had to come to terms with their own limitations. Is also assumes that the leaders of each country will be able to convince their citizens that their state stands for values and ideals worthy of emulation by others. Then, with the backing of their own citizens, the two nations could form a "partnership for peace." This partnership, resting on the pillars of disarmament, development, and democracy, "would provide the grand ambition each seems to need." With the Cold War over, the opportunities for constructive disarmament measures between the two states, at both the strategic and regional levels, have increased considerably. Another challenge for the 1990s and beyond is for East and West to collaborate not only to bring the living standards of the East up to the West, but to begin to construct a global plan for development. Still another worthwhile task would be for the East and West to unite around a common definition of democracy and to promote these ideals both in their own countries and throughout the world.

Sound preposterous? Perhaps so. Maynes admits that such a proposition at any time in the previous forty-five years would have been considered ludicrous. But the unprecedented changes in the international sphere, and specifically in U.S.-Soviet relations, have led to equally unprecedented opportunities.

27

Where Should We Go from Here?

Georgy A. Arbatov

Can We Cooperate?

...The new character of the threats to survival, particularly in the spheres of economy and ecology, demands new approaches to problems, encouraging collaboration and, in particular, the cooperation of the two greatest powers in the world, the United States and the USSR. The greatest need is to limit the military rivalry and political hostility....

Even working together, of course, our two countries cannot resolve the problem of international crises. The USSR and the United States, after all, comprise only 10 percent of the population of the planet. In the long term, our opportunities to influence the development of world events will most likely be reduced, not increased. All the same, these opportunities are very significant. The economic and military power of the Soviet Union and the United States, the breadth of their political interests, extending through virtually all regions of the planet, place upon the two nations special responsibility for the preservation of peace, the strengthening of international security, and the provision of favorable conditions for the social and economic development of all humanity.

What should be done first? It seems to me we should begin by acknowledging and surmounting old mistakes, delusions, and errors. If we look at the history of international relations in recent decades, it is difficult to resist the conclusion that the superpowers' view of the Third World as an arena of confrontation and rivalry helped to pull many of its countries into the orbits of cold war, pushing them down the path of militarization and excessive military expenditures, hastening the emergence of acute crises. To this day smouldering conflicts instigated from outside undermine the already very weak economies of a host of countries and regions.

A principled new approach is needed toward the countries where the overwhelming majority of humanity lives. It is necessary to assist the developing world not only with aid, but with a new policy. That policy should proceed from respect, from a refusal to treat the Third World as an arena of confrontation, from the understanding that it is not "ours" and not "yours." The Third World will develop not in order to please us or you, but for its own sake, for its own interests, taking its own course. The sooner everyone understands this, the fewer mistakes we will make. And the sooner we renounce our rivalry, the more effectively we will assist the world of developing countries in resolving its problems and the more we will be able to organize joint efforts in the interests of development.

Can one imagine the developing world as a sphere of cooperation rather than an arena for rivalry? With all due caution suggested by the history of recent decades, I do not consider such a prospect utopian. At any rate, I think none of the Soviet or American participants in our joint study would disagree that such a prospect now appears much more plausible than when we began the project. Before our eyes Soviet-American relations have improved substantially. In East-West relations as a whole, progress has been achieved in arms reduction; ... for the withdrawal of Soviet troops from Afghanistan and agreement has been achieved on some of the most important questions of a political settlement; in the resolution of the Kampuchea problem, light has begun to appear at the end of the tunnel. And that is not to speak of the creation of Soviet-American nuclear risk reduction centers....

...People wonder whether the current warming in relations will turn out to be another fleeting episode, to be replaced by the next attack of cold war—just as summer is inevitably followed by autumn, and then winter.

This is no simple question. We are not yet able to forecast political developments with the accuracy that characterizes weather predictions. In politics, of course, we are not observers, but participants in the events we are trying to predict. Keeping this in mind, I would risk saying that we have come quite a way since the 1970s. Three major trends stand out: the decline in the role of military power, the globalization of world society, and the democratization of world politics.

The Decline in the Role of Military Power

The past decade has seen a significant shift in the frame of mind in the political, social, and psychological spheres. Public opinion, political circles, and governments have begun to understand better the genuine character and scale of the nuclear threat. Today no responsible political figure would say that it is possible to conduct a nuclear war and attain victory. Politicians not only understand, but officially acknowledge that a nuclear war is suicide.

Even ten years ago many political figures, including those vested with government power, stubbornly refused to make such acknowledgements, which would have called in question the very idea of nuclear deterrence. Concepts were therefore invented to prove the "usability" of nuclear weapons and of "limited" nuclear war; plans were made for a "first (disarming) strike"; the "neutron bomb" was examined as a panacea, and so on. Such illusions were abandoned only slowly and with great difficulty.

The nuclear enlightenment of the politicians was assisted by the fact that the Soviet Union achieved nuclear parity and maintained it in the 1980s, despite the attempts of the United States to regain its strategic superiority. The active efforts of mass political movements and of scientists helped, especially in recent years.

The analysis of the consequences of nuclear war performed by the physicians' movement, honored with the Nobel Peace Prize, played a particularly large role, as did the "nuclear winter" effect discovered by scholars. It was scientifically proven that nuclear war spells the end of human civilization and of man as a biological species. If anybody still needed proof, that was provided by the tragedy in Chernobyl, which graphically brought home to all the indubitable truth: if we allow a nuclear war, no one will be able to hide from destruction.

Moreover, contemporary conditions have challenged the fundamental value of using military force. Humanity has now achieved a level of economic and scientific-technological development, and of social organization, such that none of the problems that gave rise to war in the past—the struggle for new lands, insufficient resources, the absence of markets, ideological and religious dogmas, social cataclysms or economic insolvency—can explain or justify the use of military force against other peoples. Even more important, military force in the contemporary world can no longer serve any rational political goals. Experience in the 1980s clearly demonstrates that it is becoming practically impossible to achieve victory even in a regional conflict (unless on an extraordinarily small scale, as in Grenada or the Falklands). Regional conflicts may last years or decades, and the costs of their conduct—economic, political, moral-psychological—far exceed the advantages that might give an illusion of victory.

A great paradox opens before us: humanity has never possessed such gigantic destructive power, and has never been so constrained in its application. Never has this power been so impotent politically, even as a means of deterrence. If I understand that my opponent realizes that neither of us can set in motion the means of deterrence without committing suicide, then the very idea of deterrence proves to be doomed. Having become mutual, deterrence becomes unnecessary. Thus arises the inescapable necessity for other, nonmilitary means of providing security.

The Growing Diversity and Globalization of World Society

The agenda of world politics is changing. People are beginning to understand that the world is becoming increasingly diverse and contradictory. In the past decade the conception was still widespread that the determining tendency of world development was the gradual erasing of historical traditions, national origins, cultural peculiarities, and ideological differences under the influence of a global tendency toward standardization and unification. This view has not been borne out by the course of history. Today the era of universal political recipes, of messianic dogmas and ideological crusades, has finally become a thing of the past.

The diversity and contradictory character of the contemporary world are paradoxically combined with the globalization of the most important social-economic and political processes. For the first time in its history, humanity is becoming a single community.

The globalization of social life is manifest on at least three levels. First of all, the border between foreign and domestic policy is gradually being erased. Social conflicts and political differences, which develop in individual societies, are increasingly crossing national boundaries.

Second, states are becoming more economically interdependent. Earlier, when the relations between states were limited to the general political and military spheres, foreign trade remained in the position of a handmaiden of politics. Today politics is often a handmaiden of trade: economic differences, problems of currency policy, and trade barriers are becoming the most important concerns at meetings of the leaders of the industrially developed countries of the West.

Third, and probably most important, the historical fates of all states are becoming unified in the face of a possible nuclear conflict (and, in principle, in the face of other global catastrophes). This unity makes necessary a qualitatively new approach to the problem of national security, which would be the distinguishing feature of new political thinking.

The Democratization of World Politics

Legal and moral factors are playing a larger role in international relations. In the past the renunciation of the norms of international law and common human morality in foreign policy in the name of a narrowly understood "realism" or "pragmatism" has led to great sacrifices and suffering, and often to defeat. But such an approach was difficult to resist while nations were relatively isolated one from another, and global threats were not hanging over the human race itself. Now that such threats (nuclear, ecological, and others) have made themselves felt, the demand will grow for legal and moral-political principles and norms of behavior that are common to all. Can states in such conditions consider themselves free from such norms? Obviously they will have to shape their policy increasingly around international law and common human morality.

At the same time public opinion has been playing a larger role in the development of foreign policy—traditionally the most elite sphere hidden from public view. The 1980s witnessed an unprecedented growth in the antiwar movement: the broadening of its composition; the increasingly informed nature of public opinion on questions of war and peace; and the strengthening of its influence on the foreign policy of states. If the establishment of more equal relations *between* states can be called the horizontal democratization of world politics, then the increased role of public opinion *within* states in questions of foreign policy is the vertical axis of democratization.

We are witnesses and active participants in a process of historic significance: the swift democratization of the entire system of international relations. The principal questions of war and peace, of foreign and military policy, are becoming the object of concern and discussion in the widest spheres of public life: among physicians and scholars, cultural and church figures, farmers and workers, students and housewives. Not so long ago these problems (especially in their nuclear dimension) were the preserve of a narrow circle of specialists and the military.

Not everyone, of course, likes these changes in world politics. One sometimes hears it said that the "fashion" for "public diplomacy" is harmful, that "everyone should mind his own business," that "public decisions should be made by responsible figures." Yet never have organized efforts to shape public opinion, at home and abroad, represented such an important sphere of foreign-policy and diplomatic efforts.

The Need to Focus on Domestic Politics

The problem of the domestic development of state and society has become more complex in all countries, large and small, industrially developed and developing. Economic development is problematic; social conflicts are acquiring new dimensions; the unresolved problems of ecology are becoming increasingly acute; national-ethnic problems are coming to the fore in many states of the world; and so on. Moreover, the tempo of change in our increasingly complex and contradictory societies is quickening, necessarily giving rise to the most diverse difficulties, disproportions, and problems. Such complex and heterogeneous societies as those of the Soviet Union and the United States are seriously affected by these phenomena.

Today, it appears, the dominant foreign policy interest of any state is the creation of the most favorable possibilities for successful resolution of its domestic problems (economic, social, cultural, and others). Clearly, in the contemporary interdependent world the tasks of domestic development (even for such large states as the USSR and the United States) cannot be resolved simply by shutting out the external world. The question is thus not whether to participate in international affairs, but how to participate in a way that facilitates the resolution of domestic problems.

Unfortunately, international relations have long done more to aggravate the internal problems of a state than to solve them. Competition did not strengthen, but weakened states, undermining their domestic potential. The rules of the game that evolved led to the substitution of artificial problems for real ones, of symbols of international influence and status for real criteria of achievement.

In recent years, however, a key question is being asked more often: ought we to compete in all spheres? Or has the time come to approach the problem of competition more cautiously and selectively?

What the Soviet Union Has Learned

In the Soviet Union the search for new rules and parameters of competition has resulted in new thinking in the foreign policy area. In the 1970s, I must admit, we in the Soviet Union moved slowly, very slowly, toward the recognition of new military and political realities, to a renunciation of outdated conceptions. Lacking initiative, we even allowed the other side to foist its rules of the game upon us in some areas.

For example, we reconciled ourselves to indolent, unpromising, and fruitless negotiations. In fact, such negotiations may have been positively harmful, for they helped the other side deceive public opinion, relieve the pressure of the antiwar forces, and inspire people with a false feeling of security....

The Americans' ability to foist upon us their rules of the game was reflected in many other areas. We responded to almost every American military program with an analogous one of our own, without carefully considering the differences in economic resources, the strategic and political realities, or even (sometimes) common sense. The very possibility of "asymmetrical reaction," of refusing to compete with the West in every concrete type of armament, only recently became established in our military-political views, as many realities and our experience were subjected to a profound rethinking.

But the problem was not limited to military technology. We began to perceive that we had unthinkingly reproduced a whole series of bankrupt elements of American military conceptions—in particular, those linked to nuclear deterrence and nuclear war. Of course, many explanations could be cited: we were lagging behind; we were compelled to catch up; and that chronic "inferiority complex," multiplied by the tragic experience of World War II (not always correctly projected onto contemporary conditions), dictated its own logic of behavior, sometimes urging us on to an unjustified policy of matching the United States blow for blow, measure for measure, in policy and propaganda as well as military affairs.

As we freed ourselves from this legacy, we reexamined our conceptions about the world and our interests as well as our approaches to many political problems. We elaborated a series of new political ideas about a nonnuclear, demilitarized, noncoercive world and a concept of a comprehensive system of international security....

... We are becoming much more discriminating in selecting grounds for competition with other countries. For example, we believe that we should compete with the United States in creating a more attractive model of social development, in providing the best conditions for the self-realization of the individual, and in resolving the problem of ecology. Such competition will stimulate both societies; unable to rest on their laurels, they will be forced to look more critically at themselves as well as their partners.

In certain areas, however, the lessons of the past have shown us that competition between the USSR and the United States is as senseless as it is dangerous. Now the Soviet Union will not be drawn into every arena of competition defined by the Americans. For example, we will not compete with America in the creation of the SDI, or in the creation of bases and "spheres of influence" in the Third World. If U.S. actions demand a response, we will endeavor to act so that the response is rational, and where necessary "asymmetrical"; it need not be bound by the traditional rules of the game and standards of confrontation thrust upon us.

What the United States Has Learned

The process of perestroika within our country is also an important international factor of the 1980s, in part because it further erodes the "image of the enemy" that was and remains an integral element of the Cold War and the arms race. Throughout the postwar period, the West as a whole has made a great deal of the so-called Soviet threat. It served as a starting point for ideology and policy, helping to justify military expenditures, to establish discipline within the country and in alliance relations, to divert attention from the West's own difficult problems. In a way, the very possibility of referring to the Soviet threat corrupted the ruling elites of the West, making it possible to divert attention from their own mistakes and failures, to eliminate the necessity to think, to doubt and to find new approaches. A struggle with supposed "absolute evil" covers a multitude of sins: when battling an unclean force, you can and should use all possible means, including those that in other circumstances would seem immoral and unacceptable.

But for precisely that reason a policy based on an image of the "enemy" carries the seeds of its own destruction. A conscious deception of others sooner or later turns into an unconscious self-deception. Political leaders become victims of their own false conceptions. And if deception of others is immoral, then self-deception is dangerous.

Today the image of the USSR is changing significantly. One can, of course, artificially prolong the life of the enemy image with the aid of various provocations and "dirty tricks," but only for a short time.

The pioneers of the Cold War will no longer succeed so easily in exploiting the trust of their public (nor, I will add, in exploiting our former secretive approach in certain security questions and clumsiness in others, whether the discussion was about our policy and our intentions, or about the other side and its policy; often our policy was depicted in a way that did not convince our own people and only gave the West propaganda advantages).

During the 1980s, I think, America has learned something. At the beginning of the decade, the United States turned away from attempts to adapt to a changing world and resumed efforts to adapt the world to its interests and to return to an old policy, not responsive to the new realities. This was its own attempt at revenge, an attempt to "replay" history. Anticommunism was again put forward as the fundamental organizing principle of foreign policy, with military force as its fundamental instrument. Psychologically, Reagan's policy was supposed to convince American society that, after the shocks and disappointments of the 1970s, America was, as it so much wanted to believe, again turning from "defense" to "offense," that everything was within its power.

The heart of the matter was that America's exceptional position (partly real, partly imaginary) had come to an end, forcing the nation to adapt to a new environment. From the very start America was much less vulnerable to outside perturbations and dangers than other countries, and much more isolated from developments in the rest of the world. After the Second World War, the nation had reached a position of unmatched power—both military, derived from the U.S. atomic monopoly, and economic—which gave it unique opportunities and freedom of action in the world economy and politics. Many Americans started believing in earnest that the "American century" and "Pax Americana" had arrived.

By the mid-1960s the situation had already begun to change. While remaining a great and strong power, the United States began turning into an essentially ordinary nation. It could no longer seek global supremacy, and became interdependent with other nations. America turned out to be as vulnerable as the rest to many threats.

For a long time Americans refused to reconcile themselves to these painful changes. Even as the realities of life forced them to start adapting to these new conditions, American policymakers (and a considerable part of the public) were still trying to figure out some way to return to the old, comfortable, and seemingly natural order of things. Those attempts reached a peak in the late 1970s and the election campaign of 1980. Against a backdrop of economic difficulties and the unusual situation of parity with the USSR, such sentiments were catalyzed by a national humiliation: the seizure of the entire staff of the U.S. embassy in Teheran as hostages for more than a year and the abortive attempts to rescue them.

Those circumstances prepared the way for the far right's calls to "make America strong again," to force the world to "reckon" with the United States again, and to regain military superiority over the USSR. At home, old values were to be restored: reducing federal social spending to a minimum, granting new benefits and concessions to corporations, deregulating private enterprise. Beginning in 1982 there was a noticeable rise in consumption and an unusually long period of economic growth. But the benefits turned out to have been mostly borrowed. Today's prosperity was obtained through credit and investments from other states at the expense of future American generations, who will have to pay the bills. Overall debt—government, corporate, and private—doubled during the years of the Reagan presidency, reaching $8 trillion, a fantastic sum even by American standards.

In foreign policy, "Iran-gate" dealt a serious blow to the prestige of the Reagan administration and to the Reagan Doctrine. America did not succeed in occupying a "position of strength" in relation to the Soviet Union, but had to return to the negotiation table, to legalize arms control anew. Despite more than $2 trillion spent on military goals, strategic parity was not shaken. The American position in the Third World was not strengthened. There is significant historical irony: the primary foreign policy success of the Reagan administration in its last two years turned out to be the summit meeting with the USSR and the agreement on the reduction of nuclear arms. The basic political asset of the Reagan administration was the INF Treaty.

What choices do the American people have in this new situation? Among those who set the tone of the emerging discussion, two tendencies are evident. First, a realistic note has been sounded, based on the understanding that economic and political realities, the internal and international position of the country, demand radical changes in many areas. They should begin at home, and with the economy. Here the choice is obvious: either consume less, invest less, or produce more. But it is not so simple. To produce more, it is necessary to invest more. Given heightened competition on the world market, investment must be directed not only to new factories, but to science, education, and infrastructure to raise the fantastic sums necessary. Will it be necessary to reduce Americans' personal standard of living? Many observers say that this cannot be avoided. But in recent years the polarization of rich and poor in the United States has intensified; the number of the poor has grown. Reagan's successors will face not a few puzzling problems in domestic policy, especially when the issue becomes one of raising taxes and reducing public spending. This necessity will force them again and again to think about all accessible economic reserves, including a reduction in military expenditures.

This pressure alone forces a definite choice in foreign policy. The advocates of the realist tendency, it seems to me, believe that the foreign policy of the United States should help solve its domestic, particularly economic problems, even at the expense of reducing appropriations to weapons and armed forces.

But the realist tendency is countered by a second strain, which I would conditionally call traditionalist. The adherents of this school come out against changes and for the preservation of the old policy, of the old order in international relations. The traditionalist camp is not restricted to the far right. A significant number of reputedly moderate (or moderate-conservative) members of the two-party traditional foreign-policy establishment are coming out against change. Many political and public figures, specialists in military and international questions, who grew up immersed in the Cold War, evidently cannot understand or accept any foreign policy outside its conceptions. Many prominent leaders are found on this side, along with important political and economic interests. The influence of the military-industrial complex makes the traditionalists a political force to be reckoned with.

Ahead lies a fierce, complex struggle of uncertain outcome. Never before has the choice been so critical. It is not the machinations of Moscow that have set this problem before America, not an individual's caprice or competing political demands, but real changes in the country itself and in the world. It cannot be brushed aside or indefinitely ignored. A choice involving radical changes is always hard to make, as we know from our own experience. Sometimes I think that America will not get by without its own *perestroika* and *glasnost*. Why glasnost? Because, in my view, the country absolutely needs a genuine, serious discussion, which can in no way be replaced by thirty-second television campaign "spots." Why perestroika? Because so much has changed that old thinking and old policy threaten to lead the country (and the whole world with it) to a deadlock, to exert the most ruinous influence on the entire international system.

Conclusion: A Fading Opportunity

The experience of the 1970s should have shown both superpowers and the world as a whole that time is the most valuable political commodity. A chance that presents itself should not be let slip, for a missed opportunity is almost always lost forever.

Historians will probably be quarreling for a long time about who carried the primary responsibility for the lost opportunities at the end of 1974, or the beginning of 1977. When we speak of truly major errors in Soviet-American relations, responsibility inevitably falls in some measure on both sides. In any case, the experience of the 1970s shows that an improvement of relations cannot be put off to next year or to another administration. Everything that can be done today must be done today.

It seems to me that both sides are beginning to understand the significance of the time factor. The negotiation and signing of the INF Treaty testify to this awakening. We will hope that this treaty becomes the first step to a truly stable, forward development of Soviet-American relations.

The idea that relations between East and West, including their competition, should be "humanized" is not new. Ever since the establishment of the Soviet government, "peaceful cohabitation" with the capitalist countries, as expressed in Lenin's words, was its preferred model of international relations. The history of the twentieth century, however, turned out to be exceptionally cruel. The conclusions of common sense too frequently gave way to crude force. Today, common sense seems to be acquiring greater material force, reinforced by inexorable economic and political necessity, by elementary interests in self-preservation. For this reason, there is perhaps a basis for looking to the future with growing optimism.

28

America Without the Cold War

Charles William Maynes

The December 1989 Malta summit between Mikhail Gorbachev and George Bush opened on an unexpected, and thus far unreported, note.

Gorbachev urged Bush to end his public suggestions that the East is now adopting "Western ideas." He argued that most of the ideas behind the East's reform efforts are not Western but universal. Bush later said to officials in Washington that, never having thought about this problem before, he told Gorbachev that he would alter his language. After all, why make Gorbachev's task more difficult?

But semantic silence even at the presidential level cannot hide the reality that throughout the bleakest days of the Cold War it was the West that championed the ideas now being adopted in the East. It is understandable that Western leaders as well as their publics now regard the growing democratization of Eastern Europe as a vindication of Western policy.

So there is a sense of triumph in the air. The world has arrived at one of those rare moments in history when everything seems to change. Questions not seriously discussed since the end of World War II are now being constructively considered. But concern is also mounting that misjudgments in policy could return the world not to costly Cold War stability but to even more costly interwar instability.

It is time to consider in detail the consequences for American foreign policy of these profound changes. It is time to debate in earnest the very different paths the country might follow in a post-Cold War world.

In one fundamental respect the new world that is unfolding contrasts very sharply with comparable periods of major historical transition. Unlike those earlier periods, no major new military threat is likely to replace the old one anytime soon. In the last half of the nineteenth century, after the rest of Europe had finally crushed a politically and militarily dynamic France, a powerful Germany emerged to challenge the European security system. In this century, after the entire world united to defeat Germany and Japan, an ideologically dynamic and militarily overpowering communist superpower, the Soviet Union, emerged to challenge the global order.

Unlike Napoleonic France or Nazi Germany, the Soviet challenger to the established order has not been crushed but contained until its revolutionary dynamism has been exhausted. And this, too, may be a reason for believing that the future holds greater promise than the past. For then the world's immediate security problem was solved through war, which tends to create new resentments and insecurities. This time, if the West has "won," the Soviet Union has not so much "lost" as changed direction. And for a variety of reasons, it seems unlikely that the Soviet leadership will or can reverse its current direction and revive the earlier revolutionary thrust. Yet without that impulse to revolution, the Cold War itself cannot revive; for it was this element of Soviet power that most frightened the West, which felt it was confronting not so much a nation-state as a radical ideology that could inspire the development of fifth columns around the world....

The Lost Sextant

Yet if there is satisfaction, there is also anxiety. For more than forty years the Cold War imparted a clarifying logic to American foreign policy that now will be missing. It reduced international politics to a zero-sum game that everyone could understand.

Both Cold War supporters and critics took advantage of this logic, which provided them a common language. Scholars could disagree about the importance for victory in the Cold War of the Western position in Laos or Zaire, but at least all knew they were discussing the same problem. As the Cold War ends, therefore, American foreign policy will lose more than its enemy. It will lose the sextant by which the ship of state has been guided since 1945....

Perhaps the most important consequence of the Cold War's end will be to deprive the American foreign policy establishment of its main organizing principle: anticommunism. For decades this principle justified every aspect of American foreign policy from the composition of its alliances to the size of its foreign aid program. Almost as important, it served as a tool to discipline critics, whether in Congress or alliance councils. Deprived of this principle, American foreign policy will lack direction. It is inevitable, therefore, that the country will face a major debate over the future course of American foreign policy.

The debate has only begun and it is difficult to anticipate all of the directions in which it might move. Nonetheless, the various participants in the debate seem to be struggling to maneuver into place three very different foundation stones on which a new foreign policy consensus might be built: national interest, democratic values, or global partnership. Each approach could provide a new logic to discipline American foreign policy. Two questions, however, arise: Which one of them will allow the country to deal most effectively with the real problems it faces abroad? And can any one of them develop and sustain the popular support necessary for an effective foreign policy?

A World Without a Great Enemy

A foreign policy based strictly on national interest would permit a sweeping retrenchment of the American presence in the world. With the Cold War over, no nation threatens American survival in any direct way.

There are five power centers in the world that, at least in the near term, determine the fate of the globe—China, Japan, the Soviet Union, the United States, and Western Europe. A major goal of U.S. foreign policy since the end of World War II has been to block the two great communist powers, but primarily the Soviet Union, from achieving a dominant position in either Europe or Japan. In the 1970s China evolved from a hostile into a friendly power. Now in the 1990s the Soviet Union is following a similar evolution.

Neither communist giant is likely to become an enemy of the United States in any foreseeable time frame. Even the tragic events in Tiananmen Square in June 1989 do not threaten a return to U.S.-Chinese hostility. Estrangement, perhaps, but China's long-term interests require it to develop a cooperative relationship with the United States and other major Western powers. Otherwise, China's efforts to modernize will fail and, if they fail, China's relative power position will decline steadily. Now with the dramatic reforms that have swept over Eastern Europe, the Soviet Union can no longer be regarded as a hostile power. It is in neither a position nor a mood to threaten Europe or Japan. Periods of greater tension may recur but the Cold War itself with its global character is over....

A foreign policy of strict national interest could also permit a drastic retrenchment of the U.S. military presence in the world. Over half of the American defense budget is designed to defend against a Soviet attack on Western Europe—the probability of which has never been high and is now effectively zero. From the standpoint of strict national interest, the American army could be slashed back to an expeditionary force designed to meet the modest military requirements involved in protecting American lives abroad, combating terrorism, and maintaining a deterrent force suitable for emergency deployment. As a hedge against Soviet recidivism, the United States might reach agreement with key European states for the pre-positioning of U.S. equipment on European soil. It could cooperate with its allies in providing sea and air support for Europe's defense. And perhaps even a token U.S. army presence could remain on European soil. But virtually all the American troops on European soil could be brought home and disbanded....

The critical question is whether the United States is capable of following a foreign policy grounded in a strict definition of national interest. America's relatively open political system ensures that public opinion will play a major role in the field of foreign policy. Given that role, it seems almost inconceivable that the United States could follow a foreign policy resting on a strict view of the national interest. Ethnic empathy toward various parts of the world, popular sympathies for the underdog, the political impact of economic issues activating new constituencies to press Congress to become more involved in the details of foreign policy—all will make a foreign policy resting solely on national interest difficult to carry out.

There is a final objection to the first grand option. Even though the Cold War is over, history and prudence dictate that at least in its early stages the coming retrenchment not be too sweeping. Just as individuals prudently purchase insurance, so should nations.

Planting the Flag of Democracy

Some analysts argue that the export of democracy should replace anticommunism as the guiding principle of American foreign policy. The operative word is "export." Virtually all American foreign policy analysts would agree that the United States should support the growth of democratic values and practices abroad. To this end they would deploy a considerable portion of the resources of American diplomacy, including financial support. American administrations have spoken and will speak out in favor of democratic values and practices in other countries, have provided and will provide political backing and financial help to democratic leaders abroad, and have tended and will continue to develop closer intergovernmental ties with states that benefit from a democratic domestic order.

But the proponents of a new crusade for democracy are not content with mere diplomatic or financial support for democratic forces abroad. Such a policy is too passive and it does not have the same expansionary impact on the defense budget. Ben Wattenberg, chairman of the Coalition for a Democratic Majority, a group that presses the Democratic party to adopt more conservative positions on defense issues, argues, for example, that embarking on a crusade for democracy can help persuade the American people to keep defense budgets high "to prevent Soviet imperial recidivism." For most of this school of thought the American invasion of Grenada or Panama, covert operations to overthrow undemocratic governments, or direct subsidies to opposition parties in other countries are all appropriate tools in a new crusade to plant democracy's flag around the world. Burton Yale Pines, senior vice president of The Heritage Foundation, suggests that even in the new conditions of détente between the United States and the Soviet Union, "America must be engaged or have the ability of engaging militarily almost everywhere in the world—including, obviously, Europe."

For forty years fear of Soviet intentions persuaded America to maintain a gigantic military machine. Will hopes for the spread of democracy now persuade Americans to retain a large military machine and to use it to pursue a crusade for political change?

Most Americans probably would be willing to defy international law and to support the use of military force to spread the cause of democracy if the cost were low.... Most Americans, like ordinary citizens everywhere, do not have the time or background to become terribly troubled over long-term costs. If the end is democracy, officials can persuade them that the end justifies the means. The average American will rely on his government to exercise good judgment in carrying out this policy. The more important question, therefore, is not whether the United States can embark on a democratic crusade but whether it should. There are several reasons to harbor doubt:

- For the first time since 1945 there appears to be a possibility of reaching an agreement with the Soviet Union about a meaningful and constructive code of conduct for the superpowers in international relations. To this end the Soviet Union has submitted several constructive proposals to the United Nations on measures to "enhance the role of international law." It would be worse than ironic if the opportunity to enter into a constructive agreement with the Soviet Union in the field of international law were lost because, at the very moment that the Soviet Union became more lawful, the United States decided to become more lawless.

- Direct intervention in a country to favor one political party or personality over another cannot be undertaken without incurring obligations that may prove difficult to fulfill. No single act did more to draw America into its disastrous commitments to the various regimes that took power in Saigon than the U.S. decision to assist forces that were planning the overthrow and assassination of President Ngo Dinh Diem. Recent CIA efforts, ultimately successful, to end the prohibition against U.S. involvement in coup attempts that might end up in the assassination of another head of state bring back troubling memories.

- A majority of the American people may support a crusade for democracy that resorts to force or covert action; but unless administrations are careful to support only real democracies rather than façade democracies, significant groups within the United States will object vehemently. A bipartisan consensus will prove impossible. America's current involvement in Central America is an example....

- A crusade to promote democracy assumes a degree of American omniscience that is lacking. Even the most knowledgeable Americans usually do not know enough about local conditions in other parts of the world for the United States to intervene effectively. (The recent democratic surge in Eastern Europe should humble all specialists, virtually none of whom predicted it.) Democracy, after all, is a social plant that adapts to the local political climate and tradition....

An Unexpected Partnership

To be fair to the proponents of a democratic crusade, however, it is necessary to acknowledge one advantage often passed over in silence. It would help bind the country together. For one curious feature of the superpower relationship is the role that a combination of ideology and economic success plays in the internal cohesion of both societies. People of many nationalities chose to come to America; people of many nationalities were forced to become part of the Soviet Union. The myth in both societies has been that the American way or the socialist model justifies the allegiance of diverse nationalities. The clear evidence that the West is increasing its economic lead has been extremely damaging to the socialist model. Evidence that the Japanese form of guided capitalism or the German path of the social market economy continues to outstrip the American economy will be very damaging to the American faith in the "city on a hill."

Because of these important myths and their role in maintaining national cohesion, both the Soviet Union and the United States have been strong ideological powers. For it is difficult to develop an ideology that one claims is appropriate to various nationalities brought together inside one country's borders and not conclude that those living outside these borders, who may even share the same language and culture, would not be better off if they, too, had the benefit of the same ideology and system of government.

Gorbachev has announced that his goal is to de-ideologize international affairs. But it seems unlikely that he can ever be completely successful unless he fails at his own reform efforts. For if the Soviet Union is able to surmount its current internal crisis, it will again believe that it has a unique message, now freshly reformulated, to carry to the rest of the world. It is likely to convey that message much more benignly in the future than in the past, but it will be unable to ignore its ideological obligations completely. Nor is the United States dissimilar in this regard. Senator Bill Bradley (D-New Jersey), for one, has argued that the United States cannot be a country of small ambitions. But can any political system have a large ambition that does not involve others?

Today both the American and the Soviet people are having to come to terms with their own limitations. The 1970s were a difficult decade for the United States and the 1980s were difficult for the Soviet Union.

Each superpower has emerged from its decade of trial somewhat chastened. Each is increasingly recognizing that the priority of the 1990s is to concentrate on domestic affairs. Each understands that as great as its power may be, in different ways each is falling behind others in critical areas, the Soviet Union quite a bit faster than the United States.

Despite this need to concentrate on domestic affairs, for the reasons already cited, each probably will be harmed internally by a total abandonment of the effort to project its values externally. Each needs to assure its citizens that their state stands for values and ideals worthy of emulation by others.

What then could satisfy the ideological need of each state yet present a constructive face to the outside world? Perhaps a partnership for peace resting on the pillars of disarmament, development, and democracy would provide the grand ambition each seems to need. Such a proposition at any time in the last forty-five years would have seemed preposterous. But Gorbachev may have made just such a partnership possible with his extraordinary address to the United Nations in December 1988. In that speech he embraced concepts of individual rights and the rule of law that make true cooperation between the United States and the Soviet Union possible for the first time since World War II. His representatives have followed up with a series of remarkable documents proposing steps within the United Nations that would permit the creation of a more stable and just international order.

It also may be a hopeful coincidence that, with the possible exception of Japan, all of the states in the world that can either protect or endanger world peace are entering what might be called an internal phase. China and the Soviet Union face daunting internal problems that are likely to siphon off their energies and attention for several decades. The United States must finally face up to social and demographic divides—sometime in the next century the United States will cease to have a white majority—that will pose the greatest test to national unity since the Civil War. Europe must concentrate on creating a more united continent and raising Eastern Europe to the level of the West. Japan with its enormous wealth must carve out a new international role for itself but that role will be less threatening to others if Japan also attends to the major social problems it faces at home—a rapidly aging population, a deficient infrastructure for a country of Japan's capabilities and prosperity, and a large, unabsorbed Korean minority.

This period of internal focus could be used to draw the world back to more reasonable levels of armed defense and to develop more enduring patterns of political and economic cooperation. Because of the Cold War, many countries have conducted their affairs since 1945 as though they were in a permanent state of siege. Armies have reached sizes unprecedented in peacetime. Almost as important as the resources wasted has been the political burden of having adopted policies capable of confronting the enemy both at home and abroad. The fact that a paranoid sense of national security in the Soviet Union has imposed barbaric sacrifices on the Soviet people should not obscure the very heavy price paid by the American people during the Cold War in terms of excessive secrecy and lost liberties. The powers assumed by the KGB were grotesque, but those granted the CIA and the FBI were often outrageous, as decades of scandal from Watergate to Irangate attest.

With the Cold War over, therefore, each side has an opportunity to engage in a significant degree of disarmament at home as well as abroad. Abroad, many bases can be closed, a large number of troops withdrawn, and key weapon-free zones created. At home, secrecy regulations can be reexamined, transparency promoted, and rights made more secure....

In the post-Cold War era both superpowers need to take steps to subject to a much greater degree of accountability and democratic control the activities of their national intelligence and internal security services. CIA and KGB budgets should be made public, surveillance files on individual citizens sharply restricted or destroyed, and rules of the road negotiated to curb CIA and KGB excesses in the field of intelligence collection and covert operations.

Internationally, the two superpowers should recognize that their opportunity to remain politically preeminent well into the next century may lie in shoring up the very institution that at different points in the Cold War each has done so much to tear down—the United Nations. For the established patterns of the Cold War and the U.N. Charter accord the two superpowers unusual opportunities for influence in the management of a new post-Cold War security system. While three other states enjoy the privilege of veto power in the Security Council, only the two superpowers have the global reach and the technology in the skies, on land, and at sea to play a leading role in a new world security system that could be based on the U.N. Charter. The general staffs of the two superpowers, therefore, should begin discussing the future role of the superpower militaries in a post-Cold War order involving peacemaking, peacekeeping, and international arms control verification under a U.N. umbrella.

The end of the Cold War may also make possible the imposition of certain qualitative restraints on the arms race in regions of the world like Africa and the Middle East. While the Cold War lasted, the interest of each superpower was usually to exploit each regional conflict to achieve some gain globally. With the Cold War over, the interest of each superpower should be to end each conflict in order to eliminate the possibility that it could evolve in a manner that would jeopardize the central relationship. Here, if one is to judge by U.S. policy toward such regional disputes as Afghanistan, Angola, Cambodia, Central America, and the Middle East, the United States seems more frozen in the thinking of the past than the Soviet Union.

As the East-West axis in world politics ceases to have the importance it once did or at least acquires a more constructive character, the key division in world politics is likely to become the North-South divide. The reasons are the relationship between poverty and people and the clash between economics and demographics....

A partnership between East and West can make it more likely that the international system will create opportunities rather than experience disruptive demographic movements. Centralized planning at the microlevel of a national economy, replacing the resource allocation function of market pricing, has been demonstrated to be a spectacular failure. But judicious planning at the macrolevel has proved to be a spectacular success. The economies that have made the most progress in the world in the last several decades have generally been states that have allowed a significant role for the state (or its central banking system) in developing the national economy—France, Italy, Japan, Singapore, South Korea, Taiwan, and West Germany.

Yet on the global scale today little serious planning is done. Each developing nation remains on its own. Often at the urging of aid officials from the developed world, each undertakes efforts that may prove futile because too many others are planning the same strategy.[1] The challenge of the 1990s is for East and West to cooperate not only in a program to bring the living standards of the East up to those of the West but to begin the very difficult conceptual work that will be required to construct a global plan for development—one that can provide the kind of information and infrastructure that permits private and public enterprise to thrive everywhere. Initially, the largest contribution in terms of energy, money, and expertise will have to come from the West but the ultimate task will require the efforts of all the world's major countries.

Is it conceivable that there could be an East-West consensus on democracy? Until Gorbachev, the answer could only have been no. Today the answer is less certain. The future of democracy in Eastern Europe and the Soviet Union is far from assured. Even if a return to the Cold War seems highly unlikely now that the communist ideology has lost its magnetic power, a return to authoritarian or military rule cannot be excluded. But the forces of democracy in communist countries have displayed remarkable resilience and energy. Steady acceptance in the East of the universal ideas Gorbachev discussed with Bush at Malta suggests that a convergence of views is possible even here. For it to be complete, however, the West will have to give greater prominence to economic rights than it habitually has. Americans in particular have defined democracy in recent years in a way that is too narrowly political and mechanistic. It is almost as though periodic and secret elections alone can bestow democracy on a people. But Americans are born in a rich and blessed land that has provided a relatively decent living to most of its citizens. For much of American history those who found that they could not make an adequate living where they were had only to move West or to appeal to the government for free land under the Homestead Act.

In other words, one essential element for democracy—an economic and social order that does not intimidate and subdue—was for much of American history provided free by government or nature to all who sought it. Yet in recent years, as the human rights debate has moved up on the international agenda, most Americans have forgotten the economic and social dimension of freedom.

The approach of the socialist countries to democracy, of course, has been far worse. The regimes in power appropriated the language of democracy while denying its reality. Freedoms were constitutionally guaranteed but never granted. And in return for this infringement of political liberty the population gained officially sanctioned economic rights but, over time, relative impoverishment because the system did not work.

It is time that East and West unite around a common definition of democracy, and Franklin Roosevelt's Four Freedoms—freedom of speech and expression, freedom of every person to worship God in his own way, freedom from want, and freedom from fear—are a good place to start. All four of these freedoms are stated or implied in the Universal Declaration of Human Rights.

A commitment by all to the provisions of the Universal Declaration and a pledge to work for their realization through the various bodies of the United Nations could provide the grand ambition that both the American and Soviet people seem to need. It could fulfill their missionary impulse constructively and peacefully. It could enrich the lives of others and prevent the return of the Cold War not simply for the next decade but for those that follow.

On which foundation is America likely to erect its post-Cold War consensus? In any age foreign policy tends to be an accumulation of nuance and emphasis. Americans may prefer one of the three options discussed but they will construct their approach to the world with elements of all three. Even during the height of the Cold War, rigorous anticommunism was not the only guide to American foreign policy. The

United States provided economic assistance to communist Yugoslavia when it defied Stalin to embark on an independent course. It entered into a tacit strategic alliance with China in the early 1970s although the political order in China was, if anything, far more repressive than the regime of Leonid Brezhnev.

Nevertheless, preferences are important. So are paradigms. Together they provide direction to a nation's citizens, who need a framework with which to understand the world. Together they provide a standard to its policy-makers, who must struggle to explain departures from the norm. Together they provide a guide for the media, which then have a clear benchmark against which to measure an administration's words and deeds.

Preferences shown or paradigms selected also have political consequences. A foreign policy based on a strict adherence to national interest could bring security at a lower cost in terms of money but perhaps a higher cost in terms of reduced vision and hardened hearts. A foreign policy based on a desire to export democracy might enhance American power in the short run, but it could lead to acting with arrogance abroad that might be dangerous in the long run. A foreign policy based on a global partnership could bring cooperative efforts in the best interests of the American people, but it would come at a cost. The two patterns of diplomacy Americans have known are isolationism and preeminence. Either maximizes America's ability to decide its own fate alone. Will Americans be comfortable with an approach that requires them to allow others a voice in America's future?

Some might prefer to avoid a choice. They might argue for further attempts to shore up the status quo, a version of the "status-quo plus" approach to foreign policy that the Bush administration initially hoped to pursue. But such caution would waste an extraordinary opportunity. For the peace dividend is not just the money that will be freed up. It is also the categories of thought that will finally be opened up. It is time for a great debate on American foreign policy, and it is not possible to have a great debate without a discussion of clear options. The most precious peace dividend is precisely the legitimacy of this debate. The country must make the most of it.

Notes

1. See Robin Broad and John Cavanagh, "No More NICs," *Foreign Policy* 72 (Fall 1988): 81-101.

About the Book and Editors

As the Cold War draws to a close, new issues inevitably have begun to surface in U.S.-Soviet relations. This reader brings together Soviet and U.S. perspectives on the broad range of challenges that both nations now face.

Within the context of a "debate" format that presents parallel U.S. and Soviet views, these timely readings illustrate areas of cooperation and conflict and weigh policy similarities and differences. Topics covered include Soviet-U.S. relations after the Cold War, military and national security debates, and the changing international economic environment. The selections also consider the impact that the evolving Soviet-U.S. interaction is having on the "new" Europe and the developing world. The volume concludes by considering the direction the superpower relationship may take in the future.

Students of Soviet and U.S. foreign policy will find this text invaluable in unraveling the complexities of U.S.-Soviet relations.

Andrei G. Bochkarev is chair of the Department of Political History at the Moscow Institute of Agricultural Engineers and 1990-1991 visiting lecturer at Northern Arizona University. **Don L. Mansfield** is associate dean of the College of Social and Behavioral Sciences at Northern Arizona University.

Index